The United States and t

Lester D. Langley, General Editor

*This series is dedicated to a broader
understanding of the political, economic, and
especially cultural forces and issues that have
shaped the Western hemispheric experience—
its governments and its peoples. Individual
volumes assess relations between the United
States and its neighbors to the south and north:
Mexico, Central America, Cuba, the
Dominican Republic, Haiti, Panama,
Colombia, Venezuela, Peru, Ecuador, Bolivia,
Brazil, Uruguay and Paraguay, Argentina,
Chile, and Canada.*

The United States and the Americas

Peru and the United States

Lawrence A. Clayton

Peru and the United States: The Condor and the Eagle

The University of Georgia Press
Athens and London

© 1999 by the University of Georgia Press
Athens, Georgia 30602
All rights reserved

Set in 10/14 Palatino by G&S Typesetters, Inc.
Printed and bound by Maple-Vail Book Manufacturing Group
The paper in this book meets the guidelines for
permanence and durability of the Committee on
Production Guidelines for Book Longevity of the
Council on Library Resources.

Printed in the United States of America

03 02 01 00 99 C 5 4 3 2 1
03 02 01 00 99 P 5 4 3 2 1

Library of Congress Cataloging in Publication Data
Clayton, Lawrence A.
    Peru and the United States : the condor and the eagle /
Lawrence A. Clayton.
        p.   cm. — (The United States and the Americas)
    Includes bibliographical references and index.
        ISBN 0-8203-2024-2 (alk. paper). — ISBN 0-8203-2025-0
(pbk. : alk. paper)
        1. United States—Relations—Peru.   2. Peru—Relations—
United States.   I. Title.   II. Series.
    E193.8.P4C58   1999
    327.73085—dc21   98-33595

British Library Cataloging in Publication Data available

To my wife, Louise,
and my children, Amy, Stephanie, and Carlton

Contents

Acknowledgments

I would like to thank a number of organizations for their assistance. The University of Alabama provided me with a sabbatical leave in the spring of 1988, which, added to a Fulbright teaching award in the fall of that same year, enabled me to continue with research both in Tuscaloosa and Lima for this book. In Lima the Department of History at the University of Lima hosted me for a wonderful semester of research and teaching—a semester punctuated by the bombs of the Shining Path making living in Peru a somewhat exciting experience in the late 1980s. The friendship and assistance of Eduardo Dargent, Felix Denegri, Marcia Koth de Paredes, Jorge Ortiz Sotelo, Raúl Palacios Rodríguez, and Fernando Rosas in Peru are deeply appreciated.

The general editor of this series, Professor Lester D. Langley, put an extraordinary amount of energy into this book, and it is a better book because of his editorial talents and unsparing standards. The errors and flaws I gladly acknowledge as my own. Professor David Scott Palmer's welcome comments and suggestions gave me the benefit of his long and intimate experience with Peru.

Special recognition goes to Professor Fredrick B. Pike, a man whose works I consider the most original in the field of Latin American history and an inspiration for a whole generation of his admirers. Fred Pike is not only an historian's historian, but a gentle and encouraging friend who never failed to prompt me—and the manuscript—forward when we both needed some gentle, but firm, prodding. Thanks Fred.

This book has its origins in the 1920s when my father, William Harold Clayton, took a Grace Line ship from New York to Iquique, Chile, to work in the nitrate *oficinas* of W. R. Grace & Co. He married my mother, Maria Rosa Reichel Lema, an *iquiqueña*, in 1930, and the two of them lived a wonderful life that stretched between the Americas for the next half century. I was in Peru before the age of three, and I have never left it in my mind and heart. Although I have passed much of my adult life in the United States, I always knew there was a good story about these two countries and how they related to each other.

My wife, Louise, and children, Amy, Stephanie, and the "caboose" Carlton, have all been a part of this book. It was begun when Amy was in high school, Stephanie in grammar school, and Carlton but a thought not even defined. Now Amy is a physician, Stephanie in graduate school, and Carlton about to inaugurate a new era in his life in the first grade. To the question occasionally asked by Louise, Amy, and Stephanie, "are you STILL working on that, Dad?" I can now answer with this gift. "It's finished, girls!"

Introduction

Ask a Peruvian about the United States and the response will be an opinion—occasionally informed but somewhat distorted. A similar query to an American about Peru usually prompts a comment about the drug trade or perhaps a vague reference to Inca mummies drawn from the latest issue of *National Geographic Magazine.*

This book is about the relations between the United States and Peru since the early nineteenth century; it is as much about points of view and perspectives as points in fact. In it the reader will find described the basic outline of these relations and the ways in which each country influenced the history of the other.

The title comes from the two birds—the condor and the eagle—that serve as national symbols of Peru and the United States respectively. Both are raptors, birds of prey, and each bird projects a certain majesty as it soars over the mountains and lakes and forests of its native habitat. The birds are wonderful, ancient symbols of sovereignty and authority. The condor's claim on the collective Peruvian imagination reaches far back into the mists of the Inca civilization that predated the arrival of the Europeans, while the eagle's place in the national life of the United States descends from ancient Roman civilization. The condor and the eagle are complex animals that have inspired myths and admiration through the ages and are apt symbols of the complex relationship between Peru and the United States.

Historical Narrative

The story of the two countries is not only one of peoples united by shared Judeo-Christian values, a commitment to political constitutionalism and republicanism, and a New World environment, but also a story of peoples divided by culture and history. Peru, for example, pos-

1

sesses a large Amerindian population and culture that is absent in the United States. Americans chose not to incorporate, but rather to eliminate Native American influences from national life.

A liberal ethic—championing the rights of the individual—has largely prevailed in the United States, while some argue that the corporate body, emphasizing the good of the whole at the expense of individual's rights and liberties, has been the Peruvian way. Americans have valued free enterprise and been suspect of the power—and tyranny—of government, while Peruvians traditionally looked to the State as the arbiter of power and influence, the core of the national body. In spite of these differences, the two shared the common experience of breaking colonial ties to European mother countries, and this experience imparted to their initial relationship a bond that has endured for almost two centuries.

The first Americans to visit Peru were probably New England whalers sailing into the Pacific in the late eighteenth century. Following them came Yankee traders during the Wars of Independence, searching not for leviathan, but for good markets, especially made profitable by wartime conditions. It was a supremely optimistic time, when Creoles and Yankees sought to dovetail their fortunes in the waves of independence sweeping across the Americas. American warships also appeared in the waters off Peru—ships sent to protect American merchantmen and to preserve U.S. neutrality in the conflict between Peruvian patriots and Spanish royalists. Early on these efforts ensnared Americans in the complicated web of loyalties and counterloyalties that marked the Peruvian War for Independence. When the liberator Simón Bolívar and William Tudor, the first U.S. consul to Peru, met, they eloquently represented points of view that optimistically stressed the common destinies of both nations but just as equally warned of their vastly different historical realities. Politically, socially, economically, and culturally, they were worlds apart. But the chasms in historical experience that Bolívar and Tudor reflected upon were gradually narrowed in the nineteenth century.

Trade between the two countries increased dramatically at midcentury, especially fed by the boom in the guano trade. Hundreds of

Yankee ships made thousands of voyages to the Chincha Islands between the 1840s and 1870s to transport the nitrogen-rich guano (seafowl droppings that had accumulated for thousands of years) back to the United States to be used as fertilizer on nutrient-depleted cotton and tobacco fields. Peru itself entered a period of economic transformation made possible by profits from the guano trade. When the guano boom finally went bust in the 1870s as the raw material was rapidly depleted, Peru went into a tailspin that led to the disastrous War of the Pacific (1879–83) with Chile.

By then the fortunes of Peru were more closely identified with American interests. The new railroads of Peru, for example, were being built largely by the American entrepreneur Henry Meiggs. New shipping lines were established, new mercantile connections made, ports and cities improved, and much of the initiative, technology, and capital issued from the United States; however Great Britain remained the dominant foreign presence in Peru until the First World War. The War of the Pacific disrupted these initiatives but did not do so for long, especially since Americans largely sympathized with the Peruvians during the course of the conflict. The story of "Casa Grace" (W. R. Grace & Co.) in Peru symbolized new ties with the United States. Founded in 1854 by William Russell Grace, an Irish immigrant to Peru, the company— whose headquarters were transferred to New York City in the 1860s— forged commercial, industrial, and maritime linkages that more closely knit the economic and, by extension, political destinies of the two nations. William Grace's brother Michael, for example, played a signal role in reestablishing Peru's financial credit and reputation in international circles in the 1880s.

The "Grace Contract" that emerged in 1890 freed Peru of the heavy burdens of debt inherited from the prewar and war years and opened the door to new investments that rapidly flowed into the country during the next four decades. It was an immensely controversial agreement that gave up segments of Peru's national patrimony—the railroads for example—to foreign ownership in exchange for the forgiveness of debts. But, freed from the bondage of debt, Peru's economic and financial fortunes took off as the century came to an end.

By the turn of the twentieth century, the American presence in Peru was increasing, especially in the extractive and agricultural sectors of its economy. Important new economic segments were developed, such as the production of copper, petroleum, and rubber, often with significant collaboration between Peruvian entrepreneurs and capital and their American counterparts. Government-to-government activities also increased, which supported and reinforced American private investments in Peru. Secretary of State Elihu Root made a goodwill tour of Latin America in 1906, and one of his most important stops was Lima; it was the first visit to Peru by an American secretary of state. A U.S. naval station was even contemplated for Chimbote, on the north coast of Peru, to help protect the Panama Canal and extend the range of U.S. defenses south of the Equator in the Pacific.

Other ties strengthened as the twentieth century unfolded, especially in cultural areas not as easily defined or quantified as in economic and commercial activities. In education and entertainment and through magazines, scientific exploration, and increasing tourism for example, Americans and Peruvians became better acquainted. The discovery of the magnificent ruins of Machu Picchu by Hiram Bingham in 1911 became the cornerstone for the development of American tourism to Peru in the twentieth century. That tourism was slow to develop, however, until the creation of fast, dependable transportation in later decades.

The high tide of American influence in Peru occurred in the 1920s under the leadership of President Augusto B. Leguía. The president was a longtime admirer of the United States, and during his long second administration (1919–30; his first ran from 1908 to 1912) he promoted a wide variety of things American, from the increase of direct American investments in a variety of public works to the betterment of Peruvian schools based on American models and run by American educators. Peruvian naval education was revamped by American naval officers invited in by Leguía to upgrade and modernize the various parts of the military establishment, including the fledgling air force. Even a portrait of President James Monroe (1821–25) was hung in the presidential palace on the Plaza de Armas in downtown Lima, perhaps the ultimate symbol of Leguía's admiration for the United States and its leaders.

Equally successful, from a government-to-government perspective, was the positive resolution for Peru of the old Tacna-Arica border dispute with Chile, which dated from the War of the Pacific. The United States sent Gen. John Pershing, the popular commander of the American Expeditionary Force to Europe during the First World War, to help broker the long-standing dispute. Pershing sided with the Peruvians, and a settlement awarding Arica to Chile and Tacna to Peru was finally reached between the two countries in 1929. Other American interventions on behalf of Peru occurred in the 1930s and 1940s, none more dramatic than that which helped ratify Peru's victory in a short border war with Ecuador in 1941 and left Peru with the lion's share of disputed territory in the Amazon region. The United States is today still one of the guarantors of the Rio Treaty of 1942 and is occasionally, such as in 1995, drawn into the fray when Ecuador reopens the old claims.

The World War II years enhanced many of the commonalities between the two countries. Victor Raúl Haya de la Torre—the founder and leader of Peru's radical political party, the Alianza Popular Revolucionaria Americana (APRA)—was drawn to the freedoms (from want, from fear, of religion, and of speech) championed by President Franklin Delano Roosevelt during the war. Even before the war, a subtle confluence of thinking among radical and liberal leaders in both countries drew them together, both looking to government as the principal force in rectifying old inequities and injustices (especially in Peru) and in addressing the new calamities of depression-era capitalism (especially in the United States). After the war a shared antipathy toward worldwide communism helped foster a common vision of a world order that led to a long period of harmony from the 1940s through the early 1960s between the two nations.

Underscoring these shared public and political sentiments were increasing U.S. investments in Peru. Some were in traditional areas, as in the expansion of mining enterprises by Cerro de Pasco, Southern Peru Copper, and Marcona Mining. Others were a combination of the new and the old. Casa Grace (the oldest and one of the largest U.S. multinationals in Peru) developed a commercial process to make paper from bagasse (the residue of the sugar-making process) at its industrial/agricultural estate of Paramonga on the north-central coast of Peru; through these actions the company launched an entirely new industry that combined the best of Peruvian and American technology. Giant retailers and manufacturers, such as Sears and Roebuck and Goodyear Tire, expanded into Peru, furthering the "Americanization" of the Peruvian economy and society (a subject explored in depth in chapter 7).

Contacts between the two countries widened, deepened, and diversified considerably in the second half of the twentieth century. A new wave of evangelical and Pentecostal Protestantism arrived in Peru, which considerably expanded the religious and cultural ties between peoples. The Summer Institutes of Languages established by William Cameron Townsend in the jungles of Peru intermingled the fortunes of Peruvian Indians, American evangelicals, and Peruvian politicians and anthropologists in fascinating, unconventional ways. More traditionally the armed forces of Peru—especially the navy and air force—became even more dependent on U.S. surplus equipment from the Second World War. With that equipment came U.S. military missions, which deepened the relationship between the military establishments of both countries.

Flies in the ointment also multiplied. Differences between the two countries were intensified by the incredibly prosperous cycle the United States entered in the postwar period—a cycle that not only further emphasized the disparity of wealth and power between the two countries but also served to underscore the great gaps between the haves and have-nots in Peru. The visit of Vice President Richard Nixon to Lima in 1958 provoked some violent anti-American demonstrations. Many Peruvians felt exploited and managed by the United States, and they hurled rocks and epithets at Nixon, calling for the end of American imperialism in Peru.

How seriously *did* the United States influence Peruvian politics? How deeply was the Peruvian economy affected by U.S. capital? These issues, and others, are examined in subsequent chapters. While such issues were given special emphasis by the Nixon visit, the inauguration of John F. Kennedy in 1961 and the launching of the Alliance for Progress that same year worked to redefine and improve the relations between the two nations over the next decade.

The alliance stressed social equality and economic development within a democratic political context. In Peru, it took many forms—in education, in agriculture, in health, and in dozens of other ways, one of which is perhaps best symbolized by the presence of Peace Corps members in Peru in the 1960s. The goodwill generated by the alliance was, however, undermined throughout the decade by the increasingly strident public debate in Peru over the International Petroleum Company (I.P.C.) and its role in the nation's history. Peruvians claimed the company had systematically despoiled Peru of one of the nation's most valuable nonrenewable resources—petroleum; I.P.C.'s defenders called the claims so much nationalistic poppycock. I.P.C., its supporters claimed, represented enlightened modern capitalism that provided everything from model communities for its workers to a rich source of tax revenues for the Peruvian government. The debate reached a crescendo in October 1968 and helped precipitate a revolution that removed President Fernando Belaúnde Terry and installed a military junta.

The Peruvian Institutional Revolution of 1968 marked a major turning point in modern relations between Peru and the United States. The generals who came to power, led by Juan Velasco Alvarado, almost immediately nationalized I.P.C. and continued to nationalize U.S. private properties, such as Cerro de Pasco, Grace, and others. Velasco also began to disengage Peru from its traditional role as a client state of the United States in such prominent areas as military equipment and training. Promising Peruvians a new role in world affairs, Velasco's government turned to the Soviet Union for major new arms needed for its army and air force. The deterioration of Peruvian-U.S. relations progressed rapidly in the 1970s as Peru turned not only to the Soviet Union but also to Eastern Bloc nations for imports and exports, for technical assistance, and for other types of assistance that marked the end of an era. By the end of the 1970s, the Soviet embassy was the largest in Peru, both a symbol and a fact of the new reality created by Velasco's intensely nationalistic regime.

The legacy of the Peruvian Institutional Revolution of 1968, however, was not as long-lasting and permanent as Velasco (who died in 1975) and his supporters would have liked. The linkages between the United States and Peru remained strong, especially in commercial and economic contacts. Peru's immense debts, created during the 1970s, were largely U.S.-controlled. The rising tide of the cocaine trade sweeping up from Latin America into the United States tied together more strongly the destinies of Peru and the United States. Peru was the world's principal supplier of cocaine and the United States the biggest customer.

From the 1970s onward, the two countries cooperated on and fought over strategies regarding how to cope with the narcotraffic. The United States wished principally to eliminate the production of coca, while Peru emphasized interdiction of the trade. The current president of Peru, Alberto Fujimori (1990–2000), insisted that eliminating the cultivation of cocaine had to be accompanied by a reasonable substitute for coca farmers. The United States viewed the vast interwoven empire of cocaine—from its cultivation to the ultimate consumers on the streets of the United States—as one nefarious empire that needed to be stamped out at its source. Peruvians quite correctly pointed out that if the consumption—principally by Americans—were addressed, the supply would naturally shrink. In the meantime the U.S. military and paramilitary presence (such as that of the Drug Enforcement Agency) expanded as joint operations were launched throughout the 1980s and 1990s to wage war against narcotraffickers.

Peruvians also disagreed sharply with Americans on another major threat to their national life—the terrorists of the Shining Path guerrilla movement. Throughout the 1980s the Shining Path waged a relentless war of terrorism against government authority in Peru and was determined to create a pure Marxist dictatorship by first eliminating the structures of government and then creating a people's republic. Tens of thousands of people perished in the war between the Peruvian military and police and the terrorists, but the United States continued to insist that drugs were a greater problem than terrorists. To Americans the corruption and insidiousness of the narcotraffic was at least as equally damaging and threatening to Peru's national existence as were the terrorists.

The election of Fujimori in 1990 electrified Peru. Suffering from raging inflation, seemingly insurmountable debt, and the persistent Shining Path, Peruvians turned to this son of Japanese immigrants for deliverance. Fujimori did indeed deliver. He initiated a massive "Fujishock" austerity economic program to control inflation and kick start the economy. He allowed the military to wage a final, exterminating war on terrorists, suspended portions of the constitution in April 1992 to better free the military's hands, and promoted his vision of how narcotraffic should be dealt with in the face of a dubious United States. Fujimori's *autogolpe* (self-coup) of April 1992 provoked the United States to temporarily suspend military assistance and give a tongue-lashing to the Fujimori government for serious violations of human rights during the military's campaign against terrorists. To many in the United States, Fujimori's acts smacked of dictatorship. For a vast majority of Peruvians, Fujimori was the welcome hand at the helm of a ship long thought to have been drifting since the late 1970s.

But in the bigger picture, the United States and Peru soon were once again marching together. Fujimori's neoliberal, economic measures—emphasizing free markets and competition—went well with the post-Communist world of the 1990s. In the fall of 1992, the leader of the Shining Path was captured, crippling that movement and vindicating Fujimori and his military tactics.

Fujimori's star truly rose in early 1997. In December 1996 another terrorist group, the Tupac Amaru Revolutionary Movement, seized the Japanese ambassador's residence and held seventy-two people hostage for more than four months. On the afternoon of April 22, 1997, an elite Peruvian antiterrorist force stormed the ambassador's mansion with explosives and automatic weapons and freed the hostages in a dramatic raid. A subtitle to an article in the international edition of the *New York Times* on April 24, 1997, summarized the world's reaction—"Hats Off to Fujimori."

How to summarize the relationship between Peru and the United

States? While this is a history book that emphasizes the historical narrative, it also analyzes the relationship over the years. There has to be some rhyme and reason, for example, to the ups and downs between Peru and the United States for the nearly two hundred years of history between the two.

Concepts and Frameworks

Within the context of Peru and the United States four major theoretical frameworks, or concepts, have been proposed that help to explain the nature of Peruvian-U.S. relations: the first framework is the asymmetrical dimension of the relationship; the second is the dependency theory, which posits Peruvian dependence on the United States based on the uneven distribution of economic and political power between the two; the third, less precise but no less consequential, framework is the ambiguous nature of the relationship between the people of Peru and the United States; and the fourth is the agreement during certain eras, or lack of agreement, in attitudes toward liberty and equality.

The asymmetrical dimension is perhaps the easiest theory to explain.[1] It is also part of the explanation in dependency theory (as we shall see). Because the United States has been the stronger partner in the relationship, it has exerted an unequal influence over Peru during the course of nearly two centuries. The actions of the U.S. government and its citizens have, for the most part, had a profound effect on the nature and course of the relationship, while neither Peru nor its citizens have had much impact on that same relationship. Most apparent in the first three quarters of the twentieth century, this asymmetry has been tempered by the changing nature of power and international politics in the last quarter of the century. The decline of U.S. hegemony in Latin America coupled with the frustration over the cocaine trade have altered the Peruvian-U.S. relationship. The asymmetry in power has remained, but U.S. efforts to exercise that power in Peru have diminished. On the other hand, Peru has been able to more assertively exert its own agenda in relations between the two, especially regarding security matters.[2]

Supplementing and helping to explain this asymmetry is the dependency theory of underdevelopment, which had great currency during the 1950s and 1960s. According to the dependency theory, the world was divided into the metropolises and the periphery. The metropolises were located in North America and Europe, where industrialization had first taken place. Those who developed and subscribed to this theory tended to see the United States as promoting underdevelopment, or dependency, by a series of conscious decisions made both in public and private circles. These decisions were aimed at maintaining the prosperity of the United States at the expense of the underdeveloped nations of the world. This meant controlling access to key natural resources, maintaining dominance in finances, promoting U.S. technological superiority, keeping the edge in strategic and military options, and, in a host of other ways, denying to the underdeveloped world the ability to rise above their circumstances, and, in essence, maintaining the Perus of the world in a "dependent" relationship.

Like all overarching theories, dependency has some basis in fact, but is flawed in too many ways to be valid. Furthermore the theory is simplistic in that it leaves out many elements, such as the behavior of the Peruvian elites who often found it convenient to ally themselves with the United States to protect their privileged position within society. And the Peruvian economy itself, as it developed in the 1950s and 1960s, was remarkably diversified, responding to internal needs as much as to external demands. Manufacturing and industrialization increased rapidly during this period, the impetus of which was more often than not national, rather than foreign, in origin and execution—which is a keystone of dependency theory. Peruvians were not simply codependent clients of the United States, but independent actors who sought their own ends, often quite successfully and independent of American wishes. The Peruvian Institutional Revolution of 1968 is the most obvious case in point, and the relations with the United States within the context and time frame of the revolution's major influence from 1968 to 1975 is explored in detail in subsequent chapters. If dependency is wanting as a general, inclusive framework, what then explains the complex relations between the two?

Rather than simply ascribing Peru's problems to the manipulation of the United States (as does the dependency theory), postdependency theory, on the other hand, looks to internal or domestic factors in Peru for the cause of its underdevelopment. This book incorporates both the dependency and postdependency theories in analyzing the relationship between Peru and the United States. In postdependency theory Peruvian elites, for example, are held as much accountable for underdevelopment as are foreign factors or dominance. Mario Vargas Llosa, the world-renowned novelist who ran for president in 1990 against Fujimori, described *dependentistas* (dependency theorists) and their reliance on the foreign card in Peru's underdevelopment as the "Great Satan" theory. Vargas Llosa pilloried the leftist intellectual elites not only for their smug assertions of a superior ideology but for their simplistic analysis. Postdependency came of age in Peru with the election of 1990, which revealed Peru's national problems to be basically a function of its own society rather than attributable in the main to foreign dominance.

Both dependency and postdependency theories contain valid frames of reference with which to analyze the long history of Peru and the United States. In some respects, however, postdependency theory is more satisfactory, for it is more flexible than dependency theory, not always trying to make the facts fit the theory, no matter how forced the fit.

Ambiguity, the third framework of this relationship, has always figured in the perceptions of one people by the other, especially from the Peruvian perspective. Over the years Peruvians have alternatively viewed the United States with profound admiration and with equally profound suspicion and dislike. They have enthusiastically sought U.S. capital and technology to develop and modernize the Peruvian economy. With equal vigor they have denounced American imperialism and capitalism as intrusive and subversive of Peruvian peoples and culture.

American attitudes toward Peru are more difficult to analyze because Peru does not figure prominently in the American consciousness. Not until the late twentieth century and the advent of the cocaine trade have Americans been exposed widely to Peru. Stories about Peru have appeared in selected journals and periodicals over the years, most notably in *National Geographic,* but the image portrayed has been highly selective. Those few Americans who read about Peru may believe its principal product is cocaine and most of its people are descendants of the Incas who live in the high sierras.

In the latter portion of this volume—especially in the final two chapters—some of the major cultural ingredients in the formation of attitudes and stereotypes are presented and analyzed. These include the gamut ranging from the drinking of Coca-Cola to the growing network of Peruvians and Americans who share information, views, and opinions on the Internet. Relations between the two peoples are determined not simply by commercial and political linkages but by the sometimes more subtle, but no less persuasive, transfer and influence of cultural, religious, social, scientific, technological and intellectual values, information, and commodities.

Attitudes toward liberty and equality (the fourth framework) have sometimes coincided, sometimes diverged over the course of two centuries. When such attitudes coincided, as during the 1920s under the regime of President Augusto Leguía, the relationship between the two countries was remarkably close, even harmonious. When they differed, especially after the Peruvian Institutional Revolution of 1968, relations soured, and conflict rather than consensus tended to be the norm. This dynamic tension between liberty and equality underscores much of modern Peruvian-U.S. relations. Many Peruvians, such as APRA founder, Victor Raúl Haya de la Torre, sought equality in a nation long dominated by the unequal distribution of power and privilege, while the U.S., in the main, supported the liberty of the individual (that support was tempered by certain events, such as the Great Depression). When the balance was tipped to one side in both countries (as in the 1920s toward liberty, toward equality in the 1960s) the sharing of a vision tended to harmonize relations between the nations. When, as in 1968 and for a few years afterward, the pendulums swung in opposite directions, relations were severely strained. By the 1990s the pendulum had swung back to liberty, especially with the overwhelming collapse of communism worldwide. Once again Peruvians and Americans appeared to view the world and its needs through a similar prism, this time emphasizing, as in the 1920s, free-market principles (neoliberal-ism), liberty, and private property. The cocaine trade and the Shining Path terrorist movement complicated this contemporary relationship. As noted above, in evaluating the relative threat to Peruvian stability from drugs and terrorists, Peruvians put terrorists first while the United States pointed to drugs, setting up a clear conflict.

Other issues in the last half of the twentieth century are important to Peruvian-U.S. relations. As suggested, economic dependence became a primary issue after mid-century while communism, and its threats, dominated the picture for several decades. Liberation theology and evangelical or Pentecostal Protestantism furthermore colored the way Americans and Peruvians viewed their worlds and each other. In 1990 a practicing Pentecostal was elected vice president of Peru, along with the second-generation Japanese-Peruvian Alberto Fujimori as president. In an historically Roman Catholic country dominated by an elite descended from Hispanic culture, this constituted a *major departure* in modern Peruvian history. And much of what was Pentecostal and evangelical came through American pathways.

Peruvian and American destinies have crossed over the last two centuries in a remarkable dance of unequal partners, yet one in which Peru has retained and indeed defined its modern identity separate from the United States, but never so separate as to be outside the orbit of the modern American empire.

1   Getting to Know You

Peru is singularly destitute of the requisite character for sustaining an elective republic. The most that could have been done at the outset, would have been to have administered a republican system in a monarchical spirit, preparing the people gradually for the unbiased exercise of the elective franchise and other civil rights.

William Tudor, 1825, first U.S. consul to Peru

Americans

In the early nineteenth century American behavior toward the emerging state of Peru reflected contradictory views—a realistic or practical point of view on the one hand, philosophical and altruistic on the other. This duality set the pattern for the two-centuries-old Peruvian-U.S. relationship.

From the practical point of view, it was in the interest of American trade and commerce to encourage the independence of Peru. Despite Spanish prohibitions, contraband and illegal trade developed in the late eighteenth century and flourished between some areas of North America and Latin America during the Napoleonic Wars.

During the Spanish-American Wars of Independence (1810–25), American traders, principally from New England ports and the Middle Atlantic states, competed with British merchants to sell their wares— everything from muskets to kegs of flour to cheap textiles—in the newly opened ports of Latin America. More resistant to the Yankee traders was the old viceroyalty of Peru, not liberated until late 1824 under the assault of patriot armies led by Simón Bolívar and José de San Martín. Nonetheless Yankee traders had already penetrated Peruvian markets.

The motivation to trade and compete in the newly opening markets of Peru was powerful among Americans who adopted the liberal belief that free trade should exist between the nations of the world. Free exchange of goods and products would presumably increase the wealth and prosperity of all parties and promote goodwill and understanding among the peoples of the world. Of no less importance was the belief that keen competition among all parties—traders, manufacturers, shippers, and investors for example—ultimately produced the most benefits for all involved. Another American assumption was the belief in unlimited resources and opportunities throughout the world. Nature existed to be conquered and exploited by man. The only limitations to the Peruvian situation were those imposed by Spain, such as monopoly laws, restrictions to trade, and so forth. That these limitations would be lifted with the end of Spanish rule in Peru made the coming of independence even more appealing to Americans who viewed Peru as a new and attractive marketplace.

American religion, politics, and individualism reinforced the notion that the United States had a special role to play in the Western Hemisphere. Almost messianic in concept, but well grounded in economic self-interest, Americans possessed a well-defined sense of mission. This belief (known as "manifest destiny" to a later generation) proclaimed that the United States had the obligation to spread the virtues of its exceptional civilization to the rest of the Western Hemisphere. The Mexican War of 1848 and the continental expansion of the United States to the Pacific coast were but two manifestations of this destiny. By the end of the nineteenth century, manifest destiny had evolved into imperialism, a potent force in the dynamic equation of relations between the United States and Peru from that time until today.

It is important to recognize the missionary dimension accompanying nineteenth-century America's sense of manifest destiny. Americans seemed committed to spreading the benefits of freedom and liberty, as they understood them, throughout the Western Hemisphere. They reinforced their devotion to these secular values, moreover, with the teachings of American Protestantism, which commanded them—as Christianity did in general—to spread the word. The serious overtures made later in the century in an effort to transform Peru into a de facto U.S.

protectorate give credence to these powerful currents of imperialism then prevailing in the United States.

Peruvians

The Peruvian reality was as complex—perhaps more so—as the American view of the world. Though both Peruvians and Americans fought wars for independence that substituted a constitutional, republican form of government for monarchy, these similarities masked profound differences. Simón Bolívar, Peru's liberator, may have been a kindred spirit of George Washington and Thomas Jefferson, but the social and cultural habits, political customs, and economic preferences of the great majority of ordinary people were often vastly different.

Peruvians' colonial heritage differed fundamentally from that of Americans.[1] The Spanish subscribed to absolutism in government, to the rigid acceptance of monarchy, and to a faith in the State and its king as the principal source of authority in the land. Religion required orthodoxy and conformity to the Holy Roman Catholic Church. Anything less meant persecution and exile. In the economic order of things, the individual accepted a world that did not change from one generation to another. Described by some as the image of the "limited good," this view acknowledged "that the available amount of wealth, goods, and resources was relatively fixed and that it was beyond human power to expand the total."[2]

By the early nineteenth century, Peru had evolved into a distinct society. At the top of the racial pyramid in Peru were the Creoles, descendants of the sixteenth-century Spanish conquistadors and their successors. They became the masters of the land and its people. Three centuries of rule reinforced the Creole sense of superiority.

Monarchists by temperament, Creoles were nonetheless comfortable with the principles of the Enlightenment that had inspired a generation of American revolutionaries. They admired those liberating doctrines that called for the elimination of titles and the social leveling of all men to the rank of "citizen" during the French Revolution. However they abhorred the execution of Louis XVI. Simón Bolívar's rule exemplified this contradictory nature. He believed that all men are equal and in the principle that sovereignty lay with the people, especially as demonstrated by the government of the fledgling United States. Yet in 1826 he wrote a conservative constitution for Bolivia that, among other things, provided for an executive elected for life. While he viewed the successful republican, constitutional experiment to the north with unqualified admiration, he was also deeply suspicious of the potential expansion of American power over the whole of the Western Hemisphere, suffocating the newly independent and embryonic Latin American identity.

Unlike North America where whites dominated the continent both numerically and culturally, in Peru, Amerindians constituted a majority of the population. The Amerindians were indigenous to America and descendants of high civilizations in the Andes. There was also an African-Peruvian population descended from African slaves introduced during the colonial period to supplement the Amerindian population devastated and demoralized by the shock of the conquest and by European diseases. From these three races there emerged others, for miscegenation flourished between the victors and the vanquished in unions both illicit and blessed—mostly the former—in the succeeding years.

Unions between conquistador and Amerindian produced mestizos. Peru not only retained a high percentage of pure Amerindians within its population, but the mestizos—often called *cholos*—expanded proportionally over the years to become eventually the dominant ethnic group. During the wars of independence the revolutionary armies depended heavily upon mestizos not only to fill the ranks but also to serve as officers. These individuals often distinguished themselves in battle. Some, such as the mestizo Andrés Santa Cruz of Bolivia, rose to the highest levels of the officer corps. Santa Cruz eventually became president of his country, as did another mestizo, Ramón Castilla, one of the stablest and most effective presidents in Peru during the mid-nineteenth century.

In the twentieth century, mestizos rose to positions of prominence and influence in Peru, bringing to Peruvian foreign policy a different vision of the world. They looked neither exclusively to Spain nor to the ancient empire of the Inca for inspiration. As the sons and daughters of both, their identity with the modern Peruvian nation—*la patria* (the fatherland) in Spanish—was more complete than either Creole or Indian. Its legacy was a frustrating but creative vision of what Peru's relationship should be with the United States.

The lot of Peruvian Amerindians changed very little in the colonial period. The Wars of Independence presumably secured their place within the Peruvian polity, as the various constitutions recognized and encouraged their participation in the progressive, democratic, individualistic society envisioned by Simón Bolívar and others of his generation. But that wish proved to be a chimera. Most Amerindians continued to labor on the land, or in the mines and workshops of Peru's highlands, subordinate to the Peruvian elites who considered them to be little more than brutes—ignorant, docile, stubborn, and sometimes dangerous.

Peruvian economic and political life revolved around the State, considered the prime regulator of life within the nation. Americans, on the other hand, saw the role of the State differently. Fredrick Pike stated it from the American point of view: "American individualism . . . has fostered an ingrained suspiciousness of government. For a society that placed its faith in individualism, logic demanded that interference with the private bargaining process be kept to an absolute minimum." The Bolivian Mariano Gamucio expressed the Peruvian point of view well: Latin American society "turns around the State"; American society "turns around the individual . . . and around business."[3] This difference in the view of the role of government in society has proved a powerful undercurrent in shaping the Peruvian-U.S. relationship.

Another phenomenon particularly Peruvian (and Latin American) was the caudillo ruler. Variously translated as "strongman," or "dictator," the caudillo was best represented by Bolívar, sometimes labeled the "first" caudillo in Peru. A military man, a powerful personality, an arbiter of power and privilege, Bolívar preached republicanism but practiced dictatorship. This apparent contradiction has bedeviled Peruvian-U.S. relations from then until now. Since Bolívar, many caudillos have presided over the Peruvian world, and have often dictated foreign policy toward the United States.

William Tudor, the first U.S. consul to Peru and a close observer of Bolívar, expected much from the liberator in the way of republicanism, constitutionality, and liberty. Yet Bolívar, the authoritarian caudillo, repelled Tudor, the republican Yankee from Massachusetts. Instead of modeling himself on George Washington, Bolívar chose Napoleon Bonaparte. Instead of championing civil authority, Bolívar chose to rule as a military chieftain. Tudor observed Bolívar in the last stages of his evolution from republicanism to dictatorship, from liberator to tyrant. His expectations of Bolivar—"animated by the most pure and lofty ambition"—were dashed by the descent of the liberator "from that lofty eminence where posterity would have recognized him, to confound himself with the ignoble herd of ambitious, usurping, *military chieftains* [emphasis added]."[4] A distaste for caudillos characterized early Peruvian-U.S. relations.

Early on American concepts of race, of the worth of revolutions, and of the Peruvian political character in general, set the matrix for American attitudes and behavior toward Peru. Conversely Peruvians looked at North America through their own prism of local and internal realities.

Revolutions, Race, and the Black Legend

The United States was born through revolution so it was natural for Americans to view the Latin American Wars of Independence with sympathy. Just as liberty had triumphed over tyranny in North America, so it should be encouraged in Latin America in those Spanish colonies suffering from long oppression by a Spain viewed as reactionary, intolerant, and tyrannical. Indeed the U.S. Constitution and other key documents were translated and widely admired and copied in Latin America. "We were their greatest example," said Henry Clay (U.S. Secretary of State under John Quincy Adams; 1824–28). "Of us they constantly spoke as of brothers, having a similar origin. They adopted our principles, copied our institutions, and in some instances, employed the very language and sentiments of our revolutionary papers."[5]

There existed other, more practical, causes for supporting the Latin American Wars of Independence, notably the great commercial instinct of Americans who viewed an independent Latin America as a market of vast potential. Notwithstanding the practical considerations, the revolutionary origins of both the United States and Peru imparted a sense of communion between the patriots of North America and the liberators of Peru in the nineteenth century.

Yet Clay's sympathetic views were not typical of those held by most American political leaders. Differing perceptions of race, for example, affected early Peruvian-U.S. relations. Americans tended to stereotype Peruvians—and most all other Latin Americans as well—as a mongrelized race with strong Negroid and Indian features; however the ruling Creoles—whites—fashioned Peruvian policies toward North America for a century after independence. Yet Americans often interacted with Peru on the basis of the stereotype rather than the reality.[6] Americans considered Latin Americans in general as racially inferior.[7] Although racism existed in both American and Peruvian societies, it took a particularly virulent form in North America, born, as John Johnson so well described it, "of a combination of emotionalism, biological taboos, and hereditarian determinism."[8]

Consul Tudor's reflections in the mid-1820s were not untypical. Andrés Santa Cruz, a mestizo from Bolivia who later became president of Bolivia and then of a short-lived Peru-Bolivia confederation (1836–39), provoked Tudor to observe that individuals of "mixed blood" were possessed of volatile, mercurial temperaments. "Santa Cruz," wrote Tudor, "has some mixture of Pocahontas blood, which mixtures are here called Cholos; is amiable and affable in his manners, but his conduct was wavering and uncertain in the progress of recent events: [he is] cursed with an unfortunate mixture of qualities, is timid, indecisive, and ambitious. . . ."[9] Furthermore Americans tended to transfer their negative images of Hispanic culture in general to Peruvian culture.

John Randolph of Roanoke, Virginia, disparaged the Spanish legacy in Latin America because it had fatally crippled the possibilities of a free, successful, republican form of government. "The struggle for liberty in South America will turn out in the end something like the French liberty, a detestable despotism," Randolph said. "You cannot make liberty out of Spanish matter—you might as well try to build a seventy-four [frigate-style ship] out of pine saplings."[10]

A few American observers were more tolerant in their estimation of Latin American prospects. H. M. Brackenridge, who took part in a special mission to Latin America in 1817, looked condescendingly upon Latin Americans as generally backward, but, like all human beings, inherently good and better fitted for liberty and self-government than Europeans.[11] Once liberty was won, the region, endowed with rich natural resources, held a great future. The United States of course stood to benefit in a practical way as these eighteen million souls turned from Europe to the United States for trade and commerce. It was hoped the new governments would be republican, but if Peruvians chose a monarchical one, that was their own affair.

The ambivalence in American attitudes toward Latin American independence was perhaps best expressed by Jefferson, who observed that "history . . . furnishes no example of a priest-ridden people maintaining a free government." Nonetheless independence was to be welcomed, for whatever governments resulted "they will be *American* governments, no longer to be involved in the never-ceasing broils of Europe." Jefferson was expressing one manifestation of the Western Hemisphere idea that held that the peoples of the Americas were special and different from their European origins. There existed a destiny formed by geographical uniqueness, providence, and historical circumstances which set the Americas apart. This general philosophical perspective tended to unify rather than divide the visions of Peruvians and Americans over the course of the next two centuries.

In the early stages of Peruvian-U.S. relations, more immediate and practical concerns dominated the relationship. Larger and deeper questions—the structure of a multiracial society, the emerging struggle between liberals and conservatives (or the modernists and traditionalists), the issue of the church and religious mission, the notion of an American system, or the Western Hemisphere idea—were subordinated to more immediate concerns. What interested Peruvian patriots and Yankee consuls, skippers, and traders were the problems of recognition, protecting neutrals' rights, and opening commercial bridgeheads between North America and Peru.

Independence and Early Relations

In the early months of 1788, the frigate *Columbia* and the smaller *Lady Washington,* both sailing out of Boston, rounded Cape Horn and entered the Pacific bound for Nootka Sound on the far west coast of North America. Storms so tore up the *Columbia* that she put in at Juan Fernandez Island on May 24. Her captain, John Kendrick, asked the Spanish governor, Blas González, for assistance in repairing his ship, which had gotten separated from the *Lady Washington* during the tempest rounding the Horn. As the Peruvian historian Félix Denegri Luna observed, "thus these Yankee mariners made the first contacts with Peru," initiating the long relationship between North America and Peru.[12]

A year later in 1789, the American whaler *Beaver* of Nantucket crossed into the Pacific, to be followed by many hundreds of Yankee whalers in her wake over the next century. Merchantmen also began to trade with the viceroyalty of Peru in this same period as Yankees and Creoles discovered and probed each other's worlds with some curiosity. Some carried dry goods, rum, brandy, naval stores, and furniture to exchange for the silver of Peru. William Shaler and Richard Cleveland visited Valparaíso, Chile, in 1802 on their way to the Pacific Northwest and Canton in China. Prevented from trading in that Chilean port, Shaler and Cleveland nonetheless were warmly received by Chilean Creoles. Before Shaler sailed, he left his Chilean friends with a Spanish translation of the U.S. Declaration of Independence and a copy of the Constitution of the United States and with a clear notion of the firm relationship between independence and prosperity.[13]

Frigate Diplomacy: The Politics
of Independence and Recognition

While relatively few Americans ventured into Peru during the Wars of Independence, those who did were generally a gregarious, entrepreneurial lot. The most numerous were whalers from such Yankee ports as New Bedford and Nantucket in search of the great sperm whales of the Pacific. By 1817–18 there were more than a hundred American whalers off the west coast of South America. Most made port stops at such places as Arica, Callao, and Paita between their long voyages into the Pacific, and many brought goods with them to trade with the Peruvians.[14]

The *Improvement* from Nantucket was a typical venture. She put in at Arica on July 31, 1821, to take on water and provisions. Anchored in the roadsteads, her officers and crew laid out their wares for visiting Peruvians. From the trunks and boxes stored in the holds below came broadcloths, gown-pieces, cottons, and linens, all hung on the rigging for a better view. Hats, hardware, powder and ball, cutlery, and other items covered the decks. The Peruvians usually paid in gold and silver specie. It was a good trade for both.[15] The Yankees were delighted to have the bullion, and the Peruvians received wares and goods either not available in Peru, or, if available, not of the same quality and price as that offered by the American ships. Or, perhaps, the novelty of buying something from abroad made the trade even more desirable to both parties. Commercial and social interchanges such as these formed the context for the earliest relations between the United States and Peru—private ventures and good trade for all parties.

American merchantmen stopped in at Callao and other Pacific ports on their way to the Pacific Northwest and China. The *America* from New York put in at Callao on April 6, 1822, loaded for the Peruvian market with four thousand barrels of flour and an assortment of other products, including paint (two hundred kegs), silk goods, cottons, bearskins, and medicines. Other American ships brought in bacon, beef, butter, sugar, tobacco, wood, quicksilver, and more flour. The Peruvians liked American products, and Americans were predisposed to favor a free Peru.

The principal problem American merchantmen faced related to the various blockades declared by the combatants, Peruvian patriots and Spanish royalists. By 1819 most of the west coast of South America was under a blockade, declared by either patriots or royalists. Both interpreted their blockades rather loosely, leading to countless seizures of American merchantmen and their ships.

U.S. naval commanders on station, such as Capt. John Downes in command of the frigate *Macedonian*, often were rather forthright in favoring the patriot cause. In 1820 Downes was anchored in Callao in an effort to protect U.S. merchantmen in that harbor when Adm. Thomas Cochrane, an English veteran of the Napoleonic Wars who was fighting on the patriot side for the independence of Chile, launched one of the boldest sea raids made during the Wars of Independence.

On the night of November 5, 1820, Cochrane's Chilean sailors and marines entered the harbor in their longboats with oars muffled to seize the Spanish frigate *Esmeralda,* which was lying at anchor in Callao. To reach the *Esmeralda* the boats passed both under the guns of the British frigate *Amphion* and the American *Macedonian* moored in the harbor.

Surprise was key. The British watch hailed the passing patriot boats and almost blew the raid. The Americans, on the other hand, let the boats pass unchallenged. In fact, the *Macedonian*'s crew quietly cheered the patriots on.[16] Cochrane and his men surprised the *Esmeralda,* quickly overwhelmed the small watch on duty, and sailed her out of the harbor, showing neutral lights to further confuse the startled Spanish garrison in Callao. The *Esmeralda* was immediately pressed into the service of the Chilean Navy.

Royalists in Callao were outraged at the complicity of the Americans. Two American sailors were killed and several wounded by the royalists the next day when they went ashore, prompting Downes to demand the arrest and prosecution of the murderers, a request to which Viceroy Joaquín de la Pezuela agreed.

Peru's declaration of independence came on July 28, 1821. It was made by the Argentine general José de San Martín in the Plaza de Armas of Lima, and it gave form to Peruvian aspirations. "Peru is, henceforth, free and independent, made so by the will of her people and by the justice of her cause which God supports."[17] Under the Argentine liberator's aegis, Peru received the trappings of a new nation: her flag, her national hymn, the beginnings of her own administrative regime, her own currency, the ships of her fledgling navy, her national library, and a constituent assembly that met for the first time on September 20, 1822. Peru was under way. On May 4, 1822, Peru's independence was recognized by the United States.[18] But the battles to establish independence in fact were yet to be won.

During the height of the military campaigns for independence in Peru in 1822–23, five to ten American ships could be found at any one time in the harbors of the west coast of Peru. Warfare almost always gives business a rosy booming aspect, and American traders—claiming neutrality—made the most of a highly profitable, albeit risky, marketplace. American merchants traded with both royalists and patriots, a practice that sometimes resulted in confrontations, fines, and even imprisonment. But the high profits more than compensated for the high risks.[19]

The problem for Captain Downes and his successors, Capt. Charles G. Ridgely and Commo. Charles Stewart, was to favor the patriots but strive to uphold a neutral's rights in the conflict between patriots and royalists. Stewart was not only instructed to favor the patriot cause but also to uphold the United States's neutrals rights with the upmost vigilance, a position that sometimes struck directly at the patriot cause.[20] (Neutrals rights is an issue related to naval warfare. Neutrals claimed the right to trade with all legitimate combatants, while the combatants themselves reserved the right to maintain blockades and thus keep neutrals out of the harbors of their enemies.) By the time his cruise ended in 1824, Stewart had so thoroughly offended patriots, royalists, and partisans of all stripes that the Secretary of the Navy felt compelled to call a court-martial to clear Stewart's good name and reputation. In essence Stewart's court-martial was the official investigation into the navy's participation in the Wars of Independence.

Stewart was cleared of all charges and vindicated. "It is impossible for any commanding officer to be in the Pacific without giving offence to the one side or the other," one member of the court, Captain Biddle, observed. "The royal party," Biddle continued, "knowing the general feelings of our countrymen, are jealous of them; the patriots, on the other hand, expecting too much, are dissatisfied." [21] Stewart's successor, Commo. Isaac Hull, commanding the frigate *United States*, arrived on station in 1824, the final, crucial year in the struggle for independence of Peru.

The Address by Monroe

President James Monroe had already articulated the premises of U.S. policy toward the Spanish-American Wars of Independence. On December 2, 1823, President Monroe declared that henceforth the Western Hemisphere was closed to further European colonization, that European powers should not interfere in the independence movements in Latin America, and that the Western Hemisphere was so transparently different from Europe that in reality "two spheres" existed, neither of which should interfere in the matters of the other.

No other statement of purpose, of intention, or of political philosophy had a greater impact on the status of Peruvian-U.S. relations over the course of the next 150 years. Monroe's message in essence cast an American umbrella over the independence movements in Latin America. [22] The flourishing commercial trade between the United States and the west coast of South America certainly prompted one aspect of President Monroe's declaration, while the patriotic cause drew upon the natural sympathies of Americans. Commerce between the United States and the South American west coast grew especially active in the years 1823–24, fueled mostly by the needs of the combatants. During that period up to ten American merchantmen were found on any given day in the port of Callao.

While Monroe's message was addressed more to Europe than to Latin America, it was the first major policy address made by the United States with respect to Latin America. In a somewhat similar vein, Simón Bolívar also expressed a vision for the Americas in 1824. In December the liberator called for a congress of American nations to convene in Panama in 1826. This "Panama Congress" symbolized Bolívar's vision of a common American heritage that needed to be cultivated, and the Congress is often considered the beginning of the Pan-American system that evolved in later years.[23]

Neither Monroe's declaration nor Bolívar's Panama Congress had much immediate effect on relations between the United States and Peru, but each expressed a vision of the future that emphasized the Pan-American context of Peru's relations with the United States. Some have interpreted Monroe's Doctrine as disingenuous, masking ulterior motives by the United States to exercise control over the destinies of Latin America. Bolívar almost always expressed himself with ambiguity regarding the United States, admiring its republican institutions but fearing its growing wealth and power. The United States, Bolívar wrote, was "destined by Providence to plague America with torments in the name of freedom."[24]

The ubiquitous Bolívar presided over the culmination of the Peruvian independence movement in 1823 and 1824.[25] The year 1824 ended with a one-hour battle fought on the breathtaking heights of Ayacucho Province situated at 11,600 feet in the Andes. This battle broke the back of Spanish resistance to the independence of Peru. Taken as prisoners were the Viceroy José de la Serna, 13 generals, 16 colonels, 68 lieutenant colonels, 484 subalterns, and 3,200 privates.[26] After the Battle of Ayacucho, Peru was independent both in name—its declaration made by San Martín in 1821—and in fact. "This memorable battle," wrote William Tudor, "secured in one day the independence of Peru and terminated the Spanish empire in America; and as this country [Peru] was the last of this continent in which Spain maintained a struggle, the world may now hope that the South American republics will be recognized by every civilized state, peace restored to the world, and the cause of freedom and national improvements obtain a lasting triumph."[27]

Private Matters: Peruvian-U.S. Relations to Mid-Century

These were noble and earnest sentiments expressed by an obscure U.S. consul who personally crafted the earliest relations between an independent Peru and the United States. Tudor was the quintessential Yankee—born to a Congregationalist minister and his wife in Massachusetts, a graduate of Harvard, cosmopolitan, and well traveled among the capitals of Europe. Equally important, Tudor was a businessman, and therein lies one key to the development of early relations between Peru and the United States.

U.S. policy toward Peru in this period was largely sculpted by consuls, chargé d'affaires, and naval officers concerned with protecting and enhancing American *commercial interests*. Policies toward the region were born of mercantile and commercial considerations, revealing a more private rather than public nature to the early relations between the United States and Peru.[28]

The American in Peru in the first half of the nineteenth century was very much a business creature, often the archetypal Yankee trader, pushing his wares and himself with vigor and conviction. The image that Peruvians first formed of Americans was through this ambitious trader. There were no Fulbright fellows, no exchange professors, no overseas students, no Peace Corps volunteers, no outlandishly dressed tourists, no mobs of diplomats and military attachés to confuse the imagery. There were only the businessmen, the chargé (the first to Peru came in 1826), the naval officers, and a few consuls.

The contrasting personalities of William Tudor and Simón Bolívar perhaps best exemplified the cultural gulf between Americans and Spanish Americans. A self-righteous republican and democrat from North America, Tudor often disparaged the authoritarian caudillo who became the dictator of Peru. Tudor was a civilian to the core; Bolívar was a military man. Tudor was ardently committed to a republican form of government—in theory *and* practice—while Bolívar governed by decrees. Tudor thought Bolívar to be tyrannical and despotic. Bolívar lectured Tudor on the impossibility of introducing true democracy to a people so ill-prepared for self-government. "It is however necessary to admit," Tudor relented, "that Peru is singularly destitute of the requisite character for sustaining an elective republic. The most that could have been done at the outset, would have been to have administered a republican system in a monarchical spirit, preparing the people gradually for the unbiased exercise of the elective franchise and other civil rights."[29]

Later American representatives to Peru voiced much the same opinion as Tudor. None reflected better Tudor's pessimism than James C. Pickett, chargé in Lima from 1839 to 1845. "I doubt much whether the Spanish Americans have gained anything by their independence, except freedom of commerce," Pickett wrote, "and . . . I doubt too their fitness, in general, for a democratic form of government and for democratic institutions."[30]

Yet there were times when the differences were bridged, however briefly. The year after the Battle of Ayacucho was a euphoric one for patriots and patriot-sympathizers in Peru. George Washington's birthday was celebrated with gusto by the Americans in Callao on February 22, 1825, and Commo. Isaac Hull hosted the festivities aboard his flagship, the frigate United States. Decks holystoned and yardarms festooned with her finest colors and pennants, the frigate presented a proud sight to the American citizens in Lima and Callao. Bolívar himself, as well as other foreign naval officers and diplomats, joined the festivities. The dress was resplendent, the day warm and sunny, for February 22 falls in the middle of coastal Peru's brilliant, rainless summer.

Bolívar still had not completely crossed his Rubicon from republican to tyrant. Hearing the toasts raised one after the other to Washington and his noble exploits, Bolívar caught the mood of the Americans as they praised General La Fayette, the beloved Frenchman who gave so much of himself in the American Revolution, and toasted other foreigners who had battled in the cause of U.S. freedom and independence.

Bolívar fondly recalled the role foreigners had played in Peru's own recent wars. He raised his glass, and all listened as the liberator made a complimentary speech to La Fayette and other friends of liberty. The toast sat well with the assembled officers, consuls, merchants, and their ladies. The day done, Americans and Peruvians returned to those practical matters that governed early relations between the two countries—commerce—and they continued to dicker and argue over their differences, principally patriot seizures of U.S. merchantmen accused of violating patriot blockades or of trading with the royalists.

Indeed the claims of U.S. merchantmen against the Peruvian government dominated Peruvian-U.S. diplomatic and commercial relations for the next quarter century.[31] These claims—amounting almost to half a million dollars—were not settled until 1841 when the Claims Convention between the two nations was signed.

Differences aside, Tudor and his successors worked to increase commerce between the United States and Peru. Tudor was joined in Peru by James Cooley of Pennsylvania, who became the first U.S. chargé d'affaires to Peru. Cooley arrived in Peru in 1827, but his visit was cut short by a bilious attack, which overcame him in early 1828. He was replaced by Samuel Larned who arrived in Peru in 1829 as the second chargé. Tudor, meanwhile, was transferred to Rio de Janeiro in 1828. In 1830 Tudor, the Yankee from Massachusetts and the first U.S. consul to Peru, caught a fever and died within a few days.

Peru's tumultuous politics frustrated virtually every U.S. effort to negotiate a satisfactory commercial accord. One of Larned's contemporaries, Commo. Jacob Jones, in command of the U.S. Pacific squadron in the Pacific in 1828, tried to take the political pulse of Peru but found it "impossible to say how many parties there are in Peru and what are their objects."[32]

From the late 1820s until near mid-century, government was based largely on usurpation of power. Military chieftains strode in and out of power, an attempted confederation between Peru and Bolivia in 1836 brought on a war with Chile, and commerce between the United States and Peru plunged in value and volume from the highs seen at the end of the Wars of Independence. Business reached a nadir of sorts in the year 1836. In that year Peruvian imports into the United States fell to $155,831 while exports to Peru dropped to $918, a figure statistically insignificant. Yet even during this depression in commercial relations, some aspects of the trade prefigured later trends.

The preference for American products was already apparent. Peruvians of the upper-middle and upper classes preferred their bread made from flour imported from Baltimore and New York—perhaps because of its quality, as chargé Larned believed or, more likely, because it was *not* Chilean. Peruvian reaction to foreign trade was, of course, not uniform.[33] Some merchants improved their lot through trade and commerce between Peru and the United States and thus were in favor of free trade and were generally pro-American. Those challenged by U.S. imports—native textile manufacturers in northern Peru, for example—wanted to keep the markets closed and protected. The latter were more likely to adopt protectionist and nationalist positions and to be anti-American.

A parallel issue between the United States and Peru was the question of recognition. Was the United States bound to recognize only duly-elected, constitutional de jure governments, or did Peruvian realities dictate a more practical recognition policy? The United States decided that all governments would be recognized as de facto governments. It was not the business of the United States to sit in judgment on the "internal affairs of other powers."[34] This was a sweeping statement of principle that governed relations between the United States and Peru for many years. "It is impossible that you can reform either the morals or the politics of Peru," Secretary of State James Buchanan declared in 1847.[35] One hundred years later, that policy would be stood on its head.

While most Americans making their way through Peru in the nineteenth century were given to trade and commerce, many were astute observers of the world through which they traveled. Several of these Americans, such as William Tudor, were learned gentlemen whose impressions of Peru helped to fashion the first images and stereotypes that Americans developed of the west coast of South America. Even before independence, young American sailors with an eye for romance and an irrepressible wanderlust were sailing into the Pacific on the whalers of New Bedford and Nantucket, bringing back the stuff of adventure, which would later be woven into such literary classics as Charles Henry Dana's *Two Years Before the Mast* and Herman Melville's *Billy Budd* and *Moby Dick*. These men not only plunged into the vast Pacific, touching in at Hawaii and other exotic ports of Polynesia, but they regularly put in at Paita in northern Peru to revictual and trade with the local inhabitants.

From Boston William Hickling Prescott delighted the world with his epochal histories of the Spanish conquests of the New World. His *His-*

tory of the Conquest of Peru, first published in 1847, was soon a best-seller, following his equally popular and powerful *Conquest of Mexico* published in 1843. Earlier, in 1829, Washington Irving published *The Life and Times of Christopher Columbus,* romanticizing a then relatively little-known figure in American history. After Irving's biography, Columbus and his venture gradually assumed heroic proportions in the American legend. By mid-century American readers were thus being entertained by spell-binding stories of such men as Francisco Pizarro, the conqueror of Peru. That country was being integrated into a hemispheric history that did not begin with John Smith and Pocahontas but with explorers and conquistadors, such as Columbus, Pizarro, and Hernando de Soto. The latter's career spanned the Americas from Peru to Florida, and he too, like Columbus, began to emerge in American letters as a romantic, dashing cavalier from the age of exploration and conquest.

The Guano Era in Peru

While Americans were being thrilled by the epic tales of conquest, a more vastly prosaic item was calling the attention of Americans to Peru at mid-century. A natural fertilizer called guano—the accumulation of thousands of years of bird droppings—was discovered by Americans and Europeans on islands off the coast of Peru. An 1824 article in *The American Farmer* appropriately noted guano's commercial prospects. "'Amongst other valuable and curious things brought by Midshipman Bland from the Pacific Ocean,' when he arrived at Baltimore aboard the U.S.S. 'Franklin' in 1824, 'was a small quantity of that celebrated manure, *Guano dung,* possessing such astonishing fertilizing properties.'"[36]

In the summer of 1841, the ship *Bonanza* arrived back home in England after a months-long voyage in the Pacific. In her holds were tons of this odiferous fertilizer. Her crew probably clambered ashore with greater than usual speed after the long voyage. The guano stunk, but it fetched a good price for the investors in the *Bonanza's* voyage, for this rich fertilizer was already known among some English farmers. Soon the word "guano" would spread across Europe and North America, dramatically transforming Peru and altering her relationship with the United States.

The remarkable properties that enabled it to rejuvenate exhausted soils attracted hundreds of vessels annually from the United States to the Chincha Islands off Peru where guano had accumulated to depths of hundreds of feet. As early as November 1841 James Pickett, U.S. chargé, had informed Secretary of State Daniel Webster that "a new source of wealth, or rather, the value of it, has been recently discovered in Peru." Pickett called it "huano," and continued, "it is found in great abundance, in some small islands [the Chinchas], a few degrees [latitude] to the south of Lima, and has been used in agriculture, for manure from time immemorial."[37]

A decade later almost a hundred thousand tons of guano were shipped to England, but U.S. demand soon surpassed this figure. Guano rejuvenated the depleted tobacco and cotton fields of Virginia, Maryland, Delaware, and North Carolina. By 1857 more guano—213,000 tons—was shipped to the United States than to Great Britain. The guano boom was then in full swing, bringing with it hundreds of American-owned downeasters and clipper ships to the Chincha Islands at mid-century. In Peru, a rising economic prosperity based on the boom formed the backdrop for increasing ties between Peru and the United States in the second half of the century. Although Great Britain continued to dominate the overall commercial and financial scene, the guano phenomenon was a harbinger of future trends. By mid-century, for example, Yankee skippers not only dominated the guano trade to the United States, but they also carried a fair share of the guano to Europe.

The 1847 Congress of Lima

As Peru's political situation stabilized under the growing economic prosperity produced by the guano boom, the Peruvian government undertook several international initiatives. On November 9, 1846, the Foreign Minister of Peru, José Gregorio Paz Soldán, issued a call for a congress of American ministers plenipotentiary to convene in Lima for the purpose of guaranteeing the security of South American nations.[38] The background to this call lay in the attempts of ex-president Juan José Flores of Ecuador to invite a European prince to sit on an Ecuadorian throne, thus establishing a monarchy in that country under Spanish or French auspices. Those nations closest to Ecuador resisted any such intervention by European powers, and the Peruvians took the lead in countering Flores's plans to launch his expedition from Europe. Furthermore the onset of the Mexican-American War in mid-1846 had alarmed several South American governments. The U.S. invasion of central Mexico in February 1847 appeared to validate Simón Bolívar's admonitions about the American threat to Spanish America.

The Congress of Lima (December 11, 1847-March 1, 1848) not only gave prominence to Peru, but brought the nature of early Peruvian-U.S. relations into focus. Though only the Pacific coast South American nations of Bolivia, Chile, Ecuador, Colombia, and Peru were represented, their goal was hemispheric—to defend South America and, secondarily, to provide for hemispheric cooperation in a number of areas, such as boundary conflicts, international aggression, duties, and tariffs. In the end none of the treaties were ratified.

Latin Americans debated on whether conferences that symbolized hemispheric solidarity should include the Anglo-Saxon nation to the north, especially now that it was pummeling Mexico into humiliating defeat. On the one hand, the United States possessed enough power and influence to help the Peruvians and their allies stop Flores in Europe before the monarchists could ever launch their expedition. On the other hand, did Peruvians wish to reach out to such a potential friend that was in the process of acquiring half of Mexico's national territory? If Mexico was dismembered today, would other countries be future targets of American "manifest destiny"?[39]

In the context of Peruvian-U.S. relations, the Lima Congress revealed a general ambivalence by Peruvians toward the United States. It was a theme never far from the surface of Peru's attitudes toward the United States for the next century and a half.[40]

Guano, Peru, and the United States

While the diplomats sparred, the businessmen, on the other hand, prospered. General trade between the United States and Peru benefited from the prosperity induced by the guano boom. Between 1851 and 1861 Peru's exports to the United States doubled in value while U.S. exports rose sevenfold, compared with exports of the previous decade. The disruptions produced by the American Civil War also failed to reverse this trend, for trade from 1861 to 1871 doubled again from the previous ten-year period. The balance of trade between 1840 and 1870 favored the United States by nearly two to one.

Exports to Peru tended to vary little in composition: coarse cottons, woolens, ready-made clothes, boots and shoes, wine and spirits, drugs and medicines, lumber, and even ice were unloaded at Peruvian ports. After guano, nitrate of soda (largely used as fertilizer as well) was the major Peruvian export, and by 1875 it had displaced guano. Smaller amounts of silver, wools (from Andean animals, such as the alpaca and vicuña), hides, bark, sarsaparilla, tobacco, wine, and spirits made up the returning cargoes.

Whaling continued to be a big business into the mid-nineteenth century. Ships from Nantucket, New Bedford, and other New England towns regularly called at such Peruvian ports as Paita in the north. In 1858 more than 660 American whalers were in the Pacific, manned by some 16,000 seamen. With such an increase in the contacts between the United States and Peru, collisions of interest were inevitable.

In 1852 some American guano speculators, led by James B. Jewett of New York, persuaded the U.S. government that the Lobos Islands off the north coast of Peru were uninhabited and unclaimed. Rich in guano the islands, located fifteen miles off the coast, could be mined freely by anyone. Peruvians hotly repudiated this point of view originally supported by the elderly Secretary of State Daniel Webster. The secretary had, in fact, been hoodwinked by Jewett and his principal collaborator, a ship captain named A. G. Benson, into truly believing that Peru did not have a legitimate claim to the Lobos Islands. President Millard Fillmore eventually was persuaded of the Peruvian point of view, and Peru's sovereignty was recognized without reservations. While the United States never questioned Peru's claims to the Chincha Islands—the principal source of guano—Americans did touch off numerous disputes that sometimes boiled up into international incidents. One such occasion involved Peru's seizure of the vessels *Georgiana* and *Lizzie Thompson* for improperly taking guano off Punta de Lobos and led to the rupture of diplomatic relations for almost a year during 1860 and 1861.

A U.S. representative in Peru, Randolph Clay, turned in his passports when the Peruvian government would not indemnify the owners of the vessels for the seizures. Cooler heads prevailed, and Jorge Basadre, Peru's premier historian, wrote that, indeed, "no animosity resulted from this affair," which was ultimately settled by the arbitration of the King of Belgium in 1862.[41]

Perhaps the rupture was inevitable, reflecting on the nature of Peru–United States relations. Randolph Clay turned in his passports as much as from the accumulation of many years of frustration in trying to obtain satisfaction from Peruvian governments for many other prior claims brought by U.S. citizens against Peru, as from the case of the *Georgiana* and *Lizzie Thompson*. In October 1860 Clay pointed out that nine claims—in addition to those of the *Georgiana* and *Lizzie Thompson*—were pending, all of which he had been trying for years to bring to settlement.

Doing business in Peru was profitable but frustrating, and American citizens invariably complained about the ethics and practices of Peruvians, both in and out of government. Ambivalence cut both ways. If Peruvians viewed the United States with a certain ambiguity, so did Americans view Peru.

The Amazon

A contemporaneous U.S. diplomatic goal was the opening of the great Amazon River and its tributaries to international navigation. Brazil and Peru were equally determined to exclude international participation in the opening of the Amazon. The tone and elements of the dispute over riparian rights echo today in the world's concern over the Amazon as a great natural resource.

When Secretary of State John Clayton asked the U.S. Navy to send a war vessel to explore the Amazon in May 1850, the Brazilians refused permission. The Secretary of the Navy then ordered two naval officers serving on board the U.S.S. *Vandalia* at Valparaíso to conduct an exploration of the great river from its sources to its mouth.[42]

Lt. William Lewis Herndon and Passed Midshipman Lardner Gibbon set out from Lima in May 1851. They climbed the Andes together before splitting up. Herndon's party struck northward to the Huallaga River valley (today one of the leading sources of coca plants) and from there descended down the Huallaga to the Marañon, the Amazon's main branch. They drifted down the Amazon for eleven months before reaching Pará on the Atlantic coast of Brazil. Gibbon turned south to Bolivia, where he was received most amicably, and then proceeded leisurely to descend the Madeira River to its union with the Amazon and thence to the sea. The subsequent two-volume report prepared for the navy was followed by a commercial edition in 1853 that delighted readers.[43] The Amazon, however, remained closed to international navigation.

Why were the Brazilians and Peruvians so opposed to free navigation of the Amazon? Perhaps the way in which the United States absorbed half of the Mexican national territory in the preceding thirty years was not too far from their minds. The Brazilian envoy Imbue Libya, who was sent to Ecuador, Colombia, and Venezuela in 1853 in an attempt to rush through treaties with these countries to close the Amazonian door to the United States, remarked that "if citizens of the United States were allowed once to establish themselves, either for purposes of trade or above, in the interior of South America, they would inevitably introduce their own institutions and renounce the allegiance of their adopted country."[44] That is indeed what happened in Mexico. Furthermore filibustering expeditions launched from the United States into Central America and Cuba were not uncommon. Perhaps Cuba would soon be absorbed into the United States. In 1855 William Walker, a filibusterer and southern expansionist, launched an invasion of Nicaragua, supported slavery there, and promoted the annexation of that Central American country into the United States. What next? Were the South Americans merely being paranoid? It seems not.

In the United States, Matthew Fontaine Maury, superintendent of the naval observatory in Washington, D.C., and brother-in-law of Lieutenant Herndon, did little to calm the anxieties of the Amazon basin countries. His overheated rhetoric set everyone on edge. Maury figured prominently at a convention in Memphis in 1853, which passed a chauvinistic memorial subsequently printed by the House of Representatives.[45] A Brazilian newspaper responded, "this nation [the United States] of pirates, like those of their race, wish to displace all the people of America who are not Anglo-Saxon." Maury had said Brazil and Peru must give way to the everlasting "principle of right."[46] In 1867, however, responding to different pressures and circumstances, Emperor Padre II of Brazil declared the Amazon open to international traffic. Peru followed suit soon thereafter and in May 1867 established the Hydrographic Commission of the Amazon to explore and prepare charts of the Amazon River system.[47]

To mid-nineteenth-century Peruvians, the more immediate threat in the upper Amazon region—called the *montaña* by the Peruvians—was not the United States but Brazil. As the rich guano beds on the Pacific coast were rapidly depleted, Peruvians looked to the montaña's potential natural resources, including forest products, minerals, and fertile lands. Conscious of their neighbors' potential designs on the region, Peruvians were also aware of their relative ignorance of the Amazon. If the montaña were to be developed, it would need a transportation infrastructure of steamboats, roads, and communications that would enable the flow of colonists, soldiers, and bureaucrats into the region—hence the decision in 1867 to create the Hydrographic Commission and the appointment of U.S. citizen John Randolph Tucker as its chief.

Tucker had already served Peru as head of the combined Peruvian-Chilean fleets in 1866 and 1867 during a short war with Spain. The ex-Confederate naval officer left for the jungle in 1867 with a small group of American and Peruvian naval officers, including Tucker's son, and

Leoncio Prado, the son of the Peruvian president Mariano Ignacio Prado. Prado later studied engineering in Richmond, Virginia, and he died a hero's death during the War of the Pacific. Other friends and contacts made by Tucker and his staff during their eight years in the Amazon were, or became, equally prominent citizens of Peru. Friendships forged in hard times and difficult circumstances (to be posted to the Peruvian Amazon was quite trying) subtly knit the fortunes of Peru and the United States into a tighter weave as the nineteenth century proceeded.

Tucker's headquarters until 1874 was Iquitos. Removed from the mainstream of national life, the natural wonders of the Amazon nonetheless attracted American scientists to Peru. When the celebrated natural scientist and New York author James Orton came through Iquitos in 1873, Dr. Francis Land Galt (Tucker's physician and a veteran of service aboard the famed Confederate raider C.S.S. *Alabama*) and his fellow ex-Confederates planned to snub this particular Yankee. In his popular *Andes and the Amazon* (first published in 1870), Orton mentioned that on an earlier voyage he had passed a steamer in 1867 carrying "the rebel" Admiral Tucker, a gratuitous insult in Galt's judgment. But Orton managed to charm the ex-Confederates during his visit by warmly seeking out his fellow countrymen.[48] The third edition of Orton's book (published in 1876) included Galt's treatise, "Medical Notes on the Upper Amazon," and much information in the *Andes and the Amazon* was derived from Tucker's Hydrographic Commission.

Dr. Galt's scientific curiosity transcended medicine. He made detailed meteorological observations, compiled a lexicon of Quechua and English, and wrote extensively on the Amerindian culture he encountered in his travels. The Smithsonian Institute, especially its superintendent Joseph Henry and the famed explorer and director of its Bureau of Ethnology, John Wesley Powell, showed an interest in the works that Galt submitted, and Galt's article "The Indians of Peru" appeared in the Smithsonian's *Annual Report* in 1877. It is considered one of the first creditable ethnographies of Amazonian Indians published in the United States and symbolized a new dimension—the scientific one— developing in the relations between the United States and Peru.[49]

Different Horizons

Orton's books in the 1860s and 1870s, the reports of the naval officers Herndon and Gibbon, and the paintings of Andean landscapes rendered by such famous American artists as George Catlin and Frederic Church at mid-century all were elements in the growing awareness of Peru and the Andean world by Americans whose interests were not only commercial and diplomatic.[50] Between the 1830s and the 1870s, American artists and scientists "discovered" the Andean world. That the Andean world was never "lost" and that man had inhabited this portion of the earth for tens of thousands of years made the awakening of interest by Americans perhaps illusionary and ironic. But it was nonetheless spectacular and is perhaps best captured in the magnificent landscape of the Ecuadorian Andes painted by George Church and first exhibited in New York in 1859.

Church's *Heart of the Andes* became the "single most important and enduring of the Latin American landscapes ever created by an American artist."[51] The painting evoked an appreciation for the Andean world shared by American artists of the period, such as Catlin, James Whistler, Louis Mignot, Titian Peale and others who traveled to Latin America. Along with the *Heart of the Andes,* other paintings—such as Church's equally beautiful rendition of the Ecuadorian volcano *Cotopaxi* (1863), Louis Mignot's *Lagoon of the Guayaquil* (c. 1857–63), Catlin's *View on the Pampa del Sacramento* (1852–57), and Whistler's *Nocturne in Blue and Gold: Valparaíso* (1866) served to introduce the magnificent vistas of the Andes and the Amazon and the deserts, lush tropical forests, and broad savannas of Bolivia, Peru, and Ecuador to the artistic American imagination.

The debut of *Heart of the Andes* at the Tenth Street Studio Building on lower Broadway caused a sensation. Thousands paid the twenty-five-cent admission fee to see a painting that drew lavish praise from both art critics ("a grand and unique work," "the complete condensation of South America") and lay spectators alike. It brought the American public into contact for the first time with a region both exotic and remote and inspired an entire generation of landscape artists to imitate Church, even while others, such as Catlin and Mignot, were already traveling through the Andean world capturing their vision on canvas for shows in the United States.

What drew these painters to the Andes? One reason was the allure of the unknown, the unexplored, a desire to be the first to plunge into one of the last frontiers on earth and record the sight on canvas. A second was the myth of El Dorado—of the incredible richness of a land and people that since the days of Columbus had intoxicated Europeans and Americans with visions of gold and silver. And a third was the belief in a terrestrial paradise that could still be found in the pristine forests and mountains of Andean America. Somewhere there existed that Garden of Eden so long ago created by God, so corrupted by the sin of man.

Such men as Church, Catlin, and Mignot were also drawn to the region by the great scientific treatises of the century, especially the monumental natural history of Latin America produced by the German scientist Alexander von Humboldt before the Wars of Independence. In 1859 Charles Darwin published his *Origin of Species,* furthering the scientific interest in Latin America.

The great archaeological and scientific issues of the age also drew artists and scientists to Andean America. Church and others painted magnificent vistas of the volcanoes of the Andes—Cotopaxi was a favorite—as they were drawn into the geologic search for the origins of the earth. Others became fascinated with the archaeological search for the origins of man in the Americas, and the ruins of the Incas and other preceding civilizations found expression in American art.

Less scientific, but no less important, was the fascination with Latin America's "exotic" nature. Whistler was inspired to paint dreamy, evocative images where the subjective, spiritual nature of the scene suffused the artist and his work. In some respects, the artists who traveled to Andean America were expanding their artistic horizons just as the United States was expanding its territorial and political horizons following the dictums of manifest destiny and imperialism.

Pan Americanism, usually associated with such political leaders as Simón Bolívar and Thomas Jefferson, also emphasized the shared geographic, cultural, and historical heritage of the Americas. American artists, through their paintings and writings, helped draw the focus of their fellow countrymen south to Latin America. The simple mechanics of travel made Peru more accessible to American visitors (although tourism is more properly a twentieth century phenomenon).

The work of U.S. artists that portrayed Andean America was the source of powerful and evocative opinions and imagery in the mind of nineteenth-century America. Through the paintings and drawings of Church, Catlin, and Mignot the magnificent landscapes, the lagoons, and the pampas came alive for American viewers. Linkages between nations and their peoples have a curious way of reflecting the true nature of man, and if we limit ourselves to the merely commercial and diplomatic we miss some of those elements which have rendered the stereotypes and images of one people so fascinating and intriguing to the other.

The exchange was not entirely one-sided with only Americans traveling exclusively to Peru and her Andean neighbors. For instance in the winter and spring of 1849, President Ramón Castilla dispatched the Peruvian brig *General Gamarra,* under the command of José María Silva Rodríguez, to San Francisco, California, to help Peruvian merchantmen caught up in the turmoil of the California Gold Rush. Rodríguez's orders were to anchor in San Francisco, gather useful intelligence, and protect Peruvian merchantmen then on the west coast of North America. This the *Gamarra* did for eight months before returning home to Callao in August 1849.[52]

By mid-century Peru had emerged from the near chronic political instability of the postindependence period. Profits from guano provided the economic prosperity that underscored political stability, and the outlines of a strong national state began to emerge. The voyage of the *Gamarra* represented a proud moment in Peru's evolution into a national state. As Jorge Basadre noted, "the Peruvian flag, honorably completing its mission where others were failing, and flying from a ship of war which had no reason to bow its head to other ships from the great powers, was, as [President] Castilla expressed himself to Congress in his message of March, 1850, the symbol of a complete transformation, given the fact that the remnants of a navy just five years before didn't even deserve the name of a Navy."[53]

Perhaps among the useful intelligence that Capt. José María Silva Rodríguez gathered while posted to California was that of the growing rift between North and South, between those who upheld slavery and those who swore to destroy the institution. In 1854 *La cabaña del tío Tom* (*Uncle Tom's Cabin*), the immensely popular antislavery novel by Harriet Beecher Stowe, was adapted for Peruvian theater and opened in Lima. The eternal theme of humankind's cruelty toward fellow humans featured in *Uncle Tom's Cabin* played well in the Peruvian capital. In 1854 slavery was abolished in Peru—the antislavery feelings and convictions intensified by this drama.[54]

Other influences from North America filtered through Peruvian society at mid-century. In July 1860 a company of four black performers from the United States, styled the "Alleghanians," made their debut in Lima playing English and American songs, opera arias, and some lighter music on their sixty-two-bell carillon and a xylophone. One of the members of the troupe was a woman. Later that year an American group called the Ethiopian Minstrels delighted Lima audiences who were more accustomed to grave and decorous Italian opera and the occasional comic French opera. The minstrels, a New York ensemble of white performers with blackened faces, played and danced to melodies and steps inspired by the African-American people of North America, who were still largely enslaved. When the minstrels returned to Lima in 1871, audiences welcomed them enthusiastically.[55]

A few Peruvian travelers wrote about their experiences abroad for a generation of fellow citizens whose knowledge about the United States was scant and often distorted. In 1862 the secretary of ex-president José Rufino Echenique (1851–54) published his *Recuerdos de un viaje a los Estados Unidos* (*Memories of a Trip to the United States*), a successor to the much more popular *Viaje al nuevo mundo* (*Voyage to the New World*; 1845). The latter work was written by the most famous of nineteenth-century Peruvian travelers, Juan Bustamante, a mestizo born along the shores of

Lake Titicaca of a Creole father and an Indian mother and who was descended from Tupac Amaru according to family legend.[56]

From 1841 until 1844 Bustamante undertook a world cruise that carried him to the Caribbean, the United States, Europe, India, and China. In the United States, he landed in New York and traveled north through Sarasota to Boston, noting the hustle and bustle of American crowds. The resulting book was more than a travelogue, however. He did not fail to learn more about his own homeland by being away from it— a lesson common to most travelers. And he encouraged his fellow Peruvians to learn more about different cultures and peoples—their character, education, and ideas; many of the ideas were good, useful, and even grand but were often lacking in his own country. Ironically Bustamante, who became one of the great defenders of the Indians of his homeland, waxed almost lyrically on European civilization: "the Europeans, born in the most enlightened part of the world, naturally can show us the luminescence we lack in the arts and in the sciences, and our efforts ought to be aimed at putting us on the same level as these cultured nations; otherwise, Independence will have been a waste."[57]

Later in the nineteenth century, other notable Peruvian writers expressed similar sentiments about the United States and its people, putative models of pragmatic behavior. If Europe was the source of illuminating ideas in the arts and sciences (much of Peru's modern medicine, associated with the life of Caetano Heredia [1797–1853], for example, was inspired and learned from the French), then the United States stood as a symbol for the progressive, industrializing, modernizing state that produced *material* prosperity.

Imperialism Old and New

The political and military fortunes of Peru and the United States also intersected in the 1860s. In 1863 two immigrant Spaniards working in northern Peru on the Talambo plantation in the province of Chiclayo were murdered in an attack instigated by the plantation's Peruvian overseer. The Spanish government demanded indemnification and an apology. When Peru wavered, a Spanish naval squadron seized the Chincha Islands in April 1864. Frightened by the prospect of losing the rich Chinchas, President Juan Antonio Pezet's (1863–65) government acquiesced to Spanish demands in early 1865. Patriotic Peruvians demonstrated in disgust against Pezet, and in November the pusillanimous Pezet was toppled from power.

By the end of the year Peru (under the leadership of a more defiant president, Mariano Ignacio Prado) and Spain were at war over the issue. Chile, Ecuador, and Bolivia joined the Peruvians in rebuking Spain's acts in the Pacific. In 1866 the Spanish squadron bombarded Valparaíso (March 31) and Callao (May 2). Old Fort San Felipe, hopelessly outgunned, nonetheless responded to the Spanish naval bombardment with spirit during a five-hour battle. The noisy, smoky battle satisfied everyone's honor before Spanish admiral Castro Méndez Núñez withdrew his fleet. Méndez might have closed the range considerably in his attempt to destroy the fortifications and city of Callao—which he had promised to reduce to ashes—had he not been aware of Peruvian torpedo defenses rigged up in the preceding months by former officers in the U.S. and Confederate navies. The Spanish fleet retired across the Pacific to Manila, and there were no more hostilities in this war. An armistice was not formally achieved until 1871 when the United States presided over a peace conference held in Washington, D.C.

Throughout this period the United States acted decisively to achieve a peaceful resolution to the conflict. While the United States declared itself strictly neutral, American sympathies were clearly with the Peruvians and her allies in the affair.[58] Secretary of State William Seward believed Spain had challenged the Monroe Doctrine and thus imperiled the independence and sovereignty of American states. Furthermore during the buildup of military and naval defenses along the Pacific, Peruvians sought weapons and technical expertise in the United States. Peru's minister in Washington, Federico L. Barreda, was especially successful in enlisting both official and unofficial American sympathy and assistance.

Barreda symbolized an important element in Peruvian-U.S. relations—he was a diplomat whose business, scholarly, or professional interests wound his nation's fortunes more tightly into the fabric of American affairs. These diplomats frequently returned to their homeland with messages of solidarity and cohesiveness to preach to skeptical audiences, less convinced of the common interests of Peru with the United States. Barreda had been in Washington since 1860. A brilliant young businessman in his late thirties, he liked the United States where he amassed a sizable fortune in his various enterprises.[59] Between 1862 and 1866 Barreda acquired war matériel in England and France, as the Union prohibited the export of arms during the Civil War.

In Washington Secretary of State Seward and Barreda argued their country's respective positions. Seward wanted peace and the Spanish out of hemispheric affairs. In fact neither side had much to gain from war. Barreda admitted as much to Seward, but the war had raised patriotism to new levels in Peru and united all parties in defense of the homeland. Peru's naval buildup also continued, a possible future plus in any confrontation with Chile, their ally at the moment, but, in truth, Peru's principal rival in the Pacific.[60]

Seward drew on the Monroe Doctrine to defend U.S. support of Peru in this conflict.[61] When Spain threatened to retake the Chinchas, disclaiming any interest in interfering with the internal affairs of Peru or with acquiring territory, Seward read the Spanish actions differently. The seizure of the Chinchas would be "injurious to many neutral states, and especially so to the United States." Or, put another way, the seizure of the Chinchas would disrupt—no matter how many disclaimers the Spanish issued—the commerce of guano, and the United States was still a big buyer of guano. Additionally the Spanish actions would violate the Monroe Doctrine. "Such a seizure and occupation would constitute an act of intervention by a European Monarchical Power in the proper affairs of Republican sovereignty in America [and] would conflict with the well understood system of the United States. . . ." And if the Spanish doggedly persisted in this strategy, the United States would find it difficult to remain "neutral in the wars which had been carried on between Spain and the South American republics."[62]

In the end the Battle of Dos de Mayo (May 2, 1866), when the Spanish bombarded Callao, proved to be the last action of the war. United States citizens had, nonetheless, become more intimately involved in this short war than merely as negotiators and diplomats on the faraway stages of North America and Europe.

Returning to Washington from London in April 1866, Barreda was instructed to find a naval leader in the United States to head the combined Chilean-Peruvian navies. Joined in an unnatural alliance against Spain, the Chilean and Peruvian governments hoped to avoid internal divisions in their combined fleets by hiring an American as leader of their naval operation. Their choice was ex-Confederate Commo. John Randolph Tucker. He assembled a small staff of other ex-Confederates, all of whom had served in the U.S. Navy before the Civil War and were professional naval officers.[63] They arrived in Peru in mid-June 1866, the first American naval mission to Peru. Tucker was appointed rear admiral in the Peruvian Navy.

Tucker took his mission seriously and worked to make his command battle-ready. Ships were dry-docked and repaired to higher standards, armament was improved, torpedo warfare techniques—based on tactics and innovations developed by the Confederacy—were upgraded, and Tucker and his officers pushed Peru's sailors to meet high professional standards. Using a combination of tact and sensitivity, Tucker sought to overcome the Peruvian prejudice against his appointment while he worked to make long-lasting improvements. Naval regulations were modernized in the areas of ordnance, signals, and fleet tactics, and Tucker's presence pushed the Peruvian Navy to a higher level of readiness.

Tucker's career as an admiral in the Peruvian navy ended ignominiously in March 1867, the result of intrigue, jealousies, and political and military maneuvering. Tucker's problem was not of his own making. Peruvian naval officers were jealous of his appointment in the face of their victory over the Spanish in the Battle of Dos de Mayo and demanded his removal. Their resentment deepened when Chilean and Peruvian civilians (among them President Mariano Ignacio Prado, who had hired Tucker) toasted Tucker and his staff during celebratory dinners.

Tucker's tenure was undermined not only by Peruvian and Chilean professional jealousies, but also by his own countrymen serving in the U.S. Navy's Pacific Coast Squadron. In the end the bitterness and rancor engendered by the American Civil War forced Tucker to resign his post in March 1867. His resignation came after a final incident regarding rendering salutes between Rear Adm. John Adolphus Bernard Dahlgren and Tucker. They had commanded opposing squadrons at the Battle for Charleston Harbor in 1865. Dahlgren and other officers of the U.S. Navy's Pacific Coast Squadron shared resentment with Peruvian officers over Tucker's command.[64]

Rivalries between northerners and southerners, between the Yankees and the "Southern Yankees," as Peruvians fondly called Tucker and his colleagues, did not surprise or rattle Peruvians very much. They understood that civil war, rebellion, and revolution were undesirable but not unfamiliar phenomena in the politics of a nation. Tucker's side had lost in the American Civil War, but the man himself was an experienced and talented leader of men. He was not stigmatized—as Dahlgren would have wanted him to be—by his cause, and he served Peru ably from 1867 to 1874 as the leader of the Hydrographic Commission, which rendered valuable, scientific service in the Amazon region.

Peru's first half century of independence was tumultuous as she unevenly advanced toward nationhood. In some respects, the United States went through a similar experience. Both countries flirted with monarchy and established strong central governments after passing through periods of intense instability where centrifugal political and military factors threatened to destroy the fragile beginnings of these new nations. Both were drawn to the models of republics and democracies and were inspired by examples from ancient history, especially of Rome before she became an empire. Bolívar and Jefferson could quote easily and knowledgeably from classic works that extolled the virtues of representative forms of democracy.

But both Peruvians and Americans faced anarchy and disorder at very similar stages in their histories. Shay's Rebellion in 1786 prodded—indeed, frightened—the Founding Fathers into junking the Articles of Confederation and convening the Constitutional Convention that led to the Constitution of 1798.[65] In Peru notable Indian rebellions in 1780

(Tupac Amaru II) and that of Mateo Pumacahua in 1814 "haunted [Creoles] for many years to come," noted the historian John Lynch.[66] While the United States accommodated republican institutions to achieve a more highly centralized and powerful federal government, Peru failed to do the same. Peru conformed nominally to constitutional, republican norms, but, in fact, rule by a series of dictators, or caudillos, marked the country's first fifty years of independence.

Part of the challenge for both the United States and Peru was to define the nature of their nationality. The American Civil War was the greatest threat to U.S. nationalism. Once that conflict was settled, the country went forward in an economic surge that took it to the level of the major world powers. The guano boom in Peru produced some economic prosperity, which was translated into political stability at mid-century. But it was a stability based on ephemeral resources. The guano supply was exhausted by the 1870s, and Peru was plunged into a disastrous war with Chile over control of natural resources in their frontier provinces. Ironically a well-defined national identity that had eluded Peru's independence-era generation was first given a strong definition by the war with Chile. In that war the United States sought to play a large role as mediator and peacemaker.

2   The War of the Pacific

Am. Intervention is all a humbug . . . Uncle Sam has backed down . . .
I am satisfied that the U.S. gov't will not use force . . . I consider
Tarapaca lost to Peru for ever.

Michael Grace, 1881

Causes of the War

For Peruvians the War of the Pacific (1879–83), fought by Peru and
her ally Bolivia against Chile, was a seminal event in Peru's development as a nation. By the end of the war Peru and Bolivia had lost huge
chunks of their national territory to the victorious Chileans. Bolivia,
stripped of her coastline along the Pacific, became a landlocked nation.
Peru, whose capital city was captured and sacked by the Chileans, was
humiliated by the defeat.[1] Like the American Civil War was for the
United States, the War of the Pacific became one of the transcending
events in Peru's modern history—as significant as the Peruvian Institutional Revolution of 1968 would later be.

Though its diplomatic intervention did not dictate the outcome, the
United States played an important role in the war. Two factors explained U.S. interests in this war, both of which foreshadowed greater
involvement by the United States in Peruvian affairs. The first was the
increasing commercial and economic interests along the west coast of
South America. The second was the U.S. determination to play a greater
role in regulating international politics in the Western Hemisphere. In
the end the United States was spectacularly *unsuccessful* in mediating
the war, especially in the face of the victorious Chileans.[2]

The war's immediate cause was the fierce competition between Chile,
Bolivia, and Peru for the guano- and nitrate-rich Atacama Desert region
shared by all three countries.[3] The dry and forbidding Atacama (which
stretches for roughly six hundred miles along the Pacific coastline) had

51

never been accurately mapped during the colonial period, and its borders remained poorly delineated after independence. After mid-century the discovery of guano, nitrate, and even silver deposits in the Atacama created new commercial interest in the region, especially on the part of Chilean and English entrepreneurs with the capital and experience to exploit these deposits on both sides of the border between Chile and Bolivia. What had formerly been a remote and distant part of Chile, Bolivia and Peru now became valuable territory.

Throughout this period the United States had evinced little interest in the issues that ultimately led to the War of the Pacific. Several U.S. naval officers made port in the region from the 1830s to the 1850s, and their reports at least kept those few interested observers in the United States apprised of the ill-defined national boundaries in the Atacama. Lt. J. M. Gillis traveled through the region between 1840 and 1852. He reported in 1855 that the border region between Bolivia and Chile in the Atacama Desert continued to be only vaguely defined.[4] Disputed boundary claims played a major role in the coming war.

Peru's rivalry with Chile for power and influence along the Pacific coast complicated the problem of ill-defined borders and newly discovered riches. An arms race in the 1860s and 1870s increased the friction and tension. Peru ordered two powerful warships from British shipyards—the ironclad *Independencia* and the monitor *Huascar*—and purchased two surplus monitors left over from the Civil War in the United States; the ships were rechristened the *Atahualpa* and the *Manco Capac* respectively. By 1869 Peru enjoyed naval superiority over Chile, an intolerable naval balance of power from the Chilean point of view. In the early 1870s Chile ordered built two powerful ironclads in Great Britain in order to gain at least naval parity, and, if possible, superiority over the Peruvians. These two vessels, the *Almirante Cochrane* and the *Blanco Encalada,* were superior in armor and firepower to the comparable Peruvian vessels.

The naval race between Peru and Chile accentuated an increasingly strident political and commercial rivalry between these two countries. Escalating prices for guano and nitrates, and development of silver mines in the early 1870s, increased the stakes. The Chilean effort to protect its nationals and their property in Bolivia through intervention in Bolivian affairs led to an escalation in the rhetoric—and eventually to war in April 1879.

Opening of Peru to European and American Entrepreneurs and Investors

How did the United States figure in all of this? In the years after the Civil War, the U.S. economic presence in Peru and Bolivia had dramatically increased, especially in technology and capital. The postwar Peruvian-U.S. trade boom continued uninterrupted until the outbreak of the War of the Pacific in 1879.[5] During the first half decade of the 1870s, all previous trade records were broken, with a heavy balance of trade in favor of the United States. Guano remained the chief export from Peru to the United States until 1875 when sodium nitrate took primacy, reflecting the rapidly depleting guano deposits and the increasingly important nitrate resources in Peru's Tarapaca region in the northern Atacama Desert.

What fueled this growing trade were not such traditional products as guano, nitrates, silver, or wool—all goods that filled the holds of American ships bound from Peru to the United States—but the export of steel, iron, and wood products bound from North America to form the backbone of Peru's most sought-after advancement in modern times, the railroad. While the British continued to dominate Peru's foreign commerce—and would continue to do so although in diminishing proportions until the First World War—the railroads opened up Peru to American entrepreneurs and trade as no other resource had before. Extracting guano and nitrates and exporting silver and wool were traditional activities that left but a small impression on Peru and its relations with the United States compared with that of the railroads.

Peruvians sought to modernize and transform their country, and the railroads were the keys to this effort. Perhaps no other Peruvian was more articulate and powerfully committed to the railroads than Manuel Prado who became president in 1872. "Who denies that the railroads are today the missionaries of civilization?" Prado wrote. "Who denies that Peru urgently needs those same missionaries: without railroads today there cannot be real material progress; and without material progress there can be no moral progress among the masses because material progress increases the people's well-being and this reduces their brutishness and their misery; without the railroads civilization can proceed only very slowly."[6]

Perhaps Prado and his liberal, progressive followers expected too much from the railroads, these "missionaries [of] material progress." But the railroads were the avatars of modernization, and they came to Peru largely through the activities of one of the most controversial, dynamic Americans to influence the development of Peruvian-U.S. relations—Henry Meiggs.

Meiggs was a native New Yorker born in the Catskills and was drawn by fortune across the continent to California during the Gold Rush of 1849. There he parlayed a load of lumber shipped around the Horn into a minor bonanza, was soon speculating grandly in real estate, and then just as quickly went bankrupt. He left California for Chile one step ahead of his creditors and the law. There he converted his winning charm and organizational abilities into building railroads, living the flamboyant life of the newly rich. He built railroads, bribed politicians liberally, and treated his workers with unprecedented respect. His romantic conquests among Chilean women enhanced his notoriety as a brilliant, accomplished rascal of monumental proportions.

In Peru Meiggs signed seven contracts between 1868 and 1871 to build more than a thousand miles of railroads. These were financed largely by revenues generated from the guano boom of the past thirty years. Though the deals that were struck, the bonds that were floated on the European markets to raise capital, and the financial negotiations in general were complex, the outcome was distressingly simple. Guano and nitrate revenues were hypothecated, or pledged, to pay off the immense loans contracted to pay for the railroads. In the 1870s the Peruvian economy withered under the battering of excessive borrowing and limited resources.

Peru's leaders had mortgaged the nation's economic future, certainly, but few had seen the warning signs. In the late 1860s and early 1870s, wrote the great Peruvian historian Jorge Basadre, Peru "once again was betting on easy wealth, on simple solutions. . . . There reigned a lottery-like spirit . . . ; [but] the iron rails which Meiggs extended 'to the clouds' ruined Peru and were the precursors, not of regeneration and progress as so many trumpeted, but of bankruptcy and international catastrophe."[7] Meiggs was a reassuring and dynamic presence. He captivated the Peruvians with ambitious plans to construct railroads from the ports into the mineral-rich mountainous interior. The government initiated vast public works to beautify and modernize Lima and Callao with broad boulevards, modern housing, new port facilities, and the other trappings and sinews of a modern metropolis.

Probably no other American has played such a pivotal role in Peruvian history as Henry Meiggs. The historian Jorge Basadre characterized him as the "man of the hour, the true power in the political, social, and economic milieu of Peru" in the 1870s?[8] Meiggs's biographer, Watt Stewart, called him the "Yankee Pizarro" after the most famous of the conquistadors of Peru, Francisco Pizarro.[9] Basadre's portrait is surprisingly sympathetic, tending to blame Peruvians themselves for being so taken by Meiggs and the grandeur of his vision and for not tempering their enthusiasm. "It isn't surprising," Basadre wrote, "that there arrived on the Peruvian scene such a man as Meiggs. What is astonishing is the lack of contrary opinion to canalize and moderate his plans."[10]

Perhaps Basadre was too critical of his fellow Peruvians, for Meiggs was a man typical of the era: buoyant, optimistic, entrepreneurial in the extreme, the charlatan and huckster mixed with the visionary capitalist and builder. Such men as Meiggs forged the modern relations, the myths, and the stereotypes between Peru and the United States. Meiggs was a charmer. He doffed his wide-brimmed sombrero to all, rich and poor, a habit that did not go unnoticed in countries like Bolivia and Peru where the class structure still divided rich and poor, white and Indian. His favorite phrases were said to be "sow with kindness, harvest the money" and "let's talk, I'm your good friend." When Meiggs was stricken with yellow fever in 1868, hundreds of his admirers thronged to his home in Lima, jamming the streets and paralyzing traffic. Even the local church bells ceased pealing while don Enrique was sick.

Meiggs's faith in the railroads and industrialization was infectious. He loved to envision great works, he loved to work, he loved to achieve his goals, he loved to make money. He was, as Basadre described him, a "messenger of that dominant and voracious race, the race of the Astors, the Vanderbilts, and others" in a land—Peru—still petrified in many ways by patterns of work and social structures inherited from the colonial period. While he loved money, he loved power and influence even more—although he was not demonstrative or arrogant in its use or display. At the banquet in celebration of the beginnings of the Arequipa to Mollendo railroad, Meiggs spent much of his time in a corner, surrounded by his engineers, talking business.

When not doing business, he was helping Peruvians in many other ways. After the earthquake of August 1868 he donated more than fifty thousand dollars to the victims. He helped build churches and houses of charity. A Christian, he nonetheless donated the land destined to be the cemetery for Jews in Lima. He equipped the newspaper *La Bolsa* of Arequipa. He was a patron of artists and writers. He was generous in the extreme, but his generosity extended far beyond simple philanthropy.

He also distributed immense amounts of money to public officials in Chile, Peru, and Bolivia, to newspapermen, and to other influential citizens. "Seed thousands to make millions" was another of Meiggs's favorite phrases; the anecdotes from this period are replete with the ingenious and fantastic system of bribes and gifts distributed by Meiggs. One friend received the gift of a two-hundred-page album, each page containing a thousand sol bill. Critics claimed Meiggs's secret list of "gift" recipients included most of the important persons of Peru and certainly of Lima—a charge that Basadre scoffed at as typical exaggeration with little substance.

Meiggs's visionary plans for Lima and Peru prompted most Peruvians to overlook his questionable practices. He envisioned wide, tree-lined boulevards connecting Lima with Callao and the seaside resort of Chorillos, projects realized many years later. He advocated the construction of low-cost, comfortable housing for the poor. He predicted Callao's future rise as the major seaport on the west coast of South America. He invested in coal, copper, and silver mines, and he promoted Chimbote on the north coast as a port with a great industrial and commercial future. Meiggs was more than an industrial catalyst in Peru's national life. "Not only economically and financially, but sociologically, Peru entered a new epoch" due in large measure to Meiggs's vision and activities.[11]

Meiggs died September 30, 1877. He was not rich, nor was he bankrupt, but his visions had become nightmares. One disturbing legacy of his ambition was the increasing indebtedness of Peru to other countries as the economy grew inflated on speculation and easy loans contracted in the early 1870s. Basadre noted that this "false prosperity" was analogous to the booming 1920s in the U.S., which presaged the crash of the stock market in 1929 and the Great Depression that ensued.

The Rise of the House of Grace in Peru

Meiggs, however, was not the only influential American in Peru during these tumultuous times that would eventually lead to the War of the Pacific. In stark contrast to the flashy Meiggs who dreamed on a grand, sometimes utopian and unrealistic scale, there stood William Russell Grace, an Irish immigrant to Peru, whose slow and steady pace built a business and a commitment to Peru that endured for more than a century.

Like Meiggs, Grace came to Peru to make his fortune. Unlike Meiggs, he stayed many years, built up his commercial house, and kept his business and personal interests in Peru years after his company's move to New York. Indeed the business that Grace began in Peru—W. R. Grace & Co.—became a fixture of Peruvian-U.S. relations for the next century. Known familiarly as "Casa Grace," more Peruvians came into contact with American institutions and products through the activities of Casa Grace in Peru than any other U.S. company.

W. R. Grace & Co.'s activities in Peru prefigured the growth of

Peruvian-U.S. economic relations for the next century. The company became the principal commercial agent of U.S. goods in Peru over the next one hundred years, as well as the principal carrier of those goods through its shipping arm, Grace Line. Casa Grace was heavily involved in the Meiggs-era construction of railroads in Peru, Ecuador, and Bolivia. The first steamships to traffic between New York and the west coast were put into business by the company in the 1890s. In 1928 the Graces, in a joint venture with Juan Trippe and Pan American Airways, established the first American-owned and -operated commercial airline between the United States and Peru, Pan American–Grace Airways (Panagra). The list of "firsts" credited to the company constitutes an extraordinary record of economic and commercial initiative and success.

William Grace came to Peru in 1852, pushed from the old country and pulled to the Americas by forces that encouraged immigration to the Americas from Europe in the second half of the nineteenth century. He left his native Ireland because it was poor, its citizens starving, and it offered little opportunity; he was drawn to the Americas because they promised to be everything that Europe was not. He ended up on the desert coast of Peru through a deal struck by his father with an Irish landowner in Peru, Dr. James Gallagher, who negotiated for Irish laborers to work his plantation.

Once in Peru, young Grace quickly disassociated himself from the other Irish immigrants who went to work on Dr. Gallagher's sugar plantation. William landed a job in 1852 with a small firm of importers, Bryce Brothers, who had a booming business servicing the guano fleet anchored off the Chincha Islands. In 1856, the name of the firm was changed to the Bryce-Grace Company in recognition of the growing importance of William Grace to the firm's increasing prosperity.[12]

Grace was a quick learner. The large fleet of guano ships usually anchored at the guano islands for two or three months. Before leaving on the long voyage around South America for the Atlantic, the ships put in at Callao to refit and revictual. Grace suggested that an old hulk be anchored at the guano islands to serve as a storeship for the guano fleet in their midst. He himself became the chief storekeeper, and the storeship was an immediate success.

One of Grace's first employees was a young Peruvian named Miguel Llaguno. He came well recommended. Llaguno was the nephew of the governor of the province of Pisco adjoining the Chincha Islands, and it was from Pisco where Grace obtained the fresh fruits, meats, and vegetables that he sold to the guano fleet from his storeship. But more important than the politically astute decision to employee Llaguno was the fact that Grace came to admire his dependable and trustworthy Peruvian employee whose demonstrated capacity and desire to work found an echo in the young Grace's own nature.

Llaguno became the first in a long line of Peruvians who joined "Casa Grace" over the next hundred years. Grace treated Llaguno like any of the multitude of his family—brothers, cousins, nephews, etc.—who crossed the seas to work with their brother/cousin/uncle in this formative period in the company's development. When Llaguno's and his family's lives were threatened during the War of the Pacific, Grace brought them to New York for the duration of the conflict, demonstrating the mixture of paternal/filial loyalty he felt toward his extended company "family."

William Grace also rapidly learned to read and write in Spanish. As a merchant he was conscious of the advantages of working in the language of his host country, and he demanded that all who joined his company—be they Europeans or Americans—learn the language of Peru. Accommodation of Peruvian customs and language became a distinctive feature of Casa Grace.

In 1866 Grace transferred his family and his headquarters to New York, leaving his brother Michael in charge of the business in Peru. Coincidentally Henry Meiggs was negotiating the first of several major railroad contracts with Peru, and the Graces became Henry Meiggs's chief purveyor of railroad supplies in the United States. The fortunes of Meiggs, the Graces, and Peru intertwined as the decade of the 1870s progressed.

William Grace expanded his business in many other fashions during the 1870s. He established the Merchants Line in 1873, the predecessor of the Grace Line, to take advantage of the increasing flow of men and materials between the east coast of the United States and the west coast of

South America. In Peru the Graces diversified their interests as such young associates as Charles Flynt, who on his own later organized the United States Royal Tire Co., pursued business with Peruvians in every way possible.[13] Importing new sugar-making mills for the growing sugar industry was one way that Flynt tied the industrial power of the United States to the needs of sugar planters in Peru. Along the way Casa Grace accumulated creditors among the Peruvian planter class who often extended themselves beyond their means. In this fashion the Graces acquired a sugar plantation in northern Peru in 1879, Hacienda Cartavio, when its owners went bankrupt. In 1927, the company acquired Hacienda Paramonga, another sugar plantation, under similar circumstances. Thus the company diversified slowly from merely being traders, to becoming shippers, ship owners, line operators, investors, and even sugar mill operators by the 1880s. On the eve of the War of the Pacific, Michael Grace acquired the exclusive right to distribute Peruvian nitrates in the United States. In sum the beachhead established by William Grace at mid-century had been considerably expanded. But just as the Graces stepped into the lucrative nitrates market, the world collapsed around the Peruvians.

For better or worse, entrepreneurs and merchants, such as Henry Meiggs and William Grace, brought the United States closer to Peru. When the war erupted in April 1879 it was not unusual for Americans—if they cared or knew about this remote war—to side with the Peruvians.

The Course of the War

From the outset the war proved a disaster for Peru and Bolivia. The Chileans took control of the sea by October 1879 and thereafter pursued a relentless military campaign against the Bolivians and Peruvians. A Bolivian army sent to the coast in 1879 to fight alongside Peruvians suffered a humiliating defeat. Peru persevered until January 1881 when the Chilean armies captured the capital city of Lima. Thereafter rear-guard, guerrilla-style activities characterized the war until the Treaty of Ancón was signed in 1883. This brief survey cannot do justice to a war that was, in the opinion of many, *the* defining event for almost a century in the modern histories of all three nations.

From the perspective of the United States, which tried six times to mediate the war on behalf of the Peruvians and Bolivians, the war was a failure of U.S. diplomacy. In fact one historian of the U.S. role in the conflict wrote that "if the results had not been so tragic and harmful to the prestige of the United States, the activities of the diplomatic corps could well be described as high comedy."[14] Chile's military and naval triumphs were matched by diplomatic successes that guaranteed that wins on the battlefields and at sea would be reflected in gains at the negotiating table.

The United States vacillated in its policy toward Peru and Chile during these crucial years. Domestic politics in the United States had much to do with this indecisiveness. The war broke out during the final two years of the Rutherford B. Hayes administration and his Secretary of State, William Evarts, was cautious and neutral toward the war.[15] When James G. Garfield was inaugurated president in March 1881, Secretary of State James G. Blaine attempted to mediate the war on behalf of Peru. By then, however, Chile's naval and military triumphs over Peru and Bolivia were complete.

The United States took a number of diplomatic initiatives, including sponsoring a meeting of the belligerents in October 1880 aboard the U.S.S. *Lackawanna* in the harbor of Arica. These meetings ended in a stalemate when the Chileans demanded more than the Peruvians were willing to concede, and U.S. diplomats could find no middle ground. The Chileans then proceeded to conduct the war with even more vigor, leading to the capture of Lima on January 16, 1881.

U.S. participation in this war occurred on many levels. Sympathy in the United States for Peru was based in part on the interests of U.S. citizens in preserving the integrity and sovereignty of Peru. While Chilean and English capital had been invested heavily in the guano- and nitrate-rich Bolivian province of Antofagasta, similar resources in the Peruvian provinces of Tarapaca, Tacna, and Arica were being developed by a combination of Peruvian, U.S., and European capitalists. For example,

Michael Grace had contracted in 1879 to distribute Peruvian nitrates in the U.S., and it was natural for Grace and others to try and protect their investments.

The west coast of South America was also a field of hot competition between U.S. and English merchants and investors. British investments would prosper from a triumph of Chilean arms; conversely the same could be said for U.S. investments in Peru. While other foreigners had a presence in the region, nonetheless, the principal foreign actors were the English and the Americans.

The provisioning of arms to the combatants drew U.S. citizens into the war, who were attracted by the immense profits that could be had and by the desire to protect investments in Peru. Furthermore Peru's old association with ex-Confederate naval officers (remember Admiral Tucker from the 1860s) was rekindled as Peruvians tried desperately to find ways to stop the better-armed and better-trained Chileans.

Not surprisingly the Graces and their young colleague Charles Flynt were soon involved in helping Peru buy arms and munitions abroad. W. R. Grace & Co. was, after all, a commercial and trading company with contacts across the United States and Europe, and its sympathies lay with the Peruvians. Even before the declarations of war, Michael Grace in Peru advised Charley Flynt in New York to be ready to fill large orders for munitions and arms. Then Flynt put his mind to the problem of getting the arms to the Peruvians.

The long voyage around Cape Horn was deemed too dangerous, for the Chileans would surely intercept anything that came near their coastline. Colombia (then still in possession of the isthmus of Panama) was neutral, and it prohibited arms traffic across its territory. The Colombians, Flynt learned, wanted to at least preserve a semblance of neutrality, so anything going through Panama would have to be disguised so as not to offend Colombian sensibilities. Flynt discovered that oilcloth, framed in the ordinary way, weighed just about the same as a layer or two of oilcloth *wrapped around a torpedo.* Conveniently Peru bought a lot of oilcloth in those days, and ten torpedoes were soon on their way to Peru comfortably nestled in the center of ten cases of oilcloth. A thousand rifles carrying the labels "agricultural machinery" were also dispatched in those hectic spring months of 1879, while cartridges for the rifles were embedded in lard barrels.[16]

The battle for control of the Pacific seesawed back and forth between Chile and Peru all during the winter and spring (April-November) of 1879. Adm. Miguel Grau waged a brilliant campaign with the powerful Peruvian ironclad *Huascar*, attacking and harrying the better-armed and better-trained Chilean Navy. In the end, the Chileans caught up with Grau. The Battle of Angamos in October established unquestioned Chilean naval superiority after the defeat and capture of *Huascar*. In the meantime Peru hurried to use the newest technologies in naval warfare. They hoped to gain the advantage in a situation that they knew was heavily weighted toward Chile. The revolution in naval warfare triggered by the American Civil War inspired Peruvian planners to look to new developments—better ironclads, submersibles, mines, spar torpedoes, and other gadgetry—to get the edge on the more powerful Chileans.

In this race for parity, such Americans as Charles Flynt and William Grace helped Peru gain access to U.S. technology. The most promising of the new weapons was the torpedo. Nineteenth-century "torpedoes" could be anything from mines to very crude and experimental self-propelled charges churning through the water with only modest amounts of direction and predictability. Within a week of the outbreak of war in April 1879, Grace had several torpedo boats and torpedoes on their way to Peru. Grace also ordered a boat built by Nat Herreschoff for $18,500 and sent it to Peru. Herreschoff later gained fame as the designer of five successful defenders of the America's Cup yachting contest.

How did the torpedoes and boats perform in the war? Unevenly is perhaps the kindest description. An attempt in Callao to torpedo a small Chilean ship was typical. The torpedo was launched and controlled by an American, Stephen Chester, from the decks of the *Huascar*. Something went wrong, as is the wont of new and untried weapons, and the torpedo circled and headed back for the *Huascar*. The prized Peruvian monitor had to scramble to avoid being blasted by its own torpedo.

Both Union and Confederate veterans served under the Peruvian flag.

Flynt recruited one ex-Confederate who had been in the torpedo service on the Mississippi. Charles W. Read had experience with the Colombian Navy after the Civil War and spoke Spanish, so Flynt hired him and took him to Bristol, Rhode Island, to help test the Herreschoff boats on Narragansett Bay. Read and an engineer, John H. Smith, sailed for Peru August 20, 1879, and, as Flynt noted with satisfaction, Read followed "their [torpedo boats'] tests in Narragansett Bay, he followed them across the Isthmus, and he followed them into war."[17] However getting into the war proved to be difficult, for American cockiness and Peruvian pride clashed head on in the next few months.

The Peruvian Navy commissioned Read a commander and he devised a plan to attack the *Cochrane* and the *Blanco Encalada,* then in port in Valparaíso undergoing repairs. If successful Read would receive a substantial amount of prize money. This rankled some proud Peruvian naval officers. Several offered to lead the attack for nothing, as did a one-legged army colonel. The Peruvians' problem, however, was not patriotism but inexperience; one American on the scene observed rather colorfully that none of the Peruvians "knew a torpedo from a Chinese stinkpot."[18]

Yet, Stephen Chester's near disaster with the *Huascar,* almost sinking the powerful monitor with its own torpedo, had done little to reinforce Peruvian confidence in the cocky American torpedo "experts." Furthermore the Americans represented three different companies, each with its own design, and the Americans bickered among themselves as well as with the Peruvians. Read and his engineer Smith, for example, were ridiculed as blockheads by Ford Snyder of the U.S. Torpedo Company team. Smith asserted that he had been a chief engineer in the U.S. Navy, but Snyder snorted that Smith was a dilapidated old Scotsman who never came nearer to being a chief in the navy than Sitting Bull did to being president.[19] Other American torpedo experts were no more successful in late 1879 or 1880. Peru's coastline thus lay open to invasion, deprived as the country was of its capital ships and unable to depend upon the disputatious Americans for results. While the Americans argued, Grau and *Huascar* met their destiny off the coast of Angamos in October.

Military and naval observers representative of such powers as England, France, and the United States closely followed the war as new weapons were tested in the firestorm of real battle. The United States, for example, still had not transformed its naval vessels from wood to iron and steel during the post-Civil War doldrums that were affecting the military establishment. The naval engagements in the War of the Pacific, especially the historic one off Angamos between *Huascar* and *Cochrane,* were closely observed, prompting U.S. officers to inform the Department of the Navy that "three recently designed Chilean cruisers outclassed the most effective United States man-of-war afloat."[20] New authorizations from Congress produced the Navy Act of 1883, which gave birth to the nation's first steel warships, the backbone of the new fleet. The lessons being learned off the coast of Peru and Chile certainly helped further the rising sentiment in the United States that a great nation had to have an effective and modern navy. While naval observers profited from the war, U.S. diplomacy moved from failure to failure.

U.S. diplomats were no more successful in promoting peace than torpedo experts were in winning the war at sea. Peru's military fronts crumbled before the victorious Chileans in 1880 and 1881, culminating with the capture of Lima in January 1881. Meanwhile a political change in Washington early in that same year altered U.S. policy toward the combatants. In March 1881 President James Garfield named James G. Blaine as his new Secretary of State. Blaine was clearly partisan toward Peru, not because he thought the Peruvians were necessarily right, but because he saw England as the hand behind Chilean aggression. And Blaine's domestic anti-British, pro-Irish sentiments were easily transferred into favoring Peru at the expense of British-backed Chile. "It is a complete mistake to see this as a Chilean war against Peru," the secretary of state said. "[Rather] it is a British war against Peru using Chile as its instrument," he concluded.[21] While that allegation was never proven, it made for good domestic consumption, and, coincidentally, aligned the United States with Peru.

Blaine's broad objectives were twofold: one, prevent territorial transfers, or, expressed in a more positive fashion, maintain the territorial integrity of nations at the peace table; and two, keep Europeans out of the peace settlements. The second objective was an attempt to invoke the Monroe Doctrine and maintain the primacy of the United States in settling inter-American affairs. The first objective was driven by desire to settle disputes and prevent wars by denying the validity of territorial transfers in the affairs of nations. This position was sometimes described by the "doctrine of immutable borders." More practically many U.S. investors in Peru, such as the Graces, did not wish to see Peru lose its southern provinces to Chile—a country that might prove more difficult to deal with when it came to honoring contracts and deals for the exploitation of such natural resources as guano and nitrates. Victorious on the battlefield, the Chileans meant to keep their captured territories as legitimate compensation for a war they felt had been brought on by the Bolivians and Peruvians. The Chileans were not intimidated by Blaine's aggressive diplomacy.

Chilean capture of Lima demoralized and divided Peruvians. President Nicolás de Piérola escaped into the rugged mountain interior to continue the fight. The Chileans accepted a presumably compliant Francisco García Calderón as interim president in February 1881, but Calderón proved intractable in accepting harsh Chilean demands. The invaders replaced him with Miguel de Iglesias in late 1882. In the mountains Gen. Andrés Cáceres and Nicolás de Piérola kept up guerrilla action. As the Peruvian political system weakened under foreign presence, social order collapsed. Race riots (aimed especially against Chinese shopkeepers and petty merchants in Lima) broke out along the coast, and Indian rebellions against white and mestizo masters erupted in the highlands. In the midst of this disorder and apparent anarchy, the Chileans demanded three of Peru's southern provinces—Tarapaca, Arica, and Tacna—as well as an indemnity to boot.

In this explosive climate, Blaine named new ministers (both Civil War veterans) to Peru and Chile in May 1881: Gen. Stephen A. Hurlbut to Lima and Gen. Judson A. Kilpatrick to Santiago. Hurlbut, a leader of the Grange movement in Illinois, actively urged greater commercial penetration of Latin American markets by American interests, especially agricultural ones. Both Hurlbut and Kilpatrick became partisans of the countries to which they were posted, lending some confusion to U.S. policy as fashioned by Blaine through 1881 and early 1882.

Blaine complicated matters in his instructions to Hurlbut and Kilpatrick when he emphasized the desire to maintain Peru's territorial integrity and to achieve a peace as soon as possible, even if that meant some loss of territory to Peru.[22] Chile, said Blaine however, must moderate its demands. The previous U.S. minister to Peru, Isaac Christiancy, had become stridently pro-Peruvian and had apparently persuaded the secretary of state that a Chilean victory would mean the ascendancy of "English over American influence on this coast . . . [and the United States] should intervene in compelling a settlement of peace on reasonable terms."[23] Christiancy even suggested establishing a U.S. protectorate over Peru if Chile persisted in its expansionist, inflexible course.

In his enthusiasm, Hurlbut led the Peruvians to believe that intervention by the United States against the intransigent Chileans was quite possible. He issued a "Declaration to the Notables of Lima" stating that the United States opposed the dismemberment of Peru, and he personally delivered a memorandum to the Chilean commander in Lima, Adm. Patricio Lynch, warning Chile not to take territory unless Peru refused to pay an indemnity.[24] Hurlbut signed an agreement with the García Calderón government to establish a U.S. naval base at the spacious port of Chimbote on the northern coast of Peru. It seemed as if the Garfield administration was poised to jump in and save the Peruvians from the rapacious Chileans. The astonished British minister in Lima, Spenser St. John, thought Hurlbut had far exceeded his instructions by essentially taking Calderón and Peru under his protection.[25] On the eve of Calderón's arrest and deportation to Santiago by the Chileans in November 1881, the zealous U.S. minister even placed part of the Peruvian archives in the U.S. legation for safekeeping.[26] Later that month Blaine censured Hurlbut for taking such extraordinary initiatives in defending the Calderón government, although the secretary of state certainly sympathized with the spirit of Hurlbut's acts, calling the Chimbote "project 'desirable' but 'not opportune.'"[27] In Peru the effect of Hurlbut's partisan behavior raised the hope of U.S. intervention. But Blaine was in better touch with U.S. political realities *and* possibilities than his enthusiastic diplomat in Lima.

As the secretary of state and his representatives were stepping up their efforts to bring the war to a conclusion, Blaine suffered a grievous political blow. On July 2, 1881, a disgruntled office seeker, Charles Gaiteau, shot President Garfield. Garfield lingered through the summer and died September 19.[28] New president Chester A. Arthur came from a faction of the Republican Party hostile to Blaine's politics and suspicious of his aggressive policies in South America. In December Arthur replaced Blaine with Frederick T. Frelinghuysen.

Before then, however, Blaine had pursued his peace initiatives on several fronts. To keep the Peruvian guano and nitrate territories intact, Blaine supported the formation of an international company in Paris by the U.S. minister to France, Levi P. Morton. This company represented Peruvian bondholders throughout Europe, and Blaine's plan was to have the company manage the Peruvian guano and nitrate fields, pay Chile an appropriate indemnity, and thus preserve the national boundaries of Peru. As a stockholder in the firm, W. R. Grace & Co. would hold the exclusive right to distribute Peruvian nitrates and guano in the West Indies and North America. From the point of view of U.S. and European stockholders and investors with substantial interests in Peru, the plan had considerable appeal.

Chileans rejected the plan peremptorily. They had conquered Tarapaca, Arica, and Tacna and were not about to yield what had been won in blood to an international firm concocted by Americans in Paris and Washington. Michael Grace sensed the resolute Chilean feelings, although he hoped Blaine's initiatives would dissuade Chile from taking all it had conquered. Nonetheless Michael Grace had an ear well tuned to the finesse of international politics. "I am satisfied," the brother of William Grace noted in July 1881, "that the U.S. gov't will not use force," adding prophetically, "I consider Tarapaca lost to Peru for ever and that the Paris gentlemen are chasing a phantom."[29]

Before leaving office in December, Blaine attempted one last initiative to forge a peace. With President Arthur's apparent approval, he appointed William Henry Trescot, a former assistant secretary of state, as a special envoy to Peru and Chile with instructions to pressure the Chileans to submit to U.S. mediation on favorable terms to Peru—that is, no cession of territory and the guarantee of neutral property rights in those territories now controlled by Chile. Blaine advised Trescot that if Chile insisted on taking large portions of Peruvian territory, the United States would appeal to other Latin American countries in mediating the peace.

Trescot arrived in Santiago on January 7, 1882, after stopping in at Lima late in December where he had been warmly welcomed by the Peruvians. The Chilean reception was more somber. Trescot spent a month urging the Chileans to conciliate, but they would not yield. The effort collapsed abruptly January 31, 1882, when Foreign Minister José M. Balmaceda told Trescot that new instructions from Frelinghuysen had superseded those of his predecessor in "very important particulars."[30] Trescot was astounded. Frelinghuysen had not only embarrassed and humiliated Trescot but also effectively ended all credibility of a peace mediated or sponsored by the United States.

What unfolded in Washington in December and the early months of 1882 is a good example of how domestic politics can very deeply influence the course of foreign policy. Blaine had numerous political enemies, sprinkled liberally among both Democratic and Republican parties. In 1882 the House of Representatives investigated accusations that Blaine stood to profit financially from supporting Peru in the war, allegedly having secret financial interests in guano and nitrate companies. Although the charges were never proven, the inquiry embarrassed Blaine who was one of the most prominent Republicans of his time.[31]

Frelinghuysen, however, was the principal culprit in the undoing of Trescot's mission to Peru and Chile. Blaine's political rivals in the Senate had asked for publication of the diplomatic correspondence regarding the War of the Pacific. Blaine allowed only a portion to be made public before he left office. Then on January 26, 1882, Frelinghuysen released all the correspondence, including Blaine's original instructions to Trescot, *and,* more important, revised instructions that Frelinghuysen had sent Trescot early in January. Trescot had not received these instructions, which effectively "canceled the parts of the [Blaine] instructions that could be construed as threatening Chile."[32]

Frelinghuysen advised Trescot that "what the President does seek to do, is to extend the kindly offices of the United States impartially to both Peru and Chili," thus reversing the firm pro-Peruvian tone of the Blaine instructions.[33] Frelinghuysen telegraphed Trescot twice on his way to South America to moderate the Blaine instructions, but Trescot was unaware of the near-sweeping reversal of his instructions until the meeting with Balmaceda on January 31. As soon as the Senate published the full correspondence on January 26, the Chilean legation in Washington had cabled Balmaceda via Paris. The U.S. special envoy to Chile was mortified to be informed of *his* secret instructions by the foreign minister of a foreign government. As one student of U.S. foreign policy observed, "to such a ludicrous pass had America's makeshift diplomacy arrived in the spring of 1882."[34]

The inability and/or unwillingness of the United States to intervene in defending Peru against Chile disturbed Michael Grace, who conveyed his concerns in a conversation with President Arthur late in 1881. Grace was convinced of the absolute lack of resoluteness in the U.S. policy toward Chile. He was disgusted. "*Am. Intervention* is all a humbug . . . Uncle Sam has backed down," Grace wrote Noel West, a Santiago colleague. He expressed even greater vehemence in a letter to his cousin in Lima, Edward Eyre: "The United States will be thoroughly hated on the west coast, will be jeered and laughed at by all the foreign legations, will be made fun of by the Chilean press, and will be thoroughly despised by the Peruvian people, who will blame them to a very great extent for the present trouble." After raising the hopes of the government and people of Peru, the United States then abruptly withdrew and left Peru open to the mercies of a victorious Chilean army.[35]

Perhaps Grace was overstating the ability of Trescot and the United States to dictate terms to Chile. When the embarrassed envoy tried to save face and his mission by urging the Chileans to be moderate in their demands, Balmaceda simply refused to discuss the matter of Tarapaca further. "Tarapaca," Balmaceda bluntly told Trescot, "is now irrevocably Chilean territory and if the United States wanted Tarapaca for Peru, then it must fight for it."[36]

Trescot packed his bags and left Santiago for Lima in March. He arrived in the Peruvian capital on March 28, 1882, one day after the sudden death of the U.S. minister to Peru, Hurlbut. Thousands of grieving Peruvians "lined the streets and decked his bier with flowers as it moved to the railway station." An Englishman said that Hurlbut "was looked upon by the natives as the Champion of the country," a sentiment that provoked such an outpouring of grief at his passing.[37]

Hurlbut's death was perhaps the perfect symbol for the bankruptcy of U.S. policy in the War of the Pacific. Just before Trescot left Peru he wrote Frelinghuysen that if the United States intended to intervene, the time to do so was now. If not, then "it was even more urgent that it make clear both to Peru and Chile the exact limits of US policy." Trescot concluded that the "current policy was an embarrassment to all parties concerned and should be terminated as soon as possible."[38]

After Trescot's mission ended in failure, Peru was effectively left on its own to determine the limits of the peace it would sign with Chile. There were few options left. Once the U.S. position became clear, Chile proceeded to push for a final settlement on *its* terms.

Treaty of Ancón

Peru now stood alone, and the Chileans moved purposefully to end the war on *their* terms. In the Treaty of Ancón (signed at the seaside resort of Ancón just south of Lima on October 10, 1883, and ratified on March 10, 1884), Peru lost her southern province of Tarapaca, rich in guano and nitrates, and acquiesced to a Chilean occupation of the two smaller provinces just north of Tarapaca, Arica and Tacna. A plebiscite held after ten years would determine their ultimate sovereignty, the victor paying the loser $10 million for the privilege of retaining the territory. That final transfer of territory did not take place until 1929, and the United States played a major role in this final settlement.

Peru lost territory that held natural resources, produced fiscal revenues, and, in some areas, included population clusters, especially in the old Peruvian provinces of Tacna and Arica. Indeed Tacna and Arica were so wedded to the Peruvian sense of national territory that the

Chileans were forced to make some concessions for the sake of the peace. Chile would, of course, have preferred outright annexation, but Peru adamantly resisted the unconditional loss of Tacna and Arica. The solution agreed to in the Treaty of Ancón helped to assuage the immense sense of loss in Peru. Ultimately Tacna would remain Peruvian and Arica go to Chile.

The effect of the legacy of the war on relations between Peru and the United States was mixed. President Arthur's message to Congress in late 1882 made clear that the United States would refrain from outright military intervention in Peru: "The power of Peru no longer extends over its whole territory, and in the event of our interference to dictate peace it would need to be supplemented by the armies and navies of the United States. Such interference would almost inevitably lead to the establishment of a protectorate, a result utterly at odds with our past policy, injurious to our present interest, and full of embarrassments for the future."[39]

On the other hand, Peru needed the support of the United States if in the future it expected to recuperate from the massive losses inflicted upon them by the war. Not only did the oligarchy want to reestablish its authority in Peru, it also required foreign capital and assistance to do so. Just the immense debt inherited from the prewar loans and war year expenditures alone—approximately $260 million—made it imperative that Peru look abroad to reestablish its credit.

Many Peruvians were embittered by the unrealistic and ultimately worthless encouragement of the United States to resist Chilean demands with respect to peace terms and territorial transfer. Peruvians, on the other hand, looked to the United States as the principal foreign power that could be called upon to mediate and lobby on behalf of Peru in future settlements with Chile. If British interests were closely associated with Chile's fortunes, then many considered Peruvian interests to be favored by the United States.

The War of the Pacific underscored the ambiguity that has often characterized relations between the United States and Peru. Though the U.S. government had proven to be a most unreliable patron, U.S. private investors and capitalists had not given up on Peru or Bolivia. In the next half century American capital and American liberal economic ideals would find a fruitful ground in Peru as it sought to reconstruct and modernize its economy in the face of such a traumatic experience with war and its consequences. In many ways the war cleared away many of the conservative, unchanging ways of the past and opened that path to the beginnings of the true modernization of Peru.

3   The Ascendant American Eagle

In the decades following the War of the Pacific, there were increasing ties between Peruvian elites—both liberal and conservative—and American entrepreneurs, traders, railroad builders, and investors who viewed the Peruvian world as a grand economic landscape to be exploited and developed. Contacts between Peru and the United States grew more frequent and varied during this period, reaching an apogee during the regime of Augusto B. Leguía of Peru in the 1920s. Leguía expressed his admiration for the United States in ways that doubtlessly befuddled other Latin American leaders. He declared the Fourth of July a national holiday in Peru and hung a portrait of President James Monroe in the national palace during a decade when hemispheric animosity toward U.S. intervention in Latin America had reached unprecedented heights.[1] But the most critical change lay in Peru's economic links to the U.S. economy. The United States replaced Great Britain as the principal investor in Peru after the First World War. The height of British investments occurred in Peru in 1925 ($125 million); however direct U.S. investments in Peru surpassed that amount to reach $200 million by the end of the decade. This represented a thirtyfold increase over the $6 million in U.S. investments in Peru in 1900—investments principally in the mining industry but also in petroleum, sugar, cotton, and wool.[2] By 1910 foreign corporations dominated the copper, silver, and petroleum sectors, while sugar, cotton, and wool production still were largely in the hands of Peruvian nationals.[3]

Just as important as the economic attraction between Americans and Peruvians, however, was an ideological component in the relationship—something more abstract, but just as important. Fredrick Pike has described its impact: "Facilitating the southward thrust of U.S. capitalism at the turn of the century was an approximation in hearts and minds between the influential classes of North America and Andean America. The United States as perceived by admiring Andean elites

74

was a country dominated by successful businessmen who operated according to the principles of the divine right of wealth and assumed that low economic status was the result of personal inferiority and moral depravity."[4]

Free enterprise and laissez-faire economics were producing enormous wealth in North America. Peruvian elites and entrepreneurs welcomed not only U.S. investors and investments but also the accompanying ideological framework that justified the prevailing trend of industrial capitalism, largely free of government intervention or oversight, in North America. Self-interest and economic self-gratification were all explained by social Darwinians as natural and good.

The natural rules of survival and competition at work among men, when allowed to run unfettered, provided the most good for the most people. Those who were fittest would survive and prosper. The rest were pulled along by the success of the best. Those left behind were condemned to poverty and subservience by their sloth, their moral depravity, and their inability or unwillingness to compete. One had but to observe nature to understand these rules. In Peru this seemed to resonate well with the prevailing social order and the emerging economic order. "Because Andean America's liberal leaders admired so much of U.S. culture as they perceived it," Pike wrote, "they were ready to afford an enthusiastic reception to American capitalists, welcoming them as frontiersmen with whom they could fruitfully collaborate in reclaiming for civilization what had long remained a vast wilderness [i.e., read, undeveloped natural resources]. This, then, was the background against which U.S. capital began its rapid penetration into Peru."[5]

The growing ties between North America and Peru took place during an era of increasing racism in North America. As American economic life reached impressive proportions, the segregation of the races had become a distinctive feature of national life. Liberal Peruvian leaders found the underlying justification for the segregation and subordination of blacks in American society quite adaptable and applicable to Indians in Peru. The supposedly brutish, indolent, passive, unteachable nature of the African American was a stereotype easily adapted from its American context to a Peruvian setting, substituting the Indian for the African American. There were countercurrents. American progressives condemned the evils of unbridled capitalism but were ambivalent about race. Peru's Indianist movement denied such racial stereotyping. The new Indianists elevated Indian culture to a legitimate, positive element in national society. But the Indianists were lonely voices in early twentieth-century Peruvian intellectual life. In the main Peruvian elites were intellectual and economic partners with entrepreneurs, such as Michael Grace, who represented the cutting edge of international capitalism along the west coast of South America. *Civilistas,* Peru's leading political party, were good friends and promoters of greater U.S. investments in Peru. Indeed "two of the most distinguished Civilista *pensadores* (thinkers), Javier Prado y Ugarteche and Manuel Vicente Villarán, regarded the United States as the model modern nation; and both hoped that Peru might one day develop a capitalist, free-enterprise system similar to that of the northern republic."[6] Michael Grace shared that vision.

The Grace Contract

Before an infusion of U.S. capital occurred, however, Peru had to overcome the legacy of war. Both Peru and the United States were debtor nations, but the United States overcame its debtor status during World War I. The Peruvian experience was different. Peru not only had an immense war debt but a debt contracted during the halcyon days of railroad building under Henry Meiggs. Complicating matters was the loss of Tarapaca with its reserves of guano and nitrates. Revenues from these resources had been largely hypothecated to servicing the railroad debt and other internal improvements. Not only had the war left a deep psychological scar on the national psyche of Peru, but it left the country in a financial morass. Attempts to raise new loans in the 1880s by the Peruvians on the European bond markets all failed. The bondholders, principally Englishmen, wanted their prior investments in Peru guaranteed before allowing fresh new loans. To break this logjam, the ubiquitous and ambitious Michael Grace devoted his considerable charm, determination, and financial genius to helping Peru and making himself wealthy, goals that Grace certainly felt were mutually complementary. The negotiation of the Grace Contract, which was signed and ratified in 1889, was complicated and aroused considerable passion in Peru. In effect Peru's future as a modern nation came to depend in part on decisions by foreign capitalists and diplomats in the boardrooms and chancelleries of Europe and North America.

In 1886 Grace formed a syndicate, the Cerro de Pasco Syndicate, to exploit railroad and mining concessions he had acquired from Henry Meiggs's heirs. Michael then sent a team of mining engineers to Peru to investigate thoroughly the Cerro de Pasco region. Grace also continued to operate the railroad, made necessary repairs, and prepared for the extension of the railway and the construction of a major drainage tunnel to facilitate mining at Cerro de Pasco. Meanwhile the principal holders of Peru's foreign debt—bondholders in England—were pursuing their interests, which, like Michael Grace's, were inextricably linked to Peru's financial problems and promises.

The bondholders' dilemma was how to redeem their investment. Peru was in no position to pay the bonds held by these Englishmen. Guano reserves had been depleted and the Treaty of Ancón had stripped Peru of the valuable nitrate province of Tarapaca. Even before the war, the principal bondholders had formed a committee to look after their interests, viewing the railroads—pledged by the Peruvians in earlier loans as collateral—as legitimate compensation for loans in default. Apparently some influential Peruvians agreed. In early 1880 the administration of President Nicolás de Piérola issued a decree granting the bondholders the ownership of all the national railroads. Though the bondholders took no action, the decree was a tacit admission on the part of the Peruvians to the bondholders' rights to the railroads.

There followed a complicated series of negotiations over the next several years between the bondholders and the governments of Chile, Peru, and Great Britain as the bondholders attempted to force the Chileans to recognize bondholder claims to guano and nitrate deposits once formerly in Peru but now in Chilean territory. By 1885 when Michael Grace bought the old Meiggs railroad concessions, an impasse existed. The

Chileans were not interested in giving away what they had won in war. Peruvians had little negotiating leverage. The bondholders could not persuade Her Majesty's government to intercede against Chile on their behalf. And the United States was undecided on how to assist the Peruvians.

At this point Michael Grace offered his services to the bondholders and in 1886 became their principal representative before the government of Peru. If Peru recovered her financial and commercial footing, Grace stood to prosper. If she remained yoked under the debt and subordinate to Chile, Grace might fail in his endeavors. The plan was simple, but its negotiation complicated. Grace placed himself between the bondholders and the Peruvian government and sought to forge an agreement that both sides would accept. The key to Grace's various proposals as they evolved from 1886 through 1889 was his insistence that any agreement between the bondholders and Peru must be "in exchange for an absolute quittal of all claims of its foreign creditors."[7]

Grace complemented his natural gifts as a mediator with an ability to understand both the hard commercial mentality of the bondholders and the fierce national pride of President Andrés Cáceres (1886–90; 1894–95) of Peru. The bondholders' initial demands were outrageous, while Cáceres's attitude was obdurate. At one point the old general groused to Edward Eyre, Michael Grace's nephew in Lima, that since Chileans now owned the guano and nitrate wealth, the bondholders should deal with them. Eyre, who was in charge of the Grace house in Lima, advised the president that successful negotiations required the granting of the railroads to the bondholders as the principal concession. Eyre's arguments drew little more than a shrug from Cáceres, who showed not the slightest enthusiasm.

"How," the president queried Eyre, perhaps rhetorically, "are we going to give them our railroads which cost us so dearly?"[8] That was a question that also troubled many other Peruvians who split on the issue as the debate heated up in the national forums of Peru. The initial demands of the bondholders—which included not only ownership of the railroads but concessions regarding coal and mercury mines, oil fields, establishment of colonies, a monopoly on all subsequent guano exports, and the right to collect customs duties at the Southern Railway terminus on the Pacific Ocean, Mollendo—outraged many Peruvians. Opponents of the negotiations claimed the demands were outright infringements of Peru's sovereignty. The colonization clauses of the proposed contract were among the most interesting, and illustrative, of the controversies surrounding the negotiations.

In the late nineteenth century, Americans saw European immigrants principally as laborers and settlers. Latin Americans shared this view, but they also recruited Europeans to help "whiten" and "civilize" the continent. Peruvians had tried to provide inducements for Europeans to immigrate, and a few Irish, Spanish, and German settlements had at one time been attempted. The results, however, had been disappointing. Now the champions of the Grace Contract were once again heralding the promise of immigration. But many found the rationale specious and unrealistic. "The projected colonization project was but a farce," said José María Quimper, a leading opponent of the contract, adding that "the age of miracles had long ago passed."[9] Quimper's pessimism proved right in the long run, for no great wave of European settlement swept across Peru; there was no leavening of Peruvian society with whiteness and no enrichment of Peru with Old World work habits, blood, or capacity for industrialized labor. But the subject of immigration stirred imaginations and fired debate within the context of the bondholders' proposals.

Not all Peruvian elites were swept up by the arguments for modernizing and opening Peru unequivocally to the streams of capitalism flowing from North America and Europe. A strong nationalist sentiment that would later become more manifest and vocal in the 1960s and 1970s reverberated throughout debates over the Grace Contract. These sentiments just as clearly colored relations between the United States and Peru as those—represented by Michael Grace and his Peruvian supporters, for example—that favored increasing collaboration at almost any cost.

One critic, Manuel Atanasio Fuentes, the interim attorney general at the time he opposed the contract, cynically observed that all the promises inherent in Michael Grace's contract were but chimeras. "Colossal enterprises," Fuentes wrote were promised upon conclusion of the contract and the settlement of the debt. "Here is a position," Fuentes said, "that all debtors would certainly favor: a creditor's representative [Grace] who not only gives his debtors generous terms, but [promises] work and bread as well. [But] we must be wary of dealing with those not born in this land," Fuentes added, "with regard to Peruvian matters," certainly alluding to Michael Grace's Irish-American background.[10]

On the other hand, President Cáceres and the Council of Ministers had decided by 1887 to support the contract, especially as Michael Grace worked to moderate the bondholders' original demands. Cáceres identified four reasons for approval in an address to a suspicious Peruvian congress: one, the need to reestablish not only the external but internal credit of the nation to release economic forces, to increase currency values, and to create new and more powerful fiscal resources; two, the need to complete the construction of the railroads and repairing and returning to regular service those in a lamentable state of deterioration; three, the importance of studying and then exploiting the riches of the principal mining centers; and four, the utility of creating new centers of population to facilitate and stimulate immigration further.[11]

In September 1887 the Peruvian Congress further complicated matters by authorizing the nationalization of certain Peruvian railroads. United States investors promptly harassed Washington with pleas to protect their railroad rights in Peru. The Graces joined the U.S. complainants. Secretary of State Thomas F. Bayard remonstrated with the Peruvian government, but the Congress, especially the Chamber of Deputies where much of the opposition to the Grace Contract centered, did not back off. Grace lectured the secretary of state not only on the illegality of the nationalizations but on the inefficiency of public enterprise. "The Peruvian government well knows," Grace wrote Bayard, "that if the roads should be taken by them and fall into the hands of government administrators, the result would be that within a few years they would not only not be extended, but the probability is that they would not be in existence."[12]

This dispute embodied one of the principal elements in the making of the modern Peruvian-U.S. relationship—the debate over the propriety and effectiveness of public versus private enterprise in Peru's economic development. In the late nineteenth and early twentieth centuries prevalent political thinking tended to favor private enterprise in this debate. But other forces and ideologies would question or directly contravene this economic wisdom in the twentieth century. The effects of the Great Depression in the 1930s and the powerful appeal of Marxism from the 1920s through the 1980s, for example, challenged the assumptions of liberal capitalism and unbridled competition. The nature of relations between Peruvians and Americans was often colored by which side of the issue—liberty or equality—prevailed in the respective nations. Peruvians historically looked to the State for adjudication and leadership in the economic and social development of the nation. North Americans, contrastingly, often suspected the State as an intrusive, meddling, and inefficient motor of economic and social development.

As the negotiations for the Grace Contract proceeded, many of these varying visions of what was best and most appropriate for a people and a nation were given voice by the supporters and detractors of the contract. In the making of the contract, thus, we have a microcosm of those elements that went into the making of Peruvian-U.S. relations for the two centuries under consideration.

Meanwhile Michael Grace had to deal more immediately with the railroad nationalizations. He argued with his Peruvian supporters that even though the nationalizations may be justified, the result was a reinforcement of the image abroad that Peru was politically unstable. "It gives another pretext," Grace said, "to the many enemies of the country to expound their theory that the country is unstable and unsafe to invest capital in."[13] "You know," Grace hammered away at his Peruvian friends, "how difficult it was to get men in Lima to join you [Denegri, to whom Grace is writing], Doctor Rosas, Doctor Aranibar, and García Calderón and others in showing the public that this project was really the only one by which the credit of Peru could be redeemed."[14]

Grace negotiated to get the U.S. government more directly involved in not only protecting U.S. investments in the Peruvian railroads but in promoting the Grace Contract itself. A special Peruvian envoy, Félix

Cipriano Zegarra, was sent to Washington in 1888 to represent Peru's interests, and Grace worked closely with Zegarra, Secretary of State Bayard, and President Grover Cleveland to achieve his goals.

Grace had little hope that the United States would intervene or intercede in what Bayard considered basically to be a private dispute between investors and a foreign government. Bayard argued that the consequences of entering into contractual obligations with an unstable government should be borne by the investors. The U.S. government was not in the business of bailing out its citizens who made bad investments or suffered the consequences of unsound business decisions. Zegarra, on behalf of the Peruvian government, assured Grace and Bayard that his country would fight rather than yield on their right to nationalize the railroads.

Bayard, for his part, knew that the United States had little leverage on Peru. William Ivins, Grace's representative in Washington during most of the negotiations, candidly wrote his boss that "the thing that staggers Mr. Bayard most, in case the worst comes to the worst, is the futility of attempting to coerce so weak and puny a state as Peru, as he fears it would only result in a long and ultimately fruitless occupation of the country and would on no account restore the values of the railroad properties."[15] Zegarra was clearly playing his strength—the very weakness of Peru—quite well.

This exchange illuminated the asymmetrical nature of the relations between Peru and the United States, but with an ironic twist to the story. Instead of the powerful dictating to the weak, the powerful finds itself unable to bring its power to bear. Relations between nations are not always dictated by power and size. Occasionally other determinants, such as long-term goals, political principles and ideals, and a careful consideration of the desire or ability of internal public opinion to sustain intervention, are often more important.

In 1888 the bondholders' committee lessened some of their demands, particularly their rights to oil fields in the north, a proposal that bondholders would name customshouse officials at Mollendo to collect duties, and a reduction of the time limit on the railroad concession from seventy-five years to sixty-six years. The crisis over the seizure of the railroads was left in temporary abeyance, for if the new contract was ratified, the railroad concessionaires, such as Michael Grace, would deal directly with the corporation—the Peruvian Corporation—slated to succeed the bondholders and carry out the terms of the contract.[16] Congress finally ratified the contract in late October 1889. When opposition members of the Chamber of Deputies had stormed out of one session in early 1889, Cáceres—frustrated by the chamber's intransigence in approving the contract—simply declared their posts vacant and held new elections. With a majority of supporters, Cáceres rammed through the contract.

Peru passed into a new era. The settlement of the national debt provided a means for recovery from the War of the Pacific and offered the nation the prospect of new economic development across a broad spectrum of activities in mining, agriculture, banking, and even beer making. But the Grace Contract remained a controversial issue among Peruvians for several generations.

In one sense—in Michael Grace's point of view certainly—it was a liberating, progressive act that enabled Peru to draw freely again upon the capitalist resources of Europe and North America. According to Quimper and the contract's critics, especially those subscribing to perspectives formed by Marxist and dependency theories in the twentieth century, those very ties with capitalism reinforced colonialism and economic dependency and thus the contract was a step backward.

The most balanced assessment of the Grace Contract was made by Peru's premier historian of the twentieth century, Jorge Basadre. Basadre felt that the contract represented the best arrangement under bad circumstances; the railroads were in a state of deterioration; the bondholders were blocking Peru's access to moneys abroad; the Chileans were in opposition to the Grace Contract; the English Foreign Office waxed hot and cold, as did the U.S. Department of State. The contract broke this impasse and by the vary nature of its solution invited foreign capital into the country. On the one hand, Basadre observed that "the unique alliance predicted between Peru and her creditors to make the country flourish dramatically did not develop." But, as Basadre noted, "nor did the pessimistic vision of the Contract's more furious and hot-headed adversaries come to pass." What happened was that "the past was liquidated and the country, thinking itself free of her overwhelming foreign debt, confronted the future in pursuit of reconstruction."[17]

The Chimbote Naval Station

In the overall scheme of relations between the United States and Peru, the Grace Contract associated Peru's aspirations more closely with those of the United States, then trying to reduce the predominant commercial and diplomatic weight of England in South America. Indeed U.S. interest in Peru was more than commercial and diplomatic. It included the possible acquisition of a naval base on the north coast of Peru in the late nineteenth century.

The possibility of establishing a major naval station on Peru's north coast first came up during the War of the Pacific when the Peruvian government and the U.S. Minister to Peru, Stephen Hurlbut, agreed to allow the United States to locate a coaling station and naval base at the spacious port of Chimbote.[18] Nothing came of this initial agreement, but in 1889 the negotiations were resumed.

The United States was expanding its naval and commercial presence in the Pacific, and it was thought opportune to have a station on the west coast of South America. In fact the U.S. Navy had maintained a small squadron along the west coast ever since the Wars of Independence, largely patrolling between Callao, Valparaíso, and ports to the north as far as Central America. As the United States gradually modernized its navy in the 1880s and 1890s and expanded its commercial horizons, the west coast of South America gained its share of attention among American planners.

Neither Peru nor the United States was ready in 1888 or 1889 to make the necessary commitments and concessions to establish a Chimbote naval station. The Peruvians would not give the U.S. territorial jurisdiction, which included the right to fly the U.S. flag, and the United States would not yield to Peru's insistence on territorial integrity. The talks continued off and on again in 1891 and 1892, just as relations between the United States and Chile were reaching a nadir over various disputes.[19] Talks resumed again after the turn of the century when Theodore Roosevelt became president.

Roosevelt was vigorously committed to a transisthmian canal across Panama and he thought a station on the west coast would help protect such a canal. In 1901 Peruvian Vice President Isaac Alzamora (who, coincidentally, was a member of a syndicate of Peruvian-U.S. investors interested in developing coal resources in the Chimbote area) suggested to Roosevelt and Secretary of State John Hay that Chimbote should again be put up for discussion. Roosevelt agreed, and Alzamora outlined the Peruvian agenda: a ninety-nine year lease of Chimbote to the United States in return for support of Peru's claims in the Tacna-Arica dispute with Chile; donation of U.S. warships to Peru; provisions for training Peruvian naval personnel in the United States; and loans to improve the port of Callao.[20]

The matter lay dormant until 1909 when Peru renewed the proposal. At the time Peru was in a territorial dispute with Brazil over the Acre region of the Amazon, rich in rubber resources, and Peru offered Chimbote to the United States in return for a guarantee of territorial integrity from the United States.[21] The Department of the Navy was, however, now not interested since the navy was transitioning to a new policy of coaling her ships at sea, thus reducing her need for coaling stations all over the world. As the Panama Canal moved toward completion (it opened in 1914), the navy argued that no further stations would be needed south of Panama in the Pacific.

Peruvian president Augusto B. Leguía continued the pressure. A dispute with Ecuador furthered Peru's desire to build up her navy, and she began negotiations with the Electric Boat Co. of Groton, Connecticut, to build submarines. Leguía made the Chimbote base proposal a part of the argument, which appealed to Secretary of State Philander Knox, who was interested in promoting the sale of American goods—in this instance, submarines—abroad. In the end Leguía was willing to concede Chimbote to the United States with few restraints, but the nearing completion of the Panama Canal made a U.S. naval presence further south unjustified. When Leguía left office in 1912, the momentum once again subsided. Besides, as some in the Department of State argued, a U.S. naval station in Peru would simply involve the United States more closely in territorial and border disputes between Peru and her neighbors and lessen U.S. independence and leverage in mediating such disputes.

As the drive for a U.S. naval station at Chimbote receded, private U.S. commercial and industrial interests were growing in Peru. Americans from the 1890s onward became involved in a variety of activities in Peru, ranging from the more traditional economic areas of mining and railroad building to sanitation, irrigation, and education. Rubber extraction along the Amazon and oil drilling along the north coast of Peru also attracted U.S. citizens and their capital. Relations broadened not only at the initiative of private U.S. entrepreneurs, traders, miners, beer makers, bankers, and textile mill operators for example, but between the agencies of the governments as well, especially as pro-American Peruvian politicians and businessmen, such as Leguía, came to power.

Mining shaped twentieth-century Peru's economic character—and some would argue her political and social conditions as well. Perhaps no other mines represented Peru's hopes and aspirations for progress and wealth than the Cerro de Pasco silver and copper mines.

Cerro de Pasco and the Peruvian Cornucopia

Cerro de Pasco Corporation became the largest U.S. investor in Peru in the twentieth century. It remained a major presence in Peru until it was nationalized in 1974. Formed by a wealthy syndicate of U.S. capitalists in 1901 to exploit the rich copper mines of the Cerro de Pasco district in the Andean highlands, the Cerro Corporation's history symbolized much of the ambivalence and ambiguity in the modern history of relations between Peru and the United States.[22]

The Cerro de Pasco Corporation was founded in 1902 by an American of Turkish ancestry, James Ben Ali Haggin. Among the investors in the syndicate formed by Haggin were J. P. Morgan, Hamilton McKowan

Twombly (of the Vanderbilt family), Phoebe Hearst (mother of William Randolph Hearst), Henry Clay Frick, Darius Ogden Mills (grandfather of Ogden Mills), and Alfred W. McCune, who came to Peru in 1900. Largely because of McCune's various efforts, in a few years the syndicate acquired the rights to a majority of the mines in the region, finished the Central Railroad to La Oroya, and constructed a new smelter near Cerro de Pasco that commenced operations in 1906. Later the Cerro Corporation expanded its operations to include the large copper mine at Morococha, and near the end of the First World War it bought out the interests in the Casapalpa mine owned by the Americans Jacob Backus (nephew of Henry Meiggs) and J. H. Johnson. By 1916 the Cerro Corporation had about $30 million invested in Peru, probably the largest investment in copper mining in the world and certainly the largest in South America.[23] Cerro was the largest U.S. corporation but certainly not the only one exploiting the cornucopia of potential wealth in Peru at the turn of the century.[24]

Attracted by the friendly investment climate created by the government of Nicolás de Piérola, which came to power in 1895, hundreds of Americans turned south to seek their fortunes, not all of them as well financed as the Cerro syndicate, but all with high hopes. In 1905 one of the largest vanadium mines in the world was discovered by accident. Indians searching for coal brought back samples from a place near Cerro de Pasco called Minasagra. American chemists found they contained high concentrations of vanadium, and in 1907, the American Vanadium Co., having purchased the Minasagra mine, began production. Vanadium was used to temper steel in a process invented only a few years prior to Minasagra's discovery. The first order of five thousand tons of vanadium from Minasagra was used in the hinges of the gates of the Panama Canal, and during the First World War, Peruvian vanadium went into the production of armaments and high powered projectiles.[25] In 1920 about thirty-eight thousand tons of vanadium were produced by Minasagra. This represented a 90 percent share of the world's production of vanadium.

Gold, too, was mined profitably during this halcyon period. In 1896

W. L. Hardison, a California native involved in oil exploration, formed the Inca Mining Company to exploit gold deposits in the Santo Domingo mines along the Inambari River on the eastern slopes of the Andes. To reach the mines, Hardison had to construct a wagon road more than two hundred miles long from the southern railroad connecting Juliaca (on Lake Titicaca) with Cuzco to the Inambari River. In 1907 Hardison's company produced more than $2.5 million worth of gold.[26]

Rubber

Peru is an Amazonian nation with varying proportions of its territory forming part of the great Amazon River basin. The Amazon came alive in the world's markets in the late nineteenth century when rubber exports expanded astronomically between 1890 and 1912, the period of Peru's greatest rubber exports. Rubber became one of Peru's most important export crops at the turn of the century as the modernizing world turned to rubber tires and components to move the bicycles and automobiles of this new age of revolutionary transportation. The boom lasted only a short time in the Amazon, subsiding almost as quickly as it rose. Nonetheless at the height of the rubber boom, rubber was responsible for 18 percent of Peru's total foreign exports before rubber plantations in Asia undermined the market for natural rubber being produced in the Amazon region.

At the center of Peru's rubber boom was the son of an American sailor who had settled in Peru in the highland city of Ancash at mid-century. William Fitzgerald had seven children, the eldest born in 1862 and christened Isaias Fermin Fitzgerald. He later changed his name to Carlos and crossed through Peruvian time and space like a comet of sorts, leaving a trail of brilliant light and garnering the nickname the "King of Rubber."[27] At the time of his death in 1897, Fitzgerald had earned a fortune from the rubber boom. Perhaps more important he had explored and charted portions of Peru's remote and inaccessible eastern Andes where the steep mountains descend into the jungle of the Atlantic river basins. Peruvians remember him not only as the "King of Rubber" but also as an explorer, as a defender of Peru's territorial sovereignty in the face of aggressive Brazilian encroachments, and as a friend of the remoter and wilder tribes of the eastern Andes and jungle region.[28]

He was educated in Huaráz and Lima where he graduated from the Liceo Peruano in 1878. His father died in 1879 on the eve of the War of the Pacific, and the young Fitzcarrald, as Fitzgerald was rendered in Peruvian Spanish, returned to the interior to trade in the Huánuco and Cerro de Pasco region. Captured during the war with maps of rivers in the remote eastern regions of the Sierra in his possession, he was accused of being a Chilean spy. He was saved from execution by a missionary who identified him. Fitzcarrald then changed his name to Carlos Fernando and took off for the deep jungle to the east. From this point until reappearing in Iquitos in 1888, he was lost to the record, but legends of a "white Indian" began to be passed along—a man who introduced civilization in the deepest jungle, a man whose intimacy with the region and its natives helped him promote the gathering and selling of raw rubber.[29] When he appeared in Iquitos in 1888, he was already the richest rubber producer on the Ucayali River system. He was then twenty-six years old and sported a patriarchal beard and a blond complexion.

Not satisfied with dominating the Ucayali system, he went on to explore the Apurímac, the Urubamba, and the Madre de Dios river systems. He discovered a short transit between the upper reaches of the Urubamba (which is a tributary of the Amazon) and the Madre de Dios (which flows to the south and east to the Rio de la Plata estuary); the transit was named in his honor, "Fitzcarrald's isthmus." The discovery was labeled "the most important geographical discovery in nineteenth century Peru" for it gave Peru immensely important commercial and strategic knowledge of an area little known to that point. Throughout his travels Fitzcarrald befriended and made allies of remote Indian tribes. They helped collect the valuable rubber, bringing the tribes into contact for the first time with European goods and civilization.

As we near another "turn of the century," and priorities with respect to nature and man take different shadings, one can question the wisdom of bringing the "fruits" of civilization to these recondite river and jungle people living where the labyrinthine eastern mountains melt into almost endless jungle and trackless savannas of the interior of South America. With civilization came diseases, the feuds of greedy entrepreneurs, the rivalries of nations, and the end of an Arcadian existence, perhaps. But, at the time, few questioned the wisdom of "conquering" nature and incorporating these people—as best as possible—into the mainstream of European-style civilization as it had evolved for almost four hundred years in the Americas. The rubber boom did not make a long lasting impression on coastal or Andean Peru where the great bulk of the population resided. In the jungle, however, the rubber boom not only produced a short-lived spurt to Peru's economic development, but it also brought people of the remoter regions into contact for the first time with large-scale entrepreneurial enterprise. Such a surge would not occur again until half a century later when in the 1970s and 1980s the cocaine drug culture once again focused the world's attention on the region.

The boom left its most visible impact on Peru's principal Amazonian river city, Iquitos. In 1912 President Leguía requested assistance from the U.S. government to establish a more modern sewage system for the river city whose population had exploded from about five hundred at mid-century to more than seven thousand by 1912.[30] The State Department recruited Dr. George Converse, assistant surgeon of the U.S. Public Health Service, and two civil engineers, Samuel Bayless and Edward Keegan, to travel to Iquitos and make recommendations. Strapped for funds, the Peruvian government could not ultimately raise the money to pursue the project.

While rubber boomed dramatically and then collapsed just as spectacularly, the impact of another mineral resource exploited in large part by U.S. citizens had a longer-lasting effect on the relations of Peru and the United States.

The Economics and Politics of Oil

Oil, like rubber, came into great demand because of the rapid technological modernization of the Western world at the turn of the century.

The internal combustion engine and a host of other machines fueled increasing demands for oil, and soon the explorer's net was cast world-wide for sources of petroleum. The early exploration and exploitation of Peru's oil fields—almost all of them discovered in the remote northern desert coast—came about in part through the initiative of U.S. citizens, sometimes acting in competition, sometimes in cooperation, with British citizens and Peruvians themselves. And the exploitation of Peru's oil resources by U.S. business interests eventually led to the most volatile conflict between the United States and Peru in the twentieth century.

As in the case of guano, nitrates, and rubber, the petroleum industry was fueled by demands largely from abroad, although the local market for kerosene helped promote oil exploration and development. In 1863 A. E. Prentice, an American working for the gas company in Lima, drilled the first well just north of the La Brea y Pariñas property on the northern Peruvian coast.[31] In 1876 two Americans, E. P. Larkin and Henry Smith, formed a partnership to develop the Zoritos fields. This company eventually was taken over by an Italian immigrant to Peru, Faustino Piaggio, who developed the Zoritos fields into a major petroleum producer—complete with its own refinery—for the local Peruvian market by the turn of the century. The larger fields of Negritos (La Brea) and Lobitos were, however, developed by U.S. and British entrepreneurs.

The Negritos oil fields were located on the hacienda La Brea y Pariñas, known since colonial days for tar pits in the region. In the seventeenth and eighteenth centuries, pitch produced at La Brea went to caulk the royal galleons for the South Seas Fleet built to the north in the Ecuadorian port city of Guayaquil.[32] After independence the property passed through several owners, and in 1888 Genaro Helguero sold La Brea to a pair of Englishmen, Herbert Tweedle and William Keswick, who then formed the London and Pacific Petroleum Company to exploit the property.[33] It should be no surprise that the ubiquitous Henry Meiggs had already prospected and drilled for oil at the La Brea site in the 1870s, establishing a refinery at Callao to manufacture and market kerosene. "By the time the Chilean navy destroyed all the oil installations in 1879, the industry was thus already dominated by U.S. capitalists," noted Rosemary Thorp and Geoffrey Bertram in their pathbreaking book on the Peruvian economy.[34]

Nevertheless even though Americans pioneered the industry, what emerged at the turn of the century was a new industry with capitalists from all three countries—the United States, Great Britain, and Peru—participating. In 1901 the last major field, Lobitos, was discovered by an Englishman, Alexander Milne, who formed the Lobitos Oilfield Company to mine the fields. Then, in 1913 and 1914, domestic events in the United States changed the configuration, and history, of the petroleum industry in Peru.

Antitrust legislation was breaking up the immense Standard Oil Company—the source of John D. Rockefeller's fortune—into independent corporations, among them Standard Oil of New Jersey. Through a Canadian subsidiary, Imperial Oil Company, Jersey Standard controlled a refinery in Vancouver that depended upon crude oil from Standard's oil wells in California, now an independent producer.[35] Looking for new sources of crude, and with the imminent opening of the Panama Canal making the west coast of South America much more accessible to ports along the Gulf and Atlantic coasts, Walter Teagle of Standard began to acquire oil properties in Peru. In 1913 and 1914 Standard Oil bought control of the London and Pacific (La Brea and Negritos) and several other smaller companies, including the West Coast Fuel Company (which controlled the distribution of oil products all along the Pacific coast countries), and incorporated them into the International Petroleum Company (I.P.C.) of Canada, a subsidiary of Standard Oil of New Jersey.

I.P.C. followed Rockefeller's strategy of consolidation and control. By the early 1920s, I.P.C. had invested almost $370 million in its Peruvian oil fields and controlled about 80 percent of the oil production in Peru.[36] The only other major producer, the British-owned fields at Lobitos, sold and marketed their products through I.P.C. The I.P.C. refinery, the port of Talara, the workplace, and the homes of I.P.C. employees became a model enclave of a foreign presence in Peru—a clean and healthy port with well-paid workers and an industry that contributed a sizable share of income to the Peruvian state. Peruvian critics, on the other hand, decried I.P.C.'s exploitation of one of Peru's principal nonrenewable natural resources.

Briefly, I.P.C. claimed special privileges exempting it from the normal claims of State ownership of subsoil mineral rights. I.P.C.'s claim dated back to 1826 when Simón Bolívar, then president of Peru, deeded the pitch mines of La Brea to one of his Peruvian friends, José Antonio de Quintana, in compensation for Quintana's financial support during the liberation of Peru. The deed apparently conflicted with Spanish law, confirmed by subsequent Peruvian law and practice, stipulating that subsoil rights were *always retained* by the Crown or State which could, nonetheless, give individuals sweeping concessions and rights to exploit mineral resources. Almost one hundred years later, I.P.C. continued to claim exemption from the general principle of mineral rights with respect to its property at La Brea. Peruvian governments vacillated, in turn trying to collect larger taxes, royalties, and other compensations from I.P.C., claiming no exemptions existed for I.P.C., and then backing off under company pressure. This pressure could be as crude as withholding shipments of gasoline and kerosene from Talara to the major domestic market of Lima (as I.P.C. did in 1918, claiming war exigencies) or as subtle as promising various presidents (Leguía among them) help in obtaining loans from the United States.[37]

When the crisis came to a head in the late 1960s, one Peruvian general charged that I.P.C. "bribed ministers, corrupted governments, and promoted revolutions." But, as Richard Goodwin, a Kennedy-era staffer who had served in Peru, noted in his recounting of I.P.C.'s history in Peru, "yet, even if this is true, it takes two to make a bribe and you cannot corrupt the incorruptible."[38] Perhaps that was a bit disingenuous of Goodwin, for, even though he strove for objectivity, Goodwin did reflect the subtle bias of a U.S. official who found the Peruvian perspective sometimes irrational and exasperating.

I.P.C. became the largest taxpayer in Peru by mid-century, and their "labor practices were a model for the country," so claimed one official of the company.[39] That was probably accurate. But, in 1928, a young Peruvian named Luis Miró Quesada ran into I.P.C., and his memory leaves a different taste in the mouth. "I first became interested in I.P.C. about forty years ago," Miró Quesada recounted to Goodwin in an interview in 1968.[40] Miró Quesada, from an old and distinguished Peruvian family, and then head of one of the leading newspapers of Peru, *El Comercio*, prefaced his remarks to Goodwin with a disclaimer. "I know America well and I have many friends there, but there is a difference between your country and the State Department—which cares mostly about the welfare of American companies. It is a great country," Miró Quesada contemplated and then continued, "but that is not the same thing as I.P.C., is it?"

This distinction was made over and over by Peruvians who challenged the acts, real or perceived, of the U.S. government in protecting U.S. rights and/or properties of U.S. individuals or corporations in Peru. In a way the Miró Quesadas of Peru were recognizing in their own fashion—and for their own ends—that the immensity and complexity of U.S. foreign policy was not the reserve of a few professionals in the Department of State, but a function of multiple private and public interests and agencies, such as the Department of Defense and even Pentecostal denominations for example, all with varying degrees of influence on the way in which the United States articulated its relations with Peru. And Peruvians found ways to appeal to this immensely varied constituency in the second half of the century.

In the 1920s, however, I.P.C. seemed regal and imperious to Peruvians. Miró Quesada returned to Peru in the late 1920s from a trip to Europe on a Grace Line ship. "We landed at Talara," Miró Quesada reminisced, "where the refinery is, and the landing papers said 'Talara-Puerto Norteamericano.' I crossed out 'Norteamericano' and wrote in 'Peruano.' When we landed, they had separate dining rooms for Peruvians and Americans. So when I got home, I began to read about I.P.C." This led Miró Quesada to some thoughts on the constant tension between the needs for foreign assistance in economic development, and the legitimate claims of national sovereignty on the part of governments. "It's not enough for an oil company to pay taxes and salaries. Peru should get a share of the profits. Once minerals are taken, they are gone. They don't grow—not like trees."

I.P.C. also represented another important face of foreign enterprise in

Peru. It was an enclave economy. Isolated by geography from the rest of Peru, located as it was on the northern desert coast, its principal links to the outside world were largely by ship through the port of Talara before roads and aviation made it accessible to the rest of the country. It was indeed an island or enclave economy, far removed, it seemed to many, from the Peruvian reality. It was an island of prosperity, good wages, and decent living conditions. It was not, it seemed, a part of Peru. Alberto Lleras Camargo, a Colombian who became president of his country in the 1960s, visited Talara while a young man touring Peru. As an I.P.C. official remembered, "Lleras looked at all our installations and had long talks with our managers. As he left, we asked him how he liked it. 'It's a wonderful, progressive place,' he said, 'but I didn't meet any Peruvians.'"[41]

Peru and the United States to the 1920s

Contacts between the United States and Peru in the early twentieth century multiplied rapidly across a wide spectrum of activities as diversified as religion, archaeology, movies, and mining. As the Cerro Corporation and I.P.C. expanded their mining and petroleum complexes, for example, the Yale archaeologist Hiram Bingham discovered one of the most stupendous "lost cities" of the Inca Empire in the jungles of eastern Peru in 1911.[42] Bingham's discovery, Machu Picchu, proved to be a mecca for American tourists who were fascinated by the remains of the once-magnificent empire of the Incas. Numerous articles and graphics by Hiram Bingham on Machu Picchu and the southern Peruvian Andes filled the pages of *National Geographic Magazine* beginning in 1912, opening up to the American reading public a vista of a world previously known only to a handful of diplomats, mining and railroad engineers, and occasional tourists who had wandered far off the beaten path. By the second half of the twentieth century tourism was growing in Peru into a major industry that linked Peru to the United States, and Machu Picchu became the principal attraction on the tourist trail.

National Geographic Magazine, under the editorship of Gilbert H. Grosvenor (the son-in-law of Alexander Graham Bell), was itself being trans-formed in the first decade of the century into the greatest purveyor of geography for the general public. Grosvenor turned *National Geographic* into a popular magazine, introducing illustrations as a major feature in 1905. By 1908 more than half the magazine was devoted to photographs, and when Bingham's first article on Machu Picchu and Peru appeared in 1912, subscriptions were climbing past the one hundred thousand mark.[43] From then until now, *National Geographic Magazine* has intro-duced millions of readers to the wonders and realities of Peru, promot-ing greater knowledge and interest in the region for American readers.

The *Geographical Review* published by the American Geographical So-ciety also provided news and findings of Peru that flowed into the United States. When Isaiah Bowman became director of the Society in 1915, he brought with him a special interest in and knowledge of the Andean region. Bowman had explored in the region as early as 1907 and had accompanied Bingham on his journey to Machu Picchu in 1911. Bowman's *The Andes of Southern Peru*, first published in the United States in 1916 (in England in 1920, and in 1938 in Peru as the first Spanish edi-tion), was a magnificent geographical treatise that included notes and observations on social and political conditions in Peru. Peru's leading historian called this work "the most notable contribution to the geogra-phy of Peru in this period . . . which contains not only a scientific trea-tise . . . but many pages with great interests for the social historian. . . ."[44]

As Americans learned more of Peru and the Andes, a few special guests, including the president of Peru, Nicolás de Piérola, sat down to watch the first "moving picture" on January 2, 1897, in the Estrasburgo Garden of the Plaza de Armas in downtown Lima.[45] The movies proved a great hit with the affluent of Lima. Within a few years movies were playing to packed crowds in the theaters of Lima, providing Peruvians with views into Hollywood's version of life—for better or worse—in the great republic to the north.

In a way some of the stereotyping in the twentieth century that came to mark the images that Peruvians had of Americans, and vice versa, was symbolized by Machu Picchu and Hollywood. The average Ameri-can who knew anything of Peru (arguably, a very small percentage of

Americans) saw Indians, ruins, and a traditional society marked by quiet Indian masses and genteel decadence among the Catholic, Creole elites as representative of Peruvian realities. On the other hand, cowboys, glamour, glitz, gangsters, aviators, seductresses of the silent screen, and an overwhelming abundance of material things—cars and money, for example—were symbols of North America distributed and touted by Hollywood.

Fredrick B. Pike explored the subject of myths and stereotyping between the two cultures in his 1992 book *The United States and Latin America: Myths and Stereotypes of Civilization and Nature.*[46] Racism, materialism, efficiency, technology, frontiers, high and low culture, and many other myths, realities, and illusions colored the images, and thus the actions, of Americans toward Latin Americans and vice versa. Hollywood as it filtered into the saloons and movie theaters of Peru was, of course, not the sole or even the most important defining image that Peruvians had of Americans. It could have been the gringo engineer, the entrepreneur, the heirs of Henry Meiggs, or the rational, scientific, can-do pioneers of railroading, steamshipping, aviation, and other outriders of technology who dotted the Peruvian landscape, or it could have been the bankers of Wall Street, toting money bags hand in hand with Uncle Sam.

A 1996 book by Thomas O'Brien, *The Revolutionary Mission: American Enterprise in Latin America, 1900–1945*, contends that U.S. corporate culture exerted a powerful influence in Latin America during this period by encouraging competition and free enterprise in such societies as Peru where cooperation and state control were the norm. Other characteristics of U.S. corporate culture, such as the premium put on profits and the accumulation of material resources, sometimes clashed with traditions and inflexible societies, producing new tensions and conflicts. A rising, consumer-oriented middle class in Peru came into being as Peru was modernized, in no small part with the participation of major U.S. enterprises. Blocked from political power by the elites, this middle class became a revolutionary element in Peruvian politics. While the impact of U.S. corporate culture can perhaps be exaggerated, it has to be reckoned as perhaps the most important external factor in the formation of modern Peruvian economic and political values. Yet ambiguity almost always characterized the values, the myths, and the stereotypes that passed back and forth between the United States and Peru.

For example, while American racists often portrayed Latin Americans as an indolent and unproductive mongrelized people with heavy doses of Negroid and Indian blood, other Americans admired the higher, more refined elites of Latin America, purely Hispanic in their racial composition, endowed with all the nobility and high sensibilities and refinement of their race. Still other Americans, especially in the 1920s, looked to Latin America as a world still in touch with nature, unpolluted by unbridled industrialism, untouched by the disease of materialism.

Whatever the case, by the early twentieth century the contacts between Peru and North America were multiplying, and no one point of this contact was perhaps more important than the completion of the Panama Canal in 1914. The opening of the Panama Canal promoted a boomlet of interest in the west coast of South America. Not only would the waterway shorten the sea route between the west coast of Latin America and North America, but the most optimistic promoters also envisioned an ocean highway of more than material goods. Cultural and social exchanges would blossom in a new era of Pan-Americanism. This augured well for the old Western Hemisphere ideal, united rather than divided by heritage and history.[47]

The inauguration of President Woodrow Wilson in 1913 also presaged a turn away from "dollar diplomacy" and held the promise for improved relations between the United States and Latin America in general. New publications began appearing in the years immediately preceding the Canal's opening. In 1912 the *West Coast Leader*, later called the *Peruvian Times*, was founded to provide news—much of it commercial—for the growing community of U.S. citizens in Peru. Between 1909 and 1913 the illustrated monthly *Perú Today* circulated in the country.[48]

During this period one individual stood out as perhaps the leading supporter of closer ties between his country and the United States. Augusto B. Leguía was born in the northern Peruvian province (called a "department" in Peru) of Lambayeque on February 19, 1863. He was educated in an English school in Valparaíso, Chile, where he was sent by his parents in an effort to help him cope with a bronchial condition. There he studied business and commerce and learned to speak English fluently. He returned to Peru shortly before the War of the Pacific and served as a sergeant in a battalion sponsored by the merchants of Peru. Though he fought against the Chileans during the ill-fated defense of Miraflores on January 15, 1881, he, unlike so many of his generation, expressed little animosity against Chile.

After the war he dedicated himself to business, especially in the area of finance and accounting. From his post as general manager of the New York Life Insurance Company in Peru, Ecuador, and Bolivia, Leguía grew closer to his U.S. contacts. He traveled to New York and London where his fluency in English undoubtedly helped him. While in England he helped establish the British Sugar Company (1896) and became manager of that company in Peru. He also organized and directed the Sud América Insurance Company and became president of the Banco Nacional del Perú.[49] His first political appointment came in 1903 when he was named Minister of Finance in the cabinet of President Manuel Candamo. He served in a number of other high-level financial posts in the next few years before his election as president in 1908. He left office in 1912, lived for a number of years in the United States and London, and returned to Peru in 1918, coming to power once again in 1919 and governing Peru until his overthrow in 1930.

Leguía was one of the most important chief executives in the formation of modern Peru. Perhaps his foremost characteristic was a decided bias in favor of and admiration for the United States. No Peruvian leader has surpassed his pro-Americanism. Those he favored with political and economic power reflected this bias. For example, during his first term in office he appointed a like-thinker, Manuel Vicente Villarán, as Minister of Justice, Culture, and Instruction. Villarán was a distinguished jurist and professor at the National University of San Marcos whose fervent liberal ideology included the commitment to massive, public education as a key to freeing the energies and talents of the people for self-improvement and development.[50] And what better model for modern, progressive, public education was there than the United States? Under Villarán and Leguía the first American "mission" arrived in 1909 to assist in this reorganization of Peruvian education. The strategy was simple—appoint American educators to key positions and give them the freedom and support to mold Peruvian institutions according to American precepts. Leguía broadened the Americanization to include a wide variety of activities, from naval contracts to financial institutions.

In 1909 and 1910, U.S. citizens occupied a number of important posts: supervisor of a special commission to reorganize the entire school system of Peru, adviser to the Minister of Education (Harry Edwin Bard), director of the Men's Normal School, inspector of the public schools in Lima, supervisor of commercial courses for Peruvian schools (certainly a reflection of President Leguía's own background in business and commerce), rector of the University of San Antonio Abad of Cuzco (Albert A. Giesecke, who held his post for thirteen years), and even inspector of girls' schools in Lima and Callao.[51] In 1920 a second wave of American educators invited by Leguía swept over the Peruvian landscape who attempted to introduce effective vocational education among other reforms in the schools and colleges. Resistance began to develop, especially among Peru's own educators, to this American "invasion" that was perceived as a threat to Peruvian values and sovereignty. Much of the objection was politically motivated, for Leguía's critics, such as the distinguished scholar Víctor Andrés Belaúnde, thought Leguía's bias toward the United States took on a subservient and demeaning tone, which undermined Peruvian independence and nationalism.

But in the early years of the century, harmony rather than discord marked the relations between Peru and the United States. In September 1906 U.S. Secretary of State Elihu Root visited Peru on his return from the third international Pan-American conference in Rio de Janeiro. The visit to Peru was the first by a U.S. Secretary of State. An accomplished orator, Root wanted to assuage and assure Latin Americans that U.S. interventions in the Caribbean and Central America were prompted by the highest and noblest intentions. His reassuring words prompted Peruvians to reciprocate with near adulatory comments. When reading some of Root's speeches, one is almost dumbstruck by the words, so filled with admiration and goodwill, especially in view of the political rhetoric of the 1960s and 1970s when it seemed that Peru and the United States could agree on little of what the world was or should be.

President José Prado y Barrera; Minister of Foreign Relations Javier Prado y Ugarteche; the Mayor of Lima, Federico Elguera; the Rector of the University of San Marcos, Dr. Luis F. Villarán; and other dignitaries praised Root. Root was elected an honorary faculty member of the Department of Political Science of the University of San Marcos on September 14; on the evening of September 11, at a gathering in the exclusive Club Unión in downtown Lima, Prado declared: "Today the American people excite the admiration of the whole world by its grandeur. . . . The American Constitution, the Monroe Doctrine, together with the policy of President Roosevelt, and of his Secretary of State, Mr. Root, voice in this manner, through the pages of history, the same language of liberty, of justice, humanity, and Americanism."[52]

Root's visit represents, of course, more than a curious historical footnote, a point followed by the counterpoint of Vice President Richard M. Nixon's visit a little more than half a century later. On May 8, 1958, Nixon was stoned by a mob of students very near where Root was made an honorary member of the faculty at San Marcos. Root's visit coincided with the apogee of like-thinking that Peruvian and American political and economic elites shared in the early twentieth century, in much the same way that Nixon's visit came to symbolize the deep differences that had developed between Peruvians and Americans by the second half of the century.[53]

President Woodrow Wilson struck even more sympathetic chords with his Peruvian admirers. Wilson's eloquence and high ideals appealed to the literate elites who governed Peru. Echoes of the patrician Wilson would ring through the relations of Peru and the United States in the early 1960s when another U.S. president, John Fitzgerald Kennedy, promoted his ideals through his plan for Latin America, the Alliance for Progress. When Wilson presented the "Fourteen Points" as his prescription for peace and justice in the world in January 1918, Peruvians enthusiastically responded. In the Fourteen Points, many Peruvians and Bolivians detected principles that would vindicate their long-held disputes with Chile over the ultimate control of territories lost during the War of the Pacific. One of Wilson's keystone principles was the self-determination of peoples. The long postponed plebiscite to determine the future of Tacna-Arica was certainly on Peru's agenda when it broke relations with Germany in 1917, thus aligning itself more closely with the United States in the hopes of getting the support of the United States and prevailing over Chile. Peruvians were almost sycophantic in their admiration for Wilson, addressed as the "Father of Peace" and the "Priest of Justice" in a long cable penned by leading citizens of Lima to Wilson early in 1919.[54] A thoroughfare in downtown Lima was renamed Avenida Wilson in honor of the president who championed international justice, morality, and self-determination. Surely those principles, when applied to the thorny territorial problems inherited from the War of the Pacific, would vindicate Peru and Bolivia.

This was naive thinking. Wrestling with its vindictive allies in hammering out a just peace in the aftermath of the Great War in Europe, the United States was little interested in the claims of Peru and Bolivia. As they sought to bring their claims before the Versailles Peace Conference, and, later, the League of Nations, the United States was rapidly withdrawing from participation in this new world forum.

The period after the end of the War of the Pacific to the 1920s was a transitional one in the relationship between the United States and Peru. Some of the most important changes were triggered by internal developments in each country as the process of modernization transformed ways of life in both the United States and Peru. In the case of the United States, modernization was manifested most strongly in the industrialization and urbanization of its citizens' lives. In the case of Peru, recuperation from the ravages of the War of the Pacific dominated national life until the end of the century. From then and continuing well into the twentieth century, Peru was more closely integrated into the world economy through increased exports of primary materials, principally such minerals as silver, copper, oil, and tin but also agricultural commodities, such as sugar and cacao. As two English economists observed: "Foreign investments can be seen as an integral part of the whole process of reintegrating Peru into the world capitalist economy after the collapse of the Guano Age."[55]

In this process U.S. entrepreneurs and corporations played a major role, gradually supplanting the preeminent role that the British had occupied in the nineteenth century. U.S. citizens not only provided capital and technology but also introduced values of competition and free enterprise that were embraced by many Peruvians, such as Augusto Leguía and his supporters. A coup in Lima on July 4, 1919, brought Augusto B. Leguía to power once again. A new era in the relations between Peru and the United States was ushered in by this second presidency of Leguía, which lasted until 1930. This second Leguía presidency reinforced the growing affinity between Peru and the United States.

4   The Leguía Years

> He even told the U.S. embassy that he wanted "to put Peru into the hands of the United States," suggesting "something in the nature of a protectorate." In return, the U.S. ambassador nominated Leguía, "the Giant of the Pacific," for the Nobel Peace Prize; he claimed the president "has the courage of Caesar, the power of Napoleon, and the diplomacy of Richelieu," and "would go down in history as one of the world's greatest men."
>
> Paul W. Drake, *The Money Doctor in the Andes: The Kemmerer Missions, 1923–1933*

The 1920s was arguably the decade of closest cooperation between the United States and Peru. President Augusto B. Leguía certainly inspired sentiments of congeniality and shared destinies that marked relations in this decade. Contacts from the most formal and warmest of diplomatic relations to multiple private initiatives arose out of a host of common interests, from investment banking to religion to pioneering aviation. Ironically this decade also produced some of the most radical political thinking about the American penetration of the country, a critique given voice by such Peruvians as the Marxist José Carlos Mariátegui and the founder of the radical party APRA (Alianza Popular Revolucionaria Americana), Victor Raúl Haya de la Torre.

Leguía's Oncenio and the United States: An Overview

Leguía's eleven-year term running from 1919 to 1930 was dubbed the "Oncenio" by Peruvians who took the term from the Spanish word for "eleven," or "once." The Oncenio paralleled the Republican resurgence in the United States, as Warren Harding, Calvin Coolidge, and Herbert Hoover governed roughly during the same time period that Augusto

Leguía was in power in Peru (1919–30). Leguía called his government the "Patria Nueva," or "New Country," and he appointed individuals who shared his ideal of promoting closer ties between Peru and the United States. To facilitate this "Americanization" of Peru he appointed a number of American specialists, administrators, and naval officers to key administrative positions within his government. The directors of the customshouses, of the tax service, of the department of education, and of the reserve bank were all Americans. A number of military and naval officers were appointed to positions such as the commandant of the naval academy. On one occasion Leguía said he wished to name an American to direct all the major branches of the Peruvian government.[1]

To many of Leguía's critics, the tying of Peru's fortunes to the United States undermined Peru's sovereignty and independence. Americanization was a crass sellout to foreign financial interests that dictated Peru's fortunes in matters not only financial but political and even military and naval as well. Furthermore, the profits arising from the exploitation of Peru's nonrenewable resources—copper, silver, and oil for example— were largely going abroad, leaving in Peru only some taxes and salaries.

To Leguía's supporters, however, the financial strength and international power of the United States was worth the effort. Peru under Leguía looked to the United States for advances on many fronts, from the mediation of the Tacna-Arica dispute in Peru's favor to the financing of massive public works projects with the goal of modernizing the nation.

Leguía, U.S. Corporations, and the Intensification of Direct Investments

The expansion of U.S. businesses in Peru in the 1920s kept apace with Leguía's determination to cultivate stronger and closer ties with the United States. The three principal U.S. companies in Peru—Cerro de Pasco, W. R. Grace, and International Petroleum Company (I.P.C.)— expanded and diversified their activities, eventually dominating the mining, petroleum, and textile industries, for example. Additionally extraordinarily diversified concerns, such as Grace, dominated international steamship transportation between Peru and the United States. They were Peru's second-leading producer of sugar, and they pioneered international air transportation in the country during the late 1920s. The National City Bank opened the first U.S. bank subsidiary, National City Company, in Peru, and the investment firm of J. and W. Seligman Company and the Guarantee Trust Company sold Peruvian bonds in U.S. markets. More directly involved were construction companies, such as the Foundation Company of New York, the principal contractor for many of Leguía's massive public works projects. Even sophisticated armaments manufacturers, such as the Electric Boat Company of Groton, Connecticut, made handsome profits in selling U.S.-made submarines to the Peruvian Navy.[2] This expansion of U.S. enterprise in Peru was not equaled in intensity or scope for the rest of the century.

Of all these businesses, none proved to be as controversial as I.P.C., the wholly owned subsidiary of the Standard Oil Company of New Jersey. In 1924 I.P.C. came into full possession of the oil fields of La Brea and Pariñas. Although the company had controlled these fields since 1913, now they owned them. Or so they thought. Many in Peru thought otherwise. The controversy was fueled by a decision made in 1922 by an international arbitral tribunal consisting of representatives from Great Britain, Peru, and the president of the Swiss Federal Court, Dr. Fritz Ostertag. The tribunal recognized I.P.C.'s right to La Brea and Pariñas and ruled that for the next fifty years, or until 1972, I.P.C. only had to pay a small tax on the property. Left undecided was the old issue of who actually owned the subsoil rights, which the prior British owners and the Peruvians had been battling over for many years.

The controversy between I.P.C. and Peru was, to say the very least, extremely complicated. Richard Goodwin, a student of the subject, wrote that "lawyers, and politicians have built reputations and careers analyzing, attacking, and defending the award of the tribunal," while Fredrick Pike noted that the "matter becomes frighteningly complex" as one probes the details, the positions, the counterpositions, the law, and the many interpretations of law.[3]

By the end of the 1920s about 70 to 80 percent of Peru's petroleum needs were being supplied by I.P.C., which had more than $60 million invested in its properties. Its production of petroleum products increased fivefold between 1919 and 1929, about 90 percent of it being exported. Dividends ran close to 40 percent of investments during the 1920s; from 1935 to 1938, the return was at least 100 percent annually.[4] I.P.C.'s center of production at Talara on the north coast became a model "enclave" economy—prosperous and with a well-paid workforce subject to the discipline and regulations of its corporate sponsor. The nature of this enclave, plus the controversy over taxes and the repatriation of profits, caused increasing tension between Peruvians and the corporation in the 1960s.

Nonetheless while some controversy bubbled to the surface surrounding the tax ruling of 1922, I.P.C. and Peru settled down to a modus vivendi in the 1920s and 1930s that struck one observer of the company as resembling the relationship between two sovereign states. "Peru was a sovereign state," noted Adalberto Pinelo in his study of I.P.C., "but within its borders there existed another state—not necessarily an American colony, but part of a multinational concern with supranational loyalties. Peru's problems with I.P.C.," Pinelo said, "stemmed not from the fact that it was an American company somehow geared to exploit Peru on behalf of the United States but rather from the fact that its parent company, Standard Oil (New Jersey), was a far larger organization and commanded more resources than the Peruvian state."[5]

In late 1930 President Luis M. Sánchez Cerro (who had overthrown Leguía earlier that year) needed money to meet the government's payroll. He turned to I.P.C. for the loan. Dramatized or not, the scene, as described by Pinelo, is amazing, certainly confirming the strength of I.P.C., and the vulnerability of Peru at the time. "In late November or early December 1930," Pinelo wrote, "the 'revolutionary' government [of Sánchez Cerro] sent its Minister of Finance to confer with the most important American in Peru—the general manager of International Petroleum." We can only conjecture on the actual conversation, but, based on U.S. Department of State records, Pinelo noted that "the minister pleaded for the company to advance secretly the Peruvian government 1.5 million soles. After urgent consultation with the company's high command, the loan was granted and the government saved."[6]

Whether the Sánchez Cerro government was "saved" or not by I.P.C.'s loan is perhaps debatable. But the fact is that I.P.C. certainly saved the day—the government was in arrears on the salaries of the army, navy, and police—and did so at a time when the Sánchez Cerro administration was publicly attacking I.P.C. in a wave of economic nationalism that had accompanied the downfall of Leguía. While Sánchez Cerro called for the invalidation of the controversial 1922 award (granting title to lands and mineral rights to I.P.C.), the collection of back taxes from I.P.C., and other popular measures, his government secretly accepted the I.P.C. loan to meet its payroll. Soon after the loan was made, I.P.C. received a monopoly on the distribution of petroleum products in Peru.[7]

These arrangements came about even as I.P.C. was being virulently attacked in public forums as well (among them the newspaper *El Comercio*, which was published by the anti-I.P.C. Miró Quesada family) and in the Constituent Assembly of 1932 that proposed to build four thousand new schools financed by the profits of a state petroleum monopoly to be created at the expense of I.P.C.

While some Peruvian politicians raged against I.P.C., the Sánchez Cerro administration received regularly 25,000 to 30,000 soles per month as loans from I.P.C. made through the Banco Italiano (renamed the Banco de Crédito in 1941 to avoid association with Italy during World War II) against future export taxes.[8] When Minister of Development Francisco Lanatta asked for more money from I.P.C.'s manager Walter Reed, Reed refused. He explained his decision to the U.S. Ambassador Fred Morris Dearing. "In view of the precarious nature of the Government, the fact that it might be forced out of office, and that its successor may not take it kindly that a foreign corporation assisted to prolong its existence by conniving with it to deceive the public," I.P.C. refused to advance any additional funds. Lanatta, however, was persistent. He persuaded I.P.C. to make another advance on the customs payments at a 15 percent discount to I.P.C. to get the Peruvian Navy's ship bottoms scraped. Lanatta then embezzled the money, which prompted the indignant Reed to confront Sánchez Cerro and a number of his ministers with the cheating behavior of their colleague. Sánchez Cerro fired Lanatta, but the pressures on I.P.C. to support the Sánchez Cerro government continued through 1932 and 1933.[9]

When a border dispute between Peru and Colombia flared up in 1932, Peru sought arms. To dampen the situation, Washington imposed an embargo on both Colombia and Peru. The Peruvians turned to Japanese and French arms makers. Peru asked I.P.C. for $800,coo worth of petroleum (to be paid off in future export duties), to trade to the French for weapons. I.P.C. balked, but the Peruvians persisted. Finally the request was turned down. The U.S. embassy contended that the deal would nullify the United States-imposed arms embargo, and, furthermore, the parent corporation Standard Oil, with properties in *both* Peru and Colombia, was not interested in advancing the bellicose activities of either country and thus jeopardizing its properties.[10]

I.P.C.'s role in Peru symbolized the ways in which multinational corporations and Peru accommodated each other in the twentieth century; they were pulled together by economic forces and, just as powerfully, pushed apart by differing political and social views of what was right and wrong. Why did I.P.C. engage in unorthodox financial arrangements with the governments of Peru? Was the corporation simply corrupt, as so many charged, wishing to play king maker in a country that, after all, was puny by comparison with the size of the Standard Oil Company of New Jersey? More probably, argues Pinelo, I.P.C. was driven to these extremes by intense international competition and the need to adapt to the "Peruvian rules of the game" if it was to survive and prosper in Peru. Not only were large profits generated by I.P.C. in Peru, but one of Standard's worldwide competitors, Royal Dutch Shell, was ready to step in should I.P.C. stumble in Peru.

Yet I.P.C. did not cooperate closely with the U.S. government in promoting and defending its interests in Peru. In fact the U.S. embassy was not privy to much of what I.P.C. did in Peru unless the corporation needed embassy support. In 1911 the Standard Oil trust was broken up by the U.S. government, and Pinelo observed that "corporate memory is long, and the dismemberment of 1911 was a very painful blow to the international oil giant." Consequently "the company informed the American embassy of its activities only when it was expedient for it to do so."[11]

But the size and power of I.P.C. in Peru made the relationship between Peru and its corporate client awkward. "Peruvian nationalists from the 'right' and 'left' never forgave I.P.C. for operating in their country as if it were a banana republic—buying off cabinet members and even total administrations, blackmailing duly constituted legislatures into submission to company demands." On the other hand, "I.P.C., for its part, could not very well accept the constant threat of fleecing promoted by corrupt Peruvian politicians. . . . The company attempted to bargain in good faith, only to discover that its concessions merely incited Peruvian chauvinism to ever more preposterous demands."[12]

By the 1960s the bitterness and mistrust had reached the point where compromise was impossible and led to the ultimate confrontation that occurred in 1968. A more immediate question is how did I.P.C. manage to survive for so long in Peru, when apparently it was targeted by so many for doing so much evil? The answer is that I.P.C. also had many friends in Peru, from the thousands of workers and employees at its wells and refineries in the north around Talara to the hundreds of Peru's well-placed industrial and commercial elite who prospered directly from I.P.C. activities. I.P.C. also waged an immensely expensive public relations campaign in Peru. But the fundamental reason is that many Peruvians benefited from I.P.C.'s presence in Peru. What drove I.P.C. and Peru apart was ultimately a matter of power, and the perception of power, in a drama that played itself out in the 1960s.

Intellectual and Cultural Influences

The influence of individuals, agencies, institutions, and other bodies—from such corporations as I.P.C. to "public opinion" informed by journalism—must be considered in any assessment of Peruvian-U.S. relations in the twentieth century. For example, such intellectuals as

Waldo Frank in the 1920s and 1930s, by virtue of their lectures, their sensitivities, and their prejudices, may have been just as influential in the making of major public policies as any memorandum drafted in the committee rooms of the Department of State by political and economic officers.

Peru's leading Marxist interpreter, José Carlos Mariátegui, for example, had a close relationship with Waldo Frank. While Mariátegui read other U.S. writers and their works (such as Robert Louis Stevenson, Henry Thoreau's essay on *Civil Disobedience*, John Dos Pasos, and Walt Whitman) his favorite was Frank, with whom he developed a long and intense correspondence.[13] When Frank made a celebrated tour of South America in 1929, he stayed with the Mariátegui family in Lima. Mariátegui cited Frank's seminal *Our America* in his famous *Seven Interpretative Essays on Peruvian Reality* which defined and analyzed Peru's problems through his own Marxist prism. The *Seven Essays* had a deep impact on the development of radical and Marxist thought in Peru. Mariátegui accepted much of Frank's spiritual interpretation of U.S. history, which stressed the primacy of the religious and mystical dimensions of American life, especially of Puritanism's role in the development of capitalism. Peruvian Marxism, thus, which was so aimed against American capitalism and imperialism, also drew inspiration from American writers such as Frank, making the relationship between Peru and the United States in the twentieth century quite complex and filled with ironies.

In another instance of intellectual and cultural influences, Haya de la Torre drew much inspiration from the revolutionary Jesus of the Bible, interpreted for Haya by a Presbyterian pastor from Scotland, John MacKay, who went on to become the president of the Princeton Theological Seminary. MacKay came to Peru in the early 1920s and, among other activities, established a school. He hired the young Haya to work in the school, and he learned from MacKay that the docile, obedient, and passive Jesus of the Roman Catholic Church possessed another dimension, that of revolutionary and emissary to the poor and dispossessed. By the time Haya founded the political party APRA (which became the most influential radical political party in Peru by mid-century), much of his symbolism and inspiration was drawn from MacKay's teachings of Jesus.

The economic presence of the United States was nonetheless always the most visible, if not always the most influential in affairs between Peru and the United States.

Cerro de Pasco

The Cerro de Pasco Corporation was well established in Peru by the 1920s. More than $40 million were invested in its mines by 1929, and like I.P.C. on the arid and barren northern Peruvian desert, Cerro's existence in the high sierra was somewhat remote and detached from the centers of power and population on the coast that were focused on the capital city, Lima.

Cerro "functioned as a virtual autonomous economic and political entity within the Peruvian nation" noted Charles McArver, emphasizing the enclave nature of this economic activity.[14] In addition to its copper and silver mines, Cerro owned coal mines, salt mines, various quarries, hydroelectric plants, and several hundred thousand acres of hacienda land surrounding its smelter. By virtue of its coal mines, for example, Cerro became the largest producer of coal in the country (85 percent in 1922), much of it used in the power plants of the copper and silver mines. The major investment was in the copper mines however. This investment represented the largest ever made in a copper mine to that date in the world, and the largest U.S. mining investment in Latin America.[15]

They were not only the largest investments, but Cerro utilized the most modern mining technologies and equipment and became one of the lowest-cost copper producers in the world. It was profitable, to say the least. Fifty-seven million dollars in dividends were distributed to shareholders between 1917 and 1930.

Cerro employed about thirteen thousand laborers and managers during the twenties. Most of the managers came from the United States, with degrees from some of the top technical schools in North America, such as MIT and McGill. In many respects, it was a remarkable enterprise. La Fundación, its principal smelter until 1922, was the largest of its kind in the world and, at fourteen thousand feet, the highest. It took five years to build (1903–8) and represented an immense investment by Cerro, but one that paid off handsomely in the following decades. Later in 1922 a new smelter at La Oroya was inaugurated with double the capacity of La Fundación.

The construction of the Oroya smelter is a good example of how U.S. technology, capital, and personnel came into Peru in the 1920s in high volume. This new smelter cost Cerro $9 million, and the company contracted with the American Bridge Company for its construction. The designer, A. G. McGregor, had designed the latest Cerro smelter in the United States. He was joined in Peru by 140 U.S. steel workers who labored alongside 1,500 Peruvians on the job. By the time it was completed, more than 240 tons of machinery and 15,000 tons of structural steel had been imported for the La Oroya smelter (whose output was 2,500 tons of copper a day when it was in operation). Everything that was needed at the 12,000-foot-high smelter was provided for: a hydroelectric station, machine and carpenter shops, foundries, water tanks, a brick plant, employee living quarters, a hospital, and recreational facilities.

Not only was Cerro one of the leading copper producers in the world, but it began producing zinc, lead, and bismuth in the 1920s and 1930s as by-products of the copper-making process. By the 1930s, lead, zinc, and silver made up at least half of the company's income.[16] It was also a railroad builder, having constructed 135 miles of track for more than $2 million, the principal line being the eighty-three mile Cerro de Pasco to Oroya segment; this line linked up with the Central Railroad, which was started by Henry Meiggs in the 1870s. Locomotives, passenger cars, freight cars, cabooses, rails, track—virtually everything associated with building and operating a railroad—were imported from the United States. Thirty U.S. railroad specialists worked with about five hundred Peruvians on maintaining and operating Cerro's extensive railroad operation, which would eventually include substantial passenger service.

In the 1920s one could board the Central Railway at the Lima station on a Monday, Wednesday, or Friday and take the spectacular ride into the high Andes along the serpentine, multiple switchbacked and tunneled railroad—the highest in the world. At La Oroya the rider connected with a company train climbing to Cerro de Pasco. The Cerro train would descend to Oroya on Tuesdays, Thursdays, and Saturdays to connect again with the Lima train.

Similar to the history of railroads in the United States, friction developed between the railroad companies and the users, the latter claiming discriminatory rates against them in favor of the big users, in this case, the Cerro Corporation itself. Small, independent mine owners and others who transported commodities on the Central Railway and the Cerro's lines called repeatedly for lowered rates, equal treatment, and even, in one extreme instance in 1916, that the railroad be expropriated. Little came of these complaints nor did Cerro make many concessions through the 1920s and 1930s.

Invariably the company battled on many fronts to preserve its privileges, while those Peruvians feeling victimized by its operations fought the company with equal intensity over the years. Indians along the railroad's right of way complained that the locomotives ran over their cattle; the company refused to pay indemnities. Importers complained that their wares sat profitless in the warehouses of Callao and Lima while the railroad took care of company business first. But one of the most serious feuds has a strikingly modern and timely tone: the claim that pollution from the company's operations at Oroya was destroying the quality of life in the surrounding region.

This was old-fashioned pollution, the three hundred-foot-high smokestacks at the smelter emitting an obnoxious mixture of arsenic, lead, zinc, sulphur, and other poisonous substances that floated over and came to rest on the rich agricultural and pastoral lands of the Mantaro Valley. "The pure, clean air of Oroya," noted Nelson Rounsevell in an article written at the time for the *West Coast Leader*, "is becoming impregnated with sulphur fumes, and the bright sunshine which has always made this the pleasantest camp on the hill is now being obscured by smelter smoke."[17]

In protest *hacendados* and native Indian communities turned to the courts, suing the company for the damage inflicted on their potatoes, barley, and other crops, as well as damage to their livestock. They claimed the land was being rendered worthless by the poisonous fumes from the smelter. The company responded by buying up many of the damaged properties, although it ran into a snag with the Indian communal lands which, by law, could not be sold. Nonetheless more than half a million acres of agricultural and pastoral lands were purchased by 1924, and indemnities were paid to the Indian communities.

Some initial pollution-control devices were installed in 1925, but an adequate system was not completed until 1942. Leguía's government insisted on some effective control in the early 1920s, but the company dragged its feet. Basically it was an expensive matter. The construction of the smelter had gone far over budget, and Cerro was unwilling to install expensive, and in some instances untested, pollution-control devices. Some critics claimed the company also wanted to depress the value of properties in the region in order to buy them cheaply, while others alleged that the company was promoting a supply of cheap labor for the mines by systematically undermining agriculture and pastoral activity in the area. Perhaps. The upshot was that by the 1930s Cerro was producing most of the meat and food crops it needed for its workforce on its own lands.

In the most objective analysis, Cerro brought income and employment to Peru. Between 1902 and 1930, for example, it probably spent $250 million in Peru in the form of taxes, wages, customs duties, investments in mines and smelters, and in other ways.[18] It developed mines that otherwise would not have been exploited because of the risk and lack of capital in the country. Cerro constituted a major link in the relations between Peru and the United States in the twentieth century. It represented and symbolized the United States to thousands and thousands of Peruvians who worked for the company, and more indirectly, to a whole nation of people.

Cerro's record in labor relations, of course, infuriated its Peruvian critics who complained of gringo brutality—the lording over of the Indian/*cholo* workers by an elite, foreign-born managerial sector who treated labor with contempt. One of the most telling insights into the company's operations came from a former U.S. employee, Harry L. Foster, who published his memoirs in 1927. Foster noted that in the Andes a white man "shall take no insolence from the Indians."[19] U.S. bosses were quick to strike Peruvian laborers who defied their orders.

However what was the nature of relations between labor and management in the United States at the turn of the century? Strikes and their bloody suppression reveal that what gringos may have been doing in Peru was not much different than what gringos were doing back home. The evolution of workers' rights to organize, to strike, to advance their interests, etc. in the United States was marked by confrontation, not compromise, by strikes and sometimes open warfare.

What was happening in the United States does not, of course, necessarily justify what may have also been happening in Peru. In his comments, Foster was referring not only to gringos, but to Peruvian whites as well, the mine owners, the landowners, the government, military, and police officials, the people who, in fact, *owned* and managed Peru in their self-interests. Overwhelmed in numbers by Indians—who they described as brutish, ignorant, dirty, suspicious, given to drunken debauchery, and in constant need of discipline and control—the Peruvian oligarches were as contemptuous, perhaps more so, of Indians as were gringos. There were exceptions. Politicians and thinkers who rose beyond the confines of self-interest, race, and caste had been speaking of edifying Inca culture and raising the lot of Indians since at least the late nineteenth century. Indeed, the Indianist movement of the 1920s sought to redeem the Indian from a past of persecution and systematic exploitation. But the Indianists, the radicals, and the more adventurous ideologues and politicians were in the minority. To the local landowner, or *hacendado,* discipline and order were indispensable in preserving civilization as Peruvian oligarches understood it. The gringo manager of a Cerro property took his experience from back home, observed the vast gulf between the whites and Indians in the Andes, and simply behaved as he figured he must. If that meant ensuring company discipline by keeping the laboring force docile and obedient, then he was willing to do so. And the local Peruvians in charge—of land, of government, of mines, of commerce—tended to support the company's maintenance of the social and cultural gap between whites and Indians that, in turn, maintained order and civilization as they understood it.

The statistics of life in the mining communities contrasted life vividly between the workers and managers. At the La Fundación smelter, workers washed coal for seventy-five cents per day, and were paid sometimes in company scrip that could be redeemed only at company stores. "It would be hard to find a dirtier town than Cerro de Pasco," wrote Thomas F. Roche in 1916, adding that Indian and *cholo* homes were indescribably filthy. On the other hand, Cerro de Pasco's club for gringo managers had a well-kept bowling alley, swimming pool, gymnasium, billiard room, reading room, library, dance hall, card room, bar, and barber shop, plus tennis courts outside. Single gringo employees at Morococha lived in one-room bachelor's quarters with heat and a communal bath.

There were exceptions, of course, to the prevailing conditions. At Casapalpa, a mining center begun by Backus and Johnson but bought by Cerro, the workers' homes were of adobe and "well-fitted and as comfortable as possible."[20] And at La Oroya, a welfare program was initiated that included night classes, medical services, and new corrugated metal shacks. The company insisted that the derogatory term "*cholo* town" be discarded in favor of "workmen's town." But, as Thomas O'Brien noted in his study of U.S. enterprises in Latin America, the company's policies "hardly constituted a full-fledged program of social welfare."[21]

When reckoning the impact of Cerro, and indirectly, that of the United States on Peru, there are two frames of reference: one, lock Cerro into its "cultural" time frame and judge it from the prevailing values of the time; or two, judge it from contemporary truths and values. Either perspective will distort the story, for, in truth, we have to judge it both ways. The results are, as human endeavors tend to be, not wholly satisfying. Perhaps examining how Cerro faced a massive crisis in 1930 may clarify our understanding of the relationship between the company and its host country.

The crisis was provoked by the Great Depression. Copper, sugar, silver, and cotton prices came tumbling down. So did the Leguía government in late August 1930. Cerro dealt with the crisis by layoffs and wage cuts to make up for downward-spiraling mineral prices on the world market, a classic corporate response to a recession/depression scenario. The response of Cerro's workers was equally predictable: unrest and strikes aimed at restoring the status quo. Also illustrated here was another classic characteristic of an enclave economy: local (Peruvian in this instance) economies that were being driven by foreign dictates (in this instance, falling mineral prices as the depression rippled out across the world).

Harold Kingsmill, Cerro's general manager in Peru, was determined to preserve his company's interests. Equally determined to preserve their livelihood were Cerro's laborers. The stage was set for a battle, and it broke out in October and November 1930 as miners clashed with government forces across the Andes.

The climax came at Mal Paso, a hydroelectric station on November 12, 1930. A group of about eight hundred workers on their way to support their comrades at La Oroya were marching across a railroad bridge over the Mantaro River where they were met by police.[22] The miners surged across the bridge, and the police opened fire. Thirteen miners and three police died in the melee. More than forty were among the wounded. The miners, enraged by the police defense of the bridge, surged through Mal Paso, looting and destroying, especially venting their anger on foreigners, most of whom managed to escape by hiding, heading for the hills, or given sanctuary by friendly Peruvians.

Three were not so lucky. Three Americans were killed, one virtually decapitated, by angry miners who blamed the company for their distress. In the eyes of many, the Sánchez Cerro government then in power was nothing more than a mere lackey to the company that seemed to be dictating to the Peruvian government.

But Kingsmill did not see it that way. To him, the Mal Paso incident was the final straw. The government was not dealing promptly or severely with outside agitators blamed by the company for the disorders. He closed Cerro's operations the next day and called all the foreign staff out of the mines and down to Lima.

A week before on November 8, the workers, organized by a Marxist-oriented union called the General Confederation of Workers, held a mass rally at La Oroya. It began with the singing of the Marxist hymn, the "International," and was punctuated with fiery calls to arms. "Tumultuous meetings," Eudocio Ravines remembered, "drew thousands of men who, for the first time heard talk of human rights. They learned for the first time, that the managers, the directors, the engineers, the foremen, were not by a law of nature the masters of the men who worked under them. They heard . . . that in other countries miners organized unions and bargained with management."[23] Within a few days, the Mal Paso incident erupted on the bridge over the Mantaro, while in Lima Kingsmill pressured Ambassador Fred Dearing to send a U.S. warship down to Peru. Dearing told Kingsmill to cool down and, rather, continue to pressure the Peruvian government to handle the rebellious miners. An American warship in Callao Harbor would only escalate the tension. Besides, "warships would be of little use at 10,000 feet," Secretary of State Henry L. Stimson remarked in a press conference in Washington on November 13. Military intervention may have been out of the question in the Department of State's view, but it did not keep Cerro and I.P.C. from making their appeals.

Closing the mines, however, did more damage to the miners' grievances and their cause than the possible presence of any U.S. warship in Peruvian waters. Kingsmill hammered away at Sánchez Cerro to meet the company's demands before he reopened the mines—arrest and remove the leading protesters and "troublemakers" from the camps and surrounding towns, continue martial law until it was safe in those provinces where the major mines were located (principally Junín), ensure the safety of foreigners, and suppress or censor anticompany media. In a conciliatory move, Cerro asked for the appointment of a government commission to study and report on living and working conditions in the company's mines.

Privately Kingsmill insisted that Sánchez Cerro remove certain ministers and prefects who were thought to be soft on the miners and/or *Apristas* and Communists. But Sánchez Cerro balked, making at least one veiled threat to run the mines himself. Kingsmill was not cowed. He castigated Sánchez Cerro's Minister of Government Gustavo A. Jiménez, for example, for failing to abide by the government's decision to remove agitators identified by the company. "There's still one mad woman up there [La Oroya]," Kingsmill upbraided Jiménez, who "claims to have drunk the blood of one gringo and she's after the blood of our superintendent Colley right now."[24]

Ambassador Dearing repeatedly counseled Kingsmill to back off. If he kept it up, the onus for the entire heated situation would be laid even more heavily on the shoulders of the company. As it was Sánchez Cerro's regime was taking much of the heat. As the repercussions of closing the mines tightened around the government like a noose, Sánchez Cerro fired Jiménez. Besides the feisty ex-minister was an unstable and chronic plotter. He later joined the *Apristas* and died in an attempt to overthrow the government in 1933. With Jiménez gone and Dearing promoting compromise, Kingsmill reopened the mines on December 12.

Sánchez Cerro was furious at Kingsmill for holding him hostage to the mines and at Dearing for pressuring him on behalf of the U.S. government to meet Cerro de Pasco's demands. He ran the country, not the gringos, and remarked that "I'll show those gringos how to run a country," in one fit of pique.[25] Sánchez Cerro certainly "ran the country," but one can argue that Cerro de Pasco "ran the mines," and who ran the mines determined much of what happened in Peru. Thousands were employed by Cerro in a country then being whiplashed by the depression. Cerro was certainly in the eye of this economic hurricane.

Casa Grace

Not all U.S. companies in Peru, however, projected the same image as I.P.C. and Cerro de Pasco. W. R. Grace & Co., or Casa Grace, projected a far different image, based, ultimately, on a unique set of premises and realities that governed its existence in Peru. Indeed when the revolutionary government of Juan Velasco Alvarado came to power in 1968, it directed much of its antipathy at the largest and oldest U.S. firms in the country, especially I.P.C., Cerro de Pasco, and Grace. I.P.C. was quickly nationalized while protracted negotiations eventually led to further seizures. One of Grace's principal negotiators, John C. Duncan, confronted President Velasco: "Why Casa Grace, General Velasco? We have built up this country. We have created wealth, not extracted it. Why nationalize Grace properties?"[26] "Because," Alvarado told Duncan, "we have to deal with all equally." Duncan felt Grace was being tarred with the same brush as I.P.C. and Cerro, while Alvarado was compelled by a revolutionary logic driven largely by nationalism.

Was Grace indeed different, as Duncan claimed in his confrontation with President Velasco? Grace had evolved by the 1920s and 1930s into a diversified international trading firm doing business from New York to Valparaíso, Chile, from Callao in Peru to Liverpool in England. It became a worldwide commodities trader in the immediate post-World War I period, buying and selling sugar, rice, jute, hides, tea, shellac, coffee, and other items across a network of trading offices that stretched across North America, Europe, and Asia.[27]

At the center of the Grace business were its ships, which were organized into the Grace Line. Between 1916 and 1920, largely due to war profits, the Grace shipping business made almost $27 million in gross profits. These tapered off to less than $1 million a year between 1920 and 1933, the decline being even more pronounced during the depression years of the 1930s. It was, in sum, a profitable business. It was also an immensely symbolic business for the stately Grace steamers (all named after saints, such as the *Santa Clara*), which came to be closely associated by Peruvians not only with Grace, but with the connection of Peru to the United States.

But its bread-and-butter business was always centered on the west coast of South America and within that region, on Peru. By the late 1920s Grace also owned more than 50 percent of the Peruvian textile business and owned and operated the second-largest sugar plantation, Cartavio, in the rich sugar-producing Chicama Valley in the north of the country. Casa Grace was the leading importer of U.S.-made equipment and technology through its IMACO (International Machinery Company) firm, and, in 1929, pioneered inter-American air travel with an airline, Panagra, founded jointly with the fledgling Pan American Airways.

Imagine a voyage on one of the famed *Santa* steamers from New York to Callao via the Panama Canal. No other vehicle—literally and figuratively—better represented the growing linkages between Peru and the United States in the twentieth century. Passengers boarded the *Santa Maria* in New York in May for its maiden voyage to South America. The *Santa Maria* employed the latest in diesel-engine design and fostered the ambiance of the floating hotel so popular with ocean travelers of the era. She measured 7,858 gross tons, carried 157 passengers, and was powered by a pair of 4,000-horsepower engines at 16 knots.

All passengers traveled first class. The *Santa Maria* was equipped with a social hall, a smoking room, children's dining and play rooms, a swimming pool, and, for entertainment, traveled with an orchestra and played the latest motion pictures. Indeed the Grace Line pioneered tourism between North America and the west coast of South America.[28] Grace also encouraged cultural exchanges, discounted travel for Latin American students and teachers going to American colleges and universities, and, in a fashion, predated the era of the "Good Neighbor" policy ushered in by the administration of President Franklin D. Roosevelt in the 1930s. In fact until the Grace Line was sold in 1969, W. R. Grace & Co., through Grace Line and Panagra (which it owned in a fifty-fifty partnership with Pan American Airways), was the principal promoter of tourism between Peru and North America in the mid-twentieth century.

The *Santa Maria* sailed May 10, 1928. The Stock Market would not crash until a year and a half later, triggering the Great Depression. A few astute economists are predicting the end of the fabulous Roaring Twenties, but nobody is really listening to them. Prosperity and good times mark the era. A Grace Line ad catches one's attention:

PERU. 38-day Cruises; through the Panama Canal (with ample time for sightseeing in Canal Zone); down South America's west coast to Callao, Peru and Lima. 11 days of stopover in Peru. Calls are made at all ports of interest and include a liberal visit to Havana. Largest, newest and fastest liners. Only $295. up. First Class—shore expenses additional. No passports required.

The ship steamed out of the bustling harbor of New York and by early next morning was far out to sea, rolling gently in the Atlantic swells, headed for the tropics.

The first port-of-call after Panama and south of the Equator in Peru was Talara, headquarters of the International Petroleum Company. Most everybody—at least most foreigners—turned out to see the new *Santa Maria*. One happy driller wrote, "An excellent buffet luncheon was served to all on board which was thoroughly enjoyed, and, as it was served in the manner for which the Grace Line is renowned, further comments are needless."[29] Then the ship headed south, following the barren, brown Peruvian coast toward Callao where its passengers arrived on May 23, barely two weeks after passing through the Narrows of New York Harbor and only about thirty-six hours after weighing anchor at Talara.

The newspapers of Callao and Lima featured the *Santa Maria* in columns and pictures. Enthusiastic guests swarmed over the ship shortly after eleven in the morning, transported by the launches and motorboats of the Grace Agency. Everyone was curious about the elegant, luxurious touches to this modern liner built especially by Casa Grace to connect better the ports of South America with New York. Yankee ingenuity and entrepreneurship were celebrated in the press, and many Peruvians no doubt wished to make a trip on the *Santa Maria*, or her sister ship the *Santa Barbara* when she makes the run between the continents.

The mayor of Callao and other government dignitaries were feted at a luncheon presided over by the general manager of Casa Grace in Peru. President Leguía's Marine and Aviation Minister, Dr. Arturo Núñez Chávez, toasts the Grace Line and makes an impromptu speech, setting the tone of the Peruvian welcome to the *Santa Maria*. Events such as these marked the eleven year administration of Leguía which, as demonstrated earlier, was so intimately tied to the United States.

From Callao the *Santa Maria* steamed south toward Chile, making ports-of-call at other Peruvian roadsteads, such as Mollendo and Arica. (One is reminded by the numerous ports-of-call that more than two thirds of Grace Line profits derive from hauling freight, the balance coming from growing passenger services.) Passengers disembarked at Callao to take advantage of a "complete sightseeing program [with] many optional sidetrips" promised by the Grace agent in Lima.

In Peru's case, the modern industry of tourism was heavily influenced by the easy access to the United States provided by such carriers as the Grace Line. While American tourists were lured from the European market by the somewhat exotic appeal of travel to Peru and South America in general, affluent Peruvians were drawn more and more away from Paris and London to New York and Washington, reinforcing the growing cultural linkages between Peru and the United States.

Major corporations such as I.P.C., Cerro, and Grace certainly played the dominant role in the development of modern relations between Peru and the United States. Another facet in the economic interlacing of the two countries that occurred in the 1920s also had long-term effects. This was the immense increase in private loans made to Peru by American bankers and financiers.

The Financial Interlacing
of Peru and the United States

Nothing is perhaps as complex as the implications of modern international financing on the relations between countries. And, sometimes, nothing is quite as important, save war or other crises of equal dimensions, in determining how these relations either flourished or deteriorated. Between 1920 and 1929 U.S. private firms and banks loaned Peru almost $100 million, which was sold as bonds on the U.S. market.

This meant that Leguía's government borrowed the money from U.S. bankers and investors, such as the National City Bank, the Guarantee Trust Co., or J & W Seligman & Co., who generated the money by selling Peruvian bonds in the United States. Leguía's government needed the capital for ambitious public works, which included sanitation projects, highway and railroad construction, irrigation projects, the purchase of arms (including two submarines to modernize the Peruvian Navy), urban improvements; finally in 1927 and 1928, the largest of the loans were made to help pay off earlier loans.

U.S. bankers and financiers were eager to make these loans. There were substantial profits involved not only on commissions but also in differentials between what Peru received for the bonds and what they were sold for on the U.S. market and in the long-term servicing of the bonds. Without going into cumbersome details, most analyses of these loans say that profits of 8 to 10 percent on the loan transactions were common.

Leguía's government was buoyed up by the loans in one sense, but the inability of Peru to repay the loans proved an immensely harmful sequel to the Leguía regime after it fell in 1930. The loans did facilitate a rapid expansion of the infrastructure of the country—roads and sanitation services for example—which facilitated economic developments and modernization in a general sense. But the consensus is that the loans proved too much for Peru to handle in the long run. By late 1930 Peru had defaulted on them. Her credit tumbled, and Wall Street responded coolly in succeeding years to Peru's projects involving international finance.

A partial explanation for Peru's dilemma was the Great Depression, which had so devastated markets and prices around the world. Peru was no more immune to these international forces than any other Western country, so the Leguía regime cannot be held accountable for the precipitous drop, for example, in the price of copper, sugar, and cotton—all Peruvian staples—on the world markets. Nonetheless Peru's closeness to the United States certainly accentuated the depression's effects in Peru.

Furthermore graft and corruption marred the transactions in 1927 and 1928. President Leguía's son Juan, for example, received almost half a million dollars in the process of loan negotiations, for which, most agreed, he did nothing other than promise not to obstruct the loan process.[30] Lavish commissions, extravagant expense accounts, and other financial rewards dotted the history of the loans. Another line of criticism focused on the many concessions and monopolies granted by the Leguía regime, and, indeed, by some of its successor administrations in the 1930s. Concessions, such as those made to I.P.C. by the Leguía administration, were thought to have seriously undermined Peruvian sovereignty. In fact Leguía was not in the back pocket of I.P.C. as his critics claimed. In 1926 for example, Juan Leguía undertook a mission to Europe to persuade I.P.C.'s rival, Royal Dutch Shell, to accept a monopoly over the distribution and sale of petroleum products in Peru, thus directly challenging I.P.C. The plan failed to materialize, for Leguía's failing health in 1927 and the Great Crash of 1929 chilled Royal Dutch Shell's immediate interests in Peru.[31]

Other concessions and monopolies made by the Leguía regime had a different result: an increase in the involvement of the State in economic development, which resulted in increased benefits for the privileged few, rather than for the many. In this scenario long-term competition and democratic processes were hampered by the short-term acts of the Leguía government. "The most negative effects of foreign credit in Peru in the 1920s," one modern student of financial history wrote, "were however, those that resulted from the expansion of foreign loans to bolster state interventionism."[32] In the 1920s more than sixty new industrial monopolies and concessions were granted by the Leguía government, in many instances to raise revenue to service the loans. These monopolies were awarded to foreigners and Peruvians alike, especially, of course, to those well placed with the government who had or could buy influence with Leguía. Concessions and monopolies, by their very nature, tended to suppress competition, and, if given to foreign firms, often discouraged local native industries.

In the 1980s and 1990s, when Peruvian economists and politicians searched for some of the underlying causes of Peru's modern economic malaise, they identified one leading cause to be the *absence* of a truly free-market economy. The State over the years had granted concessions, monopolies, and special privileges to a small minority of the population whose control prevented true competition. Thus the loans contracted between the Leguía regime and U.S. bankers and investors in the 1920s most certainly influenced Peru's economy, her politics, and, some would argue, even her society.

Some contend that U.S. bankers and financiers crassly manipulated Peru in a giant scam to enrich a few Wall Street bankers. But it's not that simple. At the other end were the hands of a man such as Juan Leguía who, according to one U.S. banker, "blackmailed us into paying him."[33] Greed does not obey national boundaries, and in the speculation craze of the 1920s, to invest in Peru was no crazier than to invest in south Florida property. Everyone expected to make easy money. If U.S. bankers acted with a wanton disregard for good fiscal sense and flung parties and payments alike in Peru to obtain the loans, the Peruvians also were lured by the gilded dollar. In the massive fallout of the Crash of 1929, Leguía lost his job, Peru defaulted on its foreign debts, civil war erupted in 1932 and 1933, and—true or not—the United States was held accountable for much of Peru's economic and political instability in the early 1930s.

The Naval Mission to Peru: The Flying Schools

When the American naval aviator Harold B. Grow flew over rebel forces led by Col. Luis M. Sánchez Cerro on August 23 in Arequipa to scatter pro-Leguía leaflets, a new high—or low—was reached in the state of Peruvian-U.S. relations. Here was a lieutenant commander in the U.S. Navy, on reserve status, flying a Peruvian Navy aircraft in defense of the government. Even the Department of State had to struggle a bit to save Grow from the court-martial that followed. What was Commander Grow doing in Peru taking part in a revolution, albeit in this instance attempting to suppress one?

As part of President Leguía's desire to modernize his navy and start an air force, he invited foreign military missions to Peru early in his administration. A French flying mission arrived and initiated a flying school in 1920, but it had little success, undermined in part by some spectacular accidents. The flying school was reorganized in 1922. Some

Peruvian pilots trained in the United States, such as Juan Leguía, Juan O'Connor and Federico Recavarren; they were joined by U.S. pilots Jack Sisson, Lloyd R. Moore, and Elmer Faucett in the military flying school, Escuela de Aviación Militar de Jorge Chávez (the Jorge Chávez Military Aviation Flying School), which shared resources with a newly organized civilian flying school called Escuela Civil de Aviación (Civilian Flying School). Great aviators from Europe visited Peru off and on during the 1920s on goodwill trips, breaking records and opening new routes, or, more practically, promoting the sales and development of their airplanes. None, however, rivaled the growing presence of U.S. aviators. Jimmy Doolittle, for example, visited in 1928 and 1929, bringing with him Curtiss bombers and fighters (Falcons and Hawks), doing aerobatics, and demonstrating the potency of air power.[34] The beginnings of civil aviation in Peru were also closely tied to U.S. aviators and fledgling air carriers.[35] Each of these links further strengthened the disposition of Peru's embryonic military and civil aviation community to view the United States as a natural partner in the development of this new form of warfare and transportation. While the new army aviation and civil aviation employed U.S. instructors and trainers, the navy went even further.

To modernize the navy, Leguía separated it from the army, endowed it with an independent ministry, and then contracted for a U.S. naval mission that arrived in Callao on September 6, 1920, aboard the Grace Line steamer *Santa Elisa.* The mission chief was Capt. Frank Freyer. He was named the chief of staff of the Peruvian Navy with instructions to direct and administer the navy. Capt. Charles Gordon Davy was put in command of the Naval Academy, Capt. Lewis D. Causey was appointed commanding officer of the Naval Division (consisting of the cruisers *Almirante Grau, Coronel Bolognesi, Lima,* and the torpedo boat *Teniente Rodríguez*), and other officers occupied similar positions.

This extraordinary access to power in the Peruvian Navy by U.S. officers had a double effect: it alienated many of the older Peruvian officers who resented the U.S. presence, but it indoctrinated a whole generation of cadets and younger officers to doing things as they were done in the U.S. Navy. Perhaps no other officer had a more long-lasting effect than Captain Davy of the Naval Academy.

As a Peruvian naval historian and naval officer wrote many years later, "in his nine years as director, Davy brought a special mysticism to his relationship with the cadets which permitted him to overcome the initial reluctance of older officers who attempted to resist the work of the Naval Mission."[36] Davy oversaw the translation of texts used at Annapolis for use by his Peruvian cadets and generally modeled changes in Peru's navy on his own experiences. Davy was characterized as "the one most dearly remembered" for his work in helping modernize this area of the navy—the training of young officers.[37] Not only did Davy help professionalize the service, but he introduced "an American way of life which was welcomed by Peruvian officers and is practiced even until today."[38]

While Captain Davy left the longest wake from his service in Peru, Lt. Cdr. Harold B. Grow, who arrived in 1923, had a much more prominent short-term profile. He was an aviator brought in by Leguía to organize and train a naval air branch and by 1928 had been put in charge of all civil and military aviation in Peru by Leguía. Grow became a close personal friend of the president, not only because of his work as a pioneering aviator—in 1927 for example he led a dangerous but successful survey flight across the Andes—but also because of his strengths as an organizer and administrator. The first domestic Peruvian airline was established by Grow in 1928 using American-built Keystone Pelican (Pronto) aircraft, and in 1928 and 1929 Grow was instrumental in helping establish the first successful commercial air operations between Peru and the United States.

During the 1920s the U.S. naval mission also assisted the Electric Boat Co. of Groton, Connecticut, selling four submarines to Leguía for more than $5 million and contributed to the modernization of the navy in a number of fields ranging from fleet organization to education. This first naval mission was formally ended in 1933, although the regime of Sánchez Cerro (which overthrew Leguía in 1930) pretty much stripped the U.S. naval officers of administrative responsibilities soon after coming to power. Recall that Captain Grow had been leaflet-bombing the anti-Leguía, pro–Sánchez Cerro forces in August 1930—right in the midst of the revolution which overthrew Leguía. No wonder a certain anti-U.S. naval mission bias was brought in by the new president!

Wings Across the Americas: Pioneering Aviation Between the United States and Peru

Less controversial, and, ultimately, with a longer-range impact on Peruvian-U.S. relations, were the attempts by the Leguía government to develop commercial aviation. Peru is an immensely diverse country geographically. Deserts, mountains, and jungles divide peoples and cultures and make commerce and exchange difficult. Yet the shadows of tiny aircraft motoring across the skies in the 1920s promised a new era of communications and transportation that many thought could overcome the wonderful, but maddening, diversity of Peru's people and geography. Perhaps national unity—long sought by Peru's leaders—could be forged, or certainly promoted with some success, by tying together better the diverse parts of the nation with these marvelous new flying machines.

Charles A. Lindbergh's solo flight across the Atlantic Ocean in May 1927 propelled aviation to the forefront of the world's attention. Not only was "Lucky Lindy" transformed, almost literally overnight, into a hero of unprecedented proportions, but everyone, it seemed at times, wanted to fly—for fun, for business, for adventure, and for profit. Peruvians with vision, and access to either money or power, also were smitten by the aviation contagion. Juan Leguía had flown with the British during the First World War and led aviation enthusiasts in his country. Foreign aviators visited Peru periodically during the 1920s, attracted by the possibility of selling airplanes and generating business but, equally, by the chance of setting spectacular records flying across the Andes, over the vast Amazon area, or setting records of distance and endurance. Lindbergh himself flew on a goodwill tour to Mexico, Central

America, Panama, and Cuba in 1927–28, while other American aviators, such as Jimmy Doolittle and Herbert A. Dargue, led missions to South America and worked the Peruvian market in 1926, 1927, and 1928. When President Leguía put Lieutenant Commander Grow in charge of all Peruvian aviation in 1928, the stage was set for the initiation of commercial aviation between the United States and Peru. However it wasn't Grow who is remembered as one of the pioneers in Peruvian aviation but a fellow named Elmer Faucett.

Elmer "Slim" Faucett arrived in Peru June 28, 1920, with a team demonstrating Curtiss Wright aircraft. He was twenty nine (born in 1891 in Savona, New York), and was smitten by aviation as a teenager. Hanging around Roosevelt Field at Hammondsport a few miles away from the family farm, he would tinker on airplanes and eventually became a mechanic for Glenn Curtiss. Flying was, however, the attraction for Slim. After a lot of observing, one day he got into one of Curtiss Wright's airplanes and took off—his debut as a pilot—and promptly got fired. However he attached himself to another branch of the Curtiss Wright group then preparing to take a team of pilots, mechanics, and planes to South America to drum up some business. Peru was on the itinerary.[39] When the Curtiss Wright group went bankrupt in 1922, Chris Dillon, another American with the team, was compensated, in lieu of a salary, with a plane. Dillon let Slim fly his plane, and the young man's career was launched, first by giving demonstration flights but then by a more dramatic launch into the skies over Peru.

In 1921 Leguía's government offered a prize for the first trans-Andean flight from Lima to Iquitos, Peru's small but important port located on the vast basin of the Amazon River. The overland trip took ten to fourteen days under the best of circumstances. Another American aviator, Lloyd R. "Dinty" Moore, had already set one Peruvian record in 1921 when he flew into the mountain city of Huaráz and, on his trip back to Lima, climbed to more than twenty thousand feet and overflew Mount Huascarán, the highest peak in the Andes. Moore, and his Peruvian copilot, César Lecca, then tried the Lima-Iquitos trip in July 1921, but they crashed outside of Cajamarca after successfully flying north along the coast to Trujillo before turning east into the Andes. Moore and Lecca escaped unhurt. "Dinty" Moore later had a long career as a pilot for Panagra.[40]

On October 5, 1922, Slim Faucett climbed into the cockpit of his Wright "Oriole" at the improvised airfield at Santa Beatriz racetrack. The Oriole was an open cockpit biplane, equipped with the bare necessities. Faucett had a map, not a particularly accurate one, to guide him through the high Andean passes surrounded by 20,000-foot snowy peaks. Half in and half out of the fuselage in his tight cockpit and swaddled in warm clothing, he pulled his goggles down and gave his crew the signal to crank up.

Off he went. For a few minutes he flew over the narrow, flat coastal plain, then quickly climbed over the brown foothills, which soon gave way to the majestic Andes. Without a radio for even rudimentary navigation, he followed his map and his flying instincts.

He made it through the high, cold windy passages and started down the eastern slopes, thawing out as he reached the lower, tropical elevations, looking for the great river below, running low on fuel but high on adrenaline. Then he hit one of nature's most perilous wonders, a giant thunderstorm that he couldn't get around. He descended lower and lower trying to get below the ominous dark clouds ahead, which were filled with lightning and violent up- and downdrafts. With the rain pelting him in the open cockpit, Faucett finally made a lifesaving decision to land. He spotted a narrow slip of sand along the mouth of Tigre River below and brought in his Oriole. The soft sand caught the tiny aircraft and pitched it forward, bending the prop as it came to a stop. Faucett escaped unhurt, but he would have to wait for a boat to take him and his Oriole the last one hundred kilometers downstream to Iquitos.

He had penetrated the Andes and pioneered the route. Within a short time the world's press, including the *Times* of London and the *New York Times,* celebrated the "Condor of Peru." The Condor, considerable aeronautical skills and proven courage notwithstanding, returned to Lima by boat down the Amazon and then by ship through the Panama Canal. Faucett augmented his business back in Lima by flying his orange-painted Oriole carrying mail and passengers along the coast to petro-leum camps far to the north, to mining towns in the Andes, and to sugar and cotton plantations stretched out along the river oases that bloomed green between the long, arid stretches of desert coastline. Faucett took the next logical step in 1928, founding his own company, Faucett Air-lines, with $25,000 in capital invested by a small group of Peruvian avi-ation enthusiasts, including Santiago Acuña, Armando Fabri, Manuel Gallagher, Pedro Winder, and Ernesto Ayulo.

On September 15, 1928, Faucett Airlines launched its inaugural flight from Lima to the northern port of Chiclayo, and then on to I.P.C.'s cen-ter of operations at Talara. Within a year Faucett Airlines added larger Stinson aircraft, which were equipped to carry eight passengers and were driven by 400-horsepower Wasp engines. In 1929 Faucett built his own field on the former hacienda Santa Cruz just south of Lima in the San Isidro district of the city. Faucett added new aircraft—or built his own to the rigid specifications needed for long-range, high altitude flying in the Andes—and spun his web across the nation. Importing only the engines and some instruments made to his specifications from the United States, in the mid-1930s Faucett fabricated wooden-framed aircraft in the workshops at the Santa Cruz Field, the first such endeav-ors in this part of Latin America. In 1937 one of his pilots, Armando Revoredo, flew nonstop from Lima to Buenos Aires, setting a new rec-ord.[41] Faucett added newer, sleeker metal-skinned aircraft to his fleet in the 1930s, keeping up with the advances in technology. After World War II Faucett put into service surplus aircraft, such as DC-3s and DC-4s, and when jets came into commercial service, he also quickly made the transition.

Peruvians became familiar with the orange and white aircraft of Fau-cett Airlines, largely run and operated by Peruvians, many of them trained for aviation careers in Peru courtesy of Faucett-supplied fellow-ships to the United States.

"Every Peruvian is in one form or another indebted to Elmer Fau-cett," eulogized the mayor of Lima, Eduardo Dibós Dammert, when Slim Faucett was buried in the Protestant British Cemetery in Bellavista on April 10, 1960. When a new airport serving Lima was inaugurated in 1962—the Jorge Chávez International Airport—the principal avenue connecting the airport to the city was named in honor of Faucett.

Faucett was a pioneer in Peruvian history, an active and progressive promoter of an industry whose value in nation-building has always been recognized. He embodied much of what was positive in the modern relations between Peru and the United States. He also lost out in one of the major aviation races in Peru in 1928 and 1929. Two days before Faucett Airlines's inaugural flight in September 1929, Dan Tobin, a pilot flying for another airline, beat Faucett to the punch.

After a brief salutation to the crowd gathered at the Santa Beatriz racetrack in Lima, Tobin taxied his four-passenger plane, specially built by Fairchild Aircraft, out to the end of the straightaway normally reserved for thoroughbreds coming down the stretch. Tobin ran his 200-horsepower Whirlwind engine through the short preflight checklist and, satisfied, turned down the track, gave his plane the throttle, and roared down past the crowd, climbing and turning north as he gained altitude. A few hours later he landed at Talara, six hundred miles north, inaugurating the first scheduled air service on the west coast of South America, two days ahead of Slim Faucett.

Nor surprisingly Harold Grow, director of Leguía's aviation services, was part of the act that upstaged Faucett. Also opposing Faucett was W. R. Grace & Co. and Pan American Airways. Faucett was up against one of the biggest transportation guns in Peru (Grace) and was challenging Pan American and her founder, the ambitious Juan Trippe, in the fledgling U.S. aviation industry seeking international markets. The genesis of Faucett's competition in Peru arose from a small outfit of crop dusters.

C. E. Woolman, a Louisiana entomologist and promoter of crop dusting in the United States, thought Peru might be a good market for crop dusters because the seasons are reversed in the Southern Hemisphere; the planes could be used in Peru when not in use in the United States. Accordingly Woolman sailed to Peru in 1926 and arranged for the first dusting contract in South America. Harold Harris, an ex–World War I aviator turned crop duster, followed the next year with four aircraft and enjoyed immense success killing army worms and other insects on the cotton plantations of the Cañete Valley south of Lima.

Harris also learned how long it took to get parts, mail, and supplies from the United States by sea to keep his planes flying. After the crop dusting season was over, he scouted other dusting jobs, and potential commercial air routes, in South America, touring Bolivia, Argentina, Uruguay, and Brazil. When he returned to New York, he promoted the establishment of a good air route from the United States to South America. Timing and access were two of aviation's great promises: materials and people could be moved rapidly, regions (such as in Peru) so remote as to be almost outside the national vision and economy could be accessed. Harris's goals found much support in the host country. There was always, of course, the military application of this new technology, and that too was never too far from the minds of planners and politicians. But the expansion of commercial aviation more than anything else captured the imagination of many Peruvians. Harris proved prophetic in championing a South American air route in 1928.[42]

In New York Harris contacted Richard F. Hoyt, a member of an investing firm in New York that was financing Pan Am and that had also recently purchased the Peruvian crop-dusting service. Harris pulled out a small map of Latin America with the potential air routes drawn in based on present and future aircraft performance. Hoyt was captivated.

"Get Trippe on the phone," Hoyt asked his secretary.

Harris wondered who Trippe was. He had never heard the name at that point.

"Trippe," Hoyt said, "come over here. I've got a fellow here who's two years ahead of us."[43] It is hard to believe that *anybody* was two years ahead of Juan Trippe. Soon their best salesman, the entomologist C. E. Woolman, was sent to Peru in 1928 not only to renew the crop-dusting contracts, but to seek a concession from the Leguía administration to inaugurate an international air service. In Peru Woolman gained the support of Harold Grow, certainly the key figure in any negotiations.

A German bid to gain the concession was throttled by Grow, clearing one hurdle for Woolman and the interests he represented. Another hurdle was Slim Faucett, with far more experience in Peru and already well known to Leguía. Faucett too sought the international concession, but with Grow supporting Woolman, Faucett's run at the major prize failed. In May 1928 Leguía awarded the contract to Woolman and his company. The contract permitted the company to carry mail, passengers, and cargo. Within a few months, the concession obtained by Woolman was transferred to Pan American. Eventually Trippe, who would have preferred to go it alone, stumbled into the giant in transportation between the United States and Peru, W. R. Grace & Co. Any improvements and innovations in transportation between Peru and the United States threatened the Grace businesses.

Would Trippe consider a partnership? Grace possessed a vast network of ships, people, friendship, and information to provide support needed for a route that by 1930 would be the *longest in the world*, extending forty-five hundred miles from Buenos Aires to Panama. To appreciate Trippe's acceptance of the Grace offer to become a partner, one must take into account the following: the average range for the best planes then available was about six hundred miles; there was no radar, indeed virtually no radio communications (radio being barely a few years old itself); only the most makeshift of landing fields existed (horse tracks were favorite options); and only a pioneer's knowledge of flying weather in the Southern Hemisphere was available. Grace's own aviation enthusiasts wanted their company to pioneer the routes. But Trippe was rapidly acquiring the concessions in the Caribbean and Central America, obtaining the critical mail contracts from the United States government that made these flights profitable. Trippe had Grace blocked beyond Panama to Miami and New York in aviation.

The two rivals agreed to half ownership in a new airline—Peruvian Airways—which acquired the Woolman/Pan Am concession. Harris, in the United States in the summer of 1928, became vice president and general manager of the new company and ordered a special plane from Fairchild Aircraft to help launch the new service.

This new aircraft, carrying four passengers and a pilot, was the aircraft flown by Dan Tobin on September 13 from the Santa Beatriz racetrack in Lima to Talara inaugurating the new service. On February 21,

1929, Pan American and Grace announced the formation of Pan American–Grace Airways (Panagra) to succeed Peruvian Airways. For the next forty years, Panagra dominated the airways between Peru and the United States, serving as one of the principal conduits for the flow of information, people, materials, and culture between the two countries. (C. E. Woolman, by the way, retired from the South American scene shortly after Panagra was founded and headed back to Louisiana where he established a small air service he called Delta after the great Mississippi delta.)

At the time Panagra was being launched, initiating a new era in transportation, an old international dispute drew to an end, closing a long chapter of hostility and enmity between Peru and Chile. The United States was very active in the protracted negotiations and maneuvers that led to the end of this dispute.

Tacna and Arica: The United States and the Resolution of Peru's Border Conflicts

Peru's territorial aspirations in the twentieth century have often been the object of U.S. diplomatic interest. This has ranged from the expression of simple goodwill to outright arbitration of border and territorial disputes. In the main the United States has supported Peru's positions vis-à-vis Chile, a tradition that goes back to the War of the Pacific when the United States sought to maintain Peru's territorial integrity in the face of the victorious Chileans. The unresolved dispute between Peru and Chile over the disposition of the cities of Tacna and Arica and their territories gave rise to the most famous U.S. arbitration of Peruvian/Chilean affairs this century.

The dispute over Tacna and Arica is a long and complicated one. Indeed "the Tacna-Arica question occupied more space in the *Papers Relating to the Foreign Relations of the United States* than did any one specific topic concerning Peru from 1908 to 1940."[44] However, boiled down from the rhetoric spun by lawyers, politicians, and diplomats for almost half a century, the issue was deceptively simple: the Peruvian cities of

Tacna and Arica located in the northern part of Peru's southernmost province of Tarapaca had been seized by Chile during the War of the Pacific, and Peru wanted them back. Chile claimed the cities as legitimate spoils of war. By the Treaty of Ancón signed in 1883, Peru gave up most of the province of Tarapaca to Chile, and Chile agreed that a plebiscite should be held in Arica and Tacna to determine their futures.

The plebiscite was not held within the ten year period that the Treaty of Ancón stipulated. Peru said the treaty had been violated and claimed the territories automatically reverted to Peruvian sovereignty. The Chileans claimed that the treaty only *suggested* that the plebiscite be held within ten years, but it could still be held in 1910 (when formal diplomatic relations between Peru and Chile were broken over the dispute, not to be restored until 1928), 1921, or whenever desired, and the treaty would be fulfilled.

Early in the 1920s the U.S. government became actively involved in this dispute. Peru claimed a plebiscite was no longer viable. The population had been so manipulated, cajoled, and intimidated by the Chileans that any plebiscite would be a travesty. Chile now agreed to a plebiscite, presumably secure in the knowledge that forty years of Chilean occupation had "Chileanized" the population enough to guarantee a Chilean victory. Matters stood at an impasse until 1925 when the administration of President Calvin Coolidge, following several years of negotiations beginning in 1922 under Coolidge's predecessor Warren G. Harding, issued an arbitration on March 4. The plebiscite should be held.

Peru was outraged. It seemed to confirm Chile's position, and no one in Peru expected a fair plebiscite.[45] To ensure fairness Coolidge's award provided for the establishment of a plebiscitary commission that included provisions for an American to preside over it and decreed strict rules to be followed in the voting—all under the jurisdiction of the commission and not the Chileans. Named as president of the commission was Gen. John J. "Black Jack" Pershing, the hero of the U.S. Army in the First World War and a much-respected soldier. Pershing's presence would prove crucial for Peru. The old soldier was, above all else, an impartial observer, and what he saw in Tacna and Arica was rather crass Chilean manipulation of the population.

On August 14, 1925, the day Pershing arrived in Arica, "[t]here was not a Peruvian flag in sight," Pershing wrote Secretary of State Frank Kellogg. There were lots of flags, but they were all Chilean. If Chile and Peru were disputing the region, where was the evidence of a Peruvian presence? "My impression," Pershing continued, "the day of my arrival was that everything was pretty much Chilean." The population was intimidated and cowed; or as the general phrased it, "this is about as near a reign of terrorism as I can imagine, and it is going to be most difficult to alter it." [46]

Pershing obviously sided with Peru in this dispute. He was motivated not by favoritism toward Peru's position but by the desire to execute justice in a fair proceeding. He quickly dispatched his observers to round up information. Many of them were Spanish-speakers from Panama and the Philippines, and their investigations revealed Chile's position to be even more suspect. The investigators interviewed people of all classes and discovered evidence of intimidation, oppression, and deportation of Peruvians by Chilean authorities.

Pershing was mad. "Mr. Secretary," he wrote Kellogg a few weeks after he arrived, "it is a situation which almost surpasses comprehension. . . . To undertake to conduct this election under the present conditions would make us the laughing stock of the world, for I have no doubt that all the countries of South America understand the conditions as they exist here better than we do . . . now." The general was especially angry with the Chileans who, in spite of flagrant abuses being uncovered, "stand up and declare that there is and has been freedom of action for all people living in this territory." [47]

The Peruvian delegation repeatedly called for neutralizing the territory—controlled effectively by the Chileans—but the Chileans said "let's get on with it." Register and vote. The result was an impasse.

Pershing grew ill, suffering increasingly from rising blood pressure and dental problems. The high blood pressure was probably brought on by his dealings with his intransigent hosts; Pershing was already plagued by bad teeth and pain before he even left for South America. His personal physician recommended an immediate return to the United States. Some have suggested this was a "diplomatic" sickness, giving Pershing a good excuse to back away from the situation, but it was not. He was sick. He was replaced in early 1926 by Gen. William Lassiter, then in charge of the Panama Canal Zone.

Lassiter came quickly to the same conclusion as Pershing. A plebiscite under the existing conditions would be a miscarriage of justice and impossible to administer fairly. He counseled that the only other way out was a diplomatic solution agreed to between the two competing parties. Frustrated by the inability to bring the dispute to a close, the United States pulled Lassiter out and declared the plebiscitary proceedings ended in June 1926.

It was a victory for Peru and was celebrated as such in Lima; the action was frustrating for Chile. Nothing had been solved, but both parties were weary of the dispute. Other parallel events were taking place that would lead to the final resolution before the end of the decade.

During the Sixth Pan-American Conference held in Havana in 1928, Peruvian and Chilean delegates in a friendly manner exchanged ideas on a possible solution. The United States, ever interested in closing the matter, suggested in July 1928 that diplomatic relations be reestablished as a prelude to a final resolution. Negotiations continued in Lima and Santiago through 1928 and 1929. Before Leguía would sign a resolution, however, he insisted that the U.S. president, newly inaugurated Herbert E. Hoover, formally propose the agreement that was actually reached in direct negotiations between Chile and Peru. Leguía knew the final settlement, although acceptable, would be targeted by his critics, for it was premised on the division of the disputed territory—Arica to Chile and Tacna to Peru. To save face with his critics and duck the popular reaction, Leguía sought to use the United States in this role. Hoover was willing. He had made an extended goodwill tour to South America as president-elect, including Ecuador and Peru on his itinerary, and he went along with the strategy.

The Treaty of Lima of 1929, awarding Tacna to Peru and Arica to Chile, settled the dispute. Chile paid Peru a $6 million indemnity and granted Peru the right of transit through Arica with a wharf, customs-house, and railroad station. It was agreed to build a monument on the Morro de Arica (a high bluff overlooking the bay) to the good relations between the two nations. Bolivia, hoping for some concessions in her drive to regain access to the sea, was pushed to the side. Both Peru and Chile agreed that no territories acquired by the Treaty of Lima could be ceded to a third state (read Bolivia) without prior agreement of both signatories, and no new international railroads could be built through Tacna or Arica without the approval of Chile and Peru.[48] The rest of the hemisphere was delighted with the end of this old feud, and the expected nationalist, anti-Leguía reaction in Lima was blunted by fixing the blame on the United States.

In fact as we near the end of Leguía's eleven year rule, the Oncenio in Peruvian history, the glow of earlier years was quickly dimming. Leguía was overthrown in a revolution late in August 1930. The Peruvian leader's overthrow was brought on in part by his dictatorial ways and corruption, but also by his close association with the United States, which was the target of increasingly strident critics who associated the beginnings of the depression in Peru with the superpower. An unpopular border rectification with Colombia, also promoted by the United States, plus the loss of Arica, further eroded Leguía's popularity, which was already waning when in 1929 he manipulated the country's constitution so that he could run for reelection. When a young officer, a mere lieutenant colonel named Luis M. Sánchez Cerro, came out of the barracks in Arequipa and declared the end of the Oncenio, few rallied around to defend the old dictator. Capt. Harold Grow's bombing run over the insurgents was perhaps symbolic of the end of the Leguía years. The paper leaflets persuaded no one to stay loyal to the dictator, but an American aviator's presence in the cockpit certainly reinforced the image that many Peruvians had of the immense influence that the United States had built in Peru under the Oncenio.

5   The Good Neighbor

> There is "scarcely a Peruvian participating in the money economy of the country who does not eat, wear, or use something processed, manufactured, or imported by Casa Grace."
>
> Eugene W. Burgess and Frederick H. Harbison,
> *Casa Grace in Peru*

The trials and tribulations brought on by the depression enveloped not only the United States but also plunged Peru into severe economic and political stress. Ironically this was the background for one of the most progressive and positive periods in the relations between the two countries. In 1933 the newly elected U.S. president, Franklin D. Roosevelt, announced his "Good Neighbor" policy toward Latin America, and, with this initiative, essentially altered the role that the United States had played in Latin America since the turn of the century.

The initiation of the Roosevelt administration and the Good Neighbor policy promoted a new agenda in inter-American affairs. Old-style interventionism was rejected in favor of collaboration and cooperation among equal American states. The devastating effects of the depression on economies across the Americas also brought traditional capitalism under attack. As the Roosevelt administration experimented with increasing state intervention in the economy and society of North America, it found sympathetic echoes in Peru, where the state had long played a dominant role in national affairs. Intellectuals across the Americas also found much in common in the 1930s as they experimented with alternative principles and models of government and society.

The Second World War reinforced commercial ties and common historical affinities between the United States and Peru. The fight against fascism emphasized the common Western Hemisphere ideals of democracy, republicanism, liberty, and other principles held roughly in common since the founding of the republics, while Peru, as a supplier of such key wartime materials as vanadium and copper, was considered an important contributor to the war effort. A border spate between Peru and Ecuador erupted into armed conflict in 1941, and the United States intervened actively in 1942 to keep the peace.

Issues related to the Cold War dominated political and diplomatic relations from the mid-1940s to the 1960s, while U.S. private investments and government-to-government assistance rose dramatically, again knitting the economy of Peru into that of the United States even more tightly. This very closeness produced in Peru a nationalist reaction that culminated in the explosive Peruvian Institutional Revolution of 1968, abruptly breaking a long pattern of cooperation and closeness between the two countries.

The Kemmerer Missions

Once upon a time foreign money doctors roamed Latin America preaching fixed exchange rates and passive gold exchange standard monetary rules. Bankers followed in their footsteps, from the halls of Montezuma to the shores of Daiquiri.[1]

Once Leguía was removed by a revolution in August 1930, an era in Peru ended. But the close relationship developed during the Oncenio between Peru and the United States continued, although somewhat frayed, through the depression era. The Sánchez Cerro government's major concern, as prices of Peru's major exports plummeted on the world's markets, was how to service the immense debt acquired from the many loans negotiated on Peru's behalf during the Oncenio. What Peru needed was a new loan to help pay off the old loans. Naturally Peru turned to the United States, and this time Peru called for a visit by the "money doctor," Dr. Edwin Walter Kemmerer, the eminent U.S. economist known for his many financial missions to Latin America in the 1920s. In the 1920s Kemmerer also embarked on advising missions to Colombia, Chile, Ecuador, Bolivia, and, finally, Peru. He was the "money doctor," and when he arrived in Peru early in 1931, he brought with him his bag of medicines, which, like most medicines that are good for the patient, did not go down easily.

"My role is exactly the same as that of a physician," the Princeton University professor said in 1931 while in Peru tending to his "patient." "I give the prescription and the treatment. If the patient likes it, he accepts it and follows it; if not, he simply throws it out the window." And Kemmerer added, "I am nothing more than an adviser."[2] But what an adviser! After his three month visit to Peru in early 1931, Kemmerer made his recommendations—with confidential copies to the U.S. embassy—to the Reserve Bank and Sánchez Cerro's government. Those recommendations were enacted in one day. Few, if any, in Sánchez Cerro's administration took the time to read them closely!

Even Kemmerer marveled at his power. "This was the speediest action we have ever had," he noted. Among the widespread recommendations enacted were a central bank, a gold exchange-standard, a general banking law, a budgeting system, a reorganization of the national treasury, a new tax code, and other measures related to customs and credit.[3]

Kemmerer earned his Ph.D. in economics at Cornell University in 1901. His base of operations was Princeton University where he taught and wrote as a professor of finance and economics for most of his professional life. Like the president of Princeton at the time, Woodrow Wilson, Kemmerer believed in the Progressive ideal of applying knowledge for the betterment of mankind. Kemmerer got started as a financial adviser to the U.S. government in 1903 when he helped put the Philippines on the gold standard. He went on to have a distinguished career, rising through the ranks of economists in the United States to the presidency in 1926 of the prestigious American Economic Association.

The goal of Peru was to obtain a new loan on Wall Street. When that ultimately failed—in spite of Kemmerer's missions, recommendations, and prescriptions—Peruvians lost interest in Kemmerer and his "medicine." Kemmerer's conservative fiscal principles and traditional financial recommendations found tough sledding in the slumping economies of the depression. Between 1928 and 1931, for example, Peru's foreign export earnings fell 71 percent. No amount of gerrymandering of the financial system could overcome that immense loss of income.

As seen above, when the Cerro de Pasco Corporation's exports and profits slid in this same period, immense stress was produced that severely strained the relationship between the Cerro Corporation and Sánchez Cerro's government.

As the depression deepened, it seemed to many that capitalism had failed both in the United States and Peru. Kemmerer's mission took on the trappings of a religious mission, with all the consequent fervor, as the search for solutions grew more desperate. The entire U.S. embassy, accompanied by the directors of the Reserve Bank and other banking mugwumps in Peru, turned out to greet the money doctor when he arrived on January 12, 1931. Not everyone was bowled over by the promise of the Kemmerer mission. "I do not think," said the undersecretary of state in Washington to one of his subordinates, the assistant secretary of state for Latin American affairs, "we should be in the position of going out and saying that he is the Moses that leads you out of your difficulties every time."[4]

Indeed the Department of State cautioned its ambassador in Lima, Fred Morris Dearing, to maintain a credible separation from the Kemmerer mission. The U.S. government would not get directly involved in negotiations between international creditors (the Wall Street bankers) and their debtors, in this case Peru. Dearing was more supportive of the professor. "While here," Dearing told Kemmerer, "the Embassy would be quietly and watchful in the background and would avoid seeming too familiar with the Mission, but [you] could count upon us for any cooperation whatever . . . in any constructive measures."[5]

APRA (Alianza Popular Revolucionaria Americana) and others who saw the old-style hand of imperialism predictably assailed the money doctor. The metaphor of a doctor prescribing to his patients and children galled many as a national humiliation. "Our financial physicians are," or "should be," one Peruvian noted, "just as able as Mister Kemmerer. But," he added sarcastically, "they are not graduated from the University of Wall Street. And that is all. With Mr. Kemmerer, it is not a matter of science. It is a matter of diploma."[6] Indeed it was. No Peruvians in the banking or financial community really expected anything new from Kemmerer. What they wanted was the imprimatur, the seal of approval, from one so well respected in the international financial and banking communities.

The *Apristas* were more outspoken in denouncing Kemmerer's mission as nothing less than another demonstration of Peru's lackeylike obeisance before U.S. imperialism. Peru needed to increase taxes on U.S. enterprises there—even nationalize the worst offenders—rather than throw more money down the rathole of imperialism by paying for Kemmerer's presence in Peru, *Apristas* believed. They upbraided Sánchez Cerro for even allowing the Kemmerer mission to take place, labeling the president of Peru as nothing more than a tool of the imperialists.

Sánchez Cerro, then locked in combat with the *Apristas* in an electoral duel for the presidency, was, however, no friend of Kemmerer. In fact the lieutenant colonel from Arequipa thought all bankers—domestic and gringo—were crooks, and that the Wall Street bankers had profited immensely and illegally from the acts of his predecessor, Leguía. Yet without a new loan from U.S. bankers, Peru simply could not service the $100 million debt contracted under Leguía. In late March 1931, Peru defaulted on that debt, and a little more than a year later in May 1932, it abandoned the gold standard, thus aborting Kemmerer's principal objectives—servicing debts and maintaining the gold standard.

Kemmerer's mission to Peru was not necessarily a failure. As Paul Drake—a student of the money doctor—noted, "while Peru scrapped Kemmerer's monetary system and never fully adopted his fiscal legislation, it preserved his banking institutions and the spirit of his orthodoxy. . . . the Central Reserve Bank . . . continued to espouse Kemmerer's principles, resisting exchange fluctuations, denouncing government deficits, and advocating an eventual return to the gold standard."[7] Indeed Peru's rather rapid recovery from the depression, which began in 1933 with rising export prices, especially cotton and sugar, gave some credence to Kemmerer's basically traditional fiscal principles. These stressed laissez-faire economics or greater free enterprise rather than increasing state control. Peruvian-U.S. relations for the three decades leading to the late 1960s were characterized by a similar vision of what was appropriate in economics.

Amazonian Frontiers

While Kemmerer was in Peru, another crisis came to a head that involved the United States. In this instance the issue was national borders with Colombia and Ecuador. Unlike deliberations over exchange rates and banking reforms that produced only hot rhetoric, this dispute erupted into some hot shooting in the Amazon region.

In August 1932 Peruvian filibusters seized the Colombian border town of Leticia on the Amazon River. For the next year, Colombia and Peru sparred over a section of the Amazonian jungle known as the Leticia trapezoid. This territory had been configured in the Salomón-Lozano Treaty between Peru and Colombia in 1922, which gave Colombia direct access to the Amazon River. Meanwhile, Ecuador chafed under these new agreements, for Ecuador too claimed disputed territories in the same region. In 1941 a border war erupted between Peru and Ecuador over the regions, and things did not go well for Ecuador. Throughout this period of dispute and resolution, the United States played a role. However the actual extent of U.S. influence and action in these various disputes—and what were *perceived* by Peruvians as U.S. intentions and actions—often proved curiously different. The United States probably did not fundamentally influence the way in which Peru's borders were settled, but the perception of U.S. friendship or lack thereof did sometimes drive Peruvian foreign policy.

The Salomón-Lozano Treaty negotiated by Leguía in 1922 rankled many in Peru. It was thought that Leguía had conceded too much to the Colombians and received too little in exchange. Although the initial treaty was negotiated in 1922, it was not ratified by Peru until 1928. That the negotiations had been held in secret and, in fact, some of the provisions of the treaty were not fully revealed even after it was proclaimed, caused suspicion and resentment among many of Leguía's critics. And many thought the United States was behind Leguía's secretive and ultimately unpopular Salomón-Lozano Treaty. How so?

One factor was U.S. compensation to Colombia for the loss of Panama. In 1903 the United States helped Colombia's isthmian province of Panama to declare her independence and thus paved the way for the building of the Panama Canal by the United States. Peruvians in the 1920s thought the United States had pressured Leguía to buckle under and sign the Salomón-Lozano Treaty, thereby helping compensate Colombia for her earlier territorial losses. Indeed between 1923 and 1928, the U.S. government made *at least* eight appeals, written or oral, to the Leguía administration to submit the treaty to the Peruvian congress for ratification. To many Peruvians, this was outright interference by the United States in Peru's international affairs.[8]

The fighting that broke out in the Leticia area in August 1932 flared off and on for more than a year. By March 1933 the Colombians had recaptured some Peruvian outposts, and diplomatic relations between Peru and Colombia were ruptured. The League of Nations was asked to mediate, and a solution was reached in May 1934 by a commission comprised of representatives from several different nations, which convened in Rio de Janeiro.

Most Peruvians felt the United States had favored Colombia in the Leticia Affair. U.S. citizens in both countries indirectly participated in the fighting by serving as aviation instructors (Colombia) or even piloting aircraft into the region (Peru).[9] In fact it was difficult for U.S. nationals and corporations not to take sides in the conflict. I.P.C., as mentioned above, was asked by Leguía to make a large loan to buy war supplies, but the big oil company refused for they were also being pressured by Colombia, where they had substantial interests. Secretary of State Cordell Hull insisted on a strict neutrality, and the United States enforced an arms embargo both on Colombia and Peru to dampen the action.

In the final agreement reached in Rio, both sides claimed victory, although Colombia probably came out with more of its positions intact. Honor and face were just as important as the nitty-gritty detail of actual treaties.

When the Peruvians withdrew from Leticia on June 23, 1933, to be replaced by a League of Nations mixed commission, honor took a front-row seat in the somewhat zany affairs of the tropical Amazon. "The Peruvian flag was not lowered. Instead," in what must be one of the most pyrrhic victories in modern history, "the flagpole was detached and carried to Peruvian territory with the flag still flying."[10] While Peruvians were toting their national banner through the damp Amazon, another border conflict festered between Peru and her Amazonian neighbor to the north, Ecuador. In that dispute, which erupted into violence in 1941, the United States moved rapidly—certainly more so than in 1932 and 1933—to force a solution.

The Salomón-Lozano Treaty of 1922 set the stage for the undeclared border war of 1941 with Ecuador. Without getting into the geographic detail of various territorial transfers, the upshot was that, after the treaty, instead of having a friendly Colombia along most of her eastern and southern frontiers, now Ecuador had to face Peru along the entire Ecuadorian Amazonian region, and Peru claimed much of what Ecuador considered was hers. So little was known of watersheds, river courses, and elementary geographic features (mountain chains, ridges, etc.) that invariably conflicting claims arose. As aerial photography and mapping improved, revealing true geographic features, the conflicts in claims became even more apparent. Recall that the *first* successful flight into the Peruvian Amazon was only made in 1923 by Slim Faucett. The Amazonian region, from the watersheds in the Andes down into the great river's upper basin, is immense and often impenetrable. The potential of finding and exploiting as yet undiscovered resources—petroleum and ores for example—of course always fueled the controversies.

In July 1941 Ecuadorian and Peruvian troops exchanged fire in the Zarumilla sector of the border. Instead of a simple spate, the conflict spread as Ecuadorian forces invaded. Peru counterattacked late in July, and in the Battle of Zarumilla, July 23–25, Peru's army overwhelmed the smaller and less prepared Ecuadorian forces.[11] Peru's army advanced across the border at will, its navy blockaded Ecuador's ports, Peruvian paratroopers captured Puerto Bolivar, and Ecuador's province of El Oro was occupied. The victory was complete for Peru, having taken more than one thousand square kilometers of disputed territory.

Supported diplomatically by Brazil, Argentina, and later Chile, the United States acted swiftly to bring a close to this undeclared war, which threatened to upset the hegemonic front the United States desired in Latin America against the Axis powers. On October 2, 1941, an armistice was signed at Talara. It was followed by negotiations in Rio de Janeiro that led to the Protocol of Peace, Friendship and Boundaries signed January 29, 1942, and ratified within a few months by both Peru and Ecuador. Of the more than sixteen hundred kilometers of border between the two, only seventy-eight remained in dispute to be resolved by a mixed commission. Assistant Secretary of State for Latin American Affairs Sumner Welles signed the Protocol on behalf of the United States, which, after the surprise attack on Pearl Harbor December 7, 1941, was especially insistent on peace in the hemisphere in order to consolidate the war effort.

Under the presidency of Manuel Prado y Ugarteche, Peru firmly supported the United States during the Second World War. The Rio Protocol was viewed not only as a magnificent testimony to Peruvian arms but also as an affirmation of U.S. friendship, which had been frayed in the 1930s by the Leticia affair.

As war broke out across Europe and the Pacific between 1939–1941, Peruvians—even the radical founder of APRA, Victor Raúl Haya de la Torre—found themselves in a somewhat ambivalent position. Peruvian nationalists, certainly aided by the victory over Ecuador, were promoting a more independent, sovereign Peru vis-à-vis the United States, while contemporaneously, many political, social, and economic sentiments shepherded Peruvians and Americans along remarkably converging, rather than diverging, paths. Haya perhaps best symbolized these ambivalent feelings toward the United States.

Victor Raúl Haya de la Torre and the United States

No Peruvians have had as much influence on modern Peruvian-U.S. relations as Augusto B. Leguía and Victor Raúl Haya de la Torre. Haya was by far more complex and controversial, and the one who left a much deeper impact on his country.

APRA, which Haya founded while in exile in Mexico in 1924, became the principal vehicle for revolutionary political action in Peru for almost half a century. APRA's anti-imperialism and radical Peruvian nationalism challenged the U.S. presence in Peru. Later, as Haya evolved toward the center of the political spectrum in Peru, APRA grew less stridently anti-American. Haya even expressed anti-Communist views in the 1940s and 1950s that echoed the anticommunism of the United States. Haya never achieved the presidency of Peru, but in 1985, his protégé, Alán García, brought the *Apristas* to power for their turn at the executive helm in Peruvian history. That García clashed with the United States on a number of important fronts—especially on servicing Peru's enormous debt of the 1980s—reminded some of the old differences between APRA and the United States.

Haya's ideology was a complex and fascinating amalgam of anti-imperialism, anticapitalism, spiritualism, Indianism, anti-Marxism, and mysticism. Above all else Haya desired to reconcile the immense differences in Peru: those, for example, dividing Indian society from white culture, the modernizing coast from the traditional sierra, and the rich from the poor. At the center of Haya's movement was his party, APRA. Its slogan, "solo el APRA salvara al Perú" ("Only APRA can save Peru"), summarized the messianic role that Haya envisioned for APRA. Furthermore Haya's early association with Protestant missionaries in Peru in the 1920s imbued the young radical with many of the symbols and strategies successful with Christian missionaries; Haya incorporated those symbols into APRA myth and strategy.[12]

One of the centerpieces of APRA ideology was the Peruvian Indian. As Peruvians looked to the Indian for insight into the Peruvian reality, they clashed with the popular mythology associated with the American reality. Such differences help to explain the different views of how Peru should meet the challenges of the modern world. If Leguía and his ardent admiration for the United States stood at one end of the Peruvian political spectrum, Haya in the 1920s and 1930s stood at the other.

Indianism in Peru goes back to the sixteenth-century Spanish invasion of the Inca Empire by Francisco Pizarro. Conquered, subordinated, and exploited, the Indian became a second-class citizen during three centuries of Spanish rule. While modern research has revealed that Indian culture retained much of its integrity and identity under Spanish rule, the general picture is not altered. Indian rebellions against white rule broke out sporadically in the highlands throughout the colonial period, the most massive being the Tupac Amaru II rebellion of 1779. Resistance and rebellion continued in the nineteenth century. In Peru, the phrase "*Indio bruto,*" or dumb Indian, fell easily from the lips of conservatives and traditionalists, who, at best, patronized the Indians, and, at worst, continued to exploit them well into the twentieth century.

Peru is also a mestizo country where the interaction of three races produced a unique Peruvian reality, one which Haya and others viewed as the true Peru. The two principal ethnic cultures—Indian and Spanish—possessed particular sets of virtues and weaknesses, often in direct contradiction. Haya's lifelong goal was to reconcile the culture of the coast—white, *cholo,* Western, and competitive—with the culture of the Sierra—Indian, also *cholo,* communal, and collective in orientation.

In the first third of the twentieth century, Haya and other Peruvian intellectuals such as Manuel Vicente Villarán and José Carlos Mariátegui developed a new—although not novel by any means—view of the Indian. The Indian was not to be dismissed as a "backward and absurd species," an *Indio bruto,* but as an inspiration for many insights into life that came from the uniquely Indian view of the world. It is not unnatural, therefore, that in the making of a Peruvian worldview, one distinct from the rationalist, empirical, scientific one of North America, there would emerge a different perception not only of reality, but, more practically, of how these two states—Peru and the United States—should relate to each other.[13]

For example, Peru's most brilliant early Marxist, Mariátegui, applied classic Marxist economic principles to Peru but "sought to formulate an indigenous brand of communism based on the ancient Inca *ayllu,*" or communal land holding. Mariátegui was not only a Marxist but an Indianist, dedicated to justice for the Indian. Mariátegui was marginalized by his radicalism.[14]

Haya, however, did not categorically reject the modernization associated with Peru's coastal culture, which embraced capitalism and individual initiative, and extolled competition and material accumulation. Haya was born to a middle-class family in the northern city of Trujillo in 1895. His father was a teacher, and Haya attended the University of Trujillo and then the national university in Lima, San Marcos.

He worked for a short time in Cuzco where he was immersed in the Indian culture and was profoundly altered by the experience. The other great influence in Haya's life as a young man was the university reform movement that swept through much of Latin America in 1918 and 1919, precisely during Haya's student days.

The reform movement was devoted to overcoming the greedy materialism and dehumanizing capitalism thought to have provoked the First World War. In Latin American universities, students attacked the most visible forms of capitalism in their world—foreign firms, foreign governments and their allies, and the old elites and oligarches. They especially attacked the old system of professors, administrators, and politicians who represented the oligarchies of Latin America collaborating with the forces of imperialism from abroad. It was an intoxicating movement that spread quickly to Peru, and Haya drank deeply at the well of anti-imperialism. Students rose up to overthrow the "agents of an insidious, antinational set of values, [those] professors systematically corrupting Latin American youth and severing it from its cultural moorings. In the university classrooms, therefore, Latin Americans must begin the struggle to liberate themselves from alien oppressors." [15] If one substitutes "Americans" for "alien oppressors," one can easily get a feel for the anti-American tone of Haya's early days.

As Haya's Indianism and anti-imperialism matured, it set him on a collision course with Leguía's vision of Peru, and, ultimately with the United States. Ironically, in the long run, Haya proved a most nimble realist rather than an unbending idealist. One further dimension to Haya's character—perhaps the most difficult to define—needs to be underscored, for it endowed him with a special quality. At the core of his personality was a communion with a mystical or spiritual dimension, which put him at odds with the average American whose nature was understood to be material, practical, scientific, and, ultimately, rational. To Haya the Indianism of Peru represented an uncorrupted spiritual center. This afforded the Indian a relationship to nature and to the cosmos, long eroded or destroyed by Western civilization's devotion to the secular, rational nature of man. In a way Haya's exposure to American Protestants in the early 1920s—precisely in the formative period of his intellectual journey—ironically reinforced his sensitivity to the spiritual world. The Methodist and Presbyterian missionaries taught Haya that the essence of Christianity was personal salvation, a *liberating* salvation that came only through the freely given grace of God. Man's response to God's grace was given through faith.

Haya discovered in Christianity a religion that deeply appealed to his spiritual sensibilities and to his thirst for a model of freedom and liberation. His mentor, a Presbyterian missionary and educator named John MacKay, taught Haya that first must come the inward conversion to Christ, and the transformation of the world would follow. Haya read the Bible and studied with MacKay, who also taught him that the Christ of the New Testament was a *revolutionary* figure whose promise was the ultimate redemption of all mankind. MacKay was most certainly not a social revolutionary, but to Haya, there emerged another face to this Jesus Christ of the old Catholic religion who taught passivity, obedience, resignation, and the love of one's enemies. Here was a lord who promised redemption, who smote his enemies, and who promised triumph in the end.

MacKay viewed the end times in spiritual terms. Haya translated the apocalyptic vision into his political party's triumphant assertion that APRA and only APRA could save Peru. Haya also learned that these Protestants set high personal examples, championed the achievement of goals by moral means, emphasized the absolute need of conversion, and put a premium on education.[16] APRA would embrace many of these strategies in its long struggle for power in Peru.

In 1931 in the midst of a bitter presidential election struggle between Haya and Sánchez Cerro, the rhetoric grew heated. While Haya moderated his position somewhat, allowing that foreign capital could remain in Peru if under strict control, many of his followers grew more strident. Haya even persuaded the U.S. ambassador, Frederick Dearing, during a meeting in September 1931 that the United States had nothing to fear if Haya were elected.[17] But APRA political tracts and some of Haya's more radical lieutenants described Peru's economy as virtually strangled by foreign (i.e., United States) control, having forced Peru to her knees in a neocolonial status. If Peru had plunged into an abyss of ruin and misery, it was on account of capitalists and imperialists. Many *Apristas* did not distinguish between foreign and domestic capitalists, identifying the cohorts of the deposed Leguía as typical oligarches in collusion with foreign interests.

APRA lost the election in October 1931, and the party quickly claimed fraud and corruption. The atmosphere was charged; that charge went off in July 1932 when a revolt erupted in Haya's hometown of Trujillo. The revolt was crushed by the army. In April 1933 Sánchez Cerro was assassinated by an *Aprista,* and APRA was declared illegal in 1936 by the new president, Oscar R. Benavides (1933–39). Many of APRA's leaders, including Haya, went underground or into exile not to emerge officially until 1945.

In the 1930s and especially in the war years of the early 1940s, an odd turnaround occurred. Haya the radical, the revolutionary, and the anti-imperialist, who had called for the internationalization of the Panama Canal and the nationalization of foreign properties in Peru, became Haya the admirer of the United States. And U.S. representatives in Peru, from journalists to members of the American Embassy's staff, began to speak of Haya as a nice fellow, one not necessarily to be damned and eschewed, but to be courted and wooed as a friend of the United States.

This change is attributed to the Good Neighbor policy announced in 1933 by Franklin D. Roosevelt. Old-style interventionism in Latin American affairs was replaced by "good neighborliness" and cooperation as the operating principles. Basically a convergence of vision occurred between Americans and Latin Americans in the 1920s but especially in the 1930s. According to Fredrick Pike, this made the Good Neighbor policy possible, and possibly even successful. Americans in the 1920s and 1930s "sought the same fusion between individualism and collectivism that Haya de la Torre hoped to find in corporatism or cooperativism. *Although the fact is little appreciated, a convergence in corporatist mythology helped achieve the rapport between North and South American intellectuals that contributed to the success of F. D. R.'s Good Neighbor policy in the years between 1933 and 1945*" (emphasis added).[18]

"Changing United States attitudes toward Native Americans contributed further to improved hemispheric relations," Pike noted.[19] It became chic for American intellectuals to glorify the Indian in their rejection of the capitalist ethic. An American Indian "New Deal" emerged during Roosevelt's administration, glorifying the communal lifestyle of the Indian. John Collier, F. D. R.'s Commissioner of Indian Affairs, based his "approach on the same assumptions that underlay Andean America's Indianism." Collier shared many of the beliefs that animated Peru's two great Indianists, José Carlos Mariátegui and Victor Raúl Haya de la Torre.

Furthermore in popular American opinion, Latin Americans were often associated with Indians. But the view that Indians were largely degenerates and impervious to civilization was changing. Rather Indians, and Latin Americans, were thought to be in communion with nature, a characteristic lost to the material, rational, soulless Americans devoted to pragmatism and business. Perhaps a new union with Latin American peoples—a people in touch with their souls and with nature—might redeem American society.[20]

The argument is wonderfully woven by Fredrick Pike to include many other elements relating to spiritual and mystical commonalities between North America and Latin America as the depression spun its black magic across the Americas.[21] The failures of capitalism invited intellectuals and politicians to think in fresh terms of the best possible political, economic, and social relationships between men and government. In this freshet of new water, such Peruvians as Haya and such Americans as the popular journalist Carleton Beals found themselves paddling in the same direction, sometimes, metaphorically speaking, even in the same boat.

Beals met Haya in 1924 in Mexico, and after visiting Peru in the early 1930s "Beals hailed Aprismo as the political force most likely to lead the land to its appointed task of national and hemispheric renewal."[22] To Haya, the mounting anticapitalism of the depression era represented a source of hope. Little less than the hemisphere's rebirth was at hand. "The conversion of Carleton Beals to the *Aprista* cause provided additional confirmation for Haya's optimistic appraisal. By 1938, moreover, Haya believed he had at least a partial convert in Frank Tannenbaum, who by then had begun a teaching career in history and economics at Columbia University that would make him one of the most distinguished Latin Americanists the United States has known."[23]

Tannenbaum and Haya met at Haya's secret hiding place in Lima on September 6, 1938. They had dinner and talked long into the evening, and the next day the U.S. chargé de affairs, Louis G. Dreyfus (ambassador Laurence S. Steinhardt was in Washington on leave), received a report on the meeting supplied willingly by Tannenbaum through the embassy secretary, William P. Cochran. Other contacts between Haya and traveling American intellectuals and diplomats (attending the Eighth Pan-American Congress in Lima in 1938, for example) reinforced Haya's impression that American regeneration was forthcoming—combining and reconciling the best of capitalism and collectivism, of materialism and spiritualism. Haya also had contact with Waldo Frank in the 1930s and early 1940s (meeting once in 1942 in Lima), each seeing in the other a redemptive, visionary person, sharing "mutually regenerationist hopes."[24]

The Paramonga Alternative

If Haya and APRA represented the revolutionary, perhaps even redemptive, visionary, and regenerative soul of Peru that echoed in certain U.S. intellectual and political circles, there was another side to the United States and Peru very much alive and thriving, and just as equally committed to its ideals. This was symbolized by the practically oriented, rational, profit-motivated, free enterprise, marketplace-driven business and commercial ethos shared by many Peruvians and Americans. Perhaps that is too unwieldy a statement. In other words, most Peruvians, and other Americans and U.S. enterprises in Peru, were not planning a political revolution or the mystical regeneration of the old system. Rather, they were building on the platforms that were already there, and, even more important, developing new industries.[25]

While I.P.C. continued to produce oil and Cerro de Pasco to mine, Casa Grace, already the dominant force in textiles and international transportation, for example, struck out in a new direction. Grace's haciendas Cartavio and Paramonga were among the leading sugar producers in Peru. But in the 1930s the price of sugar plummeted on the international markets, and the sugar quota that the United States had established for Peru in 1934 (preference being shown for Cuban sugar) remained low. So there was a surplus of productive capacity. Chile was the principal market for Peruvian sugar in the 1930s, but the Chileans could eat just so much Peruvian sugar. What to do?

Looking for alternate uses of sugar and its by-products, Grace engineers and technicians, directed by Gaston Lipscomb, an Alabama-born engineer then in charge of the small Grace technical office in New York, developed the first commercial process to make paper employing bagasse, the fibrous residue left after the juices had been ground out of sugarcane. Lipscomb directed W. H. Clayton, a South Carolina chemist managing the sugar mill at Cartavio, to do some experiments in his small laboratory there on the north coast of Peru. When Clayton reported some success, an old papermaking plant was purchased at Whippany, New Jersey, bagasse was imported from Cartavio on a Grace Line steamer, and further experiments in New Jersey proved that it could be done. Lipscomb took Clayton to Germany in 1937 where they ordered a paper machine to specifications. It was shipped in 1938 and installed at Hacienda Paramonga (about one hundred miles north of Lima) in 1939. Paramonga, unprofitable since its purchase by Grace in 1927, turned the corner in 1940. The immediate success of the first paper machine—used to manufacture corrugated boxes—prompted the continued expansion and development of the papermaking facilities at Paramonga, until by 1969 five machines were on line producing tons of paper for Peru and for export.

The Paramonga complex—expanded in the 1960s to include the production of the essential building block of modern plastics, polyvinyl chloride (the ubiquitous PVC)—is described as a counterpoint to this section on Haya and the political, intellectual, and sometimes even mystical relationship between the United States and Peru in the 1920s and 1930s. While many Peruvians were attracted to APRA and its promises of redemptive, revolutionary change, just as many Peruvians were drawn to the equally compelling attraction of a Paramonga. What Peru needed was more Paramongas. This paper-chemical industrial complex became in the 1950s and 1960s the focal point of visits by technologists, engineers, and planners from many parts of the developing world, and the U.S. and Peruvian technicians who ran Paramonga showed it off with immense pride as an example of combined Peruvian-U.S. engineering and technology.

What we are entering here—especially in the post–World War II era—is a complex phase of the U.S. presence in Peru. Petroleum workers in Talara, technicians in Paramonga, and salespeople for Sears, Roebuck (established in Lima in the 1950s) did not view the United States from the same vantage point as mineworkers in the shafts of the Cerro de Pasco mines in the 1930s. A transition was under way at mid-century that changed the tone of Peruvian-U.S. relations, and we shall examine it shortly below. However, as Paramonga installed its first paper machine from Germany in 1939, Hitler was preparing to drive into Poland and, ultimately, to set off the firestorm of the Second World War.

The War Years

The advent of the war brought Haya and the United States closer together. With the enunciation of the four freedoms by President Roosevelt—freedom from want, fear, freedom of expression and worship—Haya "grew convinced that the United States was in the throes of a profound transformation" that brought Haya's vision of Peru into accord with Roosevelt's New Deal America. The premise that "to gain liberation from want and fear, humans had to temper Western democracy's customary concern with self-reliance and accept dependence upon a strong central government, charged with the planned allocation of resources," fit into Haya's political philosophy well.[26]

Raoul de Roussy de Sales, in his work *The Making of Tomorrow* published in 1942, "stressed the difficulty of reconciling the opposing thrusts of the four freedoms. Western men would resist a 'general lowering of the spirit of enterprise,' and if governments pushed too hard in the direction of planning they would impede individual freedom, 'which, as we know, is the condition of all human progress.'"[27] Yet de Sales remained optimistic that a compromise would be achieved between the conflicting principles of liberty and equality, and Haya shared this feeling, "concluding that out of the historical space-time of America had emerged a new point of view, exemplified by the very enunciation of the four freedoms, that would create a synthesis of state planning and individual liberty."[28]

Peruvians generally lined up with the United States against the Axis powers, although Peru did not declare war until 1944. Even before 1941 the United States was actively promoting hemispheric solidarity in the face of increasing fascist ideology and influence in Latin America.

However President Oscar Benavides of Peru was not a fan of the United States, its people, or its institutions. He had spent many years in Europe, especially in France and Italy, in various military and diplomatic missions, and was disposed to favor Germans and Italians equally with Americans in Peru's relations with foreigners. Fascist in political orientation, Benavides challenged the ongoing prewar U.S. effort to create a solid, democratic Western Hemisphere front.[29]

In Peru of the 1930s, for example, the leading bank was the Banco Italiano controlled by its manager, Gino Salocchi, with fascist political sympathies and a close friendship with President Benavides. The Banco Italiano was financed by U.S., Italian, and Swiss capital and was the most popular and successful bank for the expanding urban and service markets of Lima.[30] Purchases of Italian military equipment during the 1930s by the Benavides regime were made possible by the Banco Italiano, which also counted the Cerro de Pasco Corporation among its good clients. The Banco Italiano was a sound, conservative, popular institution that serviced the financial and credit needs of Peruvian-based industries and corporations. Fascist politics aside, it made good sense for Cerro to do business with the Banco Italiano. In 1941 the bank changed its name to the Banco de Crédito to avoid the titular affiliation with Italy, and it continued to be the leading domestic banking institution in Peru through the 1950s. It was later challenged by such newcomers as the Banco Continental, bankrolled, appropriately enough, given the growing U.S. investments in Peru in the postwar period, by the Rockefellers' Chase Manhattan Bank of New York.[31]

With the election to the presidency of Manuel Prado y Ugarteche (1939–45), a close friend of the United States and democracy, the United States could count on friendship from Peru during the war years rather than the coolness of a Benavides. Prado's government cooperated very closely with the United States on a number of fronts, and, in many ways, presaged the increasing dependence of Peru on U.S. markets, U.S. capital, and on the United States in general in the second half of the century. Furthermore Peru's special envoy to Washington during the war years (he became ambassador in 1944) was Pedro Beltran, another friend of the United States who promoted close cooperation between the two nations.[32]

Peru was the ideal ally during the war. In one of its most controversial acts, Prado's government cooperated very closely with the United States in controlling Peru's sizable Japanese-Peruvian colony by arrests, deportations, and confiscation of properties. Nearly two thousand Japanese-Peruvians were deported to the United States where thousands of Japanese-Americans were also interned for the duration of the war. Internal Peruvian realities—nationalism, jealousy of the successful Japanese-Peruvians, simple greed for the properties—combined with the desire to maintain good relations with the United States to produce the tragic persecution of the Japanese-Peruvian population.

The production and acquisition of essential war materials, such as rubber, copper, vanadium, petroleum, molybdenum, chinchona bark, and other jungle products proceeded smoothly with U.S. assistance. Cotton purchases were also increased, while the Lend-Lease Program made millions of dollars worth of arms and armaments available to Peru.[33] An airstrip near Talara was built, not only to protect the oil fields of I.P.C. in the area, but to control the perimeter around the Panama Canal, so vital to the United States in maintaining a two-ocean naval presence. President Prado made a goodwill visit to Washington, and Vice President Henry Wallace reciprocated in 1943.

Wallace, who was elected as Roosevelt's running mate in 1940, was hailed by Haya as the true representative of Roosevelt's New Deal reconciling liberty and equality. Wallace wrote that "it becomes a modern duty to make individual and group interests coincide" in the new democracy and that good men should be intent on securing peace, security, and the good life. Haya felt that Wallace was the political counterpart of Waldo Frank, all three—Haya, Frank, and Wallace—sustaining the vision of the new world where convergence and harmony and reconciliation would prevail.[34]

Wallace sounded like an Indian regenerationist in his public pronouncements in Peru, with phrases that rang sweetly to old Indianists like Haya. The Indians of Peru were extolled by Wallace for "inventing the concept of social justice in America" and for their communal labor practices and agricultural prowess.[35]

For Haya, Wallace represented a number of positive American trends, such as anti-imperialism, which Haya had sensed first hand in his travels through the United States in the 1920s. A "spiritualist, visionary strain that he had encountered among certain sensitive Americans in the 1920s, beginning with Anna Melina Graves, who had been a colleague at Lima's Colegio Anglo Peruano" also triggered echoes in Haya's philosophy.[36] However Henry Wallace, Waldo Frank, and others who Haya so admired proved not so prophetic in describing the postwar world. Instead of convergence, the Cold War divided the world for almost half a century.

But Haya's good feelings for the United States endured. His obvious pro-U.S. sympathies, which angered many of his more militant followers, persisted and led to the gradual abandonment of radicalism and revolution in favor of accommodation and moderate politics from midcentury on. Indeed the glow of cooperation from the war years produced a number of long-term repercussions.

The Second World War invigorated the Peruvian economy, which benefited from increased exports to the United States and from the expansion of its own domestic manufacturing to make up for war shortages. In the United States, Nelson Rockefeller, one of John D. Rockefeller's many talented grandsons, emerged as a principal booster of Latin America. As Peru and the United States moved through the second half of the twentieth century, one of the prime criticisms of Peruvians was that few in the United States knew or cared about the needs of their country. Nelson Rockefeller went against that stream—a move that garnered some attention among major U.S. political leaders of the era.

After two trips to Latin America, Nelson, then thirty-two, approached President Roosevelt in July 1940 very anxious "that the fall of Western Europe to the Nazis that summer was having a devastating effect on the economies of Latin America."[37] Axis propaganda and perhaps even German penetration was undermining U.S. influence and interests. Roosevelt offered Rockefeller, the young scion of Republican prominence, the chance to head a new organization, the Office of Inter-American Affairs, which became "one of the glamour agencies to work for in wartime Washington."[38] The dynamic Rockefeller worked for one dollar, the eagerest of the eager beavers according to one observer. He even appeared on the cover of *Life* magazine, moving into the national limelight as a celebrity in his own right.

But the Office of Inter-American Affairs was more than a stage for Rockefeller. It was the predecessor to the "Point Four Program" announced by President Harry S. Truman in his 1949 inaugural address to make "the benefits of our scientific advances and industrial progress available for the improvement and growth of underdeveloped areas."[39] And the Point Four marked a major transition in U.S. foreign policy toward Peru and the rest of the world, for its commitment "ultimately made foreign aid a permanent element of national policy." Unlike the temporary and sporadic foreign assistance of the past, Point Four envisioned a long-term, continuous mission.

Rockefeller's initiatives presaged much of the increasingly diversified activities that characterized relations in the postwar period between the United States and Peru and Latin America generally. Inter-American trade was fostered to help the region make up for the loss of European markets, the first U.S. foreign propaganda effort was launched, and numerous cultural exchange programs were initiated.

Promoting good health in Latin America was a priority for Rockefeller. The philanthropic streak in Nelson's character came from both his father and grandfather. His grandfather, John D. Rockefeller, a ruthless capitalist titan, also supported missionaries of his generation, and, through the Rockefeller Foundation, his son and grandsons provided for large-scale assistance in medicine and public health to Latin America. Rockefeller was able to obtain major government funds during the war for public health and medicine because the efforts directly contributed to the health and welfare of Americans in the tropics, building airfields and extracting crucial war materials, for example.[40]

In Peru the organization created for combating tropical diseases and promoting health was SCISP (the Servicio Cooperativo Interamericano de Salud Pública), established in 1942 largely with U.S. funds from Rockefeller's institute. During the war years, five dispensaries were built in the Amazonian department of Loreto, nine medically equipped launches were put into service on the Amazon and its tributaries, and other improvements along the northern coast—draining and clearing swamps around the coastal city of Chimbote, for example—were accomplished.[41] Although Chimbote had little strategic value, it was selected because Peruvians viewed it as key to the commercial development of the northern coast. After the war SCISP expanded its activities to include building hospitals, promoting health demonstrations and health centers in rural back-country areas, and training health service workers both in Peru and the United States. By mid-1958 the United States had contributed almost $3.4 million to SCISP since its inception. Peru's share of the costs increased so that by 1960 the majority of the budget was coming from Peruvian sources. This was the way Rockefeller and his associates envisioned the program, one whose responsibilities were gradually transferred to the host country where it would demonstrate "the efficacy of public health."[42] Another program was established by Rockefeller's institute during the war to promote agricultural production and modern agricultural techniques. In Peru this agency, founded in agreement with Peru's Department of Agriculture, was known as SCIPA (Servicio Cooperative Interamericano de Produción de Alimentos). Agricultural experiment stations were established, the first at the jungle town of Tingo Maria in 1942. After the war SCIPA enlarged its activities to include improving livestock breeds, introducing better seeds, tools, insecticides and equipment, and establishing an agricultural extension service. By 1958 almost $13 million had been spent on SCIPA, an increasing amount of its budget subscribed to by Peru as envisioned by Rockefeller and his planners during the war.

The modern student of Peru and the United States, and of the United States and Latin America in general, tends to view the 1960s as the formative period in true "people-to-people" programs. The celebrated Peace Corps established by President John F. Kennedy in 1961 symbolized the concern of the United States with helping the developing world. But, as we look back carefully, much of this type of assistance was already being conceived and implemented during the war years.

Rockefeller's choice to head the medical area of the institute was a distinguished military physician, Brig. Gen. George Dunham. Dr. Dunham was packing his bags for Europe to serve in the coveted billet of chief physician to the U.S. Army when Rockefeller intervened and brought him on board at his own institute.[43]

Dunham, who received a Doctor of Public Health degree from Johns Hopkins University (and further training at the London School of Tropical Medicine) and with long experience in tropical medicine in the Philippines and Panama, matched Rockefeller's commitment to long-term public health programs instead of supporting patch-up jobs to meet wartime needs. Indeed the social and economic development of Third World countries (although the term "Third World" did not come into circulation until the 1950s) was closely tied, in the minds of Rockefeller and Dunham, to making basic health services available and effective. The specialists who Dunham selected to serve on the *Servicios* in Latin America were devoted, like their boss, to working closely with their counterparts in Latin America, learning the true nature of local problems as they applied the best of modern medical and agricultural practices. Education was a crucial factor in the *Servicio* programs, and the facilities and hospitals became centers of teaching for doctors, nurses, and laboratory workers. Even the quintessential American form of entertainment, the movies, were drafted into the effort of educating the public in health education.

Health films were shown in clinics, theaters, schools, union halls, housing projects, and social clubs. They were trucked into remote villages where some of the favorites were Walt Disney–produced animated shorts on infant care, the hazards of contaminated water, and the danger of disease-bearing mosquitoes. Even the Seven Dwarfs were volunteered by their creator to help with this war on disease, marching in at the end of the short animated film *Winged Scourge* to show their viewers how to destroy the nasty pests—principally the Anopheles mosquito—with the characteristic vigor and wit of Snow White's little friends.

These various programs, although driven by much altruism and idealism, always were focused on tropical areas where U.S. troops and personnel were stationed, or which might become staging areas for transporting strategic materials, a reminder that this was a wartime effort where national security was primary. In this can be seen some of the duality of purpose in the U.S. interest in Peru over the years, not just during the Second World War. Some of the interest was motivated in part by a high-minded devotion to noble ideals, but it was also well grounded in self-interest. Whether paternalistic, self-serving, or altruistic, the upshot was that hundreds of U.S. agricultural and medical experts trained and taught thousands of their Latin American counterparts, and the rewards were much more gratifying than the simple satisfaction of wartime demands.

Peru received about $2.3 million in assistance, ranking fifth in total aid after Brazil, Chile, Mexico, and Ecuador. Rockefeller and Dunham continuously broadened the scope of their mandate—officially aimed only at protecting U.S. bases and servicemen and obtaining strategic materials—to include public health in its true context—health education and health services for the public. They attracted a number of critics.

In Congress they tangled with the House Appropriations Committee. There Dunham and Rockefeller defended their actions, especially in broadening the public health program to cut across all areas of national life, not just those narrowly construed as related to the war effort.

In 1944 Roosevelt appointed Rockefeller an assistant secretary of state, and Rockefeller expanded his vision to include assistance and long-term cooperation in the fields of public health, nutrition and food supply, education, science, culture, information, transportation, and economic development, including the industrialization and modernization of agriculture.[44] There was little that "Rocky" left off.

In a memorandum to Roosevelt early in 1945 proposing to extend the life and success of the institute beyond the war, Rockefeller argued his philosophy. "These are the basic factors," he wrote the president, "which contribute to the development and dignity of the individual, a rising standard of living and the growth of democracy. Only in this way can we hope to have economic, social and political stability among the nations of this Hemisphere—without which we can never realize the permanent unity of the Americas."[45] Roosevelt shared the vision, but he was a dying man. In April 1945 he succumbed to a stroke. Rocky was soon gone from the Department of State, which was reshuffled to fit the needs of the new president, Harry S. Truman. The institute survived into the 1950s, many of its principles and goals subsumed in the Point Four Program announced by Truman in 1949 and eventually given new life through various agencies created in the 1960s, such as the Agency for International Development and the Peace Corps, for example.

Rockefeller returned to family business and politics but never abandoned Latin America. When it became apparent that the Marshall Plan launched by the United States in 1948 to restore Europe to prosperity had no Latin American counterpart, Rockefeller launched a Marshall Plan of his own design for Latin America, the American International Association. Such was the power of a Rockefeller. "AIA was to help modernize the region's educational, health and agricultural infrastructure. AIA was nonprofit and philanthropic. Its commercial counterpoise was IBEC, the International Basic Economy Corporation, Nelson's chosen instrument to deliver to Latin America the blessings of Yankee enterprise, the supermarket, mass distribution and low retail prices, all at a fair profit."[46] This was liberty to the core, emphasizing the market economy, free enterprise, and profits, all bundled with a social conscience. In fact Rockefeller's social conscience was so well developed that it prompted his successor at the State Department, Spruille Braden, to describe the Rockefeller group as possible "communist-fellow-travelers" who, if not card-carrying Communists, were, at the least, "do-gooders and one-worlders like so many in federal agencies at the time."[47] Yet, much of what would follow in President John F. Kennedy's Alliance for Progress created in 1961 echoed the principles that drove Rocky and his associates.

Rocky's IBEC initially lost $7 million of his own personal fortune in the first decade, but "he retreated, consolidated, lowered his sights, and kept the operation afloat. The failures were not necessarily those of an entrepreneur with more money than brains. *He was trying to go beyond the bottom line and to wed the profit motive to social change in foreign and often resistant cultures.*"[48]

In 1949, after four years in private life, Rocky was prompted by President Truman's Point Four to return to public life.[49] Truman appointed him chairman of a committee to advise on implementing Point Four, which had been patterned after Rockefeller's own AIA.[50] Yet the mood in the United States had changed in the wake of the Second World War. Desperate to get back to normal and on with their lives, Americans in general turned their backs on Peru and Latin America. But not for long.

6   The Early Cold War Period

The end of the Second World War brought on a profound sigh of relief on the part of the weary combatants. The next two decades was a halcyon period. The United States enjoyed an unprecedented prosperity and a rising middle class, while in Peru economic development and political stability prevailed, although coups in 1948 and 1963 temporarily disturbed political tranquillity. Until the 1960s economic and political liberty took priority over social equality, and both countries shared a similar vision.

Not everything was rosy. Peruvian exports to the United States decreased markedly in the immediate postwar period, leading to some economic dislocations, inflation, and labor unrest. By the Korean War, however, the tempo of Peruvian-U.S. trade activity once again picked up. New and increased investments by private U.S. industrial and commercial enterprises, a wide expansion of government-to-government assistance and loans (through Point Four, AID, military assistance pacts, etc.), and a common economic and political wisdom made for a period of general tranquillity and prosperity in relations. Indeed the period from 1948 to 1968 was described by English economists Rosemary Thorp and Geoffrey Bertram as "a remarkable twenty year period of [Peru's] total integration into the international system, with complete commitment to the rules of the game"—the rules-making being largely presided over by the United States.

The most obvious framework for relations during this period was the Cold War. Basically the United States and Peru believed communism was a menace to be opposed and destroyed. Furthermore many in the United States thought their country was endowed with an exceptional nature that should be shared with the world. Peter Marshall, the chaplain to the U.S. Senate during the late 1940s, wonderfully captured this mood in his sermon "The American Dream." "World events," Marshall said, "today are forcing us, whether we realize it or not, to rediscover the meanings and the significances of the things that make America *different* [emphasis added] from other nations . . . the hope of a world weary of war, heartsick and hungry."

"Ours is a Covenant Nation [with much] to give to the rest of the world," Marshall continued, hammering home his message that "America [is] good enough to lead the world, to make the American Dream of equal opportunity for all men come true."

Finally he stated the message with startling clarity, summing up the feelings of his age. "We have to give more of the only thing, after all, that makes our life different from theirs, namely, our ideals, our faith, our philosophy of life, our concept of human dignity, our Bill of Rights, our American Dream." [1]

Yet this high-reaching goal often conflicted with other realities, giving Peruvian observers good reason to label U.S. foreign policy as somewhat cynical. Sometimes dictators in Latin America, such as Manuel Odría in Peru (who ruled from 1948 to 1956), helped promote vital U.S. economic and political interests. Odría's regime was procapitalist and anti-Communist and not particularly democratic. Yet the United States accommodated Odría, as it did numerous dictatorships in other parts of Latin America from the 1940s through the 1960s, because *in the main*, they served U.S. interests, even if sacrificing political democracy while doing so.

Heavily dependent upon the export of minerals, the Peruvian economy became even more closely tied to the United States' economy and sensitive to the fluctuations in the world market. When the import of minerals to the United States declined in the period 1945–50, Peru's economy slumped. Stimulated by the Korean War, mineral exports increased, and Peru's economy rose. And when the United States curtailed imports in 1957 for example (ending a policy of stockpiling key raw materials), Peru's economy sagged again. Tied into a capitalist economy and driven by free-market forces was akin to being on a roller coaster, with someone else determining the curves, the ups, the downs, and the timing of the ride. It was exhilarating at times, immensely frustrating at others. The frustrations led to one of the most fascinating and disruptive incidents in the modern history of Peruvian-U.S. relations—the visit of then Vice President Richard M. Nixon to Peru in 1958. Other bumps on the road kept the relationship from lapsing into happy tedium.

Ten years earlier in 1948, when the Marshall Plan was declared for the restoration of Europe, Peru took offense. In February 1948 the Peruvian Minister of Foreign Relations, Enrique García Sayan, criticized the plan for failing to take into account the Latin American *"problematica,"* in the jargon of the times. In other words while all the efforts of the Marshall Plan were aimed at restoring Europe to a productive and prosperous region, what would become of Latin America?[2] Latin America had furthered its industrial capacity during the war. What would happen when Europe began to regenerate its productive, industrial capacity, especially with such a large infusion of American assistance? The answer—rhetorical—was that the Latin American industrial base—slender and vulnerable at best—would simply not be able to keep up with a recovered Europe, and Latin American industries would once again be put at a competitive disadvantage to Europe. This proved to be correct.

The Peruvians suggested that the Marshall Plan needed to be amended to accommodate Latin America's needs. While Latin America stood to benefit in the short run from the export of raw materials and commodities to Europe, in the long run, it would fall even further behind. Here was a short, but clear, statement of the dependency theory that became so prominent in explaining Peruvian—and Latin American—underdevelopment in the 1950s and 1960s. Raúl Prebisch, an Argentine economist, popularized this theory, which claimed that Latin America was underdeveloped because of a structural dependency upon the industrialized world. To overcome this gap in development, import substitution was suggested as the most appropriate strategy—build or manufacture what had previously been imported, and many of the "dependent" structures would begin to fall. It was especially important to free Latin American economies from the vagaries of the world market. Dependency theory was already well under way as a way of explaining Latin America's relative lack of industrialization and modernization when the Marshall Plan came along and seemed to ignore Latin America in favor of restoring Europe.

What is interesting is the Peruvian proposition that the United States had gone off half-cocked in its determination to restore Europe and had not fully studied the implications of the policy in the Western Hemisphere. The continuing, and deepening, dependence of Peru and Latin America on North America thus produced a conflicted closeness between the regions. But, while differences existed between Peru and the United States on the Marshall Plan, the two generally agreed on their anticommunism stance. This provided a common perspective for an entire generation.

This shared view undergirded the increasing investments and presence of the United States in Peru from mid-century to 1968. Private sector development was in full swing in Peru in the 1950s and 1960s and was promoted by the governments of both Washington and Lima, which viewed economic development as a bulwark against communism.

Perhaps the most ardent anti-Communist in Peru at mid-century was Victor Raúl Haya de la Torre. At one time Haya had been the most combative, anticapitalist, anti-imperialist among Latin America's political leaders. But he was never pro-Communist. In fact, Communists and *Apristas* were bitter competitors in Peru. "I've been to Russia," wrote Haya, "and seen their nationalism; they're convinced they're going to save the world; it's almost mystical," he added, perhaps ingenuously, since the party he had created, APRA, was supported heavily by mystical underpinnings. "Yet their standard of living is inferior to the American, and the little they have acquired has been done at the expense of their liberty. They have bread without liberty. APRA, on the other hand, offers "bread *and* liberty. . . ."[3]

A few years later, in January 1953, the U.S. Secretary of State, John Foster Dulles, stated *his* position vis-à-vis communism, which summarized the nature of the Cold War from the American perspective: "Soviet Communism believes that human beings are nothing more than somewhat superior animals. . . . That the best kind of a world is organized as a well-managed farm. I do not see how, as long as Soviet communism holds those views, there can be any permanent reconciliation. This is an irreconcilable conflict."[4]

"Dulles," wrote a pair of his biographers, "had come to unshakable convictions of a religious and theological order. Like the religious warriors of the sixteenth and seventeenth centuries, he saw the world as an arena in which the forces of good and evil were continuously at war. Like them, he believed that this was the contest which supremely mattered."[5]

"Dulles was an American Puritan[,] very difficult for me, a Lutheran[,] to understand," Albrecht von Kessel, the West German minister in Washington, said. "This partly led him to a conviction that Bolshevism was a product of the devil and that God would wear out the Bolsheviks in the long run."[6] Indeed for Dulles it was nothing less than a religious war, with the stakes much higher than mere economic and political survival.

Here is a potent duo in the equation of relations between Peru and the United States at mid-century. Both countries were committed to destroying the Communist menace to their countries or parties and to realizing their national destinies beyond the yoke of communism, godless to one and tyrannical to the other. Furthermore as noted above, Communists were APRA's leading competitor among labor and student constituencies in Peru and thus a double menace.

"APRA's position is clear," a party directive stated in 1947, "and without reservations. We are opposed ideologically to all imperialism, but denounce, at the same time, the demagogic attempt by the Red or Black Internationale to label this position hostile to the United States. We know the difference between total imperialism, [or totalitarianism] which is not only political and economic, but racist—and an economic imperialism that exists within a democracy, but an imperialism that can be combated and stopped using those liberties which democracy gives and guarantees."[7]

The choice then was between democracy and totalitarianism, a distinction made clear as early as May 20, 1945, when the APRA leadership called upon all Peruvians "of good will, without distinctions and capable of working sincerely for the public good to defend together our Democracy in a great national campaign against the totalitarianism from Moscow."[8] Haya's career thus becomes even more important in defining the relationship between the United States and Peru, for if the distinction between totalitarianism and democracy was the one favored by Washington, it was also the one fostered by Haya and his party.

Haya's career perhaps embodied more irony than most others in modern Peruvian history. He traveled widely through Europe in the 1920s and spent time in the Soviet Union. His impression of Russia under communism was mixed. He was impressed by the "vast and profound national enthusiasm," by a vital and committed youth, by a "vivid faith in the future," but was appalled by the rigidity of Marxism-Leninism.[9] Haya rejected the Soviet brand of communism, and this rejection helped determine the evolution of Peruvian-U.S. relations from then to the end of the century.

Haya's rejection was complex, embodying personal ambition as well as ideology and much of it need not detain us here. Basically Haya associated communism with the Russian world; he came from another world—the one of the Indians of the Andes, the one of Creole Hispanicism of the coast, the one where time and space were different from that in Russia. Later he would develop his own theories about Peruvian space and time. In these theories Haya attempted to reconcile the many extremes in Peruvian society into one political program. From these reflections there emerged the modern configuration of APRA.

On a practical level, Haya's party worked to eliminate Communist control over student and workers associations. In 1944 the Confederation of Peruvian Workers was taken over by the *Apristas,* who also came to control student political organizations at the University of San Marcos and expanded their influence over faculty organizations. Anticommunism for APRA was more than ideological rhetoric: it was about political power, although in Peru a pro-U.S. attitude could get a political activist in trouble when nationalist sentiments were running strong.

For example, in 1946 and 1947, President José Luis Bustamante y Rivero's administration, supported by *Aprista* members in the Peruvian Congress, signed a contract with I.P.C. to explore and exploit new petroleum reserves in Sechura. The Sechura Contract was attacked by a strange coalition of Communists and capitalists. Bustamante and APRA were accused of betraying the national interests, of toadying to the United States and I.P.C. When a major critic of the contract, Francisco Graña Garland, the publisher of *La Prensa,* was assassinated January 7, 1947, *Apristas* were immediately singled out as the culprits. APRA struck back. The Communists were accused by APRA of being the real assassins who were following orders directly from Moscow with the intention of discrediting APRA.

Meanwhile Haya was traveling through the United States in 1947 and 1948, where he gave a series of talks at U.S. universities. While traveling and lecturing Haya met with Walt Disney in Hollywood and talked with Alfred Einstein at Princeton. When he returned to Peru, the *Aprista* newspaper, *La Tribuna,* assured its readers that Haya had been received as one of the most notable men in the world, comparing him in stature to Roosevelt or Ghandi. Even given journalistic hyperbole, there is no doubt that at mid-century Haya represented Latin American radicalism more notably than anyone else in the hemisphere. That he met with two of the most famous men in America, one the pioneering cartoonist and the other the most important physicist since Sir Isaac Newton, certainly gives *La Tribuna*'s claims some credibility. That Disney was a profoundly committed conservative in his politics endows the meeting between the *Aprista* and the creator of Mickey Mouse with a significance beyond mere curiosity.

Haya's politics in the 1950s sought the strengthening of ties with the United States. Colleagues and critics within the party chided Haya with the news that the Good Neighbor policy was dead, and interventionism was once more in vogue. But Haya was not easily dissuaded from seeing Marxism as the most dangerous competitor of APRA, not simply ideologically, but, as we have seen, practically as well. Furthermore Haya continued to view Washington as APRA's friend, encouraging the United States to take strong positions against militarism and dictatorships, such as that of Odrías, for example. And if Washington could be convinced that democracy was the best defense against communism, well, there stood APRA, representing democracy against militarism and dictatorship in Peru.[10]

In fact the Eisenhower administration in the 1950s did not discriminate rigidly between Latin American dictatorships or democracies, as long as they were anti-Communist. By the 1960s this rigid anticommunism was moderated by critics within the United States, such as J. William Fulbright, chairman of the powerful Senate Foreign Relations Committee.

In his best-selling *Arrogance of Power,* which appeared in 1966, Fulbright argued that American policy makers simplistically identified revolutions with communism. In fact Americans were of two minds toward revolutions: on the one hand, they feared the phenomenon; on the other, they supported social reforms that often came in a revolutionary format in Latin America.[11] Fulbright identified this ambiguity in American thinking, with a dominant strand of democratic humanism (the altruistic, idealistic strand) and a lesser, but durable, strand of intolerant Puritanism, which, in this instance, was well represented by Dulles's intransigence on communism.

The shared vision of communism was more than an ideological construct that united some intellectuals and politicians in the United States and Peru. It had a very practical dimension, well exemplified by the modern military and naval relations between Peru and the United States.

Modern-Era Naval and Air Force Missions

In the anti-Communist, Cold War framework, the Peruvian military establishment grew in importance during the 1960s and was truly challenged in the 1980s by the Shining Path terrorist movement. How these institutions were woven into the larger tapestry of Peruvian-U.S. relations from the 1940s to the 1970s informs us considerably on the nature of the relations.

While the U.S. naval mission—so closely associated with the Leguía regime—was somewhat discredited in 1930 with the overthrow of Leguía, the links between the U.S. Navy and the Peruvian Navy were only frayed, certainly not broken. The naval mission was reestablished in 1938 by President Oscar Benavides, himself an army general, to renew the progressive development of the navy started in the 1920s and to combat growing Italian influences in that service. Benavides had trained with the French before the First World War and was a confirmed Francophile. This U.S. naval mission, staffed by four officers initially, lasted in some form until 1946. Each of the officers, as in the 1920s, held actual rank in the Peruvian Navy, such as chief of naval operations, inspector general, fleet commander, and in various directorates.[12] The naval mission continued after 1946, but its members only served in advisory and technical roles, no longer holding command and rank in the Peruvian Navy.

The ties forged earlier between the navies of the United States and Peru served as a foundation for increased cooperation in the post–World War II era. World War II surplus U.S. destroyers and smaller vessels were acquired by the Peruvians, and, beginning in the 1950s, joint tactical exercises commenced between the two navies. In 1968 the Peruvian fleet consisted of two cruisers, two destroyers, three destroyer escorts, and four submarines. Except the two cruisers acquired from Great Britain, all were from the United States. The close relationship between the navies was symbolized by the training of Peruvian naval cadets at the U.S. Naval Academy. Since the Second World War, Annapolis reserved three spaces every four years for Peruvian nationals, and these were always filled.[13]

Old habits were even revived for a short while in 1948. An aborted revolt against the government of President José Luis Bustamante y Rivero compromised hundreds of naval officers and men who had conspired unsuccessfully with the APRA party to overthrow Bustamante. In the general fallout, many officers were forced into retirement, including the director of the Naval Academy. In his place U.S. Navy captain Gordon A. MacLean was appointed to run the academy, while Lt. Cdr. Jack Roudebush was appointed to administer the Naval War College.[14]

Peru's Air Force also forged close ties with its U.S. counterpart in the post–World War II era, although perhaps not as intimately as those between the navies. The bulk of the air force's weaponry came, as in the case of all the armed forces, initially from surplus U.S. arms left over from the Second World War. By the 1950s and 1960s, newer jet aircraft and trainers, such as Korean War era F-86s jet fighters and T-37 jet trainers, were also added under the Military Assistance Program (MAP) signed between Peru and the United States in 1952. Occasional purchases from other arms manufacturers—a squadron of British-made Hawker Hunter fighter bombers in the late 1950s and a small number of French-made helicopters in the same time frame—supplemented the acquisition of U.S.-supplied equipment. The equipment, including a steady flow of spare parts, auxiliary gear, and supplies, was supplemented by intensive training of Peru's air force personnel on U.S. bases both in the United States and the Panama Canal Zone. Almost five thousand Peruvian Air Force officers and men took courses or were trained on U.S. bases between 1952 and 1968 for example. "One result of all this exposure to U.S. instruction is that Peruvian military schools have largely adopted U.S. techniques and methods of teaching which have helped to improve the quality of their own graduates."[15]

But training in the United States and exposure to American culture did not necessarily guarantee a pro-American attitude. In 1968 ten of the fifteen top Peruvian Air Force officers had studied or trained in the United States. Were they predisposed by this exposure and training to view the United States favorably in the course of U.S. relations with Peru? Yes, in some instances, and most definitely no, in others (as we shall see below when we examine the "tuna/fishing wars" between the United States and Peru in the 1950s and 1960s, and at what happened when the Peruvians sought to modernize their air force in 1967 and 1968).

The military training and travel programs were not entirely one-sided. An interesting set of exchanges took place in the 1960s and 1970s where a small number of U.S. military officers studied in Peruvian institutions, giving U.S. officers insights into Peruvian priorities and lifestyles. Curiously neither the Peruvian Air Force nor Army had made extensive use of the quotas provided for them in the U.S. Air Force Academy (Colorado Springs) or the U.S. Military Academy (West Point), in contrast to the navy's relationship with the U.S. Naval Academy (Annapolis).

The U.S. Military Missions to Peru

While the influence of the United States was particularly large in the Peruvian Navy, and substantial in the Peruvian Air Force, it was the Peruvian Army that dominated the military establishment. When the military intervened in politics in the modern era—by Sánchez Cerro in 1930, by Gen. Manuel A. Odría in 1948, the coup of 1962, the Peruvian Institutional Revolution of 1968, the Alberto Fujimori *autogolpe* (also referred to as the "autocoup") of 1992—and produced contretemps in Peruvian-U.S. relations, the interventions were led, or supported, by the army. The navy and air force could be useful allies, or irritating critics, but it was the army that forged the history. What was the relationship between the U.S. military and the Peruvian Army?

The Peruvian Army traditionally sought its models in Europe, not the United States. French military advisers had been in Peru in one fashion or another since 1896, and scores of Peruvian officers, such as the general and president Benavides, had received their training, their inspiration, and their models from France. After World War II, Peru's military refocused their concentration on the methods of the United States rather than France. The disastrous military defense of France in 1940 against the German juggernaut certainly diminished the attraction of studying French strategy and tactics. The onset of the Cold War also brought Peru into closer contact with the U.S. military establishment as international communism threatened the hegemony of the United States in the Western Hemisphere. The plain dominance of the United States in post–World War II hemispheric politics and economic structures also drew the Peruvian military into the orbit of the United States. Not only were the new doctrines of total war associated with atomic age weaponry being developed in the United States, but, more practically for Peru, conventional training and equipment were being made available by the United States. Later, especially during the 1960s when counterinsurgency became one of the principal concerns of the Peruvian military, the United States again became a source of not only doctrine but training.

The Military Assistance Program (MAP) signed between Peru and the United States on February 22, 1952, was the linchpin of the modern relationship between the two forces from then until the early 1970s (although the first sixteen-man U.S. military mission began working in Peru in July 1944). The MAP raised the level of military aid, loans, and outright grants from thousands to millions of dollars. In 1952, for example, military aid was $100,000; in 1956, it totaled $9.1 million. From

1952 to 1967, MAP delivered to Peru $73.2 million, the third-largest program in Latin America after those in Brazil and Chile.[16] That Peru received so much can be ascribed to a number of factors: to continue support of the strong anti-Communist stance of President Odría's regime; as a recognition of the high rate of U.S. investments in Peru producing such strategically important minerals as copper, lead, zinc, and vanadium, for example; and, equally important, to preclude the deployment of U.S. troops to the region as had been necessary during the Second World War.

Traditionally the Peruvian military had had a dual mission: one, to protect and defend the nation against external aggression (read Chile and Ecuador for all practical purposes in the latter half of the twentieth century); and, two, to provide for internal peace and order. After the triumph and consolidation of the Fidel Castro Communist regime in Cuba in 1960, a supplement to the second role developed: confronting and combating Communist, or Communist-inspired, guerrilla revolutionary movements. Concomitant with this latter role was the growing realization among Peruvian officers that a long-term response to internal subversion and insurgency had to include the promotion of social and economic development. Peru's problems in the distribution of wealth and power were apparently insurmountable to the politicians. These caused insurgency movements, such as in 1965, which threatened not only law and order, but the existence of the military as an institution. Given the failures of the politicians, and the needs of the nation, the military increasingly viewed itself as the best institution to promote social justice and economic development to reduce and eliminate the circumstances that gave rise to poverty, inequality, injustice, and, in the end, insurgency movements. The implications of such thinking would result in an amazing revolution in October 1968.

In 1965 a combination of Cuban and Communist-inspired revolutionaries in Peru led by Luis de la Puente Uceda and Héctor Béjar declared a Cuban model revolutionary *foco* (band or cadre of revolutionaries) in existence to prosecute a people's war, and, additionally, to end the influence of the "Great Monster of the North" (i.e., the United States) in Peru. That revolutionary effort lasted about seven months and was largely confined to the Sierra before being suppressed by the army in a campaign that claimed perhaps as many as eight thousand peasants killed and thousands of acres scorched by napalm. Significantly Peru's counterinsurgency units had been largely trained in U.S. bases, receiving both doctrine and weapons to prosecute this new type of warfare.

Since 1949 Peruvian officers had been training at the U.S. Army's School of the Americas in the Panama Canal Zone or at the Army's Special Warfare Center and School at Ft. Bragg, North Carolina. Between 1949 and 1964, more than eight hundred soldiers trained there, and from the early 1960s, a number had completed the internal security courses that included counterinsurgency, jungle operations, airborne training, civic action, and psychological warfare. The Peruvian Army formed an elite counterinsurgency unit under the command of Col. Gonzalo Briceño Zevallos in the early 1960s and many Peruvian officers were eager to demonstrate their unit's capability when insurgency movements erupted in 1965 in the Peruvian Sierra. Even CIA-trained operatives were employed in the successful campaign of 1965, which, along with a policy of taking few prisoners and the use of napalm, emphasized the military's urgency to stamp out this guerrilla movement.[17]

By the mid- to late 1960s, Peruvian military officers, many of them trained in the United States, had been moving away from their traditional roles as defenders of the nation (from external threats) and defenders of the status quo (in league with the old oligarchy), to a more progressive, interventionary role in the nation. This stressed new solutions to a society still divided by race, geography, and class. In 1950 the Center for Higher Military Studies (*Centro de Altos Estudios Militares*, or CAEM) was established, modeled loosely on counterparts in France and the United States (the National War College), to study national war doctrine and how it related to basic national problems. Although officers who passed through CAEM were not the sole, or perhaps even principal, architects of the radical military-led revolution of 1968, CAEM was certainly a seedbed of thinking on how the military should participate in and promote national development, social justice, and economic equality.

Yet the Peruvian military was not quickly transformed into the government agency so dedicated to social reform and economic justice that seized political power in the 1968 revolution. Soldiers were professionals who sought U.S. military assistance to prepare themselves to better fulfill their mission, which could be defined in many ways—from the protection of national borders to revolutionary land reform. Disputes with Ecuador over Amazonian boundaries called for a modern, well-equipped traditional military establishment, while saber-rattling with Chile was a proven method to obtain more training and materials.

What happened in 1967, however, represented a significant departure in the relations of the U.S. military with their Peruvian counterparts. In 1967 President Fernando Belaúnde Terry (1963–68) requested from the United States the sale of Northrup F5A Freedom Fighters, an aircraft created especially for export to modernize the air forces of U.S. allies. However, the administration of Lyndon B. Johnson tried to dissuade the Peruvians from purchasing such costly armaments, suggesting instead that economic and social projects take priority in national expenditures.[18] The Peruvians next turned to the French and began negotiations for the sale of twelve highly sophisticated, supersonic Mirage V fighters. The move prompted the U.S. Department of State to approve the sale of the Northrup F5s. But it was too late. Peru was already in an advance state of negotiations with the French, and the about-face by the United States simply irritated an increasingly nationalistic Peru. The deal with France cost the Peruvians about $20 million. In the summer of 1967, the Johnson administration slashed the Military Assistance Program for Latin America, causing further deterioration of Peruvian-U.S. military relations. Several U.S. public officials were quoted prominently in the Peruvian press at the time of these negotiations. The Peruvians were "[p]racticing international blackmail," harrumphed Sen. Wayne Morse, "by buying supersonic fighters outside the United States." Peru would have to fight its "guerrilla bands with machetes and . . . stones" Rep. Silvio Conte said.[19] Daniel Masterson, a specialist on the Peruvian military, observed, "The [F5/Mirage] controversy undermined United States-Peruvian military relations which reached a low point during the [Gen. Juan] Velasco [Alvarado] administration [1968–75] with the expulsion of the United States military mission."[20]

Other points of friction further aggravated deteriorating Peruvian-U.S. military relations. The controversy over the future of I.P.C. reached a climax in 1968, and a long-standing fisheries dispute continued unresolved as Peru adamantly claimed a two-hundred-mile territorial extension of its sovereignty out to sea, while the United States fought to keep the seas open to its fishermen. Superheated rhetoric punctuated and colored *all* relations between the two nations at this stage, with the U.S. Congress passing or invoking various amendments (the Symington Amendment, the Hickenlooper Amendment, the Conte-Long Amendment, the Pelly Amendment; all are discussed below) that put the squeeze on countries like Peru that threatened U.S. interests (read I.P.C. in Peru's case) or contravened U.S. foreign policy (for instance the purchasing of Mirages instead of F5s).[21]

It should be remembered that the Peruvian military, especially the army, possessed long professional and sentimental ties to the French military establishment. Peruvian officers had associated themselves with the American military since the Second World War, but they did not sever their links with the French, or the British, as suppliers of materiel. As Peruvian nationalism increased in the 1960s, so did the desire to move away from dependence upon U.S. arms and instruction. From the perspective of the U.S. military, even more worrisome was Peru's military turn to the Soviet Union for arms and equipment in the 1970s. That in itself was not only an historic departure for Peru's military but a fascinating experiment in the development of Peruvian nationalism vis-à-vis its relations with the United States.

The Fisheries Dispute

"In the predawn hours of February 14, 1969, an English-built Peruvian PT boat, armed with machine guns and 20mm cannon fore and aft, began shadowing United States tuna vessels 40 miles off Peru's coast. At dawn the naval vessel headed for the *Mariner* and collided with the vessel in an attempt to board her. . . . The Peruvians then landed a boarding party which guided the damaged San Diego-based seiner to Talara where her captain was forced to buy a license and matricula, and fined, the total coming to about $10,500."[22]

The Peruvian PT-boat then turned on the *San Diego*, another U.S. tuna boat, and raked her with machine-gun fire that destroyed the windows in the pilothouse, damaged the radio and radar antenna, and barely missed the captain. The U.S. crew hid below decks and let the boat run on automatic pilot while the Peruvians fired upon the fisherman. What was at stake in this incident were two conflicting principles, one held dear by the United States, and one recently staked out by Peru and some of her Latin American neighbors, such as Chile, Ecuador, and Costa Rica. In 1947 and 1948, Chile and Peru (and later other Latin American nations) extended their claims to sovereignty over their seas and its resources two hundred miles out from their coastlines. The United States maintained that the freedom of the seas doctrine precluded any such sweeping declarations beyond the traditional three- and twelve-mile limits. From this basic difference there bubbled up a dispute between Peru and the United States that festered like a boil from the 1940s through the 1980s.

The Humboldt Current that sweeps up from the Antarctic along Peru's coast provides a rich environment for a number of valuable fish, including the anchovy and tuna. The anchovies are caught largely for fish meal, while tuna and other species are processed for more widespread consumption. By the 1950s Peru was the leading producer and exporter of fish resources in the world, so rich were its waters in anchovies. In the 1960s it was not unusual for eight or nine million tons of fish to be exported annually.[23]

Peru came into conflict with the United States when it decided to protect its maritime resources two hundred miles out from its coastline. The United States objected from military, strategic, commercial, and scientific perspectives. From a military point of view, the United States claimed Peru's unilateral declaration implied control of the seas to a distance of two hundred miles. This compromised a critical freedom of the seas thought to be crucial for U.S. national security. The scientific access and management of the world's resources seemed to be at stake as well, although Peru countered that it could scientifically and rationally manage maritime resources as well as the United States or any international body. Furthermore the presence of U.S. tuna boats in the waters claimed by Peru brought the two countries into direct conflict.[24]

From the 1950s through the 1970s, Peru occasionally seized U.S. tuna boats to validate its claims, while the United States continued to deny the validity of Peru's territorial claim. Various pieces of U.S. legislation provided for the reimbursement of fines incurred by the tuna boats, and by 1969 the U.S. government was suspending military assistance agreements as each incident contributed to increasing friction.[25] The estrangement in 1969 and 1970 following the I.P.C. crisis and the first acts of nationalization on the part of the new revolutionary government worsened this long-standing dispute over territorial waters.

Ironically the United States finally accepted the concept of the two-hundred-mile limit. In 1984 the administration of Ronald Reagan extended the United States's claims to various marine resources out two hundred miles—in effect vindicating Peru's position, which by then had been adopted by virtually all Latin America. Yet the United States—as of 1995—had yet to ratify a 1982 United Nations–sponsored law of the sea. The reluctance of the United States to do so is based largely on the interpretation of deep sea mining regulations rather than being a general rejection of the two-hundred-mile concept.

Protestants in Peru

"It seems clear that Haya's [Victor Raúl Haya de la Torre] acquaintance with evangelical Protestantism was not a negligible influence," wrote one historian of Methodism in Peru.[26] Another scholar reflected that under the tutelage of John A. MacKay, a Presbyterian educator in Peru in the 1920s, Haya not only "began to read the Bible and thus to familiarize himself with one of the greatest sources in all literature of regeneration myth and symbol," but "to look upon Christ as a revolutionary and to see in religion a means for basically altering the world." Haya "acquired a new perspective on religion and a renewed conviction that it was possible to change the world through recourse to supernatural power."[27] Indeed when Haya founded the Alianza Popular Revolucionaria Americana, he shaped it "as a religion, [not forgetting] what he had learned from his employer and confidant [MacKay] at the Colegio Anglo Americano."[28]

Influence, defined by *Webster*'s, is "the power of persons or things to affect others, and the effect of such power." Within this definition Protestantism in its many forms, from traditional Protestantism to evangelical, Pentecostal Protestantism, had a profound effect on these two nations while their people formed and developed politically, intellectually, socially, and spiritually, and, ultimately, as they related to each other.

During the nineteenth century few Protestants reached Peru, and even fewer Peruvians went abroad to be possible carriers for introducing new ideas and new denominations into their country. British merchants and their families living in Callao, Lima, Arequipa, and other cities were the first to import Protestant churchmen to minister to their subjects, to perform marriages, to administer the sacraments, and to bury the dead. From midcentury onward other Protestant emissaries began to arrive, but this time not only to minister but to witness. They came as Bible salesmen, as representatives of mission societies (especially Methodists and Presbyterians), as educators who understood that the key to conversion was education. For these Protestant missionaries, learning to read the Bible not only brought one into direct contact with one's Savior, but also was the first link in the long chain of learning that was the key to any modern, progressive man.

While some attempts were made to establish missions before the 1890s, none were successful before the arrival of Thomas Bond Wood, his wife, Ellen, and his three daughters in August 1891. The Presbyterians had established a mission in 1884 under the direction of J. M. Thomson and E. C. White, but it ended in 1886 for lack of financial support. Characteristically, however, the two men had opened a high school as part of their endeavor. Between 1883 and 1886, two missionaries representing the American Bible Society, Andrew Milne and Francisco Penzotti, sold over 5,000 Bibles from Piura in the far north to Tacna and Arica in the south. They were struck by the hardship and widespread poverty in the wake of the disastrous War of the Pacific, but they were equally satisfied that there was a great thirst for the Protestant message. Although Peru only officially tolerated Roman Catholicism, the missionaries went about their business without any official interference until Penzotti was thrown in jail in 1890 for distributing Protestant literature and promoting Protestantism.[29]

Penzotti's experience—he was released in 1891, the same year the Woods arrived—illuminated one of the early areas where Protestants "influenced" the course of Peruvian events. Many liberals in Peru considered freedom of religion as necessary to promote modern commerce, business, industry, and politics. Foreign investors, technicians, and other immigrants would be attracted to Peru if the nation welcomed not only capital and working hands, but tolerated other religions as well. The Woods struggled for an official declaration of freedom of religion for twenty-two years before they returned home in 1913. Two years later Peru provided for freedom of worship, thus fulfilling one of the most cherished goals of missionaries to Peru.

From the 1920s Protestants in Peru were represented by members of the Free Church of Scotland (Presbyterians), the Christian and Missionary Alliance, the Evangelical Union of South America, the Church of the Nazarene, the Seventh Day Adventist Church, and the California Holiness Mission. Of these, the Methodists and Presbyterians were the most active. Fervent social gospellers, they were devoted to the personal conversion of all to Christ and to ministering to the needs of the whole person.

Protestantism's first important impact on Peruvians came with the social gospel movement, which called for the redemption of society through personal salvation. If all were successfully called to a Christian life—born again in terms of scripture—then peace and harmony would ripple out through a society torn by the troubles and dislocations of modernization and industrialization. Social gospellers were social activists, which explained their involvement in the U.S. Progressive movement in the late nineteenth century. They stepped out of their communities, established social programs, and ministered to the poor and displaced. After spiritual conversion, they were devoted to social action—the YMCA, settlement houses, child labor laws, etc.—and to education as the secular counterparts of the inward conversion to Christ. They viewed Peru and her problems as great challenges.

In twentieth-century Peru, perhaps no other problem has been discussed, defined, analyzed, and debated more than one labeled the "Peruvian problem." Peru's greatest historian, Jorge Basadre, called it the problem of Peru's true identity. Victor Andrés Belaúnde, one of the country's most fertile thinkers and a cornerstone of Christian democracy in Peru, entitled two of his most famous books *La realidad peruano* (*The Peruvian Reality;* 1930) and *Peruanidad* (*Peruvian Character;* 1943), as he pondered the Peruvian reality. Appropriate definition of the Peruvian identity—white, *cholo,* Indian, coastal, Andean, corporate, Hispanic, Incaic—might enable the nation's leaders to prescribe the best political and economic system and to articulate a uniform ideology that will guarantee freedom, liberty, work, and dignity, Belaúnde believed.

Consideration of Protestantism in Peru provides an oblique insight into what many viewed as the essence of the Peruvian problem. "We share the opinion of Unamuno, Francisco Garcia Calderón and others," John MacKay, the Presbyterian missionary, opined, "that the religious problem is the main problem of the country and we contend that its solution would give the key to the solution of other problems. The Renaissance has to be in the soul and be manifested in the newer, or if it is wanted, old type of saint."[30] Belaúnde expressed similar beliefs in calling for a spiritual renewal. Certainly economic justice was a sine qua non for the health of the Peruvian body politic and society, but economic justice was not enough. As the historian Jeffrey Klaiber noted, Belaúnde was interested not only in justice but also in forging a nation and a community. Purely secular answers were inadequate. "For him, it was necessary to organize the nation on spiritual and moral bases, inculcating the ideals of service for the common good above every other interest."[31]

We already saw in the previous chapter where the lives of the Presbyterian pastor John A. MacKay and the young Peruvian radical Victor Raúl Haya de la Torre intersected. MacKay came to Peru from Scotland as a missionary and soon founded a school, the Anglo-Peruvian Colegio. Haya found employment there teaching part time to meet expenses while attending San Marcos University and directing the Popular Universities founded by him and other young idealists to bring education to the masses. Two kindred spirits, Luis Alberto Sánchez and Raúl Porras Barrenechea, also taught at Dr. MacKay's school. Sánchez went on to a brilliant career as writer and critic, and APRA stalwart, and Porras Barrenechea became one of Peru's premier historians. Coincidentally Sánchez's doctoral thesis presented at San Marcos in 1922 was entitled *"Nosotros"* ("Us"), a literary study in search of Peruvian reality. Porras, less politically active than Haya or Sánchez, taught at the school until 1934. Under MacKay's Protestant tutelage, and in gatherings at Porras Barrenechea's home, they met to discuss literature, politics, and religion and shared their growing discontent with Leguía's Peru.

Leguía not only seemed to be courting Americans slavishly, but in April 1923 the president was planning to attend a public ceremony conceived by Archbishop Emilio Lisson to consecrate Peru to the Sacred Heart of Jesus. Haya rose in protest. The result was a series of marches and protests sponsored by Haya and others in late May 1923 against Leguía and Lisson's proposed dedication. Haya called for true religious freedom in the land, a rewriting of the constitution to reflect this, and the elimination of many of the old Catholic privileges.

Haya had learned much about religious freedom and liberation at Dr. MacKay's school where the young radical was a favorite among teachers and students. And the older Presbyterian was an ideal tutor. MacKay came to Peru via Madrid where he had studied Spanish and Spanish literature, especially the Spanish mystics. After arriving in Lima in 1917, he enrolled at San Marcos where he wrote a doctoral dissertation on the religious thought of Miguel de Unamuno.[32] MacKay instructed the young Haya not only as MacKay knew the Bible but also from his understanding of the profound spiritual values inherent in Spanish culture itself. There emerged for Haya the Christ of the social gospellers—a Christ who was not only redeemer and savior but a revolutionary who championed the poor. This was not a Christ of suffering and resignation, but a Christ who called on changing the world.

"He [Haya] later made the discovery," MacKay remembered, "that in the writings of the Old Testament prophets and in the teachings of Jesus were more incandescent denunciations of oppression and wrong than he or his companions had ever made."[33] Fredrick Pike, in his biography of Haya, noted that "Haya began to read the Bible and thus to familiarize himself with one of the greatest sources in all literature of regeneration myth and symbol."[34]

According to Pike the Book of Revelation, relying heavily on symbolic language and filled with the noise of redemption and retribution—the "fire and brimstone" so often referred to by students of the Bible—especially appealed to Haya, whose rhetoric often was as hot as the verses of Revelation.

MacKay taught Haya that sometimes the duty of an educator was to "attack everything in society that seems responsible for the suffering and backwardness of men." This was pretty radical, but not revolutionary according to Pike. MacKay was not a social revolutionary, but rather he was devoted to the inward revolution in man when he accepts Christ as redeemer and savior. Through love, kindness, charity, and a strict discipline, the inward transformation would ultimately radiate outwards and transform people as a whole. Or, as Pike phrased it more felicitously, "once he put himself in touch with the divine spirit, beginning by reading the Bible, man would undergo transformation; his life, according to MacKay, would begin to 'give out music as sweet and harmonious as the legendary music of the spheres.'"[35]

Haya saw it slightly differently. He wanted to change Peru, and through MacKay, learned that Christ and the supernatural powers ascribed to him and his believers were powerful weapons. When Haya went on to found and mold his political movement, APRA, "he would not forget what he learned from his employer and confidant at the Colegio Anglo Peruano."[36]

Or, as Jeffrey Klaiber writes, Haya also went on to associate two phases of life—religion and revolution—that he had previously thought incompatible.[37] Haya built his party around this principle: that revolutions must be imbued with religious fervor and even endowed with religious symbols and imagery.

Was MacKay's student simply borrowing the symbols and methods of Christianity? Had he undergone the internal conversion, the "born again" experience, so crucial to the Protestant way, at least as MacKay and other Protestant missionaries to Peru understood it? Perhaps. Perhaps not. But Haya *did* accept many elements of Christian teaching.

Haya told his students at the Popular University of Vitarte that legitimate Christians practiced justice, truth, love, and forgiveness. "The Apostolic Roman Catholic Religion," Haya addressed his students, "is not just candles and flowers. What aroma is more pure than that of a generous action? What flame is more ardent than the fire of love which is practiced."[38] After burying those killed in the May 1923 protests, Haya "brilliantly analyzed Christ by exalting the purity of his doctrine and superiority of his ideals of humanity and justice which were not in line with the absurd prejudices and methods in use."[39]

Love, humanity, justice, and discipline flowed easily from Haya's mind and heart as he learned more and more about the revolutionary, loving Christ from MacKay. Haya was not, however, ready to reject his patrimony, his inheritance as a Peruvian reared in a Roman Catholic tradition, albeit one extremely conservative until waves of reform swept across the Catholic landscape in the second half of the century.

Among Haya's early teachers was not only John MacKay, who later became president of the Princeton Theological Seminary, but Emilio Lisson, the man who became Archbishop and decided to consecrate Peru to the Sacred Heart of Jesus. Haya had studied English and natural sciences in Trujillo with Lisson. When Lisson was installed as Archbishop of Lima in 1918, Haya accompanied his uncle (a priest), Samuel Octavio Haya, to greet the new archbishop. Lisson's private secretary was none other than Uncle Samuel Octavio.[40]

On May 3, 1923, Lisson and Haya appeared on the same program to inaugurate a new school for worker's children in Lima. Lisson remembered his former pupil well and stayed to chat. "Revolutions are by nature destructive Victor Raúl," the old teacher lectured one of his aptest, but most critical, students.

"Excellency, you dignify your calling by coming here to bless the school and to address social problems," Haya responded, praising his old mentor. "But," he continued, in a more challenging tone, "revolutions are not all destructive your Excellency. The French and Russian

Revolutions were creative after a destructive stage. The very Reformation was revolutionary, but creative."

"I prefer revolutionaries of the heart and spirit," Lisson responded. "True revolutionaries, such as Saint Vincent de Paul, not your secular saints, a Gonzalez Prada, who voices revolution, sows destruction, but does not cultivate the tender plant of love and order and discipline taught by our Saviour."

Haya rose to the occasion. "Christ too was revolutionary your Excellency. I read the Gospels and the apostle Paul and I see a man and his Master overturning the old, establishing the new. Where is that spirit today?" Haya asked somewhat rhetorically. The encounter, according to observers, was not unfriendly, eliciting a "strong sympathy for both speakers."[41]

Meanwhile Haya found that his relationship with MacKay was more valuable than simply as a forum for free expression and a conduit of learning. When Haya and his Popular Universities were hounded by the Leguía regime in October 1923, he took refuge in the Miraflores home of his Presbyterian tutor. There he was arrested and eventually deported, beginning an exile that carried him through Central America, Mexico, the United States, and Europe, all the way to Russia through England, France, and Germany, before returning to the Americas in 1931. In 1929 MacKay visited Haya in Berlin where his old pupil assured him that a new book in the works would be filled with quotations from the Bible.[42] Although that book never appeared, MacKay was satisfied that Haya still retained an immense enthusiasm for the Bible.

In this early period of Protestantism in Peru, the contacts were few but important, none perhaps so dramatic as those that flowed between the Presbyterian John MacKay and the young radical, Haya. For MacKay the relationship with Haya had a mutual dimension, for the pastor drank from the well of Haya's radicalism as well, learning first hand what the realities of Peru truly were. MacKay represented the first of two waves of Protestantism that arrived at Peru's shores in the nineteenth and twentieth centuries. These early, "traditional" Protestants—Methodists, Presbyterians, Seventh Day Adventists—were social gospellers, reformers, and "liberal" in the twentieth-century political definition of

that word. They were not revolutionaries, but they believed that cooperation among individuals in a truly free society would lead to spiritual
regeneration, and from that would flow national regeneration. These
were also Progressives whose links were clearly with the modernized,
capitalistic society from which they sprung. But rather than conveyors
of the most nefarious forms of capitalism and imperialism that Haya
and his cohorts damned with much vigor, they conveyed the solutions
to the ills of capitalism and modernization within a Christian, pacific
context.

MacKay brought to Peru and to Haya a revolutionary message that he
defined as an inward expression of a desire to follow Christ rather than
as a political movement. Given the religious conservatism of the time in
Peru, MacKay and his Protestant brethren were considered liberal and
even radical.

The second wave of Protestants arrived in Peru in the 1940s and
reached major proportions in the 1960s and 1970s. Initially identified
with the Summer Institutes of Languages founded by William Townsend Cameron, this second generation of Protestants swelled in numbers with the arrival of the Pentecostal and evangelical sects. Unlike
their predecessors, they were conservative and distanced themselves
from political battles. Their influence has been in the transformation of
the way new Peruvian Pentecostals and evangelicals live their daily
lives. Before the Pentecostals, but paving the way for them, were the
evangelical or faith missions from the United States to Peru. The most
prominent and perhaps the most controversial of these was established
in Peru in 1945 under the auspices of the remarkable American missionary educator Townsend.

Summer Institutes of Languages/
Wycliffe Bible Translators

Townsend (1896–1982) was the son of a poor Presbyterian tenant
farmer and his wife from North Carolina who sought his destiny in California. He was driven out of the post–Civil War South by debt, drought,

and falling agricultural prices.[43] Young Townsend attended Occidental College, founded by prosperous, Presbyterian citrus growers, on a minister's scholarship; he dropped out in the midst of World War I to sell Bibles in Guatemala under the sponsorship of the Central American Mission. In Guatemala he encountered a multitude of Indian languages and dialects. Knowing Spanish was simply knowing the language of the overlords. To properly evangelize one needed to learn the language of the Indians. From this conviction was born the Wycliffe Bible Translators (WBT), organized by Townsend in a summer camp in Arkansas in 1934. The WBT was named in honor of John Wycliffe who in the fourteenth century first translated the Bible into English. In 1942 WBT was transferred to the University of Oklahoma.

To better penetrate Latin America, which was still very much Catholic and suspicious of Protestant evangelism, Townsend incorporated a second group called the Summer Institutes of Languages (SIL), which was publicly nondenominational and strictly devoted to studying and translating native dialects. As David Stoll described it in his excellent study of the SIL/WBT group, "by going into the field as Summer Institute linguists rather than Wycliffe missionaries, they obtained long-term contracts from anti-clerical and Roman Catholic governments alike. In exchange for language studies, literacy work, and other services such as the 'moral improvement' of Indians, governments allowed a linguistic institute to operate wherever it pleased."[44] The SIL/WBT strategy was first implemented in Mexico in the 1930s, moving into other parts of Latin America, including the Peruvian Amazon, in the 1940s.

The first SIL was established in 1945 at Yarinacocha near the town of Pucallpa on the Ucayali River, one of the leading tributaries of the Amazon flowing northeastward along Peru's eastern jungle borders. Pucallpa was the end of the road for Peru's first transandean highway and a logical launching point for SIL/WBT's linguistic and missionary work among Peru's Amazon Indians. Pucallpa was probably first settled by Franciscan missionaries in the mid-nineteenth century, who were also attracted by its proximity to Peru's Amazonian Indians. Townsend's camp was located near an oxbow lake, enabling quick access via pontoon-equipped aircraft. Indeed linguistics and air transportation soon determined SIL's success in Peru, so much so that "the base-airplane-bilingual school evangelizing machine became a model for other branches as far away as the Philippines."[45]

How did the Peruvian government stand to benefit? Basically they viewed the linguistics schools as helping to socialize and introduce the Indians into the mainstream of Peruvian life and thus promote national integration. Over the course of the next half century, that is in fact what SIL/WBT did do. They were agents of change and integration, usually enjoying official support. They also set in motion a tremendous controversy, especially among some anthropologists and Indianists in the revolutionary 1970s, over the side effects of Uncle Cam's (as Townsend was known to his friends and colleagues) institutes. It seemed to some that the institutes were destroying native customs and culture as Indians were gradually brought within the circle of Peruvian national life. The institutes not only provided a written language, but they evolved into centers of trade and commerce, which broke down the old isolation of the Indian tribes as they joined the market economy. The defenders of the institute rejoined by claiming that the newly acquired Christian faith and especially the newly taught skills empowered Indian peoples with the ability to adjust and not to be overcome by the advance of "civilization" (represented by oil exploration and colonization of the Peruvian Amazon, which was proceeding rapidly in the second half of the twentieth century).

How effective were the institutes? In Peru they worked in at least 32 languages and by the early 1980s had organized more than 12,000 pupils in 210 communities in bilingual schools. They were reaching, in effect, perhaps as many as one third of an Amazonian Indian population of about 150,000, and the schools were tremendously successful and popular among the Indians.[46]

The very first contract for the SIL was negotiated by Kenneth Pike in 1943 with the Minister of Education Enrique de la Rosa. The contract, like subsequent ones, was to provide for the study of indigenous languages, to prepare primers, to help the government authorities interpret in the region, to organize language courses, to discourage "vice by all means," and translate "books of great moral and patriotic value."[47]

In exchange, the SIL obtained visa and import privileges, the right to operate airplanes and radios, and an office in Lima. Nothing overtly was said about Bibles and Christianity. In fact Peru's Catholic hierarchy would not challenge the SIL until 1953 when an interesting debate flowered in the Peruvian press.

The SIL found much favor among Peru's indigenists and friends of the Indians. The most prominent Indianist of Peru, Luis E. Valcárcel, defended the SIL vigorously against its critics as they emerged in the 1950s and afterward. Valcárcel, like others of his generation, had evolved from a revolutionary framework to a more moderate position in analyzing Peru's problems. His earlier work, *Tempest in the Andes* (1927; reprinted in 1978), contended that "the solution to the problem had to come from the Indians themselves rather than those who had dominated them for centuries."[48] A companion of Jose Carlos Maríategui, Peru's leading Marxist theoretician of the 1920s, and a lifelong *Aprista,* Valcárcel would not on the surface appear to be a prime candidate for friend to a U.S. institute sponsored by, among others, conservative California businessmen, and one promoting, albeit quietly in the beginning, a Protestant evangelization of the Amazon.

Valcárcel served as Minister of Education in the Bustamante administration and was styled by Fredrick Pike as one of the leading examples of a new school of "respectable Indianists" in Peru. Rather than attempt to revolutionize the Indian, the new Indianists, such as Valcárcel, sought to take the best of the Indian's communal lifestyle and preserve it within a framework of state authority—in other words protect and preserve the Indian from above, by a series of measures instituted and governed by the central government. In this fashion Indians, long thought to be naturally obedient to higher authority, would be best protected within a country whose dominant values led to the denigration and exploitation of its indigenous peoples.[49]

There developed a natural alliance among Peru's indigenists and the SIL. In the face of traditional values that contended the Indian was by nature brutish and incapable of ever being transformed fully into a rational, free actor in the life of the nation, Townsend, Valcárcel, and others viewed the Indian as "upliftable," although Uncle Cam's vision was as much spiritual as temporal. Townsend was voted into the prestigious Peruvian Indigenist Institute, the first American to be so included, and enjoyed a long and close association with many of his indigenist peers in Peru.

The U.S. government cooperated fully with the SIL in these early years. It helped Townsend acquire a Grumman Duck amphibian from the U.S. Navy, promoted visits from Peruvian legislators and the Peruvian military to SIL camps in the Amazon, and utilized Point Four (a U.S. government assistance program) and U.S. embassy resources for these and other endeavors. The most astute but critical student of the SIL/WBT, David Stoll, wrote that in this period the U.S. embassy (through Ambassador Prentice Cooper) thoroughly muddled "the distinction between private and official U.S. sponsorship, its own 'linguistics school mission' and the U.S. Government's servicios, or 'missions' expanded under the Point Four programme." [50] Yet this kind of criticism is itself a bit disingenuous, since "official" and "unofficial" U.S. activities in Peru had historically been interlaced in many ways. Any embassy's mission, whether it be the United States or the French or the British, was to represent its government, to acquire information, and to ensure that the legitimate interests and rights of its citizens were protected. This included promoting U.S. enterprises in Peru, and the SIL was most certainly an enterprise.

Townsend's establishment of the Jungle Aviation and Radio Service (JAARS) in 1948 opened up new avenues for the institutes. The first pilot, Larry Montgomery, was recruited from a U.S.-Peruvian military mission. Among the JAARS's first Catalina amphibian aircraft, two were sponsored by Christian businessmen in Southern California, one by the Bible Institute of Los Angeles, one by Henry Crowell, heir of Quaker Oats, and one by the Moody Bible Institute of Chicago. [51] In the mid-1950s the JAARS not only flew for the SIL/WBT projects, but it also provided transportation for oil companies exploring in the Amazon and even occasionally was called upon by the Peruvian military and civilian authorities to reach remote areas, where SIL-trained translators could be expected to help as well.

In 1953 the Spanish Franciscan Vicar of Ucayali, Monsignor Buenaventura León de Uriarte blew the whistle on the SIL. On the pages of one of Lima's leading newspapers, *La Prensa,* the Franciscan charged that SIL was nothing but a front for Protestant evangelization. Townsend's response was published alongside the Franciscan's charge.

"How could a scientist," Townsend asked, "who believes in our loving Jesus Christ live among human beings who worship the boa and . . . not tell them anything about Christianity?" That beginning cast Bishop Uriarte's accusation in something of a self-serving, Catholic versus Protestant sectarian tone.

"We do not carry out evangelical work," Townsend continued, "because the Institute has a mission of scientific character and not a religious end." However Townsend certainly admitted to being a member of the Wycliffe Bible Translators, although he maintained the independence of that entity from the Summer Institutes of Languages.[52]

What was going on here? Was Townsend an out-and-out liar as the bishop, and some other sharp critics, claimed? In a *National Geographic* article, Townsend explained.

"We're not really a religious organization," Townsend the linguist and Indianist said, "but we do introduce the Indians to Christianity by translating part of the Bible," Townsend the missionary explained.[53]

Townsend placed the secrecy of SIL's mission within the context of scripture. On numerous occasions, Jesus in his ministry cautioned his disciples, and those he had miraculously cured, to keep these acts a secret. If his mission on earth were prematurely revealed, it could be compromised. Much of scripture is, of course, open to interpretation, and can be read a number of ways, but Townsend viewed his ministry as one that also could be compromised by premature revelation. God's work was being accomplished, not by outright deception, but by separating the secular dimension (translation, linguistics, schools) from the religious dimension represented by the WBT.

There is much more to this extraordinary element in the history of contemporary Peruvian-U.S. relations. The bilingual schools, for example, enjoyed an unparalleled reputation among Peruvian indigenists. Efrain Morote Best, the rector of the University of Huamanga in the early 1960s and a leading leftist educator and indigenist, was a longtime friend of the SIL. Catholic schools were still trying to force Indians to stop being Indians by suppressing their languages, enforcing the speaking of Spanish, denigrating Indian ways, and extolling white/*cholo* culture. Morote admired the SIL's bilingual schools, on the other hand, which represented a "revolutionary step from the educational and social point of view because Indians could be taught basic subjects in their own languages, in their own communities and by other Indians."[54]

In the mid-1950s Morote, working for the Ministry of Education in the Marañon Valley, encouraged SIL-trained translators and their Indian teachers to emphasize arithmetic and promote cooperatives. This was considered subversive by local landowners and bosses whose practices were revealed, by the newly found tool of simple arithmetic, as dishonest and deceptive. Morote's professional journey as an educator eventually propelled him to the rectorship of the University of Huamanga in 1961.[55]

Ironically the man who viewed the bilingual Christian teachers of the SIL institutes with such admiration was also the man who gave Abimael Guzmán Reynoso—the founder and leader of the Shining Path terrorist movement—his first professional appointment as a member of the faculty at Huamanga.[56] Supported by increasingly leftist, Communist elements among the students and faculty, Morote ousted Fernando Romero in 1962 as rector in a tight election decided by just one vote. When Guardian Mayorga, a philosopher, unexpectedly departed in mid-1962, Morote recruited the bright, young Guzmán as a replacement professor of philosophy in the education program. Morote hoped to replicate SIL's bilingual school approach among the Quechua-speaking Indians of the Sierra and was supported by Francisco Miró Quesada, Belaúnde Terry's Minister of Education in 1964.

One of Townsend's bright young subordinates, Donald Burns, then occupying a chair of linguistics at Huamanga, was put in charge of the Quechua project in 1964. It lasted until 1970 when revolutionary fervor forced Burns and his wife, Nadine, out of Peru.[57] The revolutionary government proposed to end the contracts between SIL and the government when they expired in 1976. Peruvians would then be in charge of SIL, and SIL would have, in effect, been nationalized. SIL was standing in the way of "revolutionizing" the Indians.

Not so said many of SIL's supporters, both within the U.S. embassy

and among SIL's many friends in Peru. In April and May 1976, two pe-
titions were published in the Peruvian press supporting SIL. They were
signed by more than 120 prominent Peruvians, including Luis Valcárcel, Jorge Basadre, Francisco Miro Quesada, Mario Vargas Llosa, retired
military officers, prominent businessmen and academics, and even two
Catholic priests.[58] As the regime of President Morales Bermudez (1974–
80) reversed some of the most radical directions taken by the Velasco
government, SIL once again regained the security of a government tolerant of its activities. And when its old friend Fernando Belaúnde Terry
was reelected president in 1980, Townsend was awarded a medal for
SIL's contributions in helping to bring the Amazon into the mainstream
of Peruvian national life.[59]

How do we evaluate SIL/WBT in the context of contemporary
Peruvian-U.S. relations, and, more specifically, as an example of U.S.
Protestantism's presence in Peru? What was it that attracted Peruvians
of all political, social, and economic stripes to Uncle Cam's institutes?
Was it their anticommunism? Was it their rigorous devotion to preserving Indian languages and Indian customs? Was it, perhaps in the hearts
of many, the Christian nature of the whole endeavor? Were the institutes successful?

"The Summer Institute," wrote David Stoll, "has demonstrated that
Amazonian Indians can run their own school system, which is no small
achievement." Could Indians be running all that? "Ironically," Stoll
commented, "SIL itself was proving that Indians could run all that."[60]
That they could was in no small measure due to the small army of translators and missionaries from the United States who devoted themselves
to concord, learning, and Christianity among Peru's jungle Indians.

The Role of U.S. Private Enterprise in Peru

In an insightful book on the United States and Peru published in 1964,
James C. Carey entitled chapter 10 "The Mighty Dollar at Work." Here
he focused on U.S. private investments in Peru since the Second World
War. It is perhaps one of the most important chapters in his history of

relations between the two nations, for it described the economic context that is arguably one of the most significant in modern relations between the two countries.

Carey found that about one-third of Peru's gross national product came from foreign enterprises, mainly U.S.-owned or -controlled ones. The mineral sector accounted for about 10 percent of Peru's national income, and Americans held the highest percentage of ownership in this crucial industry. I.P.C. controlled about 98 percent of petroleum production, while U.S. businesses owned two-thirds of all direct foreign investments in manufacturing and more than half of all foreign ownership in agriculture. Peruvian ownership still predominated in agriculture and manufacturing, although, as noted, the highest foreign participation was American.

In the postwar years, mining and petroleum continued to dominate U.S. investments in Peru, although they were not the most visible. Encouraged by the liberal Mining Law of 1950, which benefited foreign capital, the giant Cerro de Pasco Corporation increased its investments in Peru in the 1950s.[61] Cerro expanded its lead-zinc refinery at Cerro de Pasco and Casapalca and began open-pit copper mining at Cerro de Pasco. In a joint venture with ASARCO (American Smelting & Refining Company), Cerro became a minority partner (22 percent) in SPCC (Southern Peru Copper Corporation), which was created by ASARCO (51 percent of SPCC) in 1952 especially to open up a giant new copper mine at Toquepala.[62] By the time Toquepala came on stream in 1960, SPCC had invested more than $250 million, then the largest investment by a U.S. corporation in Peru. In the early 1950s, another U.S. corporation, the Utah Construction Company, came on the scene, enhancing the presence of U.S. investments in Peru even more.

Utah Construction, along with the Cyprus Mines Corporation and a number of minority shareholders that included the wealthy and powerful Prado family, created the Marcona Mining Company in 1952 to exploit the iron ores of the Marcona deposits in southern Peru. A beginning in the iron and steel industry had been made in 1943 when the Peruvian government formed the Santa Corporation to construct and manage a steel mill in Chimbote. The iron ore would be mined and shipped from the Marcona deposits nine miles from the coast in southern Peru. Sending bulk iron ore from the Marcona deposits by sea over long distances was an innovation that eventually worked well for the Marcona Company. But the Chimbote heavy industrial complex that the Peruvians envisioned, centered on the steel mill, was slow in getting started, eventually almost going bankrupt before Marcona came on the scene in 1952. By the 1960s Marcona, SPCC, and the older Cerro de Pasco were all comfortably in production, although dissatisfaction among some Peruvian political circles with taxes, concessions, and profits generated by the U.S. corporations provoked not a little criticism and much public scrutiny.

Of the three—called the *gran minería* in Peru since they dominated the mineral industry—Cerro was the oldest and best established. After World War II, Cerro continued to diversify and expand. By 1951 it had removed the name "Copper" from its title because the company was actually producing more zinc and lead than copper. It moved aggressively in mining supply endeavors, either with controlling or minority interests, in areas such as explosives, welding rods, steel castings, refractory bricks, and expanded in metal manufacturing plants making wire and cable and lead alloys, for example. It obtained oil and gas concessions in the Peruvian jungle and aggressively expanded in other parts of the world. By 1970 Cerro was Peru's largest private enterprise, employing seventeen thousand people, the largest employer outside of the Peruvian government.

SPCC developed Toquepala, a truly fascinating operation high in the Andes. The mine is located at 8,500 feet and a 114-mile railroad had to be built to the sea where a port and smelter were constructed near the town of Ilo. In 1970 it was the second-largest U.S. investor in Peru with a payroll of almost four thousand people.

Marcona, the third of the *gran minería*, developed a system to move iron ore directly (palletized or as slurry) from the mines to the coast via conveyors or slurry line, a distance of nine miles. There Marcona vessels transported the ore to steel mills overseas, the bulk going to the United States during this period. Marcona enjoyed a relatively good relationship with both the state-owned Santa Corporation with its steel complex at Chimbote and the Peruvian government itself. Increasing demands for better terms from the government were always negotiated with Marcona before the expiration of current contracts, and the government's share of Marcona, through Santa, increased gradually so that in 1970 it was anticipated that Santa would own 50 percent of all of Marcona's production by 1982. That never happened, as Marcona was nationalized in 1975, becoming Hierro Peru.

U.S. investments in Peru were certainly not limited to the mines of the *gran minería*. The post–World War II climate induced many U.S. corporations—among them Goodrich, Goodyear, and Sears—to locate in Peru, joining the older companies, such as the ubiquitous W. R. Grace & Co., which by 1954 had been in Peru for a century and continued to grow and diversify. Grace was perhaps the most interesting, and certainly most diversified, U.S. firm operating in Peru in the middle twentieth century. Although its investments in millions of dollars was fourth in rank behind the *gran minería* and I.P.C., Grace employed more than ten thousand people in Peru, second only to Cerro. More telling was the range of Grace activities, from aviation to paints, steamshipping to papermaking. Grace's operations included two sugar plantations, the paper and chemical complex at Paramonga, the premier air and sea transportation lines between Peru and the United States, and other production endeavors that included candy and crackers, liquors and fish meal, trucks and textiles. Casa Grace was thoroughly associated with the indigenous Peruvian economy. Many of its activities were with Peruvian partners, even more thoroughly "Peruvianizing" Casa Grace's character.

Grace continued to expand and diversify in Peru in the 1950s and 1960s, even given its retrenchment and withdrawal from Latin America in general in the 1950s and 1960s. While the Paramonga paper complex was expanded, experiments led to the development of a new industry. Grace engineers, chemists, and technicians from the United States and Peru developed a process to produce polyvinyl chloride (PVC) from alcohol, a by-product of the sugar-making process. PVC is the basic building block of the modern plastics industry (most commonly produced from petroleum), and by 1965 the Paramonga chemical industry was producing PVC for widespread use throughout Peru. This was in addition to the manufacture of paper from bagasse (a process also pioneered by Grace at Paramonga) as well as the production of chlorine for water filtration and other industrial uses. Paramonga, indeed, became a technological showplace demonstrating the ability of a Third World nation to invent, manufacture, and compete in a very sophisticated industrial fashion. Lest this be seen as an enclave of a U.S. company, where technology and specialists from the United States simply ran the show, Charles Goodsell remarked that in 1968, or one year before the revolution, "Peruvian nationals were almost completely in charge" of the Grace plantations Cartavio and Paramonga, and in Cartavio, also the site of a new paper plant, "not a single American resided except for occasional visiting consultants. . . . At Toquepala," SPCC's principal operation, Goodsell noted, by comparison, "operations were almost entirely directed by Americans."[63]

Casa Grace's place in Peru *was* different from that of SPCC, I.P.C., or Cerro. While profits were always a high priority, Grace was nonetheless a builder and contributor of new wealth, rather than simply an extractor of nonrenewable resources, such as were Marcona, SPCC, I.P.C., or Cerro. In some instances the latter corporations were also "good corporate neighbors," and they did add to the national wealth by injecting large amounts of vital capital and technology not generally available in Peru. But they also came under intense scrutiny and attack in the 1960s by Peruvian economic nationalists who perceived those corporations as basically parasitic rather than critical for Peru's national development.

Given the immense diversity of U.S. investments in Peru, were they in the main welcome or not? "The merits of United States investments," James Carey clearly phrased the question, and its difficult answer, "have constituted a source of disagreement. Some Peruvians would like greater investment and some would wish for less."[64]

A decade later, Charles Goodsell framed it slightly differently. "To what extent is national independence compromised by foreign capital?" he asked. "Are there lasting effects on the political system?" The answers spanned the spectrum of opinion.

On the one hand some Peruvians felt that foreign investments contributed to "economic imperialism," and "national independence is compromised and even destroyed, and . . . a lasting effect on the political system is servility to the capitalists and their government." On the other, Goodsell, for instance, found that many Peruvians considered modern corporations to be politically weak and defensive given the strong structures of the state and public opinion.

"The local political environment," Goodsell noted, "is so hostile . . . that the corporations steer clear of politics, conscientiously obey local laws, and confine themselves to public relations and charitable good works in an effort to improve their image."[65] Obviously the subject of U.S. investments in Peru, and their effects, bridged a wide gulf of opinion.

The least controversial U.S. company continued to be Casa Grace. The company seemed to flow into every area where there was a business need in Peru, often pioneering new fields.[66] In 1934, for example, when it became clear that the Las Palmas airport in Lima could no longer accommodate a growing Panagra Airlines and its newly acquired portion of Slim Faucett's operation (Panagra acquired 25 percent of Faucett's stock in 1938 to avoid direct competition), Panagra helped build Limatambo Airport. Limatambo was the gateway to Lima for thousands of passengers over the years, serving as Lima's principal airport until the inauguration of the new Jorge Chávez Airport in Callao in 1962. Panagra in fact built airports and landing strips all around Peru to make aviation possible and profitable from the 1930s onward. A Dutch immigrant to Peru, Bill Peper Nicols van Meurs, was in charge of Panagra's ambitious airport construction.

"Van Meurs's job," Goodsell wrote, "was to make his way personally to wherever Panagra wanted a ground facility, which in some cases meant going in on foot and muleback." After surveying a suitable site, van Meurs hired local labor, including *cholita* women, to help with the excavation and leveling of the runway and taxiway. To guide his crew, van Meurs staked the ground with red and white flags. "Dig at the red flags ladies," van Meurs told his crew, "and dump at the white flags." "What shall we use señor?" they sometimes asked. "Your petticoats will be just fine," the thrifty Dutchman responded.

Landing strips were built at Talara, Paita, Piura, Chiclayo, Pacas-mayo, Trujillo, Paramonga, Huacho, Cerro-Azul, Pisco, Ica, Nazca, Are-quipa, Ilo, and Tacna. Not all were dig and fill, as this writer can testify. The landing strip at Paramonga's paper and chemical complex was a smoothed section of the adjoining sandy beach, hard by the breakers crashing in from the Pacific.

As Panagra's operations developed and the aircraft became larger and heavier, the important strips were paved and other facilities, such as ra-dios, power, and weather stations, were added. A small passenger ter-minal also occasionally adorned the aerodromes to provide some com-fort for travelers.[67] Eventually all these installations were turned over to the government for maintenance and operation, although as late as 1952 Panama paid for an instrument landing system and high-intensity run-way lights at Limatambo.

The *gran minería*, I.P.C., and Grace were, of course, not the only repre-sentatives of U.S. capital and technology in Peru. In 1943 a rubber plant was established by Goodyear at the urging of a local Goodyear dealer, Eduardo Dibós Dammert, who later twice served as Lima's mayor. Goodyear became an immensely successful manufacturer of automo-bile and truck tires and tubes and was going strong even after the rev-olution of 1968.[68]

In 1955 the giant U.S. retailer, Sears Roebuck, opened its first store in Lima in the suburb of San Isidro. When it first opened, 80 percent of its merchandise was imported. By the time of the revolution, more than 90 percent of its merchandise was made in Peru, reflecting a Sears pol-icy of integration into the local economy as fully as possible.[69]

One of Nelson Rockefeller's companies, the International Basic Econ-omy Corporation (IBEC), sponsored another retailing enterprise, called *"Todos"* or ("Everything") in Lima. Todos Supermarket, built next to Sears in San Isidro, helped pioneer not only U.S.-style mass retailing but brought the pleasures and perils of suburban shopping in a mall-style environment to *limeños* (residents of Lima), although the first true malls would not be built until the 1970s.

Relations between the United States and Peru from the 1940s were profoundly shaped by the presence of U.S. capital, technology, entrepreneurship, marketing techniques, and other American economic and cultural elements introduced in this period. It is difficult, however, to judge the effects of this major U.S. presence in Peru. The skipper of a tuna boat from San Diego, being chased out of Peru's territorial waters or paying a big fine for fishing within those waters, was worlds apart in his thinking and culture from an American engineer working side by side in partnership with a Peruvian engineer in the chemistry labs and paper mills of Paramonga. A Slim Faucett constructing aircraft in Peru specifically designed and built for flying from short airstrips into high-altitude locations possessed a different perspective from a Cerro de Pasco corporate executive making decisions in the Colgate Building in New York that affected worldwide operations. Faucett, for example, imported the engines (Pratt & Whitneys), instruments, and propellers from the United States and then fabricated the rest of the specially designed aircraft in his own shops at an airfield in the suburb of San Isidro. The first such plane, christened "El Chico," carried 8 passengers, cruised at 140 mph, and climbed to 20,000 feet. Thirty were built between the 1930s, and in 1947, all of them were painted the brilliant orange colors that was Faucett's colorful trademark.[70]

While the U.S. presence in Peru—from Protestant missionaries to mining engineers and aircraft builders—was constantly diversifying and expanding, internal Peruvian historical forces were themselves undergoing a remarkable transformation. In 1968 the Peruvian military, long a conservative force in society, overthrew the government and proceeded to embark on a radical program of nationalization that brought it into direct conflict with the United States.

7 The Peruvian Institutional Revolution of 1968

"Please don't burn that limousine,
Don't throw tomatoes at the sub-
marine.
Think of all we've done for you.
You've just got those exploitation
blues."

Richard N. Goodwin, "Letter from Peru," *The New Yorker*
(May 17, 1969), quoting from the "ballad of student dissent"
made popular by Bob Dylan in the 1960s

Early in the morning of October 3, 1968, special forces under the command of Col. Rafael Hoyos Rubio broke into the presidential palace and took President Fernando Belaúnde Terry into custody. Thirty tanks encircled the palace. The invaders hustled the protesting Belaúnde to a waiting jeep. From there it was a quick trip through a sleeping metropolis to the Jorge Chávez International Airport at Callao where a plane was being readied to take the Peruvian leader into exile in Argentina.

On the same day Belaúnde's captors delivered a "Revolutionary Manifesto" calling on all loyal and patriotic Peruvians to support the beginning of a new era. The Peruvian Institutional Revolution of 1968 was launched. It had a profound effect on Peruvian-U.S. relations for the next decade as Peru's leaders, largely coming from the army, sought to carve out a new destiny.

The revolutionary government came into conflict with the United States in numerous areas. While the underlying causes of the revolution went deeper than the growing frustration with the International Petroleum Company's control of the country's economy, the long-standing and deep presence of the United States in Peruvian affairs was *thought* by many to have precipitated the revolution. Sometimes the *perception* of reality was more important as a motivator and an activator than the reality itself. This is perhaps no better illustrated than in the area of U.S. corporate influence in Peru's internal politics and economy. Charles Goodsell framed the question in a series of hypotheses in his book *American Corporations and Peruvian Politics:* Did U.S. corporations actively participate directly in Peruvian politics? In areas where American employers were the principal employers (such as in the I.P.C. and mining enclaves), did corporate management dominate local political life? On the other hand, did the activity of some American entrepreneurs and corporations have the unintended, long-term, beneficial net effect of adding to the political, social, and economic integration of Peru?

The Influence of Foreign Corporations in Peru's Internal Life

The 1950s and 1960s, wrote Goodsell, were "a second golden age for American business in Peru," the first being in the 1920s under Leguía. Other scholarly studies, such as the detailed economic history of Peru by Thorp and Bertram, *Peru, 1890–1977,* give ample evidence of the extraordinary expansion of U.S. business investments in Peru during this period. "Dollars Flock to Peru," hailed *Business Week* magazine on October 11, 1952. "Why Peru Pulls Dollars," the equally prestigious *Fortune* magazine explained in November 1956.[1]

From the onset of Odría's presidency in 1948 to the overthrow of Belaúnde Terry in 1968, Peruvian leaders sought actively to foster industrialization through export-led development. While major mineral and petroleum exports were largely in the hands of U.S. corporations, much of the increasing industrialization in Peru occurred through U.S. investments, or, with increasing measure, through joint Peruvian-U.S. business alliances. New mining and industrialization laws in the 1950s actively promoted foreign investments. Between 1950 and 1970, direct U.S. investments in Peru rose from $145 million to $691 million, perhaps even higher if one uses different scales of measurement. And, as noted above, the range of U.S. investments was quite wide. Although petroleum and mining represented the largest proportion of capital, such U.S.-based companies as W. R. Grace, Sears, Goodyear, and others manufactured and marketed a wide range of goods for not only internal consumption but also for export from Peru.

Most of the top twelve American subsidiaries in Peru were rather closely controlled by the parent companies through ownership and staffing of the top managerial positions, especially in the key areas of operations and finance. Although the vast majority of staff and managerial positions were held by Peruvians—almost 98 percent on the average for all American companies operating in Peru—the key decision-making positions, or those at the top of the business hierarchy, were in the main held by Americans, with certain exceptions.

"What really matters in business organizations," Goodsell noted, "of course is who occupies the highest jobs."[2] Goodsell concluded that U.S. control of U.S. investments and capital in Peru of the 1950s and 1960s was very great, even though the *percentage* of Americans employed in these corporations had dramatically diminished over the years. Sears started with twenty-one Americans in 1954 and had only two on its payroll in 1969. Southern Peru Copper's American managers were reduced by more than 50 percent in the 1960s, and W. R. Grace's American managers were demonstrably scarce in Peru.

Though nationalist Peruvians often condemned the economic impact of these American corporations on Peru, the facts indicated that in the aggregate, U.S. investments, output of goods, jobs created, and taxes paid accounted for 10 percent or less of the total gross economic activity of Peru. What mattered most to Peruvian critics of the U.S. economic presence was not its size but its distorting influence on the national economy. Although U.S. corporations only paid about 10 percent of Peru's taxes in the aggregate, the *top* tax-paying enterprises were all American-owned. Another example comes from foreign trade. The United States continued to be Peru's principal trading partner through the 1960s, absorbing 35 percent of Peru's exports and providing more than 30 percent of its imports. And more than 50 percent of Peru's exports—including oil, minerals, sugar, and fish meal for example—were produced by U.S. firms.

Goodsell noted that "as a primary source of foreign exchange, these [export] earnings are essential to Peru in order to buy imports and meet innumerable other external financial obligations."[3] External financial obligations is the long way of saying debts, and Peru had more than a billion dollars in debt in 1969. That debt increased considerably in the 1970s under the revolutionary government's policies.

In certain key areas of economic production, such as mining, U.S. companies dominated the businesses. SPCC produced more than two-thirds of Peru's copper, Marcona mined all iron ore, and Cerro produced more than half of the lead, zinc, and silver in Peru in 1968. Goodyear produced more than two-thirds of Peru's tires and tubes, Grace produced almost all of Peru's paper and cardboard, and I.P.C., of course, dominated the petroleum industry, producing about two-thirds of all petroleum products.

The argument made by the leaders of the Peruvian revolution was that Peruvian dependence upon the United States must be either ended or reigned in. Their views generally reflected those made elsewhere in Latin America, especially from the 1940s onward, when the "*dependentistas*" came to the forefront to explain the relative underdevelopment of Latin America with respect to North America, and, later, to a Europe recovered from the Second World War.

According to dependency theory, the world was divided into the metropolises and the periphery. The metropolises were located in North America and Europe where industrialization had first taken place. Those who developed and subscribed to the theory tended to see the United States as promoting underdevelopment, or dependency, by a series of conscious decisions made both in public and private circles. These decisions were aimed at maintaining the prosperity of the United States at the expense of the underdeveloped nations of the world. This meant controlling access to key natural resources, maintaining dominance in finances, promoting technological superiority, keeping the edge in strategic and military options, and, in a host of other ways, denying to the underdeveloped world the ability to rise above their impoverished circumstances, and, in essence, maintaining the Perus of the world in a "dependent" relationship.

Like all overarching theories, dependency has some basis in fact but is flawed in too many ways to be a valid generalization. Furthermore our description is too simplistic for it leaves out many elements (as discussed earlier in the introduction), such as the behavior of the elites of Peru who often found it convenient to ally themselves with the United States to protect their privileged position within Peruvian society. And the Peruvian economy itself, as it developed in the 1950s and 1960s, was remarkably diversified, responding to internal needs as much as external demands. Manufacturing and industrialization increased rapidly in this time frame, and it was more often than not national in origin and execution, rather than responding to foreign priorities, which is one of the keystones of dependency theory.

U.S. companies in Peru were perceived by some Peruvians as the primary actors in keeping Peru in a dependent relationship to the United States. These companies employed various "avenues of access" to power, including lobbyists, the national legislature, political parties, interest groups, and direct contact by corporate executives. Of all these the last was the most successful vehicle for "influencing" events involving U.S. companies. That is to say, U.S. executives, or top Peruvian managers of U.S. companies, spoke directly with presidents and ministers to get across their points and influence decisions. In this scenario little had changed since the days of the early 1930s, for example, when the manager of Cerro de Pasco in Peru, Harry Kingsmill, spoke candidly and often with Sánchez Cerro and his ministers during the crises of that period.

Private and corporate gift giving to political parties and candidates is common in the United States, of course. In the Peruvian context cash payments by U.S. companies may have been common, but they did not always have a common purpose. Some moneys were payments from a U.S. company, for example, for services rendered to an underpaid Peruvian bureaucrat in the customs office; other payments could be construed as a mild form of corruption, or simply the expression of a reward mechanism common, acceptable, and legitimate in the Peruvian/Hispanic cultural context.[4] Small payments to bureaucrats were simply a normal way of business life. Larger amounts to high-ranking government officials, on the other hand, constituted bribery.

The small payment was called a *"coima"* in Peru. It is a fee or tip for a service performed, expediting business, giving the payer some advantage. It is as old as business civilization. It is called "speed money" in India, "dash" in Africa, and the famous *"mordida,"* or little bite, in Mexico. While bribes were not uncommon in earlier phases of Peruvian-U.S. relations, they had grown less common by the 1950s and 1960s. In fact U.S. firms in Peru were little inclined to take the chance of tarnishing their image, not from any superior or high redoubt of business morality, but because it didn't make sense.

In one interview this author did a number of years ago, an upper-level Grace executive, John C. Duncan, said that Casa Grace long ago (perhaps as early as the turn of the century) decided to stay out of Peruvian politics, and, by extension, refrain from the behavior that one could describe as either high-level payoffs or bribery.

"Why?" I asked.

"The Peruvian political scene changes so fast," Duncan said, "that to support one faction was to endanger your interests when they were replaced, through elections or revolutions. So, we made it our business *not* to play the political game."[5]

U.S. businessmen, and their Peruvian counterparts holding high managerial positions in U.S. firms, did actively try to tip the scales in their favor. However they did this through public relations campaigns for example, but not through high-level bribery on any appreciable scale.

Ironically the company that pursued the most active, widespread public relations campaign—I.P.C.—also suffered the worst image in Peru in the 1960s. On the other hand, the firms with the lowest profiles—Grace and Anderson Clayton, for example—emerged in public opinion polls as contributing, rather than detracting, from Peru's national life. Grace successfully merged its interests with those of Peru, utilizing Peruvian imagery, Peruvian themes, Peruvian names, and, in short, the symbols and reality of Peru, to market its goods and services in the nation.

I.P.C. published a wonderfully attractive and informative magazine called *Fanal* (*Lantern*) on a quarterly basis that featured Peruvian art, history, education, and contained no political commentary or company propaganda. Expensive color documentaries were produced by I.P.C. for showing in Peru's theaters and on television, contests were held, charities supported, and relief provided during times of national disaster, such as the earthquake of May 1970 when a number of U.S. firms pitched in to help the Callejón de Huaylas devastated by the earthquake. The image of I.P.C. as a good neighbor and corporate friend was promoted with a big budget and an ongoing, high-level public relations campaign. And I.P.C. was the first major U.S. firm nationalized by the Peruvian generals who came to power in October 1968. I.P.C.'s *earlier* corporate behavior stalked her in the 1950s and 1960s like a persistent shadow, frustrating the attempts to develop a new image based on the model corporate citizen.

Company Towns in Peru

Outside of the primate city of Lima, many of the U.S. firms interacted on a more intimate level with Peru and her people. *Limeños* tend to think that the world of Peru begins and ends along Rimac River valley where the river nourishes the rich valley before flowing into the Pacific Ocean. But in the mineral mining camps of the Andes, in the towns and villages located near the great oil deposits on the arid, northern coast, or in the coastal region of sugar and cotton plantations, Americans and Peruvians worked side by side exploiting some of Peru's richest natural endowments, and creating some of the most fascinating scenarios in the long and complex association of Peru and the United States.

The "company town" is not a novel term. A creation of the industrial revolution, the company town was a community dominated by one industry that attracted workers and families whose livelihood depended upon the company's operations. The principal employer—the company—dealt with its workers mostly as it pleased, and the range of that treatment was wide, from brutal exploitation to benign and even enlightened paternalism. As Peru industrialized in the twentieth century, conditions in these towns slowly improved. The rather close and even intimate association between the U.S. capital and its Peruvian hosts most frequently took place in "company towns," often in remote places where Cerro, I.P.C., Grace, SPCC, Marcona, and other American companies directly worked with Peruvians and their resources.

The early history of company towns in Peru typically reflects the raw and brutal nature of capitalism that virtually all nations passed through. In previous chapters we discussed the violent confrontations, for example, in the early 1930s between management and labor in the company towns of Cerro de Pasco. These confrontations were not extraordinary or unusual in the history of industrial capitalism.

By the 1960s, or the period immediately preceding the revolution of 1968, eight Peruvian communities of varying sizes were identified as U.S. "company" towns. In six of the eight towns, the top man in charge was an American. Only in the two Grace plantations of Cartavio and Paramonga was a Peruvian in charge.[6] About 60 percent of the managerial class was Peruvian in the towns taken together. The remaining percentages, 26 percent and 15 percent, represented the United States and other foreigners respectively. The populations in these towns were overwhelmingly economically dependent on the U.S. company. Most of the property, private and commercial, was owned by the companies.

The I.P.C. "company town," Talara, was the *least* controlled by the company by 1968. In a deliberate attempt to reduce the heavy paternalism of the company, land and buildings (the stadium for example) had been ceded to the municipality, the company's theaters sold, and in-town land set aside for private residential development. "Beginning in the 1940s," Fredrick Pike noted, "I.P.C. had served as a trail blazer for other U.S. firms operating in [Latin] America as it moved to become a model employer by showing solicitous concern for its workers. As a result, the company won worker loyalty to such an extent that its labor force backed I.P.C. rather than the Peruvian government at the time of nationalization."[7]

On the other hand, the Grace plantations Paramonga and Cartavio, and the SPCC mining camps Toquepala and Pueblo Nuevo, were almost entirely dependent economically upon the companies, almost all property belonging to the U.S. firms. Access to nearby communities somewhat reduced the totality of this scenario. Other company towns—La Oroya (Cerro), Cerro de Pasco (Cerro), and San Juan (Marcona)—fell in between the extremes, regional and historical factors moderating each situation. Cerro de Pasco, for example, was an ancient Indian settlement before the Americans arrived and retained an identity distinct from the corporation.

As befits the nature of company towns, much of what consisted of public entertainment, news, communications, and other social and cultural life was provided by the company. Movies and newspapers were distributed and published by the companies. While the companies provided upbeat news of their activities, the overall local, regional, or national news content was not particularly slanted or distorted by company public relations. The movie theaters typically were divided in the same way management divided employees in the towns. Upper-level managers and their families, for example, were given choice seats in the balconies. "Staff," or lower managers, obtained better seats than the "*empleados*," white-collar workers, who, of course, had better seats than the workers, or "*obreros.*"

In Paramonga in the 1950s, the Peruvian manager of the plantation lived in a substantial hacienda-style home, surrounded by a high fence and well guarded by large dogs, the descendants one would presume of the ferocious war dogs introduced in the sixteenth century by Francisco Pizarro.[8] American technicians and managers, as well as their Peruvian counterparts, lived in more modest but quite comfortable homes aligned on a road from the main factories (sugar and paper at that time; chemical by the 1960s) to the oceanfront. *Empleado* housing was even more modest, and the one story, depressing, dusty accommodations of the *obreros* were humble in the extreme, described by Goodsell as "small, multiple, unpainted, and without running water."[9] On the other hand, Talara, San Juan, Pueblo Nuevo, and Toquepala "make a quite good impression if one values such features as decent housing and an attractive physical environment."[10]

The wide variations in accommodations, entertainment, architecture, and general appearances were, again, typical of an immensely diversi-fied U.S. presence in Peru. Cerro de Pasco's housing was probably the worst, but by the 1960s the company also possessed some of the best in new apartment buildings at La Oroya and an entirely new town near Cerro de Pasco. The new town, San Juan Pampa, shined in comparison to the old one, but *pasqueños* resisted the company at every turn. Car-tavio and Paramonga were old settlements even before Grace began op-erating them, and when the company did build worker housing in those early years, "concepts of human decency were very different."[11]

I.P.C.'s settlement at Talara was atrocious when I.P.C. assumed con-trol from the English London & Pacific company in 1913. Plagues of smallpox, bubonic plague, and beriberi periodically swept through the camps where rats lived comfortably cheek by jowl with the workers. There was no treated water, and a six-bed clinic and two doctors were provided for a community of more than twenty-five thousand people.[12] Little had been done to improve conditions when a devastating malaria epidemic swept through the camps in 1925. New York headquarters sent its medical director to Talara. The American physician was shocked by conditions. Subsequently a new water plant was built, inoculation programs instituted, and worker quarters were destroyed and rebuilt. Twenty years later conditions were once more lamentable. A study in 1945 showed that more than half the workers lived in wooden homes without lights and water, taking community baths and using commu-nity toilets. In a masterful piece of understatement, the study concluded that "many of the worker's quarters are painted a dull brown color, which, coupled with the nature's drab, sandy surroundings, present a very unpleasing aspect."[13]

To its credit, I.P.C. responded with an impressive amount of corpo-rate conscience. Peruvian architects were hired, among them a young fellow trained in architecture at the University of Texas, Fernando Be-laúnde Terry (who would later become Peru's president), and between 1952 and 1954 a new city, complete with new homes, schools, recreation facilities, and a shopping mall, was built. Flimsy, shabby, and over-crowded multiple family dwellings that marked the old Talara were replaced by single family, brick homes. New hospitals and clinics, immunization on a regular basis, and increased sanitation transformed Talara into a modern company town.

Throughout the 1950s and 1960s, virtually all U.S. companies sought to "depaternalize" the nature of the company towns. In other words, the level of economic, social, cultural, and even political dependency was reduced as companies sold off housing, turned over civic responsibilities, sponsored privately or community-owned stores, and even encouraged labor syndicates and unions. It is a fascinating chapter in modernization, in this instance replacing the paternalism of the past with a modern relationship between management and labor, one based on freedom, contractual agreements, and, ultimately, promoting more of a partnership in the workplace. The new way did not always work. In some of the company towns, individuals were not particularly interested in giving up the security of the corporate mantle—free electricity, free housing, and other perquisites—for the independence, and responsibility, of going it alone. In others local community development projects took off quite well, such as replacing the old company stores with consumer cooperatives, inculcating a new independence of action.

The process of depaternalization was quite uneven. In the Grace plantations, field-workers were reluctant to give up their weekly rations of meat, rice, and salt in exchange for food coupons. The system was more than a century old, introduced when the first Chinese coolies were imported into Peru to work in the cotton and sugar plantations. Serving five and seven years as indentured servants, the coolies were paid in part by weekly and, in some instances, daily food rations. When the coolie system was ended, the practice continued. In the old I.P.C. town of Negritos, sold when company operations were consolidated at Talara, the residents resented paying for water and power that they had formerly received gratis from the company. That experience slowed I.P.C.'s rush to depaternalize. What seemed logical and rational from the company perspective was sometimes construed as mean-spirited and derelict among workers and *empleados* not really prepared for independent living.

In another instance, however, I.P.C. helped to rebuild the small fishing village of Cabo Blanco, twenty miles north of Talara. Cabo Blanco had surfaced on the American literary scene when the celebrated American novelist Ernest Hemingway flew to Cabo Blanco in April 1956 to help film *The Old Man and the Sea*, his last great novel. The story's protagonist was a simple Cuban marlin fisherman fighting off sharks trying to make a meal of his catch. Except the marlin off Cuba would not leap or jump for the cameras. So Hemingway and the film crew flew to Peru, where, off Cabo Blanco, some of the great marlin of the world were known to sport.

Hemingway and his crew fished for thirty-two days from just after dawn "until it was too rough to photograph and the seas ran like on-rushing hills with snow blowing off the tops," according to Hemingway.[14] When the crew finally hooked into some marlin, the fish would not jump. Disappointed, they left Cabo Blanco, where one Hemingway biographer—who was either ignorant or was invoking "literary license"—described the hotel where Hemingway and the film crew had stayed as "luxurious."[15]

I.P.C. workers knew Cabo Blanco well. Luxurious it was not. A desalinization plant was located on an adjacent beach, and I.P.C. personnel occasionally fished the deep, cold waters off Cabo Blanco where the Humboldt Current swept up along the coast. The hamlet, however, was primitive. No water, sewage, or electricity flowed through the wooden shacks where residents, pigs, and cattle all shared the same spaces. Dead fish and fresh dung stunk and added to the squalor, although fishermen, endowed by nature with such a wonderful fishing ground, only had to fish two or three days a week to make a living. When Dr. Guillermo Gorbitz, I.P.C.'s medical director at Talara, was asked whether I.P.C. would help build a church, the physician went one step further. "Why not rebuild the whole town?" he suggested, no doubt having been assailed on occasional visits to the hamlet by the smells of rotting fish and raw sewage, a potent combination. A nearby petroleum tank farm probably added the noxious odor of oil to an already vile mixture of fish and sewage.

The town formed a committee, named its most prestigious citizen, the owner of the small hotel-bar where Hemingway had stayed, as chairman, and agreed that it would be a good idea to rebuild the town. I.P.C. supplied much of the materials and machinery, and the work began. Pens were built to separate the animals out of living quarters, and the old wooden shacks were torn down and replaced by homes built from cinder blocks that the villagers themselves manufactured on the beach. I.P.C. asked for some compensation, so the village voted a self-imposed tax that was collected by an extra day of fishing. When a price tag was added to the water from the desalinization plant, the local governing committee added its own markup to increase its revenues.[16] Cabo Blanco was happy with I.P.C.

Life in the company towns was leavened by other new forces in the 1950s and 1960s. Many idealistic young American priests traveled the long road to Peru to promote social and economic justice, and some logically enough migrated to the company towns. Indeed in the 1960s the wave of American priests, many of them members of the Maryknoll Order, reached a high tide in Peru. Almost 70 percent of all American priests in Latin America were in Peru.[17] They sought to raise standards of living and clashed in numerous places with companies that felt they were moving as rapidly as possible to improve living conditions, given the limitations imposed by local cultural patterns and the necessity to produce profits. Maryknolls and managers were both Americans, but with distinctly different priorities, making the easy generalizations levied by dependency theorists against the United States sometimes difficult to reconcile with the realities of the U.S. presence in Peru.

Labor unions, encouraged by U.S. companies to learn to seek the benefits of collective bargaining, colored labor-management affairs in the company towns rather differently from the normal context of labor-management relations in Peru. Encouraged to seek nonpolitical ends, the unions focused on wages, benefits, work schedules, and the like, and they were quite successful in many instances. The very success of these U.S.-modeled unions caused concern among the old governors of Peru. They felt the State was losing its paternalistic control and dominance of the laboring man whose new independent-minded unions looked to themselves rather than the government in Lima for their livelihood and welfare.[18]

Despite the new image created by U.S. companies, which bore little outward resemblance to their ancestors at the turn of the century, heated and sometimes protracted disputes still arose. In the 1960s the Cerro Corporation decided to move the town of Cerro de Pasco to gain access to rich ores known to exist under the old town. They could only be mined profitably by open-pit mining, so the old town had to be torn down. With this move the company was committed to building a first class new town, San Juan Pampa, in every way materially better than the old one. Generous terms were extended to everyone, from homeowners to store owners, and the company would build everything—houses, plaza, civic buildings, schools, a church, and even a university. With indoor plumbing and modern architecture, it was to be a picture-perfect, planned-from-the-beginning new town.

But few wanted to have anything to do with this new town. They liked the old winding streets filled with memories, the beloved church whose steeples, bells, and statues reminded the people of their antique faith. The new church, for example, was designed by a Swiss architect and looked like a giant A-frame. Pleasing to the European or American eye, it was an eyesore, a foreign object in the midst of the *pasqueños*.[19] The old church had to be demolished in the dead of night with members of the Guardia Civil cordoning off the site. Anguish accompanied the move to the new town. The company eventually built a replica of the old church in the new town of San Juan Pampa to make amends. "San Juan Pampa," Goodsell noted, "is many times more attractive than the old town by almost any conceivable standard of material welfare, but it had been imposed on its people."[20]

The impact of U.S. companies in Peru extended, of course, far beyond the confines of company towns. I.P.C.'s presence in fact reached throughout Peru wherever petroleum products were sold. The ubiquitous "Esso" logo represented to Peru the long arm of imperialism, with all its negative connotations. That for a long time the mother corporation of I.P.C. was named the "Imperial" Oil Company smacks of a rich irony, perhaps underscoring the power of words in matters of influence and perception.[21]

But there was another aspect of the U.S. corporate presence in Peru that proved immensely positive in Peru's national development. Peru's leaders had long sought to integrate a nation divided by geography, race, and historical circumstances into highly distinct regions. Inadvertently, but certainly not indirectly, U.S. companies brought national integration more closely to being realized in modern Peru.[22] The history of this aspect of the U.S. presence in Peru goes back to the nineteenth century (and has been examined in previous chapters). For example, Henry Meiggs and Slim Faucett helped pioneer railroading and flying, respectively, in Peru, two of the most obvious means of integrating a nation by extending networks of communications across previously isolated regions. Through Pan American–Grace Airways (Panagra), Pan Am and Grace contributed directly to the communications infrastructure of Peru—from building airstrips to installing navigational aids across the nation, used not only by Panagra and Faucett, but by other air carriers as they developed after mid-century.

Another U.S.-sponsored air service within Peru was provided by the Jungle Aviation and Radio Service (JAARS). In the late 1940s and 1950s they had more than a dozen planes in service that transported not only the missionaries but commercial traffic, such as U.S. oil company teams exploring for petroleum. JAARS also occasionally gave a lift to the Peruvian military into remote parts of the jungle, until then only penetrated by American translators and missionaries employed by the Summer Institutes of Languages and the Wycliffe Bible Translators.

In the realm of transportation, entities such as Grace Line, I.P.C., SPCC, and Marcona provided lighterage services and improved port facilities at various roadsteads along the coast. The petroleum and mineral companies built piers and facilities at such places as Talara (I.P.C.), Ilo (SPCC), and San Juan (Marcona), while Grace Line provided tug and lighterage service all along the coast. This was especially important since Peru possessed few natural harbors, and ships (of Grace Line or other lines) had to anchor offshore and transfer cargo via tugs and lighters at most of the open roadsteads.

The other modern form of transportation in which U.S. companies participated, and sometimes initiated, was road building. The record, though, is spotty, and roads sponsored or built by U.S. companies contributed little to "national" integration, if by that term we mean truly linking disparate and isolated parts of the nation together. The immense geographical barriers of Peru and the needs of the companies limited these efforts. For example, the roads built in and around Talara by I.P.C. basically only networked the company's oil fields and refineries. Likewise roads built by Marcona and SPCC were largely to connect their mines and towns to the Pan-American highway. Some of the Cerro Corporation's roads stand out for the incredibly difficult terrain they had to conquer in the high Andes. Other efforts, notably one led by the U.S. entrepreneur Robert G. LeTourneau, were aimed at opening up parts of the jungle area on the eastern slopes of the Andes to colonization and development.

LeTourneau's trajectory in Peru brought together some fascinating elements. In this instance Christian evangelization was tied in with road building and heavy equipment testing in an experiment that, in many ways, is still ongoing in Peru. LeTourneau, a Longview, Texas, native, made his fortune manufacturing heavy machinery and then spent much of it on Christian fundamentalist causes. An eccentric, he liked to fly around in a converted World War II vintage B-26 bomber and relied closely on his link with God for business decisions. "God," he said, "is chairman of my board of directors."[23]

LeTourneau reached Peru in 1952 through his friendship with William Cameron Townsend, who, as discussed earlier, founded the Summer Institutes of Languages and was a noted Protestant educator and evangelical. LeTourneau was soon introduced to President Odría, who liked the Texan's plan to open up the jungle area around Pucallpa with his huge earthmoving equipment. LeTourneau agreed to build a road from the Central Highway to the Pachitea River, a navigable tributary of the Amazon.[24] In return he was given a sizable concession of jungle land south of Pucallpa to colonize and develop in return for building the road. And, of course, LeTourneau would also be propagating the faith among the Indians. The town of Tournavista that was built to accommodate the project contained not only schools, a church, store, clinic, power and sewer systems, two airfields and a water treatment plant, but also an Indian Bible Institute to spread the missionary gospel among the Indians.

LeTourneau finally built his road, but the work required almost five years, for the annual rains and mud slides were almost more than even his heroically sized earthmovers could handle. The projected development of the jungle did not take place. Beef cattle were introduced successfully, and a handful of colonists were in place by the late 1950s and 1960s, but the jungle proved a tough place to pioneer on the scale that Bob LeTourneau had envisioned. Only with the coming of the cocaine trade in the latter third of the century did these jungle valleys and lowlands become more accessible to the rest of the nation. Ironically the notorious drug trade of the 1980s and 1990s has probably done more for the integration of the jungle into the national psyche than all prior efforts.

The "Affair Nixon"

While LeTourneau and Townsend were looking after the material and spiritual development of Peru in the 1950s, the vice president of the United States prepared a trip to Latin America in 1958 that included Peru. Richard M. Nixon was greeted in Lima with rocks and epithets, symbolizing another face of Peruvian-U.S. relations, one marked by discord and anger, that presaged the role the United States was destined to follow in the revolution ten years later.

"You are cowards, you are afraid of the truth!" the vice president shouted at the jeering mob of students. Nixon stood in his limousine with his legs braced by his secret service chief, John T. Sherwood; the car slowly backed away from the mob gathered outside the gates of the University of San Marcos on the morning of May 8, 1958. The students responded in kind.

"Nixon get out! Go home," they shouted, with an occasional "Death to Nixon!" thrown in for emphasis.[25] One rock caught Sherwood in the mouth, breaking off a tooth. Nixon exalted in the confrontation. His ambassador, Theodore C. Achilles, was terrified by the fury of the encounter. The old battler against communism was once again confronting his foes, challenging them to talk, to defend their diatribes with facts, to listen to him respond from his profound faith in the American way that he knew was far better than godless communism. Why else would there be such a violent, angry mob meeting the vice president of the United States, if not one inspired by a small, cultish minority of Communist activists?

From San Marcos the motorcade drove on to the Catholic University where the reception was more civil and appropriate. Some students registered their displeasure at having to host Nixon, but the vice president finally found a relatively peaceful assembly of students with whom he could dialog. They talked about many things, and in the give and take that ensued between Nixon and the students many of the controversial issues between the countries were vividly portrayed.

The U.S. policy of stockpiling zinc and lead for national security had ended in 1957. Accordingly worldwide prices for those two ores plummeted, and Peru suffered, for lead and zinc accounted for 15 percent of its foreign earnings. How could the United States be so callous in this regard? Wasn't this just another demonstration of imperialism and dependency? Why wouldn't the United States recognize Peru's two-hundred-mile territorial limit? This was a legitimate expression of Peruvian sovereignty and to constantly oppose it was an affront to Peruvian nationality.

Why did the United States continue to support dictators in Latin America, even still selling arms to one of the most notorious dictators in Cuba, Fulgencio Batista? The United States spoke of democratic values and freedom but did not act that way. Was not the famed guerrilla fighter, Fidel Castro, promising a new freedom, a new social and economic justice for Cubans, as he waged his war from his havens in the Sierra Maestra mountains against the U.S.-supported Batista?

What about social justice and economic equality for Peruvians themselves, so long divided by race and wealth into a nation of very few haves and very many have-nots. What did the United States propose to do to help Peru in this area? Would the United States support land reform, for example, or oppose it in league with the patricians of Peru who still arrogantly controlled most of the land and wealth in the countryside?

Why did the Japanese receive preference in the U.S. fish market, and the Peruvians did not? Why did the Cubans receive preference in U.S.

markets for sugar, and the sugar quota from Peru was not increased? Was not a rising cost of living in Peru due, in fact, to many attitudes and actions of the United States?

"What is the United States going to do Mr. Vice President?" was the general tenor of questioning. What indeed?

Nixon admitted that the United States could do more to help under-developed countries economically. Politically, the vice president said that "it was not sufficient to demonstrate that communism is bad. We must also," he added thoughtfully, "prove that liberty and democracy are better."[26]

Some Peruvians made it clear to Nixon that it was the *Apristas*, and not the Communists, who hurled rocks and spat and jeered at him that morning at the doorsteps of San Marcos. Indeed *Apristas* controlled much of the student government. In the wake of the incident, a number of the radical leaders apologized for the violence but not for expressing their points of view. Many in the Peruvian press applauded Nixon for his bravery and pluck in the face of such a violent confrontation, al-though the historian Jorge Basadre reflected that such grandstanding may have been part of the vice president's modus operandi. It gave him notoriety and publicity, and, after all, it *was* anticipated that he would be the Republican presidential nominee in the 1960 election.

Following Nixon's visit, the loud and sometimes rancorous debate be-tween Peru and I.P.C. continued, further underscoring Peru's perceived dependency upon American capitalism. I.P.C. had been arguing for some time for petroleum price increases. Peruvians already paid the lowest price for gasoline anywhere in the Western Hemisphere, and I.P.C. could no longer sustain such artificially low prices and continue to invest in finding and developing new oil fields. I.P.C.'s operating costs were rising, exports were falling, and Peruvians had to pay more. Peruvians responded to this corporate wail with extreme skepticism. They viewed I.P.C. as simply an extension of the giant Standard Oil of New Jersey, which had annual revenues *three times* greater than Peru's gross national product, an impressive statistic that made I.P.C.'s public groaning rather incredulous in the view of many Peruvians.[27] Besides, they argued, I.P.C.'s profits in the past had been so high that the com-pany could well afford a few lean years.

Despite the rancor associated with Richard Nixon's trip to Peru in 1958, Peruvians demonstrated that they were of two minds with respect to the United States. Some wished for more sympathetic and fairer—at least in the Peruvian point of view—treatment from the United States. Others resented the continued dominating presence of the United States in Peru, especially through such giant corporations as I.P.C. and Cerro de Pasco.

The character of the U.S. presence was complex and diverse, leading to often strikingly divergent views among Peruvians. The U.S. government supported San Diego–based tuna fishermen that hurt Peru, but the United States also provided technical assistance in agriculture, medicine, and other areas. The growing presence of Protestant evangelicals, such as Townsend's Summer Institutes of Languages, threatened traditional Peruvian Roman Catholicism, but it also was a "new" religion welcomed as a liberating influence in a traditional society. Peruvians stoned Richard Nixon one week and applauded Leonard Bernstein in concert the next.

By the end of the decade, new winds were blowing across the hemisphere. Fidel Castro captured Havana on January 1, 1959, with his ragtag, bearded revolutionaries and sent Fulgencio Batista packing. Within a year Castro was leading Cuba down the road of true Marxism, linking up with the Soviet Union. And in November 1960, a youthful senator from Massachusetts squeaked through to victory over Richard Nixon, restoring the Democrats to power, rekindling in Washington some of the high idealism and activism of the early Roosevelt years, only this time within the setting of the titanic struggle between communism and the free world.

The Alliance for Progress Era

Mention President John F. Kennedy and Latin America in the same breath, and one almost automatically conjures up the Alliance for Progress. The alliance was conceived of by a consortium of political, business, and educational leaders called together by the president-elect to brainstorm at Harvard University in December 1960, and its establishment was announced formally by President Kennedy March 13, 1961. Two imperatives drove the alliance: one, the threat of communism in Latin America, especially given Castro's rise; and two, the renewed spirit of social and economic justice that drove the Kennedy administration.

Basically the alliance sought to undermine communism and promote democracy by attacking what were perceived as the roots of communism, and revolutionary discontent in general, in Latin America: social injustice, economic inequities, political dictatorships, and their concomitants—hunger, poverty, underemployment, and frustration with a system that did not deliver what people wanted.

"[Latin] American people need homes, work, and land, health and schools," President Kennedy said upon announcing the alliance, and the United States aimed to deliver. Kennedy intended nothing less than to eliminate hunger and illiteracy in Latin America. Land reform and tax reforms were musts on the agenda as well.[28] These massive social and economic reforms could only be accomplished within a framework of free, democratic structures.

"Progress yes," Kennedy said, "tyranny, no," he added, thereby directly challenging the policies of several of his predecessors who tolerated dictatorships, as long as they were friendly dictatorships.

"Liberty and progress walk hand-in-hand," Kennedy said, challenging his listeners. The alliance would be different. Indeed it was perhaps the last crusade of the United States to remake Latin America in the American image. Or, as Fredrick Pike phrased it, the "Americanization of Latin America" was under way.[29]

The basic ingredients of a happy and prosperous American people—individual freedom, self-reliance, and the spirit of competition—needed to be inculcated in Latin America if the region was to march out of underdevelopment and dictatorships.[30] Create a stable and prosperous nation of individualistic capitalists, and "they would not only become good democrats and reliable anti-Communists; they would also become purchasers of U.S. goods."[31] Thus, reflecting for a moment on the Alliance for Progress and Peru, it could be expected that U.S. companies in Peru would be supported by the U.S. government in this era. That proved to be true, and, as we shall see below, only too true when the controversy between I.P.C. and the Belaúnde administration increasingly came to occupy center stage in the mid- to late 1960s.

The formal alliance was declared in August 1961, after a meeting of the American states at Punta del Este, Uruguay. The Charter of Punta del Este embodied the principles enunciated by Kennedy, and, equally important, the United States pledged $11 billion (two-thirds from public funds, the balance from private ones) in assistance over the course of the next ten years. Goals were set (a minimum economic growth rate of 2.5 percent per year for example), agencies created (the Peace Corps, the U.S. Agency for International Development), and existing institutions, such as the AFL-CIO, integrated into the effort. AFL-CIO organizers and administrators were drafted, for example, to help create independent unions, encourage collective bargaining, and reduce or eliminate the old union's dependence upon old-style paternalistic governments. It was all part of a grand scheme.

By 1968 the alliance had run out of idealistic steam and actual monies, but it served as the framework for Peru and the United States in the 1960s. Agrarian reform, for example, was long a goal of both revolutionaries and reformers, and it was thoroughly integrated into the alliance's agenda.

Agrarian Reform and the United States

In Peru through the mid-twentieth century, more than 75 percent of the land under cultivation was owned by less than 1 percent of the population. Almost all twentieth-century reformers and revolutionaries in Peru, and, indeed, throughout Latin America, fervently fought to redistribute the land from those few who owned it to those many who worked it. The history of land and its use in Peru is long, complicated, and fascinating. By the 1960s, under the goad of the idealistic alliance and even before then in an experiment (examined below), the United States sought to make land reform a reality in Peru.

There were hedges and reservations on the part of U.S. advocates, but land reform was thought critical to making Peruvian society more just, making material and psychic prosperity available to the masses, not just the privileged elites. APRA, for example, had long made land reform one of its most important goals. APRA celebrated virtues of land reform as the mechanism for restoring dignity, prosperity, and equality to the great mass of Peruvian Indians and *cholos* still marginalized by a system justly described as feudal even through the mid-twentieth century.

One of the dreams of some social scientists is to somehow put their knowledge, or their theories, to work outside the classroom. In 1950 a professor of anthropology at Cornell University proposed to a Peruvian government agency, the Instituto Indigenista Peruano, that a hacienda named Vicos in the high Andean valley of the Callejón de Huaylas be made the subject of a long-term experiment in change and improvement.[32] Professor Allan R. Holmberg had been doing research in the region under the auspices of the Carnegie Corporation. His friendship with Peruvian colleagues Carlos Monge, Manuel Velasco Núñez, and Mario Vásquez of the Instituto Indigenista, plus the continuing support of Carnegie and Cornell, paved the way for turning Vicos into something of a laboratory of modern, applied social anthropology. Vásquez spoke Quechua, the language of the Vicos Indians, which was an indispensable tool for any anthropologist doing research among the indigenous peoples of Peru. The stage was thus set.

In 1951 the Peru/Cornell project leased the Vicos hacienda from its owners, a private charitable institution, or *beneficencia,* of Huaráz, the capital of Ancash. The 19,000-acre Vicos lay in the shadow of the magnificent 21,000-foot Huscarán, the highest peak in the Peruvian Andes. The *beneficencia* typified a form of absentee landownership in much of Peru. Churches, schools, and other institutions, as well as individuals, were largely absentee landlords who usually leased or rented the land. Little was invested in making the land more productive, in the welfare of its workers, or, in short, in the long-term interest of the land and the men who tilled it. The Indians of Vicos, the *vicosinos,* were immensely conservative and distrusted outsiders. Their hacienda was usually rented to the highest bidder whose interest was in making money as quickly and expeditiously as possible. The Indian workers were at the bottom of this pile, receiving pitifully low wages and a bit of coca to chew.

When the Peru/Cornell project organizers suggested in 1955 or 1956 that the *beneficencia* rent the hacienda directly to the Indians, rather than through the project, the trustees of the *beneficencia* flatly refused. The Manuel Prado y Ugarteche government in 1956 had to expropriate Vicos from the *beneficencia* and then provide a loan for the new owners who were expected to repay the *beneficencia*.

What did the Peru/Cornell project accomplish? Did it successfully transform the ancient hacienda into a community of cooperative, prosperous landowners, with a "new spirit of independence and hope" as James Carey phrased it in the early 1960s when reviewing the events of the past decade.[33]

In the first year of the project its gringo/Peruvian administrators were barely able to gain even a hint of trust and confidence from the Indians whose experience with outsiders was based on exploitation and abuse. "Let's talk about problems," the social scientists and agronomists said. "What problems?" would be the short, quiet, door-shutting response from the Indians.

Gradually and persistently, a bridge was opened between the two, not by making philosophical or political points, but by commonsensical strategies, such as suggesting a new and better seed potato and providing access to insecticides and fertilizers. That is the way to communicate with farmers, and, to their credit, the Vicos administrators never moved rapidly or theoretically beyond the confines of the Andean reality. The second year a new school was constructed, with teachers provided by the Peruvian government. Later a potable water plant and an electric generator were installed, in each instance community labor and assistance being drawn upon to closely identify the improvement of life with self-help.

The project also helped draw the *vicosinos* into the modern mainstream of Peruvian life. Isolated by geography, by language, and by historical circumstances, many Vicos Indians did not recognize the name of the Peruvian president Odría in 1951, or even what the word "Peru" referred to.[34]

"Today [in 1972]," wrote William Mangin, an anthropologist who served as field director of the project in 1952–53, "it would be rare to encounter the kind of isolation that was common then. . . . Indians have found out about the nation and about themselves." They learned Spanish, at least those aspiring to rise in the community, some traveled around Peru selling potatoes, others served in the army, and a few even traveled to the United States on trips sponsored by AID and the farmer's union.

By the early 1960s, after all U.S. personnel had departed, Vicos served as a model of sorts for the many other self-improvement agrarian projects launched in the 1960s. Once thought to have been unique, as Fredrick Pike noted, Vicos "provided only one among dozens, even hundreds, of examples of peasant communities that were 'digging their own way out of their Andean isolation, punching through their own farm-market and access roads, bridging the gullies that cut them off from the national economy, providing school rooms for their children, quarters for their local officials, and starting on the task of providing basic modern public utilities.'"[35]

In the process of improving or reforming life in the agrarian sector of Peru, the United States provided much of the agricultural credit in the 1950s and 1960s, and through such agencies as the Peace Corps, even a little of the manpower. Most of the credits and moneys were aimed at improving existing structures, however, rather than at land reform itself. Irrigation schemes (Quiroz/San Lorenzo in the region around Piura in the north), a fishing cooperative at Chimbote, and agricultural production and planning for southern Peru all received U.S. assistance in the prealliance period.

In the 1960s AID spent $12 million in technical assistance with the goal of increasing the food supply and distribution. The National Agrarian University at La Molina just outside of Lima was expanded and upgraded at all levels, from the physical campus to the level of instruction of its faculty and students. Contracts with U.S. universities, such as North Carolina State and Iowa State, brought in dozens of technical experts to Peru to assist in a wide variety of agricultural objectives, from planning to implementation. Millions more were made available by AID in other areas of agriculture, in transportation ($20 million), and in housing ($13.5 million).

Curiously John Strasma, one of the most reliable observers of the alliance phenomena, wrote that "the role of the U.S. government and of U.S. companies during this period was not great."[36] Perhaps in the context of the overall Peruvian economy, U.S. aid was small. U.S. companies, after all, only accounted for about 10 percent of the gross national product of Peru. But, as we have seen through Goodsell's analysis of U.S. companies, it could be an immensely important 10 percent, depending upon how one looked at its composition and focus. The *gran minería* of Cerro, Southern Peru Copper, and Marcona, for example, was viewed as having a disproportionate influence in the export sector of Peru's economy. And, as we shall see shortly below, holding back some of this AID-funded assistance during the I.P.C.-Peru crisis proved perhaps even more telling than the impact of the actual assistance itself.

The Alliance for Progress in Peru was more than agriculture, although the largest proportion of assistance to Peru was targeted at the agrarian section. Education, housing, public administration (modernizing taxes for example), labor development, public safety, and numerous other areas received U.S. funds, loans, and/or technical assistance. After agriculture one of the principal areas of assistance was education. To deliver assistance at the primary and secondary level of education, AID contracted with the Teacher's College Columbia University (TCCU) to work with the Peruvian Ministry of Education for a five year period between 1963–68. The agenda was impressive and wide-ranging, from developing a modern system of vocational education to increasing the effectiveness of rural education. Much planning was done, experts dispatched, reports filed, and then, as one jaded observer wrote, "the U.S. advisers settled into their relatively unproductive routine."[37] Various difficulties plagued the TCCU teams, none more telling than the periodic freezing or withholding of funds in the mid- and late 1960s as the U.S. continued to put pressure on Peru to settle the I.P.C. crisis.

In higher education, funds made available through the Interamerican Development Bank, itself funded in part by AID, were applied to upgrading faculties and resources throughout the traditional university system. Science, technology, engineering, and agriculture were the principal recipients of various funds, used for everything from building laboratories to sending scores of Peruvians to the United States to continue their studies. Even new institutes were created. Through an AID contract, Stanford University helped establish a graduate-level business school called the Escuela Superior de Administración y Negocios (ESAN) that blossomed into the premier graduate-level business school in Peru in the next three decades.

While an immense amount of goodwill was being generated through the various programs of the Alliance for Progress, one unbearable American thorn remained in the flesh of Peru: I.P.C.

The Peruvian Revolution of 1968

"No people can live in dignity," said one of Peru's generals involved in the revolution, "and with respect for its sovereignty . . . when it [the government] tolerates the insolent arrogance of another state within its own frontiers." "We were the largest taxpayer in Peru and our labor practices were a model for the country," sniffed an official of I.P.C. in reply. To which the U.S. embassy added, "I.P.C. was always very generous, and honestly worked hard to reach a settlement [with Peru]."[38]

The revolution of October 3 led by Gen. Juan Velasco Alvarado was triggered by the inability of the Belaúnde government to bring I.P.C. under Peruvian control, although the facts of the matter rather bizarrely demonstrate that in the four or five months preceding the October revolution, I.P.C. virtually capitulated to all of Peru's demands.

At the core of these demands was the insistence that I.P.C. yield on its claims to the subsoil rights at its oil fields in La Brea and Pariñas. During the negotiations of the 1960s, especially picking up in intensity after Belaúnde was inaugurated July 28, 1963, Peru upped the ante. I.P.C. characteristically resisted, but it slowly acquiesced to Peruvian demands. When Peru claimed, for example, that I.P.C. had illegally operated the oil fields for more than fifty years, and, in fact, owed Peru an astronomical sum—$600 million—in back taxes and profits, I.P.C. objected, but then agreed that perhaps even this point could be negotiated. If I.P.C. renounced its ancient claims to La Brea and Pariñas, would the Peruvians agree to a long-term concession enabling I.P.C. to continue in

Peru—utilizing oil from the old I.P.C. properties (perhaps given to Peru)—for I.P.C.'s refineries? Would Peru renounce its claims against I.P.C.—including the bill for back taxes and profits—if I.P.C. renounced all prior positions it had taken with regard to its unique claims at La Brea and Pariñas?

Of course the negotiations did not take place in a vacuum. Indeed when one reviews the bare facts, it seems that a reasonable solution could have been reached between Peru and I.P.C. in 1963 and again in 1968, based on the willingness of both sides to make compromises in their positions. But the history of I.P.C. in Peru heated the exchanges in a fashion that almost leads one to the phrase "inevitable." Was the demise of I.P.C. in Peru inevitable?

Examine the role, for example, of the U.S. government during the "affaire I.P.C." In 1962 the Kennedy administration did not recognize a military junta that ousted President Prado on July 18. At issue was what was basically a Peruvian problem. The military refused to countenance the possibility that their old nemesis, the APRA party, would come to share political power after a tight presidential election held earlier that year. Given Peru's electoral laws, Manuel Odría—one of the three presidential candidates—once again would be elected to the presidency, only this time with the support of Haya and the *Apristas*. The military favored the reformist Fernando Belaúnde Terry, who would be blocked from the presidency by the accord between Odría and the *Apristas*.

The Kennedy administration balked at the coup, especially since Belaúnde clearly represented the reformist option so dear to alliance planners. In the immediate wake of nonrecognition, the United States suspended all but humanitarian aid to Peru. A member of the Peruvian junta tried to assuage U.S. concerns by promising to respect all U.S. properties and investments in Peru. Besides, Peru argued that the U.S. policy was inconsistent and hypocritical given the fact that the United States had quickly recognized a military coup earlier that year in Argentina. Kennedy eventually backed down, especially when assurances were provided by the junta to the Organization of American States that constitutional liberties would soon be restored and a new election held in June 1963. Belaúnde would go on to win that election.

On August 17, 1962, the United States recognized the junta, but in its recognition statement referred to internal Peruvian politics.[39] This rankled the Peruvians who issued a strongly worded statement protesting the American announcement. *El Comercio,* one of I.P.C.'s most vocal critics in the country, warmly supported the junta's stand. Relations were restored, but the lingering effect of having to bend the knee to U.S. pressure did not sit well with the generals. The issue of I.P.C. was bandied about by some junta members during their year in office as something that needed to be settled decisively and rapidly. The mixture of petroleum and the Peruvian military would prove lethal to I.P.C., especially during Belaúnde's presidency when the president moved neither decisively nor rapidly to solve the I.P.C. problem in the minds of the generals.

The U.S. policy toward Peru with respect to I.P.C. between 1963–68 was contradictory, confusing, and ambivalent. In effect U.S. policy was dictated by whomever was occupying the post of Assistant Secretary of State for Inter-American Affairs, as well as by changing domestic circumstances in the United States. The result was an amazing lack of continuity in policy that confounded the Peruvians.

When Belaúnde was inaugurated in July 1963, Kennedy's coordinator for the Alliance for Progress, Teodoro Moscoso, flew to Lima to offer the new president generous assistance and aid. It seemed like a propitious moment for moving ahead together. Belaúnde was committed, through campaign promises, to solve once and for all the I.P.C. matter. The Kennedy administration furthermore was not committed, either by law or disposition, to assisting I.P.C., nor was there ever any evidence presented in the period that I.P.C. specifically asked for government intervention. The Hickenlooper Amendment *had* been passed by Congress in 1962, and it would loom over relations between Peru and the United States in 1969 and 1970 after the revolution; it did not affect, however, I.P.C.'s negotiations with Peru. Hickenlooper was aimed at cutting off assistance to countries that had expropriated U.S. properties without just compensation. I.P.C. had neither been expropriated nor nationalized in 1963, although certainly the threat was in the air.

John Kennedy was assassinated November 22, 1963, in Dallas, Texas.

His successor, Lyndon Baines Johnson, appointed a fellow Texan, Thomas C. Mann, as new Assistant Secretary of State for Inter-American Affairs. With Mann's appointment, there came a reversal of U.S. policy toward Peru and I.P.C. This set the stage for one of the oddest scenes in the long history of Peruvian-U.S. relations.

"Mann decided to suspend all foreign aid to Peru," wrote Richard Goodwin, a one-time Kennedy staff member, "until Belaúnde reached an agreement with I.P.C." So far so good. Then, as Goodwin remembers, the matter was kept basically secret from the Peruvians. "Foreign aid was suspended without delivering an ultimatum or even telling Peru that aid had been stopped," wrote Goodwin.

"The idea," one U.S. official said, "was to put on a freeze, talk about red tape and bureaucracy, and they'd soon get the message." The official went on to say, somewhat incredulously, that "unfortunately they believed we were as inefficient as we said, and it took about a year for them to get the message."[40]

In fact assistance was frozen for almost two years as Belaúnde's government continued to negotiate, unsuccessfully, with I.P.C. Belaúnde almost reached an agreement with a new I.P.C. general manager, Fernando Espinosa, named in early 1964. Espinosa was Cuban-born and a long-time executive of I.P.C.; he was described as urbane, well educated, more of a diplomat than a businessman.[41] Almost groomed by disposition and education to the job, he got along well with Belaúnde, and they reached an accord in mid-1964. Belaúnde worried that the opposition, especially the *Apristas* and the anti-I.P.C. daily *El Comercio*, owned by the powerful Miró Quesada family, would sabotage the tentative agreement.[42] So Espinosa helped Belaúnde by dealing directly with Haya and getting a verbal agreement that APRA would cooperate. However, with Luis Miró Quesada, the old lion of the family, Espinosa made no headway. Angered to the point of fury by the seeming intransigence and logic of Miró Quesada's opposition to I.P.C., Espinosa even considered filing a libel suit against the newspaper, only to be dissuaded by I.P.C.'s Peruvian lawyers.

Although in his eighties and somewhat fragile toward the end of his long personal war with I.P.C., Don Luis Miró Quesada was a formidable opponent. Miró Quesada had a long and intimate acquaintance with the English-speaking world, having begun his schooling as a young boy in an English school. Later, when he wrote his doctoral dissertation in literature at the University of San Marcos, he chose the theme of "Calderón de la Barca y Shakespeare." The titles of his dissertations for his Ph.D. in political science reflect his interests in the modern problems of Peru: "La moderna crisis social" ("The Modern Social Crisis") and "La cuestión obrera en el Perú" ("The Labor Problem in Peru"). He gravitated toward journalism and after obtaining a law degree went to work with his father publishing *El Comercio.* He served in a number of high-level public positions, both elected and appointed, distinguishing himself as an innovator in education in Lima and in reforming the teaching of education at the university level. But his love was journalism. And his nemesis was I.P.C.

"It's not enough for an oil company to pay taxes and salaries," he said. "Peru should get a share of the profits." After all, unlike trees or other renewable resources, "once minerals are taken, they are gone."

Pressed to justify his intransigent stand against I.P.C., Don Luis defended his position. "I am a nationalist. There is nothing wrong with that. I am anti-Communist," he continued, observing that "they have some good criticisms, but they do not have liberty, and that is the most important thing to men. Especially to journalists."[43]

Nationalism and liberty. These were key principles in Miró Quesada's opposition to I.P.C.: nationalism because I.P.C. seemed to have subverted the exercise of legitimate Peruvian sovereignty over its natural resources; and liberty, for it seemed that I.P.C., supported by the U.S. government, had deprived Peru of its liberty to pursue its destiny.

But it was more than the sometimes impersonal forces of nationalism, liberty, and other principles that drove this argument between I.P.C. and Peru. It was people, such as Luis Miró Quesada, who saw a different "truth" from the managers of I.P.C.

When Jack Ashworth, the general manager of I.P.C. in Lima in 1959, found himself on the same aircraft from Lima to New York with Miró Quesada, Ashworth tried some personal diplomacy. "Please don't try to persuade me," Miró Quesada told Ashworth. "You are the General

Manager of I.P.C. and you do well to defend your Company. I am the Editor of *El Comercio,* and I do well to defend my country. You have to be responsible to your share-holders. I have to be responsible to my readers." [44]

"This is the way it is," I.P.C. officials peremptorily told one Peruvian lawyer representing his client before the company. "They [I.P.C.] didn't even want to talk," the lawyer said, obviously frustrated and angry. "They just walked out." This seemingly imperious behavior on the part of I.P.C. infuriated Peruvians. I.P.C.'s acts did not particularly sit well with other members of the American business community in Peru either. "They got what was coming to them," said one U.S. businessman after the revolution of 1968. "They had bad public relations," noted another American in Peru, in a statement that Richard Goodwin correctly labeled as a masterful stroke of understatement. [45]

The gulf between I.P.C.'s and Peru's view of the world widened irreparably during the 1960s. I.P.C.'s manager during this period, Espinosa, met with President Belaúnde on at least sixty occasions, but Espinosa was still astounded by Belaúnde's misunderstandings of the relationship between Standard Oil and the U.S. government.

Belaúnde, so Espinosa gathered from his many meetings with the president, was operating "under the assumption that the United States government was very much under the influence of American business, particularly Standard Oil (New Jersey)." This assumption was so well entrenched that Espinosa "got the impression that Belaúnde actually thought that the only thing needed for a resumption of aid was a telephone call from Standard Oil's president to Lyndon Johnson." [46]

The politics of the situation were not so simple, as Espinosa suggested. Belaúnde, who had studied in the United States and no doubt was aware of some of the major elements in American history, may have recalled—or had it recalled for him by his advisers—that in the past, such U.S. capitalists as John Pierpont Morgan *had* been able to influence U.S. policy with a phrase, a phone call, a loan. On the other hand, Lyndon Johnson had cut his political teeth on Franklin Roosevelt's New Deal era, and New Dealers were not particularly sympathetic to big business in America. Lyndon Johnson did believe in big government, but he certainly was not a lackey of big business. Those times had passed. Besides, in the summer of 1965, Johnson was cranking up the war in Vietnam, firing the opening salvos of his War on Poverty, and ensuring that the civil rights movement was given power through passing the immensely controversial and time-consuming Civil Rights Acts of 1964 and 1965. What happened to a small subsidiary of the giant Standard Oil in Peru did not concern L. B. J.

And, in the overall financial scheme of Standard Oil, I.P.C. hardly counted for much either. By the 1960s its investments in Peru had been amortized, its profits were small, and certainly an agreement with Peru should have been negotiated. But the agreement that was finally negotiated did not come until 1968, for the country and the company continued to spar and punch rather than negotiate through 1965, 1966, and 1967.

A considerable factor in this dispute was honor. Both corporate pride and Peruvian nationalism had more bearing on the situation than anything related to the simple facts of the case. Goodwin claims that ultimately the U.S. government could have promoted a settlement. "Only United States policy," Goodwin observed, "could have reconciled these diverging perceptions, for only the United States could command the respect of both I.P.C. and the Peruvian government." "This force," continued Goodwin, "was not brought to bear, and today's crisis [his article appeared in 1969] is in large measure a result of that failure."[47] Perhaps. Perhaps not. Could the United States have safely steered the tricky shoals of pride and nationalism?

Espinosa negotiated with a vast range of individuals representing all shades of Peruvian public opinion as he tried to forge a solution. In one exchange with a Peruvian senator, Espinosa discussed the issue of back taxes. Did I.P.C. owe Peru hundreds of millions of dollars on back taxes never paid from the company's profits? After considerable persuasion, Espinosa convinced the Peruvian senator that I.P.C. did not in fact legally owe the back taxes. Then, Espinosa recollected in an interview given in 1971, the senator still insisted that the company make a settlement of $50 or $60 million and end the controversy.

"But we have proved there is no debt," Espinosa argued.

"Maybe so," the senator shot back in frustration, "but the matter of the debt is a national psychosis!"[48] Psychosis is defined as "a major mental disorder in which the personality is very seriously disorganized and one's sense of reality is usually altered." To be fair a collective mental disorder should not be substituted for nationalism as one of the principal agents of discord between Peru and I.P.C. What is perhaps most suggestive of the situation is that two different sets of realities governed here—one viewed through the prism of Peru, and one through the corporate lens in Coral Gables, Florida, the headquarters of I.P.C.

The Peruvians insisted that I.P.C. make restitution for defrauding the nation over the long course of I.P.C.'s presence in Peru. I.P.C.'s management in Coral Gables would no more take responsibility for what had happened three or four decades ago than holding Peruvians of the 1960s accountable for what Leguía and Sánchez Cerro did in the 1920s and 1930s.

"For the group of men," I.P.C. historian Adalberto Pinelo wrote, "who had been responsible for their company's policy during the last thirty years, the men who had made Talara grow from a miserable village into a bustling and prosperous industrial city, it was hard to admit that they had been defrauding the Peruvian nation all along. . . . No private corporation can disburse fifty million dollars as therapy for a national psychosis."[49]

Then, early in 1966, the new Assistant Secretary for Inter-American Affairs, Lincoln Gordon, was appointed. U.S. policy again switched after Johnson adviser Walt Rostow traveled to Peru and received assurances from Belaúnde that Peru never intended to take I.P.C.[50] Aid was resumed, but by now Belaúnde's domestic economy, exacerbated by a dwindling export sector, was beginning to erode his political power.

A cyclical recession in 1967 forced the devaluation of the Peruvian currency, the sol, and fueled inflation. Land reform, so crucial to Belaúnde's progressive reform program, had been blocked by the opposition in the Peruvian Congress, raising frustrations of those promoting a real and ongoing program of social and economic justice. Intermittent U.S. assistance, much of it in the form of loans directed toward land reform programs, further interrupted this process. No one seemed very happy with the president. The devaluation of the sol produced a sudden increase in prices, not matched by salaries, and the lower and middle classes suffered a short but intense period of anguish and economic hardship. Belaúnde's government did initiate a series of deflationary efforts, and some progress was evident by 1968, but the general consensus of many Peruvians by then was that the president hardly had control of the country.

The Peruvian purchase of French-made Mirage jets in 1967, discussed above, once again tripped the wire on U.S. aid. U.S. assistance and loans were drastically cut in response to Peru's rejection of U.S.-made jet aircraft. A series of scandals in 1968 over smuggling rocked the administration, although Belaúnde himself was untouched.

Who was in charge here? Many thought that foreign firms were dictating Peru's economy, and thus were causing the woes. And at the center of the foreign firms was, of course, I.P.C.

In 1967 I.P.C. chose, at a most unpropitious moment, to apply for an increase in the government-fixed price of gasoline. The reasoning was simple. The devaluation of the sol meant that I.P.C. was selling gasoline at a loss, albeit a small loss. Furthermore I.P.C. was having to import gasoline to meet the demand in Peru that was now outstripping production. So I.P.C. asked for an increase in the price at the pump. It was logical. How could the company stay in business operating at a loss? Why should it continue to import gasoline to sell at a loss?

Peruvians saw it differently. Gen. Julio Doig Sánchez, then Belaúnde's Minister of War, angrily summoned Espinosa to a meeting. "If you stop importing gasoline, we seize La Brea," Doig Sánchez told the manager of I.P.C.[51] Espinosa, aware of rumors beginning to circulate in the capital of a possible military coup, stalled for time.

"I need to travel to Coral Gables and consult," he told Doig Sánchez.

"Why go so far to talk? Use the phone," the general snapped.

Convinced that the generals were serious, I.P.C. backed down on its threat. Within a few months, however, I.P.C. was quietly allowed to increase its prices.

Sitting in on the conference between the manager of I.P.C. and the minister of war was Gen. Juan Velasco Alvarado. He became the army chief of staff in March 1968 and the leader of the revolution that ousted Belaúnde on October 3 of that year.

Velasco Alvarado tightly controlled his fury. He was no stranger to I.P.C. As a young mestizo boy growing up in a modest home in Piura in northern Peru, he was familiar with the power that I.P.C. wielded in the region. In 1941 Velasco, as an infantry captain, was assigned the task of commandeering I.P.C. vehicles to move his troops to the front against Ecuador. Captain Velasco was told to cool his heels for about twenty-four hours as the local managers checked with their headquarters. Some think Velasco's later intransigence with I.P.C. was fueled by this incident.[52]

Velasco headed a military cabal of about a dozen middle- and high-ranking officers who were already planning to overthrow Belaúnde. A number of forceful internal or domestic reasons drove this coup. Belaúnde's failure to make progress on land reform, the continuing economic crisis, in-fighting among the leading political parties, and the military's own growing sense that the national destiny could only be fulfilled by the military institution—disciplined, apolitical, in touch with the mass of Peruvians' needs and desires—all contributed. The storm with I.P.C., however, escalated the growing frustration of the military with Belaúnde's inability to deal with the perceived problems of the nation. In effect the I.P.C. affair was the accelerator of the revolution.

But the military was almost deprived of its favorite whipping boy at the last minute. In July 1968 nationalist rhetoric heated up, and rumors of an impending coup to be followed by the swift expropriation of I.P.C. dominated the *limeño* imagination. Right then I.P.C. gave in to virtually all Belaúnde's demands.

On July 25, three days before Peru's national independence day when Belaúnde was expected to make a sweeping declaration of expropriation, a manager of I.P.C. walked into the office of Belaúnde's minister of development. I.P.C. would transfer La Brea and Pariñas to Peru and renounce any rights over the subsoil. In return Peru was asked to drop all claims against the company—back taxes and debts—and sell the crude oil from the newly nationalized fields of La Brea and Pariñas to I.P.C.

so that it could continue to refine and distribute petroleum products in Peru.

"I.P.C. agrees to all of that?" the Peruvian responded incredulously.

"Yes," came the reply. "It's everything you were asking for."[53]

Belaúnde went before Congress on July 28 and announced triumphantly that the I.P.C. affair was finally settled. La Brea and Pariñas belonged to Peru. I.P.C. could continue refining and marketing petroleum, but the land and subsoil were now Peru's. The deal was done. Some small details had to be hammered out, but they would soon be negotiated and the transfer of properties accomplished. Among the details was how much I.P.C. would pay the Peruvian state oil company, Empresa Petrolera Fiscal (EPF), for crude oil from La Brea and Pariñas to be refined by I.P.C.

Peru's negotiators were led by the president of EPF, Carlos Loret de Mola, a mild-mannered businessman who had never engaged in politics but was well schooled in the petroleum business. Belaúnde had announced that he would fly to Talara on August 13 to sign the final agreement, putting the pressure on the negotiators for I.P.C. and Peru to reach a final accord before then. The final deal kept sticking on one point: whether I.P.C. would agree to a price set by the Peruvians on the crude oil it was to buy from La Brea and Pariñas.

Lawyers, politicians, and technicians crowded the presidential palace for two weeks, wheeling and dealing in an increasingly hothouse pressure. When negotiations reached an impasse, Belaúnde urged Loret de Mola to continue. Loret de Mola was negotiating with I.P.C. nose to nose, and the Standard Oil Company could be tough.

"Standard Oil never gets out of any place without getting all its money," one I.P.C. negotiator stated flatly to the Peruvian, "and the same is going to happen here. . . . Here are our conditions," Loret de Mola was told. The conditions seemed to contradict what Belaúnde had told Congress a few days earlier. "Your President shouldn't have gone before Congress the way he did, because he deceived the people," the I.P.C. official told Loret de Mola when the Peruvian negotiator pointed out the contradictions in I.P.C.'s conditions and the President's message.[54]

Negotiations took on a special air of urgency the night of August 12.

The next morning Belaúnde was scheduled to fly to Talara to sign the agreement. Logically there simply had to be an agreement. But as the talks pushed into the dawn hours of the thirteenth, the negotiators could still not agree on the price I.P.C. would pay for the crude oil.

Espinosa, thinking perhaps the last details had finally been hammered out, went home around two in the morning to prepare for the dawn flight to Talara later that day. The phone rang a few minutes after Espinosa got home. "If you don't come back," Belaúnde's Prime Minister, Osvaldo Hercelles, ominously told Espinosa, "there'll be an expropriation." The case was still open.[55]

Belaúnde's staff called and woke U.S. Ambassador John Wesley Jones. "You have to negotiate to a conclusion," Jones told Espinosa. "Otherwise, Belaúnde will expropriate." Indeed the cabinet had already approved a decree of expropriation at an emergency meeting at three in the morning.

Espinosa returned to the presidential palace near dawn and the contract was finalized. Loret de Mola signed the ten-page document in one room. Espinosa did the same in another room. Then, in a somber mood, wearied from the tension of protracted negotiations, the group rode through the streets of Lima to the awaiting presidential aircraft. There, joined by Belaúnde, cabinet members, and other political officials, they took off for Talara. Later that day Belaúnde signed the Act of Talara, declaring the case closed once and for all. La Brea and Pariñas was—finally and irrefutably—Peruvian.

There was, however, a small fly in the ointment. On September 10, Loret de Mola appeared on national television and claimed there was a page eleven to the contract. On this page a minimum price for crude oil had been specified. Page eleven had been sabotaged by I.P.C. and left out of the final agreement.

El Comercio jumped on I.P.C.'s alleged foul play. "Grave Accusation by Loret de Mola," the headlines screamed. "The Contract Signed August 13 Was Altered and a Page Is Missing."[56] The rest was downhill for Belaúnde's government and for I.P.C. Critics of Belaúnde and I.P.C. jumped all over the contract—and not just the missing page eleven. Jungle concessions, continuing rights to operate and expand the refinery, and other real or perceived flaws in the contract were magnified by the missing page controversy. On October 3, 1968, the army seized Belaúnde in the palace and sent him packing.

"The armed forces of Peru," the revolutionary manifesto released by the junta on October 3 declared, "assume the responsibility for the management of the state in order to guide it definitely toward the attainment of national objectives. . . . Conscious of the desires of its citizens," the manifesto read in justification of the revolution, "and of the unprecedented need to put an end to the financial chaos, administrative immobility, improvisation, surrender of the national wealth and its exploitation for the benefit of the privileged few as well as the loss of the principle of authority and the incapacity to carry out the structural reforms for the well-being of the Peruvian people and the development of the country," the armed forces acted.[57]

On October 4, a decree nullified the Act of Talara, and on October 9, another decree followed, expropriating not only La Brea and Pariñas but I.P.C.'s refinery at Talara as well.

"The revolution is on the march," General Velasco Alvarado told the Peruvian people in a national address on the day of expropriation. As Peruvian soldiers and sailors took over the installations, Velasco rallied the nation. "The problem of La Brea and Pariñas has constituted a terrible wound for more than fifty years," Velasco said. "It is a chapter of opprobrium and shame in our history, an outrage to our dignity, our honor, and the sovereignty of the nation."

"So," Velasco continued, "the Armed Forces, closely tied to all Peruvians in one authentic national fraternity, once again meet its obligation, initiating with this act a revindication of our sovereignty and our dignity which will remain as a precious legacy for our sons." And, to distinguish Peru's attitude toward I.P.C. as opposed to foreign investment in general, Velasco added that "[we do this] as evidence of our affirmation of revolutionary goals, those very same goals which not only respect but encourage foreign investments which are in keeping with Peru's best interests."[58]

On February 6 the revolutionary government presented I.P.C. with a bill for almost $700 million, a figure fixed as the value of petroleum extracted from La Brea and Pariñas since 1924. The remainder of I.P.C.'s assets were seized that same day and were held until I.P.C. settled the bill. The expropriation was complete.

Was there a page eleven? Richard Goodwin explored the incident and came to the conclusion that there possibly did exist a page eleven signed by Loret de Mola, but that it never was seen by Espinoso. It was removed by one of the lawyers—Peru's or I.P.C.'s—since Loret de Mola insisted that a guaranteed price for La Brea and Pariñas crude be included in the contract, and Espinoso just as adamantly refused to negotiate a fixed price. As Loret de Mola recalled, he inked in the following on a blank sheet, page eleven: "In any event, the price for crude oil shall be no less than $1.0835." He signed the page. However the final Xerox copies of the contract contained only ten pages. Page eleven was missing.

To make the agreement work, Loret de Mola needed page eleven, which he got. Just as surely Espinoso would not agree to a fixed price. Therefore someone must have removed page eleven from the time Loret de Mola signed it in one room of the presidential palace near dawn of August 13. The original was then taken to Espinoso, sans page eleven, and he signed. Then the original disappeared, to be replaced only by the ten-page Xerox.

As noted on many occasions, the facts of the case in this instance carried considerably less weight than the perception of what actually transpired. We may never know the facts, but we do know what was perceived to have happened. It was enough to precipitate the end of the Belaúnde regime and the beginning of a remarkable revolutionary government for Peru.

And, in the context of the United States and Peru, I.P.C.'s long presence came to an end. Equally important a new era in Peruvian-U.S. relations was born. The new revolutionary government was careful however to distinguish between I.P.C. and other foreign investors in Peru, claiming that I.P.C. represented a unique case.

One has only to review the table of contents of a book containing President Velasco's speeches and declarations between 1968 and 1970 to appreciate the magnitude of I.P.C. on Peru's national consciousness.

Interspersed with such subjects as "autonomy," "colonialism," "peasant communities," "cooperativism," "dependency," and "economic/social development" was the unique category of the "International Petroleum Company" which sat, alphabetically, between "independence" and "social injustice." No other corporation, no other private or public entity, merited such an entry. There was also an entry for the "Act of Talara" and "Talara" as if to underscore the fixation of Velasco and other military officers on I.P.C.

The revolution not only knocked the wind out of the mostly comfortable relationship the United States and Peru had enjoyed to 1968, but it promoted a small growth industry in academic circles determined to explain and analyze what had happened. Perhaps the academic boomlet represented a maturing of the relationship.

In May 1970 a former Peace Corps administrator who helped create and direct the first Peace Corps programs in Peru organized a major conference on Peru. The result was a book published in 1972 and edited by the organizer, Daniel A. Sharp, *U.S. Foreign Policy and Peru*. For ten dollars one could obtain articles and comments by U.S. and Peruvian scholars, politicians, and statesmen on those subjects they defined as important in Peruvian-U.S. relations: among those were U.S. relations with the Peruvian military, the fisheries dispute, international lending agencies, the United States and agrarian reform, Indians, diplomatic protection of U.S. business in Peru, the foreign private sector in Peru, U.S. labor policy, Peruvian educational development, U.S. church-financed missions in Peru, Peru's relations with the United States and national development policy, and U.S. aid to Peru under the Alliance for Progress.[59]

Other studies exploring the relationship followed, including Charles T. Goodsell's *American Corporations and Peruvian Politics* (1974), an insightful study by a political scientist into the mechanisms of power and influence. A year later *The Peruvian Experiment: Continuity and Change Under Military Rule* (1975), edited by Abraham Lowenthal, appeared. Lowenthal had served in Peru as a Ford Foundation official between 1969 and 1972. He organized a group of social scientists in a seminar in New York in 1973 sponsored by the Council on Foreign Relations to explain the course of the Peruvian revolution. Lowenthal's lead article gave a hint of one of the principal themes: "Peru's Ambiguous Revolution." Other subjects included redistribution of income, squatter settlements and policy innovations, transforming the rural sector, land reform and social conflict, continuity and change in Peruvian education, political ideology, and foreign investments in Peru. The focus was clearly on Peru and her revolution, rather than on the United States and Peru, a relationship that, as we shall see in the last chapter, had been temporarily eclipsed by the direction and momentum of the revolution. In 1983 Lowenthal coedited with Cynthia McClintock a second appraisal of the revolution more than a decade after it had begun. *The Peruvian Experiment Reconsidered* drew heavily, as did the first volume, upon the views of political scientists and economists, although more Peruvian points of view were included in this volume. It was published in translation in Peru in 1985 as *El gobierno military: una experiencia peruano, 1968–1980,* by the Instituto de Estudios Peruanos. The title testified to the intimate relationship that Peruvians had with the military and the revolution's thrust, objectives, achievements, and failures.

The magisterial, pioneering work on the United States and Peru in this immediate postrevolutionary period came from historian Fredrick Pike, who was commissioned in the early 1970s to do a work on the United States and the Andean nations for a series published by Harvard University Press. Titled *The United States and the Andean Republics: Peru, Bolivia, and Ecuador* (1977), it was more than a history of relations between the United States and the Andean nations. Pike explained the context and culture of these relations and opened up an area of understanding heretofore little examined by historians and other social scientists. In a sense Pike's probing, brilliant, controversial analysis of cultural types and stereotypes in North America and Andean America pushed the subject of the United States and Peru into a different plane. In Pike's analysis the way people lived, thought, and acted out their lives were as important as the movement of capital, diplomats, and shifting world events.

A year later two English economists, Rosemary Thorp and Geoffrey Bertram, published their *Peru, 1890–1977: Growth and Policy in an Open*

Economy (1978), which broke with tradition and the old rhetoric of economic dependency in many ways. It defined Peru's modern economy—especially with respect to U.S. investments—as often including a vital, dominant domestic strand that was not particularly subservient to foreign interests or demands.

The Peruvian Revolution of 1968 had called into question much of the reigning wisdom and prevailing values that had governed relations between the United States and Peru. The revolution promoted the dependency theory that ascribed to the United States many of the ills of modern Peru. Goodsell's *American Corporations and Peruvian Politics* examined the politically explosive charge that U.S. corporations participated actively and directly in Peruvian politics. Goodsell—like Thorp and Bertram in their economic history—challenged the rhetoric of dependency by positing a series of hypotheses and then submitting them to an empirical test.

Finally in 1986 the Centro Peruano de Estudios Internacionales (CEPEI) sponsored a symposium on the relations of Peru with the United States. The proceedings were published the next year as *Relaciones del Perú con los Estados Unidos* edited by Eduardo Ferrero Costa. Sponsors included the Ford Foundation, the Friedrich Ebert Foundation, the Banco Continental, USIS, and several Peruvian governmental agencies. And, as its predecessor of 1972, *U.S. Foreign Policy and Peru*, the focus once again turned on the relationship between the United States and Peru, reinvigorated by the problems of debt and drugs.

While the expropriation and elimination of I.P.C. in Peru's national life represented the end of an era, it also, of course, opened up a new one. For that we turn to the last chapter.

8   Contemporary Times

"The only successful multinational that ever was developed in Peru . . ."

Attributed to President Alán García of Peru in reference
to the business of cocaine

After the revolution, Peru followed a new foreign policy that brought it directly into confrontation with the United States on a broad front. Some major points of friction involved compensation for expropriation of American properties and investments, the continuing fisheries disputes, and a rejection of the United States as traditional military supplier. When a new military government, less radical than the Velasco regime, came to power in 1975, much of the rancor in the relationship subsided. The increasingly uncontrollable debt and the rise of the cocaine trade were injected into the debate as new elements in the 1970s and 1980s.

Forces at work during the presidencies of Fernando Belaúnde Terry (1980–85) and Alán García (1985–90) continued the trend, begun during the revolutionary years, of moving away from the long and deep association with the United States that dated back to the Oncenio of the 1920s. Peru and the United States clashed in the 1980s on major issues of debt, human rights abuses, Central America, the Falklands War, and drugs, for example. And, as U.S. economic power in the world at large grew relatively less imposing, so did the dependency of Peru upon the United States. The old gross asymmetry in the relationship between the two countries began to erode. As Abraham Lowenthal, a noted observer of relationships between the Americas, noted, by 1980, "the United States exerted less dominance in the Western Hemisphere than at any time since World War II."[1]

Although this trend was moderated somewhat by the immensity of the Latin American debt crisis of the 1980s—much of it owed to U.S. institutions—it nonetheless signaled a new direction in relations between the United States and Peru. Fredrick Pike reflected on this trend of declining U.S. influence in his *United States and Latin America: Myths and Stereotypes of Civilization and Nature*.[2]

Yet the end of the Cold War and the triumph of U.S.-styled democratic capitalism brought a new realignment in world politics. The United States emerged in the eyes of many Peruvians as a model and leader, and neoliberal capitalism was adapted as national policy by many Peruvian leaders of the 1990s. The election of 1990 brought many of these new trends into perspective.

When the son of Japanese immigrants was inaugurated as president on July 28, 1990, a new era in Peruvian life dawned. Not only was Alberto Fujimori the first Japanese descendant elected to a presidency—other than in Japan—in modern world history, but he turned Peru away from the socialism and statism of the past two decades and worked to invigorate and restore the economy by applying free-market principles. He also freed the military to wage a successful and final war on the Shining Path terrorist movement.

Other issues brought Peru and the United States into close contact in the 1980s and 1990s. Perhaps the most dramatic was the increasing production of cocaine in the Andean region—principally in Peru and Bolivia—to be sold in the growing markets of North America. As the United States sought to bring drug use under control, it put pressure on Peru and Bolivia to crush, or, at the very least, diminish the supply. Major disagreements ensued between the United States and Peru over objectives and tactics, although they shared the general goal of eliminating the *"narcotráfico."*

The immense debts incurred by Peru in the 1970s led to a decade-long crisis in the 1980s that brought the United States and Peru to loggerheads. In 1985 the new president of Peru, Alán García, announced that Peru would pay no more than 10 percent of its income to service the debt, effectively defaulting and triggering a serious crisis with its American creditors.

The collapse of Marxism around the world in the late 1980s also colored Peruvian-U.S. relations, especially in light of the long struggle in

Peru to eradicate the most pernicious Marxist terrorist movement in the Western Hemisphere, the Shining Path. The capture of Abimael Gúzman, the founder and leader of the Shining Path movement, in 1992 and the gradual destruction of the movement drew Peru out of the stagnation and despondency that characterized much of the 1980s. Symbolically perhaps, Peru's fall and climb has been largely accomplished through means not dependent upon U.S. actions or interventions. In determining the greatest threat to Peru's integrity and democracy, the two differed basically over cocaine and terrorists. Peruvians viewed the Shining Path as the principal threat to their existence, while Americans put the emphasis on eliminating what they considered to be the most pernicious threat to Western culture—drugs. And in the war against the terrorists, Peruvians were severely criticized by American agencies for human rights abuses.

Economically the United States remains the largest trading partner for Peru, but the predominance of earlier times has waned as Peru has diversified markets for its exports and attracted capital from non-U.S. sources.

Curiously, even given all the disagreements over debt, drugs, and human rights, a congruence of vision is setting the context for more harmony than discord between Peru and the United States as the century nears its end. As in the 1920s, private enterprise, free-market principles, and a reduction in the social and economic apparatus of the State dominates the leading economic and political principles in both countries. Or, put another way, the renewed emphasis on liberty rather than equality is once again undergirding the relationship.

The election of a Japanese-Peruvian as president of Peru in 1990 and again in 1995 symbolized this dimension well. Fujimori represented to many Peruvians the power of the Japanese character to triumph and rejuvenate, to act honestly and efficiently, to release the energies of a people by freeing them from the old politics and economic formulas. The prowess of Japanese capital and industry in not only remaking Japan, but in expanding Japanese economic power in the world, was not lost on Peruvian voters. In another sense even while borrowing from one of the most conspicuous success models of modern times, it was a look inward for direction and inspiration. The brand of Peruvian nationalism that emerged in the late twentieth century looked to the United States and Japan for models of political stability and economic growth. But these were only two of many models to study. Peruvians were all the while searching, as Haya did all his life, for the truly authentic "Peruvian" way. That, indeed, was what Gen. Juan Velasco Alvarado set out to do in 1968.

The Revolution and the United States

The revolutionary government of Peru from 1968 to 1975 was generally antagonistic to the United States and U.S. enterprises in Peru. There were some exceptions, but the general thrust was clear: Peru developed a new foreign policy, and it challenged the old assumptions and old relationships that had previously underscored and governed the relations between the two nations.

At the core of this new foreign policy was the determination on the part of Peru to end its dependence upon the United States. This clearly nationalistic stance drew much inspiration from the dependency school of analysis. Many of Peru's social and economic problems were laid upon the doorstep of foreigners, foreign investments, and foreign priorities, which in most cases meant Americans. Domestic reforms across a wide spectrum of activities—from a massive redistribution of land to the nationalization of many key industries—were driven by peculiarly Peruvian perceptions and needs, but in almost all cases also affected U.S.-owned enterprises.

Peru also sought to carve out a new position in international affairs, and that meant, in fact, turning away from the old alliances and understandings with the United States. The American military mission, for example, was expelled from Peru in 1969, and throughout the 1970s the Peruvian military bought large quantities of arms from the Soviet Union.

The overall effect was clearly disruptive. "Early policies of the revolutionary government," wrote Ronald Bruce St. John, "especially those intended to reduce Peruvian dependency on the United States, served to heighten tension between the two states."[3] "Confrontation with the United States," agreed Helan Jaworksi, "marked the entire seven-year period" of General Velasco's presidency.[4]

The Peruvian military bought large amounts of sophisticated arms from the Soviet Union throughout the 1970s. What did Peru intend to do with these arms? They included Sukhoi SU-22 fighter bombers, SAM-3 surface-to-surface missiles, T-55 tanks, and other advanced military equipment heretofore not available to Latin American military establishments. What troubled the United States was the shifting emphasis of mission as conceived by the Peruvian military.

"What was disturbing," noted Col. Raymond Kaufman, a U.S. Army officer (retired) with long experience in Latin America, "was the shift of the armed forces' traditional doctrine of internal defense development to one that could project an offensive capability towards its neighbors."[5] Long-standing border disputes with Ecuador and Chile could erupt into hostilities, a scenario that Washington viewed as possibly disastrous for regional stability. As the centenary of the War of the Pacific neared, Peruvian rhetoric heated up, and it seemed as if the Peruvian military was indeed bent on retaking Arica and recapturing a sense of honor lost in a war fought almost a hundred years earlier.

"The Peruvians established major bases and airfields in the south near Tacna," Kaufman wrote, "and deployed two armored divisions equipped with the latest Soviet equipment, including artillery and sophisticated air defense units, within striking distance of the Chilean border."

At the same time, army units in the north along the Ecuadorian border were being upgraded and reinforced. As the Peruvian Army moved to a higher state of preparation and readiness, security in and around military bases was tightened, and esprit and morale among the officers and troops was running high. The troops were also being readied for the shock of battle. While jogging through the peaceful resort town of

Chorillos on the outskirts of Lima, Peruvian troops could be heard chanting,

> Ataca Arica,
> No es nada
> Es una batallita.

> Attack Arica,
> It's nothing,
> A little skirmish.

Intense pressure from Jimmy Carter's administration, plus Chile's certain willingness to defend its territory with everything at its disposal, helped defuse the situation, and as the centenary passed, so did the crisis. It is somewhat ironic that during and after the original War of the Pacific, the United States was Peru's ally, trying to maintain Peruvian territorial integrity in the face of the victorious Chileans. And, in the Tacna-Arica settlement of 1929, Peru's best friend once again had been the United States. The assessment of Chile's aggressive behavior by the principal U.S. mediator, Gen. John J. "Black Jack" Pershing, helped Peru substantiate its claims that Chile had made a neutral plebiscite impossible.

While the Peruvian military rattled its newly acquired Soviet sabers in the 1970s, the "ambiguous revolution" continued to evolve in other areas.[6] Regarding Peru's opinion of U.S. investments in the country, the term "ambiguous" most definitely applies. Velasco made it clear in his declarations and actions that Peru's dispute with I.P.C. did not extend in a paranoic mantle over other U.S. investments. But Peru's new rules on capitalism and investments inevitably brought Peru into conflict with other U.S. companies.

Velasco's doctrine adopted early in the revolution stated that "natural resources and basic industries would be reserved for state enterprise." In other nonbasic sectors, foreign investments would "be channeled through joint ventures or private companies, subject to a fixed period of reversion to the state once the total investment and an acceptable return have been covered by profit."[7] What did this mean? How were foreign investments translated into works of value for Peru? The Velasco Doctrine meant that the State would determine with greater precision how private enterprise, both domestic and foreign, could operate in Peru. It was, as economist Shane Hunt observed, not a new element in economic nationalism; the revolution did go beyond rhetoric and began translating some of its doctrines into actions. Some examples of how this led to clashes with the United States follow.

Perhaps the most serious tools the U.S. government had fashioned to deal with expropriation and economic nationalism were a series of amendments—usually to foreign aid bills—in the previous two decades. These amendments, such as the Pelly, the Hickenlooper, and other target-specific bills (passed with a particular situation in mind), aimed to put pressure on such countries as Peru for actions against U.S. interests in those countries. Withholding foreign aid, interrupting the flow of military equipment, reducing quotas on imports (such as Peruvian sugar into the United States), and a number of other tactics were applied by these various amendments.

The election of a new administration in Washington within a month of the October 1968 revolution in Peru must also be taken into account. In November Richard M. Nixon was elected, and on January 20, 1969, the former vice president was inaugurated the thirty-seventh president of the United States. By early 1970 most U.S. foreign aid to Peru had been cut off, and Nixon's administration was freezing Peru's access to international sources of credit.[8]

The war of words and credits between Peru and the United States escalated in February 1969. San Diego–based tuna boats had long been battling with Peru over the two-hundred-mile limit. Between 1953 and 1970 more than thirty-five tuna boats had been seized by the Peruvian Navy and forced into port to pay substantial fines, some as much as fifteen thousand dollars. The Pelly Amendment to the Foreign Military Sales Act of 1968 was but the latest in a series of congressional efforts to protect the U.S. fishermen by reimbursing them for fines, reducing aid to those countries levying the fines, and discontinuing military assistance to such countries as Peru.

On February 14, 1969, the tuna boat *Mariner* was stopped and seized by the Peruvians on the high seas. Her partner, the *San Juan,* refused to be boarded and was machine-gunned by the Peruvians. Friends of the American tuna industry were outraged. "I urge you," Congressman Thomas Pelly of Washington implored President Nixon, "to provide naval protection to our fishing fleet on the high seas."[9]

While the U.S. Navy was not dispatched to protect the tuna boats, Nixon's administration did invoke the Pelly Amendment and suspended military sales to Peru. Peru retaliated by expelling forty-one members of a U.S. military mission in Peru and threw cold water on a proposed visit by Gov. Nelson Rockefeller of New York on behalf of the Nixon administration.

On February 17 Peru also signed its first trade agreement with the Soviet Union, one of many new initiatives in this direction that signaled a further degradation of the old relationship between Peru and the United States. By 1973, for example, more than 15 percent of Peru's sugar was being bought by the U.S.S.R., China purchased 10 percent of copper exports, and both Cuba and China were importing Peruvian fish meal.[10] Tuna boats continued to be seized throughout 1969. Although talks rather than machine guns punctuated the dispute throughout that year, no resolution was achieved. Peru would have its two-hundred-mile limit. And, just as surely, the United States kept contesting it, until, as described above, in the 1980s the United States accepted the basic principle of a two-hundred-mile territorial zone long championed by Peru and other Latin American nations.

One of the most ironic seizures made by the revolutionary government in 1969 is that of Casa Grace. The chain of events was set in motion by the declaration on July 24, 1969, of a long-awaited agrarian reform decree of the revolutionary government. It was aimed largely at breaking up the nearly feudal system of land holding that still prevailed in Peru. So it was addressed to the Peruvian *campesino,* a kind of generic term for the peasant farmers waiting for the revolution to begin.

"From this day on," President Velasco addressed the nation, "the Peruvian campesino will no longer be a pariah, an outcast living in poverty from the womb to the tomb who looked impotently on an equally bleak future for his children. From now on, the Peruvian campesino will be truly free, reaping the fruits of the land he works, treated justly by a society and nation where he never more will be, as he was until today, a second class citizen, a man to be exploited by his fellow man."[11] It was a ringing address, calling for an end to *latifundia* and *minifundia* (parcels of land), providing an outline for a land reform more extensive than any other in Latin America since the Cuban Revolution. "The Agrarian Reform Law," Velasco added with vehemence, "will be applied across the nation, without exceptions which might favor particular groups or interests."

Squarely targeted by the agrarian reform law were the Grace plantations Paramonga and Cartavio. As large sugar plantations, they were to be nationalized and turned over to cooperatives of workers and employees. Yet they were also industrial enterprises, producing paper and a variety of chemical products, such as polyvinyl chloride, chlorine, and a number of other industrial products. The raw material for these industrial activities came from the sugar grown on the plantations. Very early on there developed a conflict between Grace's view of continuing successful operations and the view of the revolutionary government.

Grace did not think it could operate efficiently or profitably if its primary source of raw material was managed by the new government cooperatives being set up to run the agricultural business of the plantations. Besides, why were their plantations being expropriated? The Grace plantations were producers of wealth, of jobs, of taxes, of new technology.

There were to be no exceptions was President Velasco's answer. In 1970 the government appraised the two Grace estates at $10.1 million. Grace said they were currently worth $26 million and could only be replaced with an outlay of $46.7 million. Additionally the method of compensation was unacceptable to Grace. The Peruvian government would pay Grace largely in bonds that would not mature for twenty to twenty-five years, pay an interest rate of 5–6 percent, and were nonredeemable unless invested in industrial projects approved by the government.[12] In other words from Grace's point of view, they were to be compensated with useless, and largely worthless, bonds. The stage was set for a confrontation.

Another ironic twist to the situation arose from Grace's overall corporate profile. Since the 1960s it had been selling off its Latin American properties and investments as it concentrated its presence in the specialties chemical industry in the United States. For example, in Chile, where Grace had long been present, the company had sold virtually all its properties when the socialist government of Salvador Allende was inaugurated in 1970. Grace had been selling its properties and enterprises, valued at more than $70 million, all over Latin America to its former employees. Grace Line, certainly the most visible symbol of Casa Grace in the public's mind, was sold in 1969 to a Greek shipping tycoon, ending more than a century of trade and sea transportation by Grace between the Americas. And Pan American–Grace Airways (Panagra), the pioneering inter-American airline, was sold to its old competitor Braniff Airlines in 1966.

But Peru had been the exception. In Peru Grace was still expanding. Peru thus was an anomaly in the restructured W. R. Grace & Co. of the 1960s and early 1970s. It was a company that had divested across all of Latin America, a company that was focusing its activities in the United States and Europe; but it was also a company still inexplicably intermingled in Peru's national economy and life. Why?

Good profits and sentimentality kept Grace in Peru. There was the feeling among its managers that Casa Grace was immune from nationalization. After all, it was thought of as a Peruvian company, was it not? Not really. It certainly was not in the minds of the generals pushing the Peruvian revolution to the left. Casa Grace's headquarters was in New York City, no matter how many managers, employees, staff, and workers it employed in Peru. And besides, if large haciendas, large corporations, anything major associated with the old oligarchy—native born or foreign owned—was being subject to the intense focus and intervention of the revolutionary government, why should Grace be exempted?

In 1971 Grace executives proposed that a set amount of money be withheld from sugar bought from Peru by the United States. This money—fifteen dollars per ton was suggested—would then be placed in a reserve to compensate owners of expropriated properties (such as Paramonga and Cartavio, for example) that had not been properly compensated (so claimed by Grace).[13] Grace did not promote a reduction in Peru's sugar quota, then approximately 435,000 tons per year; but once the ball got rolling in various committees in the U.S. Congress, the desire to punish Peru picked up momentum. The sugar quota was eventually reduced to 392,000 tons and was done so with language that castigated Peru for the expropriation of I.P.C. Congressmen were, however, not simply motivated to chastise Peru. A bit of American politics worked its way into the equation. Louisiana, the largest producer of sugar in the United States, stood to gain from reducing foreign sugar quotas, and, surprise, Sen. Russell Long of Louisiana was chairman of the Senate Finance Committee that made the recommendation.

Between 1970 and 1973, other U.S. firms, such as Cerro de Pasco, Anderson Clayton, and subsidiaries of International Telephone and Telegraph and Chase Manhattan Bank, were also expropriated.[14] In retaliation the Nixon administration froze Peru's access to new credits. So, desirous of consolidating its gains and obtaining new loans to proceed with its ambitious social and economic programs, Velasco's regime entered into productive discussions that resulted in the so-called de la Flor–Greene Agreement of February 19, 1974.

For $150 million—in a deal largely worked out by the United States Export-Import Bank, the World Bank, the Inter-American Development Bank, and private U.S. banks—the outstanding debts from Peru's acts of expropriation were settled. Grace, Cerro, some fishing enterprises, and even I.P.C. were among those paid from this fund. In return the lines of credit frozen for four years to Southern Peru Copper (SPCC) to finance the development of the immense Cuajone copper mines were released. New oil exploration by Occidental Petroleum Company into the northern jungles also was initiated during this period. After 1974, but especially after 1975 when President Velasco was replaced by a more moderate military regime led by Gen. Francisco Morález Bermúdez (1975–80), a modus vivendi was reached regarding U.S. capital.

The old order, typified by the vastly different approaches of a Casa Grace and an I.P.C., was gone. In their place old and new capital had to work within different parameters set by the national government. The extreme statism introduced by the revolution moderated under the second military regime of Moralez Bermudez. The State grew even less intrusive throughout the 1980s when civilian rule was restored (in the presidencies of Fernando Belaúnde Terry and Alán García), and, finally, State intervention was largely discarded as a political and economic strategy by the administrations of President Alberto Fujimori, who returned the country to a free-market model.

The Peruvian National Debt

In the meantime Peru acquired a massive foreign debt, much of it owed to U.S. banks and lending agencies. When Belaúnde Terry was overthrown in 1968, Peru's foreign debt was approximately $700 million. When he returned to power in 1980, the debt had increased to nearly $1 billion, or about fourteenfold its 1968 value.[15] And, by the time Belaúnde ended his second term in 1985, the foreign debt had advanced to $1.4 billion.

All these figures can be meaningless unless given context and translated into lay terms. In Peru from the mid-1970s through the 1990s, the cost of living went up and the standard of living went down, in large measure due to the inordinate debts contracted by the government. By the late 1980s, Peru's standard of living, especially among the Indians and *cholos* of the sierra, was barely above the level of Haiti (whose standard of living is the lowest in the Western Hemisphere), measured by such standards as infant mortality, caloric intake, and other measures of human health or misery.

The debt was not the sole cause. Peru's continued dependence for its income and prosperity upon exports—such as copper, silver, oil, and fish products, for example—was notoriously subject to international demands. During this time period, demands tended to be depressed in many of Peru's principal export markets, and prices dropped accordingly, in some instances precipitously. Oil dropped from $30 a barrel to $16 per barrel, copper from $1.30 per pound to $.60 per pound, and silver from $40 an ounce to $6 per ounce.[16] Such natural disasters as earthquakes and the periodic appearance of El Niño (the warm current that massively disrupts the fishing environment off the coast) rocked Peru. But the debt loomed over all other factors, bedeviling the nation with hyperinflation, un- or underemployment, stagnation, and other signs of a languishing economy. So where did it come from?

The easiest, and perhaps the most obvious, answer is that the debt was created by borrowing. In the case of Peru, borrowing began to pick up momentum in the early 1970s as the revolutionary government took initiatives in many different areas, which necessitated new moneys. The state nationalized many sectors of the economy, such as the fish meal industry, the banking industry, the mining sector, the petroleum industry, and electrical and telephone systems. It then created new and expensive bureaucracies to run these state-owned enterprises. Often driven by nationalism rather than marketplace rules, these new entities operated at huge losses. The state borrowed to make up for the losses. Here is a major element of Peru's debt.

In its drive to free itself of U.S. domination and carve out an independent position in world politics, the military turned to the Soviet Union for weapons in 1973. Over the next twelve years, the Peruvian military acquired more than $1.6 billion worth of Soviet military equipment.[17] The Soviet Union gave Peru easy credit terms for these purchases. Indeed Peru's other creditors, many U.S. banks and international lending agencies, also extended to Peru generous loans in the early and mid-1970s.

"The international banking community," wrote Peruvian senator Felipe Osterling, "inundated us with petrodollars," the term denoting the immense profits generated by the petroleum producers of the world in the early 1970s.[18] "The producing countries," Osterling explained, "placed their money in banks. And these banks relocated, rather quickly I would add, those dollars in Latin American countries. It was a sort of drug addiction."

In other words immense profits generated by the world's oil markets made lots of cash available, which was then loaned as rapidly as possible to such countries as Peru. One needs money to make money, and one of the best ways of doing this is to loan it and charge interest. There were lots of petrodollars around in the 1970s, Peru's basic exports were rising in value in the same time period before collapsing in the late 1970s and 1980s, and the borrowing was easy. And the Soviets made military equipment easily available to the Peruvians. Peru bought jet fighters, tanks, helicopters, artillery, rocket launchers, missiles, and other weapons. Soviet advisers and Soviet technicians came with them, and the Soviet presence expanded in Peru. "The level of technical cooperation between Peru and the Soviet Union," Daniel Masterson, a prominent U.S. authority on Peru's military establishment, observed "[was] second only to Cuba in the Western Hemisphere."[19]

When the Velasco regime came to an end in 1975, so did the heady period of borrowing. Peru slowly slipped into a recession, and then into an economic depression that lasted until the 1990s. Other problems contributed, naturally, but none quite so dramatically as the debt.[20] Ironically as Velasco's intensely nationalistic regime broke the old ties with the United States, new ties were forged through the somewhat invisible but silken bonds of international finance. And most of the debt was owed to private U.S. banks or international lending agencies, such as the International Monetary Fund (IMF), whose tough fiscal policies more often than not reflected U.S. policy. One of the most abrasive points of contact in modern relations between Peru and the United States occurred precisely on account of the debt.

When Alán García addressed the nation as its new president on July 28, 1985, he dramatically announced that Peru would pay no more than 10 percent of its export earnings on the huge debt. To service the debt properly would have required more than 60 percent of foreign earnings, and, in fact, the Belaúnde administration had been quietly reducing debt payments since 1983. But García made it public policy, throwing the gauntlet down at the feet of the international and U.S. financial communities.

García took his agenda before the United Nations in September 1985, declaring that the IMF's policy of demanding severe austerity measures was nothing short of colonialism.

"The IMF," García said heatedly, "calls for austerity only in poor countries, while favoring the most powerful nation [the United States] on earth."[21] The "most powerful nation on earth" reacted predictably.

New loans from private U.S. banks were put on hold, military assistance was temporarily halted, and by late 1986, the IMF, the World Bank, and the Inter-American Development Bank all suspended further loans. Peru was cast out in an international financial limbo, joining Vietnam, Zambia, Somalia, Guyana, Sudan, and Liberia. By 1990 when new elections were held, Peru was in its worst depression since the aftermath of the War of the Pacific.

The election of Alberto Fujimori as chief executive of Peru marked a radical departure in Peruvian politics and ushered in a new era in Peru's national life. The "Fujimori Phenomenon" that swept the new leader into power in 1990 opened up for examination all the major issues of the times between Peru and the United States.

Fujishock: The Peruvian Presidential Election of 1990

Peru's voters delivered a stunning victory on June 10, 1990, to Alberto Fujimori, a presidential candidate virtually unknown three months before. The odds-on favorite in the first round on April 8 was Mario Vargas Llosa, Peru's most celebrated writer. He is an author whose works have been translated all over the world, has written numerous classics of modern Latin American literature, such as *Aunt Julia and the Scriptwriter* and *The War of the End of the World,* and is a man whose creativity and brilliance may someday earn him a Nobel Prize in literature. Vargas Llosa was, in fact, well known in the United States among the reading public.

During the second round of voting on June 10, however, Peruvians chose Fujimori, the fifty-one-year-old former rector of the National Agrarian University, a descendant of Japanese immigrants to Peru. He was a man the pollsters and pundits dismissed as a newcomer, a populist, a man whose Asian ancestry put him well beyond the pale of realistic possibility. On June 10 Fujimori trounced Vargas Llosa by more than fifteen percentage points.

Fujimori was inaugurated on July 28, Peruvian Independence Day. He also celebrated his birthday, endowing him with some of the aura one might bestow on an American "born on the fourth of July." That he was reelected in 1995 marked perhaps an even more significant turn in Peruvian national life, confirming Fujimori's policies and actions, many of which caused considerable tension in Peruvian-U.S. relations.

A few weeks before his inauguration Fujimori traveled both to the United States and Japan to secure financial support for his country. Peru promised to implement an economic austerity program in return for readmission to good standing in the world of international finance. The United States, Japan, and Spain promised a bridging loan of $2 billion to cover Peru's defaulted loans (she actually owed more than $20 billion, the highest amount per capita in Latin America) to the IMF and other financial agencies.[22] The switch was on.

Less than two weeks after his inauguration, Fujimori announced the first of several new economic measures that were soon dubbed the "Fujishock" by Peruvians. Fujimori, in fact, enacted much of the program for economic recovery preached by Vargas Llosa. It was austere in the extreme, putting to work orthodox economic principles. But many thought the very viability of the country was at stake. Peru was suffering from a raging hyperinflation—more than 3,500 percent per annum—massive drops of more than 50 and 60 percent in the purchasing power of average Peruvian wage earners, chronic losses by state-owned enterprises (more than $1.2 billion), and other factors that made life miserable, unpredictable, and hopeless for many Peruvians.

Indeed in a review of the state of Peruvian archaeology, Richard L. Burger, an anthropologist from Yale, wrote rather matter-of-factly that "the prosperity of prehispanic Peru stands in stark contrast to modern Peru. In many regions, the canal systems, terraces, and ridged fields made it possible to cultivate at least 35 percent more land than at present. Whether this discrepancy is due to social, technological, economic, or environmental factors is a question that is of as much interest to the Peruvian government as to archaeologists."[23]

"The key elements of the [Fujimori] program," wrote Bruce St. John in his excellent history of Peru's foreign policy, "included a liberalization of foreign trade policies through elimination of exchange controls, a lifting of restrictions on most imports, and a deep cut in tariffs. . . . Most important, the government ended price controls and subsidies in effect for decades. As a result, Peru experienced its steepest one-day price increase in the twentieth century, and the popularity of Fujimori plummeted among his poorer constituents."[24]

With Fujimori's turn to free-market principles, Peru also turned to the United States seeking a better relationship. Not only did the free-market principles reflect a similar ideological framework for nation building, but Fujimori realized that the cooperation of the United States was crucial in reestablishing Peru's credit abroad. Peru and the United States were, however, not relating simply on the plane of debtor and creditor from the 1970s onward.

In the last quarter of the twentieth century Peru's economic woes were compounded by two phenomena: the rise of a virulent terrorist movement, and the rapid development of the international cocaine trade. The Shining Path and the cocaine trade both threatened to subvert the established order of government, and the United States became intimately involved in the attempts to control both, especially the cocaine trade.

The United States and the Shining Path to Cocaine

The twin vices of terrorism and drugs that threatened to overwhelm Peru in the 1980s impinged upon Peruvian-U.S. relations in an odd fashion. The Shining Path was a totally autochthonous, indigenous Peruvian movement whose existence only remotely concerned most Americans. The rise of the drug trade, called *narcotráfico* in Peru, on the other hand, was intimately tied to life in the United States, so much so that the United States was "identified as the primary power player in policy, consumption, and economics related to the cocaine issue" by one student of the drug phenomenon.[25]

Around 1983 and 1984, the Shining Path became part of the cocaine scene in Peru, and the separation between the two evils blurred. U.S. insistence on the defense of human rights also became an issue as Peru's military waged a bitter campaign against Sendero Luminoso (the Shining Path). The violence of Sendero was matched by the military's determination to exterminate the movement. Thousands of civilians were slaughtered by combatants on both sides. Cocaine and the Shining Path did not share any obvious similarities, but they did became principal elements in the relationship between Peru and the United States in the last third of the twentieth century.

No other terrorist movement in Latin America generated so much violence and interest in the Western Hemisphere than the Shining Path, whose official title, the Peruvian Communist Party in the Shining Path of José Carlos Mariátegui, provides some clues to its origins and ideology.

"The Shining Path," wrote David Scott Palmer (who was a young Peace Corps volunteer assigned to the University of Huamanga in Ayacucho in September 1962), "has been something of an enigma since its inception almost twenty years ago."[26] That perhaps was one of the classic understatements in the growing field of "senderology," or those dedicated to studying this violent, revolutionary movement.

The secretive, sectlike Sendero owes its origins to an odd but lethal combination of Maoist Marxism and native Peruvian Indian nationalism that originated in the 1960s. A small group of intellectuals at the University of Huamanga in the city of Ayacucho gathered around a professor of philosophy, Abimael Guzmán Reynoso, who formally founded the Shining Path in 1970 as a splinter group of the Peruvian Communist Party. On May 17, 1980, Shining Path initiated the armed conflict by burning ballot boxes in a small village in the province of Ayacucho. Sendero went underground and committed itself to the violent overthrow of the government through terrorism. Between then and 1992, when Guzmán was captured and imprisoned, more than twenty-five thousand souls perished in Sendero-inspired violence. Why?

That is the question that senderologists have devoted themselves to since the early 1980s. Why Sendero? Before 1980 Abimael Guzmán, nicknamed "Presidente Gonzalo" by his fanatical followers, was but a cipher on the far left fringe of Peruvian politics. Before Sendero, a shoving, shouting crowd was considered a "violent" act in the context of Peruvian politics and society. Within a decade of Sendero's firing of the ballot boxes and first assassinations, violence had spread out from Ayacucho and become endemic in Peruvian life. That violence was the subject of probes by U.S. and Peruvian journalists and writers who filmed, photographed, and wrote about Sendero for magazines as diverse as the *New Yorker,* the *New Republic,* the *New York Times Magazine,* and *National Geographic.*[27] Television documentaries exposed particularly brutal episodes in the history of Sendero's war on Peruvian society; U.S. congressional hearings were held on the phenomenon; and Peru surfaced in the American conscience in the 1980s and 1990s as a violent, terrorist-prone society, certainly to be avoided by tourists. Peru was the target of human rights activists and the subject of social scientists searching for the roots of violence.[28]

Indeed Sendero became a near metaphor for evil, but an evil that many Peruvian and American senderologists could almost explain given the great gulfs that still existed between the haves and have-nots of Peru. In their search for the roots of Sendero, many agreed that the severe economic stress of the late 1970s and 1980s finally dissolved the fragile notion of the caretaker state in Peru—the idea that through all perils and disasters, the state would somehow provide succor and relief. But not all agreed on whether it was the state's authoritarian, centralizing tendencies or its inherent weakness that opened the window for Sendero.

For some of Sendero's ideologues, the United States represented a whipping boy. But Sendero was usually more critical and contemptuous of Cuba, the Soviet Union, and even China after Mao Tse-Tung's death (in 1976) for abandoning true Marxism. The sharpest vituperation was saved for the misinterpreters of Marx rather than for the heart of capitalism itself, the United States. Presumably it was far worse to commit ideological apostasy rather than simply be in the opposing camp. Besides beating on the United States in Peru in the late 1970s was like beating on a dead horse. Since the revolution of 1968, the State in Peru had pretty much dictated a nationalist path for Peruvians. So, if blame were to be placed, it would have to be internally, and *Senderistas* thus turned with a vengeance on their own compatriots.

What did Sendero seek? One important Sendero tract called for "[a] single, irreplaceable new society without exploited or exploiters, without oppressed or oppressors, without classes, without state, without parties, without democracy, without arms, without wars."[29] If it sounds idealistic, it was, in the extreme, as were the devotees of Sendero and Presidente Gonzalo (whose other nicknames were Dr. Puka Inti, Quechua meaning "Red Sun," and "Shampoo" by his younger followers because the leader washes brains).[30]

Guzmán's career from a boy born out of wedlock in 1934 in Arequipa to his rise as the inspirational guru and leader of the most violent terrorist movement in the history of the Western Hemisphere is fascinating. Guzmán's career evolved from student to professor to Marxist revolutionary mostly outside the orbit of relations between Peru and the United States. When Guzmán went abroad in the 1960s, he traveled to China where the cultural revolution taking place there reinforced his dedication to orthodox, unswerving Maoist Marxism. His battles in Peru were not against I.P.C. and U.S. companies but against deviations from the Chinese line of Marxism. In the 1970s he fought the reformist military government that stole much of Sendero's thunder. Until 1980 when Sendero went underground, "Presidente Gonzalo" fine-tuned his party, purging the opposition, inculcating the ideas and the methods of Maoist doctrine into his cadres. And, in one of the richest ironies of the times, Guzmán even had a brilliant Japanese-Peruvian man, Luis Kawata Makabe, serving as his leading lieutenant until his ouster by Guzmán in 1976.[31] A spellbinding teacher, Kawata recruited students at the University of Huamanga with immense success before his fall from grace and eventual imprisonment for much of the 1980s. In 1990 almost toothless, his "skin all dried out and stretched over his fragile face," and draped in sad, worn clothes, Kawata witnessed the victory of a fellow Japanese-Peruvian, Alberto Fujimori, whose trajectory to power was so radically different from his own.[32] The divisions in Peruvian society itself were put into such sharp relief by the fortunes of these two first-generation Peruvians of Japanese descent.

Just before Sendero went underground in May 1980, Guzmán enjoined some of his followers who were still wavering. After all, the cultural revolution was dead in China, revisionists were in control in Moscow, Havana, and other Marxist nations, and Sendero seemed isolated. Precisely at this juncture Guzmán prevailed.

"They came to see themselves," said Gustavo Gorriti, a Peruvian journalist and one of the most astute recorders of Sendero's rise and fall, "as the center of world revolution . . . by stressing the primacy of ideology, it [the Shining Path] showed that as long as an organized party maintained the correct line, communism would recover and conquer in the end."[33] And to bolster his cohorts as they prepared for battle, Guzmán turned to an American writer.

"He read excerpts," Gorriti noted, "of Washington Irving's all-but-forgotten 1850 book, *The Life of Mahomet,* to show how several desert tribes when moved by an intense conviction could conquer a great part of the world in one generation. He was persuasive, and the war began a month later."[34]

Few predicted the escalation of violence that followed when Sendero went underground. As far as the United States was concerned, Peru's problems were largely economic. After all, democracy had just been restored by the election of Fernando Belaúnde Terry in 1980, and Ronald Reagan's new administration was focused on Nicaragua, Central America, and the Caribbean, rather than on Peru and South America. In 1979 the Sandinistas overthrew the old Somoza dictatorship in Nicaragua and ushered in a new Marxist government in that small country. For much of the next decade, the Reagan administration targeted the Sandinistas in Nicaragua. Jimmy Carter had introduced the primacy of human rights as a foundation of foreign policy in his inaugural address of 1977, but in Peru of 1980 there were few abuses. Most of Carter's sanctions had been taken against the military regimes in Chile, Argentina, and Nicaragua by suspending or eliminating bilateral aid, while Bolivia, Paraguay, and El Salvador were chastised by U.S. lawmakers abstaining or voting against loan proposals.[35] Peru was clean. Certainly there was the debt, and an ever-increasing flow of cocaine from South America into the streets of the United States, but as Guzmán took his minions underground to slay the dragons and beasts of capitalism and injustice, the rest of Peru remained naively unaware of what was in store.

Sendero plunged Peru into a fifteen-year nightmare of violence and terror. Sendero was committed to liberating Peru from all despotic, corrupt politicians, so local elected officials were especially targeted for intimidation and assassination. In the election of 1990, for example,

Sendero shot up or bombed the campaign offices of *all* the major political parties, demonstrating a contempt for the political process in general. Much of the indiscriminate killing was attributable to the Peruvian military's equal determination to extirpate the Sendero movement as it gained momentum through the 1980s.

Sendero's favorite weapon was dynamite, for many *Senderistas* (or *terrucos* in the local argot) were miners, or sons and daughters of miners. They not only hit the police, the army, and local administrators but also the power pylons strung across remote parts of Peru. Especially after 1988, when Sendero began infiltrating the larger urban areas, large sections of the capital city of Lima were often plunged into darkness by Sendero's dynamiters. This served to remind coastal Peru—an export-oriented, cosmopolitan, quasi-industrialized society—that no one was safe from Sendero's reach, and equally important, that the national government was impotent to protect them. With at least half of Peru's population susceptible to Sendero's call for radical revolution, the threat to political stability and social order in Peru was palpable.

How to neutralize the Sendero movement occupied the attention of many Peruvians in the 1980s. Terrorism ranked right alongside unemployment and poverty in an opinion survey commissioned in Peru by the U.S. Information Agency (USIA) in the late 1980s.[36] Coincidentally drugs and the drug trade ranked very low as a matter of concern among most Peruvians. The reverse situation prevailed in the United States: the drug trade was a major issue in contemporary American society, while terrorism was but a blip on CNN's international report.

In a far-ranging article published in the *New York Times* on July 31, 1983, Mario Vargas Llosa sought to explain how and why eight Peruvian journalists were murdered by peasants in the remote sierra village of Uchuraccay in the province of Ayacucho. This article brought the violence of Sendero before the United States for the first time in a widely read forum. Vargas Llosa believed the journalists were mistaken for *Senderista* terrorists by the local peasants who took justice into their own hands. The culpability, the writer argued, lay with a system that forced the Indians into poverty and adversity, with the consequent increase and acceptance of violence as a part of their culture.

Violence had become near endemic in Peru by the late 1980s. The theme was taken up in *La Boca del Lobo,* an engrossing film that appeared in Lima theaters in November 1988. It was produced by the Peruvian Francisco Lombardi, whose first critical success was a film based on Vargas Llosa's own *The Time of the Hero.*

An intense, bearded man then in his late thirties, Lombardi looks like Francis Ford Coppola, the producer of one of the classic films based on the Vietnam War, *Apocalypse Now.* Perhaps the resemblance between Lombardi and Coppola is deliberate on Lombardi's part, for *La Boca del Lobo* was also an intense, stomach-churning movie about war. Like *Apocalypse Now* and other classics of the Vietnam War, *La Boca del Lobo* does not rest easy with its viewers. Its images keep reoccurring in the mind's eye.

The film focuses on a small Indian village in the high Peruvian sierra that is caught in the middle of a war between the *Senderistas* and the armed forces of Peru. While the army bears the brunt of the war, marines, civil guards, and police are all involved.

Both the army and Sendero are determined to destroy each other, and the film relentlessly explores the escalation of violence. A platoon of soldiers, commanded by a psychopathic lieutenant, arrives in a small, isolated town where Sendero has been active. The town's inhabitants, almost entirely Indian, become unwilling participants as Sendero terrorizes the small troop by butchering and dismembering those soldiers they are able to capture. The soldiers, largely mestizo or whites from the coast, are hardened and brutalized by the violence, and they turn on the local population with fury. Every Indian is seen as a Sendero collaborator, and the end of the film is chilling.

Why the awful violence? Pregnant women were dragged out of their homes at night, butchered, and dismembered before their husbands and children; suspects were rounded up and shot casually without evidence; executions conducted with sticks of dynamite blasted people into formless chunks of blood and tissue. The violence was not limited to clashes between the army and Sendero, but it enveloped the civilian population also. Whole villages were wiped out as Sendero or the army got caught in the fury of recriminations, and the spiral of hatred rose.

Guzmán was captured September 12, 1992, in Lima in a brilliant piece of detective work led by Gen. Antonio Ketín Vidal, the head of DINCOTE, a special investigative arm of the national police. Taped by his captors in a sound bite that was broadcast by CNN, Guzmán waxed defiant.

"You can kill a man," Guzmán told Vidal soon after his capture, "but you can't kill this," he continued, tapping his head.[37] The bearded, middle-aged man with a paunch was described by one writer as a "flabby, splayfooted, and solemn" individual, hardly the image of the semiheroic, terrifying, charismatic leader of the terrorist movement that had ignited the country in a conflagration of civil war.[38] But there was a fire and intensity in Guzmán that even his capture, no matter how humiliating, could quench. Garbed in near cartoonlike prison stripes and confined to a cage in one celebrated interview allowed with Peru's reporters, Guzmán lectured them on imperialism, exhorted his followers to maintain the faith, clenched his raised fist defiantly, and struck off a few bars of the "Internationale," the old theme song of international Marxism. The scene smacked of a country carnival, complete with a wild and caged animal, but it was not a circus. For Guzmán and the Shining Path, there was no possibility of compromise, no middle ground. In Peru it was either Shining Path or destruction, and this absolute intransigence had endowed the movement with its internal coherence.

Although much of Guzmán's motivation was autochthonous and his ideology driven by Maoist Marxism, the United States was never too far from the consciousness of *Senderistas.* David Scott Palmer recalled Guzmán well. Palmer remembers that Guzmán's first political victory at Huamanga was his masterminding the removal of the Peace Crops in November 1963. In the Shining Path's ideological and practical evolution, the United States stood on the path to the liberation of Peru from corrupt capitalism. The Peace Corps, no matter how well intentioned an agency, was nonetheless of U.S. origin. The dogmatic inflexibility that characterized later acts of Sendero was amply demonstrated in this harbinger.

Palmer became one of the leading "senderologists" in North America, remembering with a certain bittersweet nostalgia how he learned to view Peru from the periphery inward. He admitted that he could "respect the dedication and zeal of the Shining Path leadership as it tries to forge a new and more meaningful reality for peripheral Peru's long-suffering citizenry." However he could not condone "Shining Path's obsessively destructive methods," which he labeled "abhorrent."[39] That was the dilemma that Sendero posed for thoughtful Peruvians and Americans.

When Alberto Fujimori became president in 1990, he realized that if the war against Sendero was to have some chance of success, the military and police forces had to be freed of judicial and congressional restraints. On April 5, 1992, he suspended Congress and much of the judicial system. He proceeded to rule largely by decree with the support of the military, and as it turns out, with a large majority of the Peruvian people behind him. Fujimori had, in fact, invoked a traditional Latin American political tactic, an *autogolpe,* or "self-coup," to get a firmer grip on power. The United States predictably deplored the *autogolpe* and suspended for a time all but humanitarian assistance.

Within six months of the *autogolpe,* Guzmán was captured. With Presidente Gonzalo imprisoned, many proclaimed the end of Sendero Luminoso. Severely crippled, terrorist activity dropped for the next three years. Meanwhile Fujimori had to devote himself more fully to the one issue that the United States would not let up on, the one issue Americans felt was far more important than terrorism or debt in the contemporary relations between Peru and the United States. And that issue was the drug issue.

Clear and Present Danger

> O cuál es más de culpar,
> aunque cualquiera mal haga.
> El que peca por la paga
> o el que paga por peca?

Who is more to blame,
Even though both do wrong.
He who sins for pay,
Or he who pays for sin?[40]

In 1990 the acknowledged king of "techno thrillers," Tom Clancy, published *Clear and Present Danger,* an instant hit and best-seller. Made into a film starring Harrison Ford, *Clear and Present Danger* explored the way in which the U.S. military was going to stop the drug traffickers. The film explosively roamed across the drug landscape, from deep within the secretive halls of the Pentagon to the jungles of South America, its heroes duking it out with the drug lords in the best Clancy fashion. Laser-guided bombs, electronic warfare, tension, whiz-bang action scenes featuring the latest in submachine guns, and the good guys and bad guys clearly drawn, it is Clancy at his best. And to many Americans, the stereotypical image that comes to mind when imagining a Colombian or a Peruvian is one straight out of a Clancy book or movie. Travis McGee, writer John D. MacDonald's immensely popular hero of many novels, also fights the drug lords and their evil machinations in serialized books, such as *The Lonely Silver Rain* and *Cinnamon Skin,* entertaining millions of readers.

When the average American reader or moviegoer looks south of the border, he or she really does not have to look any farther than Miami. There the streets, villas, and condominiums are populated with drug lords, "Latino" types sporting Dior shirts and Gucci shoes, a Rolex on their wrist, a gold chain laying against a hairy chest, tinted glasses, tanned and dark-eyed, ready to wheel and deal.[41]

The nefarious drug trade reaches right into Hometown, America. Writer Robert B. Parker's popular protagonist, Spencer (the prototype for the television series *Spencer for Hire*), travels to Wheaton, Massachusetts, in *Pale Kings and Princes,* investigating a murder in a small town described as "the biggest cocaine distribution center above the Mason-Dixon line."[42] Cocaine seems everywhere: in the form of powder for the affluent baby boomers and their children and as crack for the less affluent street junkies of New York and Los Angeles. Cocaine use has exploded, and more than 60 percent of all cocaine is produced in Peru. In 1975 the coca leaf growers of the Upper Huallaga Valley (UHV) of Peru produced about four thousand metric tons of the leaf. In 1980 that amount increased to about eighteen thousand metric tons, and in 1990 production of the leaf was probably in excess of eighty thousand tons — the vast majority of it being processed, refined, and marketed as powder or crack in Colombia and destined for consumers in the United States.[43]

Where does cocaine fit into the equation of modern Peruvian-U.S. relations? At the very center is this writer's guess, outweighing the issues of debt, terrorism, and democracy, largely because cocaine directly affects American life. Other such issues as debt, human rights abuses, terrorism, and constitutional rule appear only as fleeting blips in the minds of most Americans and as quick sound bites on American television.

In a fashion the export of coca to the United States is but one facet of the long economic relationship that Peru has had with the United States since the guano era of the mid-nineteenth century. Just as Americans discovered then that Peru possessed an immensely valuable fertilizer, Americans of the 1970s discovered that the coca plant of Peru produced a marvelous narcotic that satisfied the psychological and physiological appetites of millions of Americans. Like guano, the use of coca was, however, not unknown among Peruvians. And unlike guano, which was largely depleted within four decades, coca is a renewable resource, constantly expanding in production.

Coca leaves have been chewed for hundreds of years in Andean America. The growing and chewing of coca in Peru is not illegal. Occasionally, over the past five centuries, it has been prohibited, banned, taxed, and condemned, but it never has been successfully suppressed. A little lime is added to the coca to catalyze the release of chemical properties, and the casual Indian chewer looks much like a southern farmer or sharecropper in the United States of one or two generations past, going about his daily tasks with a wad of tobacco firmly plugged into his cheek. In the sierra of Peru, a wad of coca helped pass the day or night, suppressing hunger if one was working long hours in the fields or the mines, guarding against the cold of the mountain nights.[44] It was a mild narcotic largely relegated to the Indian population and was a cultural stigma associated with the Indians.

Modern science discovered that the cocaine alkaloid, extracted from the raw coca plant leaves, possessed powerful painkilling qualities that turned it quickly into a popular anesthetic in the United States in the early twentieth century. Cocaine by the 1920s was produced in large quantities for distribution by pharmaceutical firms. It was habit-forming, however, and controls were established to try and prevent addiction.

Cocaine belongs to the same chemical family as nicotine, caffeine, and morphine. The coca leaves are mixed with hydrochloric acid, and when heated produce cocaine hydrochloride. This form of salt is then mixed with various adulterants and can be administered or taken in different forms. Cocaine produces a rush of euphoric excitement. Dopamine, a neurotransmitter or chemical messenger, is released by cocaine's activation of nerve cells in the brain. This leads to feelings of pleasure, heightened alertness, and increased motor control. It also produces excitation, insomnia, loss of appetite, increased heart rate, increased respiration, and increased blood pressure. Cocaine addiction, or repeated use, leads to chronic fatigue, convulsions, depression, irritability, loss of sex drive, memory problems, nasal bleeding, paranoia, severe headaches, increased body temperature, and, in some cases, death.[45]

Cocaine usually is either inhaled as a powder or smoked as crack, a concentrated form of cocaine, in a pipe. The latter is extremely addictive in a short period of time. Simple to make and not particularly costly, cocaine became the "drug of choice" in the United States during the 1970s and 1980s, although by the time cocaine reached users there, a tremendous "value-added tax" was being charged by everyone involved in the trade, from the producer of raw paste in the Upper Huallaga Valley to the cocaine cartels of Colombia that refined and marketed the drug in the United States.[46]

In 1982 President Ronald Reagan (1981–89) declared a "War on Drugs." Reagan and his vice president and successor George Bush (1989–93) would have more success in bringing the "Evil Empire," the

Soviet Union, to its knees than in eliminating the flow of drugs from Peru to the United States over the course of the next decade. In the process of escalating the War on Drugs, the United States militarized the conflict, declaring in 1986 that the drug trade was a threat to the security of the Americas (in a speech made by Ronald Reagan on April 8, 1986) and put increasing pressure on Peru (and the other drug-producing and trafficking countries—principally Colombia and Bolivia) to stop the business of narcotraffic at its source. The emphasis of the United States throughout the 1980s and into the 1990s was on destroying or crippling the supply sector. This came into direct conflict with Peru's view of the problem—no amount of eradication at the source could ever shrink the trade until the United States got the demand under control.

Summing up the thinking of most Peruvians on the subject, Vargas Llosa said, "I think one must accept the premise that the responsibility lies equally on the countries that produce and those that consume." "Production exists," Vargas Llosa continued with the Peruvian perspective, "because a market exists, a near irresistible goad to produce. Farmers can increase their earnings fivefold, tenfold, sometimes one hundredfold by planting coca instead of traditional crops."[47]

"I don't think the policy should be totally repressive," he said, basically questioning the emphasis on eradication by the United States. "Mutual responsibility must be translated into mutual cooperation. It should be a policy aimed at stimulating the conversion of crops from coca to alternatives, and for that to work one needs strong economic incentives. That is the only way. One cannot simply condemn farmers alone—by destroying their crops, their livelihood—to accept the cost of destroying the system."

Then, echoing the position that Fujimori took after his election in 1990, Vargas Llosa said that "incentives and repression must go hand in hand." Fujimori's insistence on a strong program of crop substitution and incentives for the coca farmers ran directly counter to U.S. policy aimed principally at eradication. Much to the chagrin of the United States, Peru in 1990 and 1991 refused to acknowledge the primacy of U.S. interests. The enormity, and complexity, of the business in Peru precluded a simple eradication and interdiction campaign. By the late 1980s the Upper Huallaga Valley's approximately three hundred thousand farmers were devoted largely to coca production. Trafficking in cocaine was indeed a worldwide business.

"In the mid-1980s," wrote Renssalaer W. Lee III in one of the best studies of the cocaine trade, "South American cocaine traffickers probably earned a minimum of $5 billion to $6 billion yearly from sales in international markets."[48] In Peru millions of dollars (the amount depends on how it is figured) were pumped into the local economy of the Upper Huallaga Valley (UHV), providing jobs, income, and security. Cocaine dollars rippled out through the nation, producing many effects, not the least of which was increasing corruption.

"In Peru," Lee noted, "Reynaldo Rodríguez Lopez, a trafficker who was a trusted adviser to Peru's top police officials, owned a travel agency (International Tourist Services) that served as a cover for his cocaine smuggling operations."[49] Corruption was one problem, but making a living was, arguably, more important to the average "little person" in the cocaine-producing regions of Peru.

Most are familiar with the fantastic fortunes made by some of the most celebrated drug traffickers, such as Pablo Escobar of Colombia (killed in December 1993), who reputedly had amassed a personal fortune of more than $3 billion. What about the little guy in the UHV? Field hands there made twice the wage they could expect in licit agricultural endeavors in the area. Those who stamped the coca leaves into paste, *pisadores,* made even more than the leaf pickers. Some *pisadores* made about forty dollars a day. Schoolteachers made twenty-three dollars a month. Peruvian Army enlisted men assigned to the UHV made ten dollars per month while the salary for a general in the Peruvian Army was about two hundred dollars per month in the worst days of Peru's economic depression in the late 1980s.[50] The temptation to succumb to the blandishments and moneys of the drug traders was overwhelming.

"In Peru," Lee wrote, perhaps in understatement, "the pattern of corruption can be very complex. In mid-1988 . . . traffickers paid roughly $12,000 in bribes for a load of cocaine base flown out of the Uchiza district in the Upper Huallaga Valley: $5,000 went to the military command

of the district, $5,000 to local offices of the civil guard (the national po-
lice), and $2,000 to various community organizations thought to be
fronts for Sendero Luminoso."[51] Some put Sendero's take as higher,
$6,000 to $15,000 per flight, and the annual take of the Shining Path's
operations in the Upper Huallaga Valley at anywhere from $10 to
$100 million.[52]

Everyone seemed to be corrupted by cocaine. But what is corruption?
Could terrorists such as the Shining Path be "corrupted"? Did Peru and
the United States have a different perception of corruption? It seems so.
In an earlier chapter we discussed the notion of *"coima,"* a word for a
prevalent form of fee-taking, sometimes labeled bribery, in Peru. The
fact that cocaine induced massive bribe-taking was undisputed. Where
the United States and Peru differed, according to one study, is that in the
American perspective, "corruption is widely perceived as being principally responsible for the failure of states to curtail the flow of drugs to
the United States."[53] Reduce or eliminate corruption, and, presto, the
supply is reduced or eliminated and the cocaine problem is solved. But,
"corruption" to the American often translates into "livelihood" and
"survival" to the Peruvian.

"Drug trafficker payoffs to police," observed Ethan Nadelmann,
"tended to be considered not in the context of meager government salaries but as government corruption, pure and simple. As a consequence,
the label of corruption was attached to economic transactions that were
viewed by many Latin Americans . . . as normative rather than corrupt
behavior."[54]

Clearly two visions of "corruption" were being projected on the drug
trade—one from the U.S. cultural perspective, and one from the Peruvian end. This is not to say that Peruvians accepted high-level corruption as a routine part of their life. In the 1980s and 1990s Peruvian presidents periodically purged members of the police and armed forces
guilty of the most flagrant abuses. Corruption at a very high level, and
often done in such an open fashion, directly challenged the legitimacy
of government itself. It was a more subtle challenge than the Shining
Path, but a no less insidious one, threatening to undermine the fundamental principle of rule by law in general, and more specifically, to
break down the very essence of discipline in the military. And in the

United States in June 1995, several former federal officials in the Department of Justice whose jobs were to identify, find, and prosecute narcotraffickers were themselves indicted for conspiracies with the drug cartels in the district of southern Florida.[55]

Complicating the problem, or, if one views the world from the perspective of the Shining Path, enhancing the opportunities, was the collaboration that developed in the UHV in the early 1980s between the terrorists and the narcotraffickers, from the lowly coca farmers to the high-powered middle men who transported the paste out of the UHV north to Colombia. Shining Path followers were in the valley as early as 1980, and by 1983 were promoting alliances—based partly on persuasion and partly on terror—with the drug traffickers.[56] As U.S. efforts to eradicate coca crops or interdict the supply lines, or both, became more frequent in the 1980s, the terrorists found it easier to persuade the growers and narcotraffickers that the Shining Path was acting in their interest, protecting them from the national police and their gringo allies.

Militarized, antinarcotics operations were organized with greater and greater frequency from the mid-1980s onward. Funded by the United States and often manned by U.S. personnel, Operation Bronco in 1984, seven major Operation Condors between 1985 and 1987, Operation Snow Cap in 1987, and Operation Support Justice in 1991 all reflected the growing U.S. interest. In 1989 a new base at Santa Lucia in the UHV was built to house three hundred men and nine helicopters with $3 million from the United States. A fifteen-hundred-meter runway—the longest in the UHV—was constructed and protected by a minefield and watchtowers. U.S. pilots flew the helicopters. The war against drugs was becoming "militarized." In early 1989 the new Bush administration's Secretary of Defense Richard Cheney "publicly proclaimed that detecting and countering the production and trafficking of illegal drugs was a 'high-priority, national security mission' for the Pentagon."[57] The armed forces, not simply the Drug Enforcement Agency and other federal agencies that had been involved in the drug wars, were committed with ever-increasing frequency.

"The apparent [new] model for the U.S. military in the Andes," wrote another American drug trade specialist, Donald Mabry, "is a work of

fiction." Tom Clancy's *Clear and Present Danger,* which pits U.S. special-
ized light infantry troops inserted into Colombia against the drug armies, represented the most "militarized" of scenarios—U.S. troops injected straight in country to do battle. As Mabry noted one of the most
visible and successful models was Operation Just Cause in December
1989. There the military dropped in on Panama and, like a giant posse,
captured the notorious drug trafficker, Gen. Manuel Noriega. Various
drug "summits" (Cartagena 1990; San Antonio 1992) were held. These
summits brought together President Bush and Andean heads of state
and focused squarely on the principal issue between the United States
and Peru and her neighbors—the drug trade. For Peru, however, the
principal threat to her national security and well being was not drugs.
Terrorism, poverty, unemployment, and inflation all outweighed drugs.
But efforts to control the coca industry became enmeshed in the war
against terrorism, making the antidrug campaign even more complicated in the equation of Peruvian-U.S. relations.

In Peru, furthermore, rivalries between the national police and the
army played into the hands of terrorists and narcotraffickers. The police
were charged with the war against drugs, while the military focused
on the terrorists. But as the campaigns fused in the UHV, chains of authority, lines of command, and simple jealousies between the police
and army confounded antidrug and antiguerrilla operations. Funds,
for example, supplied by the Drug Enforcement Agency (DEA) were
channeled through the police into antidrug campaigns in the Upper
Huallaga Valley, but those funds could not be applied by the army to
counterinsurgency operations. The results could be nightmarish.

On the night of March 27, 1989, Sendero launched an assault on the
police post at Uchiza, a major population center in the UHV. Desperately the police radioed for assistance. They knew military units were
only minutes away by helicopter. The police were in direct communications with their boss in Lima, Armando Villanueva, then minister of the
interior and head of the national police. Villanueva could not get his
own Peruvian air forces or the DEA helicopters based at Santa Lucia to
rescue his embattled police. At dawn the police surrendered to the terrorists, who then shot all officers on the main plaza but pardoned the

lower ranks. Sendero's red flag with the hammer and sickle was raised on the town flagpole.

The air force and DEA claimed its helicopters were not equipped for night operations, and so they listened on the same frequency, as did Villanueva, throughout the night as the police succumbed to the terrorists. Furthermore many growers in the UHV were no friends of the police who were their principal antagonists. Earlier that month the United States had finally prevailed upon the reluctant Peruvians to test a new chemical weapon, Spike, in the war on cocaine. Spike was the herbicide Tebuthieron manufactured specifically by Eli Lilly to eradicate coca plants. Theoretically it spared other foliage. Sixteen acres were destroyed in a test, but coca growers and traffickers viewed the whole experiment as a threat to their livelihood concocted by the police and the Americans. The year before, more than five thousand acres of coca had been eliminated by Peruvian crews using U.S.-made weed eaters, transported to the coca farms by U.S.-made helicopters manned by U.S. crews, and all largely funded by the DEA. This made it much easier for Sendero to penetrate the valley. The terrorists posed as friends of the coca growers, as defenders of people's liberties against the American imperialists and their allies, the corrupt police and national government. In this way the war on drugs played directly into the hands of the terrorists.

For most of 1989, from February through September, the intensity of Sendero's activities in the UHV forced the withdrawal of all Peruvian eradication crews and their DEA advisers. García's government was losing control of the valley. In April the government declared the area an emergency zone and turned control over to the army. "Lima's concerns," observed José E. Gonzales, "in other words, shifted from the drug war to the guerrilla war."[58]

For a while Uchiza was a Shining Path city.[59] But not for long. Within a few days a strong detachment of the army, commanded by Brig. Gen. Alberto Arciniegas, retook Uchiza. The veteran terrorist fighter meant business. He ordered the colors of Sendero struck from the flagpole before the assembled citizens in the town plaza.

"The compañeros [Sendero's nickname in the UHV] will kill us, take reprisals," some complained. "If the Peruvian colors don't fly in our plaza," the general responded, "I'm the one who's going to kill you; not with knives, but with helicopters that will destroy the entire town." If the citizens cooperated, on the other hand, he said, "you can count on my protection and support."[60]

Arciniegas soon had the valley under his control. He pursued the terrorists without respite but backed off the coca farmers and traffickers. That was not an army problem. Ensured of his cooperation, the farmers and traffickers in turn gave Arciniegas theirs. U.S. officials were furious as the coca traffic resurged.

Melvyn Levitsky, Assistant Secretary for International Narcotics Matters in the Department of State, testified before the Permanent Subcommittee on Investigations of the U.S. Senate that Arciniegas was corrupt, cooperating with the drug traffickers, taking bribes, and thus breaking up the efforts of the DEA and national police. Arciniegas was outraged and struck back in the press denying personal complicity.

But the facts showed that the army had to cooperate in some fashion with the drug growers and traffickers. Some of the military's success against the terrorists had been financed by funds generated by the drug enterprises themselves. Arrests made in 1990 of army officers protecting drug flights simply revealed that corruption was inevitable with so much money flowing into the country at a time of desperate economic straits for Peru. The economic crisis, compounded by the war against terrorism, drugs, and corruption, endowed the election of 1990 with a special urgency.[61]

Models for Development

That sense of immediacy turned Vargas Llosa in his presidential campaign of 1990 into a radical of sorts, championing free enterprise based to a large extent on the U.S. model with such enthusiasm that his critics labeled him a fanatic of the right. Fujimori played on that theme brilliantly, portraying Vargas Llosa as the spokesman for the old elites and politicians. But Fujimori was being disingenuous, for he too was committed to deconstructing the elaborate state controls put in place by the military regimes of the 1960s and 1970s. "Privatization" was the buzzword of the 1980s in the Americas, and it was the U.S. model— complemented by conspicuous successes in other nations, such as Britain, Spain, and Japan—that most middle-of-the-road Peruvians looked to.

"Spain is a good example," Vargas Llosa said, "of how one country is very intelligently taking advantage of foreign investments in general, and U.S. investments in particular. And this is very interesting, because it not only occurred under a government that might be labeled right-centrist, but it has continued under the succeeding government, one certainly labeled left-centrist. This government [that of the socialist prime minister Felípe Gonzales] has not only maintained the politics of its predecessor, but has stimulated foreign investments."

Vargas Llosa also looked to Asia for models. "Look at the Asian countries," he said. "They have stimulated foreign investments that have contributed heavily to their economic take-off. It's very evident that those countries have benefitted from large foreign investments."

Closer to home Vargas Llosa found encouraging economic models in Chile and Bolivia, two neighbors whose destinies have been interwoven tightly into Peru's history. Both formed part of the old Spanish viceroyalty of Peru and were subordinate provinces of the empire governed from the viceroy's capital at Lima. Lima's Creole aristocrats never quite forgot they once were the lords of the Spanish empire in South America, while Chileans and Bolivians still bristle a bit at Peruvian haughtiness.

Chile had passed through a remarkable period of economic recovery since the socialist presidency of Salvador Allende (1970–73) was overthrown in a coup led by Gen. Augusto Pinochet. Taking many cues from Milton Friedman's Chicago school of economics, Pinochet and his advisers reduced the role of the State in the economy, opened Chilean markets, and encouraged the influx of foreign investments. For many years, however, the open economic model meant a closed political system. Pinochet governed with a tight hand and, until October 1988, when he allowed a plebiscite to take place on his presidency, political liberties were in scant supply in Chile. Pinochet himself was voted out of power in December 1989.

Vargas Llosa, like so many Peruvians, admired the Chilean economy, but was wary of endorsing the political means to that end. "I don't cite the case of Chile," he says, "largely because I am very critical of its politics and of the Chilean dictatorship [under Pinochet]. But, from the economic point of view, it is a very interesting case. Chile has had, very evidently, an intelligent policy, stimulating and attracting foreign investments which have, in turn, benefited Chile a great deal."

In the mid-1980s Bolivia had the dubious honor of joining a few other countries in modern history to reach hyperinflation. When Bolivia's inflation rate peaked at about 22,000 percent per annum, the government of President Victor Paz Estenssoro bit the bullet and enacted a program of extreme fiscal and economic stabilization.

Vargas Llosa and other Peruvians admired the results. "More than 380 million dollars have been repatriated into Bolivia—taking it out of the banks of Miami and bringing it back to Bolivia. That can only take place with a change in policy which effectively provides security and guarantees a decent earning on one's money. There is no other remedy. The threats, the state control, etc. have never functioned. It only encourages people to take their money out, further impoverishing the nation."

"I think this economic catastrophe," Vargas Llosa said, returning to Peru's problems, "can have the positive effect of opening our eyes— those of public opinion and the general public—to the folly of setting up an autarchic system in this era of the internationalization of the economy, of culture, of communications. I think the Peruvian public will come out of this vaccinated against certain ideologies such as economic nationalism, autarchic economies, and come out of it with a modern and practical attitude towards the theme of foreign investments."

"Foreign investments" in Peru, of course, means those made by the United States—Peru's principal trading partner for the better part of the twentieth century and its principal investor. In the election of 1990, while attention was riveted to the most visible problems of terrorism, inflation, unemployment, and an economy generally in tatters, the rela-

tionship with the United States was never far from the surface of underlying solutions being offered by candidates Vargas Llosa and Fujimori.[62]

Peru and the United States in the 1980s and 1990s

The United States remains Peru's principal trading partner, although
the presence of Japan, Germany, and Britain, for example, is on the rise
in Peru, creating a diversity long sought by Peruvians. Nonetheless
in 1990, Peru still exported three times more to the United States than
to its nearest rival—Germany—while imports from the United States
were four times in excess of those from Germany. Japan, Britain, and
Brazil followed Germany as leading recipients of Peruvian exports,
while imports came, after the United States, from Argentina, Germany,
Brazil, and Japan.[63] Clearly, even if the immense issue of the narcotraffic
were removed from the equation, the close economic relationship between Peru and the United States that has prevailed since the Oncenio
of the 1920s continues.

The Reagan administration's conservative economic and political
emphasis (deregulation at home and pushing the Cold War to victory
abroad, for example) generally was looked upon with favor by 1990
presidential candidates Vargas Llosa and Fujimori. However, some issues in the previous ten years had rocked the relationship, which Bruce
St. John, in his book on Peruvian foreign policy, rather carefully analyzed as "strained but probably as good as could be expected."[64]

The "strain" came in a number of areas during the Belaúnde and García administrations. García's famous "10 percent" stand on the debt
certainly exacerbated relations, while both the Belaúnde and García
administrations publicly criticized Reagan's Central American policy,
which was aimed at overthrowing the Sandinistas of Nicaragua. Peru
threw its support behind the Contadora Group, which promoted a separate, negotiated settlement to the Central American crises. During the
1982 Falklands/Malvinas War, Belaúnde openly sympathized with the
Argentines, calling the U.S. support of Great Britain "blind and anach-
ronistic," a position not guaranteed to generate much goodwill in Wash-

ington.[65] And human rights abuses by the military constantly drew the attention of American and international human rights organizations, such as Americas Watch, Ecumenical Committee on the Andes, Amnesty International, and other groups with access to power and public opinion in the United States.

The killing of eight Peruvian journalists at the remote village of Uchuraccay in 1982 was featured in a probing, intense thirty-five minute film entitled *Fire in the Andes,* which was widely distributed in the United States. And the massacre of inmates in the Lima prisons of Lurigancho, the Santa Barbara Women's Prison, and the navy's island prison of El Frontón in June 1986 set human rights activists aflame. In a history of contemporary events, James Rudolph noted that "the brutality and scope of these events shocked even the violence-inured limeño population."[66] Yet the almost daily brutal assassinations of members of the police, the armed forces, and innocent victims by Sendero was sometimes overlooked by zealous U.S.-based human rights activists who apparently had tacitly accepted the Sendero view of Peru. Not so Peruvians.

In 1988 the appearance of the Peruvian-made film, *La boca del lobo,* described above, highlighted and condemned violence in all its many ugly manifestations—although some thought the movie was *Senderista* in sympathy. Perhaps they did not see the movie. This writer watched the film one evening in the suburb of Miraflores in the fall of 1988. Suddenly the screen flickered and abruptly went off, plunging the theater into darkness. Emergency lights, powered by a small generator kept by the theater, came on and everyone quietly and in orderly fashion filed out of the theater, receiving a receipt for another showing. Sendero's power pylon bombers had struck again in the hills and canyons beyond Lima's immediate vicinity, once again plunging a part of the city into darkness. I came back the next week to see the film. Its focus was on brutality. The effect was sobering, ominous. In such an atmosphere, Fujimori and Vargas Llosa tilted for the grand prize in 1990, and, as noted, the United States was never too far from the rhetoric and ideology of the campaigns.

Vargas Llosa, for example, insisted that peace, and prosperity, would only follow by reaching out to the United States. "I am convinced of the necessity of a close relationship between the United States and Latin America in general," he said, "because Latin America needs American economic and political collaboration, not only for economic development but for the consolidation of the democratic system."

Fujimori's contribution during the campaign was to avoid the United States publicly and focus on Japan instead, although his first trip abroad after the election was to Japan *and* the United States to negotiate with the international banking establishment regarding Peru's debt.

Vargas Llosa was less fussy in his admiration for the United States or in encouraging a think tank called the Institute for Liberty and Democracy (ILD) from receiving U.S. support. Both the U.S. Agency for International Development and the Center for International Private Enterprise (funded by the National Endowment for Democracy established during the first Reagan administration) have supported the ILD. The institute was established in 1980 by an economist named Hernando de Soto to explore the problems and suggest solutions for Peru's complex economic issues. Accepting U.S. assistance—directly or indirectly—carries with it certain risks for Peruvian politicians, but Vargas Llosa did not flinch. Besides, he did not subscribe to what he colorfully described as the "great Satan" theory of American imperialism. Instead he viewed Peru's own elites as the source of many of Peru's modern ills, an ironic twist given that his association with those elites probably hurt him fatally in the election.

From Vargas Llosa's perspective, American policy toward Peru had been to then largely determined by U.S. private companies operating in the country, rather than by the priorities of the government in Washington, D.C. One could argue, however, that by 1990 the narcotraffic was driving U.S. policy more than any one other factor.

"Private interests [U.S. companies] can be interpreted, in many instances," Vargas Llosa said in a professorial manner, analyzing the relationship between U.S. capital and the Peruvian state, "not to have contributed to the national interests of Peru. But I don't hold, necessarily, the American companies culpable. Rather, it was the Peruvian state for not determining rules and norms which would have favored Peru." It was this immense bureaucracy, privileged and inefficient, which both

Vargas Llosa and Fujimori attacked with reformist zeal in 1990. Both aimed to essentially dismantle the state apparatus and reinvigorate the economy by the application of neoliberal principles.

Vargas Llosa looked to other world leaders and their policies for models; Great Britain's Prime Minister Margaret Thatcher and her thinking on cultivating a "property-owning democracy," which itself resonates with Jeffersonian style and substance, was studied by Vargas Llosa.

"Today property is still in the hands of very few people. What we need to do is make property owners of all Peruvians. That is fundamental. Where there is no direct experience of property, it is very difficult for the idea of liberty to take root. We want to make Peru into a country of property owners and entrepreneurs. We have to massively distribute Peruvian property. That will sustain the democratic way. And Peru has the ability to do so. There is an immense public sector that can be privatized, applying appropriate social and technical criteria, to distribute property massively, both in the city and in the countryside."

In the end Vargas Llosa desired passionately to democratize his country, sounding very much like a Jeffersonian democrat as he championed the values of the common man and extolled the virtues of private property ownership. To achieve his vision, he argued that some basic cultural changes had to occur.

"Fundamentally, we have to foster civic responsibility, and encourage a change in the culture of the country. To give Peruvian democracy a chance, a vitality that it needs, we need to persuade all Peruvians that our problems can only be solved by us, that they cannot be resolved from above, or from afar."

In fact Fujimori adopted virtually all of the Vargas Llosa proposals into his program for the redemption of Peru. The one exception was that of a basic division with Washington on drug policy.[67]

Fujimori and the Americans, 1990–95

The final campaign had opposite effects on the candidates. Vargas Llosa seemed worn down, while Fujimori, riding the crest of "Fujimania" in Peru, gained momentum. The usual political controversies plagued the final campaign. Both Vargas Llosa and Fujimori were accused of evading taxes, but there were no smoking guns to leave any lasting damage on either. Not surprisingly religion played a role in the campaign as well.

Fujimori is nominally a Roman Catholic and Vargas Llosa an agnostic. The major role in the religion issue was played by the growing number of Protestant evangelicals in Peru who supported Fujimori. Today there are more than one million Pentecostal Protestants in a general population of twenty-two million. The number has doubled in the past five years, and the largest denomination, the Assembly of God, has more than one thousand churches in the country.

Fujimori rallied the Pentecostal Protestant support very effectively. His running mate for second vice president was Carlos García García, a Baptist preacher and president of the National Evangelical Council of Peru. More than 25 percent of Fujimori's party's (Cambio 90) congressional slate were either ministers or members of a Protestant sect. Much of the very successful door-to-door campaigning was done by evangelicals in support of Fujimori. The association between the Pentecostals and the U.S. religious right certainly reinforced the tendency of the first Fujimori administration to favor the conservative political and economic trajectory that it took.

Not long after his inauguration, Fujimori committed the country to a tight program of conservative economic measures to end inflation and restore Peru's standing before the international financial community. He started measures to privatize the economy, to promote foreign investment, to increase tax revenues, encouraged free competition, and, in sum, turned Peru toward a free-market economy. The short-term results were predictably harsh. "Fujishock" replaced "Fujimania" as the favored label of a president who turned Peru dramatically away from the state interventionism of the 1970s into a model post–Cold War, neoliberal state of the 1990s. In many ways a congruence of vision was once again being restored between the United States and Peru under the Fujimori administration. Liberty once again triumphed over equality, and this common political context helped Lima and Washington weather some rough spots over the next few years.

While Fujimori and the Bush administration marched in step regarding the economic plan for Peru's revival and restoration of her international credit, they differed on how to address narcotraffic. During his campaign Fujimori insisted that economic incentives must be a priority to wean the coca farmers from growing the plants. Fujimori even initially rejected $35.9 million in U.S. military assistance negotiated by the García government earlier in 1990 to wage war on the traffickers by expanding bases and supporting the Peruvian military with logistics and advice. The president-elect contended that it was an economic problem that had to be faced with alternate development plans and crop substitution strategies rather than simply military eradication efforts. In late June, however, Fujimori said he might reconsider. By October 1990 he was more firmly committed to his supply-side strategy on dealing with narcotraffic. It was emerging as the Fujimori Doctrine and was not popular in Washington.

It was also clear, however, that Fujimori would have to accommodate to some extent U.S. priorities in the war on drugs if collaboration on other fronts, such as the critical one of reopening Peru's access to international lending agencies, was to succeed. It was equally clear to the Bush administration that Peru's priorities had to be addressed if any movement on the drug front was to be made. The Fujimori Doctrine stressed alternate development, crop substitution, land titling for coca farmers, and access to credit, while the United States favored programs of repression and crop eradication. In May 1991 Washington and Lima signed a new antidrug agreement that responded to the Fujimori Doctrine, providing assistance along a broad front that included economic, political, and social areas, as well as addressing the military and security threats that the United States viewed as primary.[68] It was a broad agreement, encompassing human rights, structural adjustment and alternative development, security, interdiction and prevention, corruption, ecology, international markets, external debt operations, and virtually every conceivable approach to reduce the narcotraffic.

Less than a year later, on April 5, 1992, Fujimori performed a classic Peruvian political *autogolpe*. He suspended the judiciary system and dissolved Congress. The courts were labeled corrupt and inefficient, while Congress was obstructing Fujimori's efforts to bring about structural reforms and, equally important, was blocking an all-out war on Sendero. The United States reacted predictably to the Peruvian Samurai's caudillo-style coup: all assistance except humanitarian was suspended until constitutional order was restored. And in the UHV, Fujimori gave the Peruvian military a free rein to interdict the drug traffic. The air force was given control of all flights into and out of the UHV. The entire valley was once again placed under military control, and the campaign against the Shining Path was sharply escalated across the country.

That Abimael Guzmán was captured within a few months of the coup is no accident. The terrorists struck back quickly. They murdered four Peruvian pilots and two police officers in Lima within hours of a military court's judgment sentencing Guzmán to life imprisonment in January 1993.[69] But Shining Path's strength dwindled through 1993, 1994, and 1995. Fujimori's decrees allowed for quick arrests of Sendero suspects with little evidence and for summary judgments by anonymous judges to prevent reprisals so frequently executed under the old judicial system. Pardons were offered freely to induce defections from the Shining Path, and thousands turned themselves in by November 1994. More than three thousand people died in Sendero violence in 1992. That number was dramatically reduced to a little less than seven hundred in 1993.

In the presidential election of April 1995, Fujimori won a resounding landslide victory over his closest rival, former Secretary General of the United Nations Javier Pérez de Cuéllar, confirming the overwhelming support that Fujimori has received for his policies. Sendero attempted to massively disrupt the elections as a show of force. But they did not show up. Although random bombings and assassinations still were taking place in 1995, it seemed like Fujimori's regimen—reducing inflation from 7,000 percent in 1990 to 15.4 percent in 1994, and expanding the economy so it was the fastest-growing economy in the world in 1994—

meaning jobs, employment, and security for many—had stripped them of much of their rationale. The freedom of the military and police to run down the terrorists also hastened their demise. Nonetheless such a long-lasting and pernicious movement with such devoted partisans cannot be said to have been eliminated totally in a country where, in spite of all Fujimori's efforts, inequities in the distribution of resources and power still startle the visitor and student of the country.

And the narcotraffic? It will probably be with us far longer than the terrorists, observed historian Donald Mabry. A new agreement was signed between the United States and Peru on May 12, 1995, to promote alternative development and economic growth in the coca-growing zones. Forty-four million dollars were to be devoted over a period of five years to support such programs as technical assistance to create new jobs, to study alternate crops, to provide financial advice and assistance, to establish agroindustries, and to protect the environment. This is more than was invested between 1981 and 1993 (aside from the millions directly pumped into the police and army for direct eradication, destruction, and interdiction), and prompted the U.S. ambassador in Lima, Alvin Adams, to state enthusiastically that the program in alternate development was one of the largest in the world. Meanwhile in the U.S. crack cocaine was moving into the rural South, leading to sharp increases in crime.

The actual war on drugs can become heated, especially with so many high-tech, secret missions being sponsored or actually executed by the U.S. military in Peru. On April 24, 1992, a U.S. Air Force Hercules C-130 flying along the northern Peruvian coast was shot at by a Peruvian Air Force, Soviet-made Sukhoi SU-22 attack jet on patrol near the military base at Talara. The rapid decompression caused by the strafing sucked one U.S. crewman out of the aircraft and sent him to his death thousands of feet below. The Hercules was able to return to its base, never having established voice contact with the Peruvians, even while monitoring the international distress frequencies of 121.5 (civilian) and 243.0 (military), which should have prevented the incident.

Typically the versions of the incident differed. The United States said the Hercules was clearly marked, flying a prescribed route at a certain prearranged altitude, and in international airspace, beyond the Peruvian coastline. The Peruvians said the C-130 was not marked or identifiable, that it was on a secret mission, and had strayed from its assigned altitude.

That little was made of the strafing incident is testimony to the close cooperation between the Peruvian military and the U.S. drug enforcement efforts in Peru. Yet the solution to the drug enigma remains unsatisfactory in the relations between the two countries, perhaps underscoring the differing worldviews of the participants in this business. Can the struggling coca farmer of the UHV have much in common with the cocaine consumers of an affluent North America whose very affluence is almost the world's stereotype for the good life?

Another point of contention between Peru and the United States involved a periodic border dispute between Ecuador and Peru that erupted once again in January 1995. The United States was one of the original guarantors—along with Chile, Argentina, and Brazil—of the 1942 Rio Treaty that defined Peru's frontiers along her northern border with Ecuador. The stream of events is long and complicated, but essentially Ecuador wanted unimpeded and sovereign access to the Amazon, and Peru's claims to the region conflicted with Ecuador's. The border in question was along a remote section of the Andes called the Cordillera del Condor and the Upper Cenapa River region. Ecuador had been modernizing its armed forces for more than a decade—especially after a skirmish in 1981 went badly for Ecuador—and in January 1995, Ecuadorean units pushed into the region to challenge Peruvian outposts. The Peruvian military, distracted by the long war against terrorism, failed to dislodge the Ecuadorean troops and equipment and a ceasefire was established, again overseen by the Rio Protocol guarantor nations.[70] In fact all agreed that Ecuador bested Peru in this exchange, although the preponderance of military power still lay with Peru.

The United States has deliberately maintained a strict neutrality in this border dispute, one of the oldest in Latin America. But when tensions run high, so does the nationalist spirit in both countries, and the United States's interests in the region are jeopardized. These interests include the "sanctity of international treaties, the peaceful resolution of conflict, the friendship of two nations that are keys in the war against narcotrafficking, the nonproliferation of high-tech weaponry, and the pursuit of democracy and free trade in the Hemisphere."[71] The solution is the final demarcation of the border in accordance with the Rio Protocol. In fact only about seventy-eight kilometers of border remain in dispute, but that is enough for nationalists on both sides to keep the pot stirred. It may seem like an insignificant border spate, but as one observer wrote, "the border dispute has totally dominated bilateral relations between Ecuador and Peru," and more important, has overshadowed "the numerous social, economic, political, and environmental topics where there exists a community of interests and a need for greater cooperation."[72]

Other Cultural Contacts

Cultural, intellectual, religious, or even spiritual elements also impinge on the relations between these two nations and peoples. The influences can be as profound, perhaps even more so in some instances, than in the more easily identifiable political, social, and strategic areas we are accustomed to emphasize.

Often ignored are these other cultural contacts in the relations between the United States and Peru. For example, did the book *The Bridge Over San Luis Rey* by Thornton Wilder weave a vastly different image of Peru that contrasts with the world of terrorists and drugs so violently portrayed by Tom Clancy in *Clear and Present Danger*? Certainly. Wilder's 1928 Pulitzer Prize–winning book is about fate and destiny in the human condition, calling our attention to eternal truths, all set in the exotic, remote world of eighteenth-century Peru where Spaniard and Indian existed as if in two different worlds.

Clancy's book is a fast-moving, techno-thriller, clearly distinguishing for us the good guys and the bad guys. Although largely set in Colombia, the imagery and stereotypes are equally applicable to Peru.

Which book draws a better picture of Peru for the American reader? The one where the slender, Inca rope bridge over the deep, narrow canyon of San Luis Rey snapped and plunged a few travelers to their deaths, thereby setting Wilder to ask himself the great question: Why? Or do we sublimate and put ourselves into Clancy's book, imagining ourselves chasing evildoers up and down the coca valleys of Peru, flying the fast helicopters, spraying machine-gun fire on drug planes trying to get off landing strips hidden in the jungles of the Upper Huallaga Valley? Which image do we carry of Peru?

More than ten million readers receive *National Geographic Magazine* each month, and the images of Peru in those pages may reach more people on a regular basis than even the wildest, most violent news of the drug wars in the press. In a sampling of the seventeen articles featuring Peru published in the magazine since 1970, more than half focused on the Indian nature of Peru, carrying such titles as "Titicaca, Abode of the Sun," "The Lost Empire of the Incas," "Mystery of the Ancient Nazca Lines," and "New Tomb of Royal Splendor, the Moche of Ancient Peru." The remainder were geographical in content, "Amazon—The River Sea," "The High Andes, South America's Islands in the Sun," or provided some insight into Peruvian realities, such as "The Two Souls of Peru," "The Incredible Potato," and "Silver, A Mineral of Excellent Nature." Rounding out the selection were two articles on sports, "Kayaking the Amazon" and "Roaring through the Earth's Deepest Canyon."

Granted, *National Geographic,* by very definition is an apolitical, geographically oriented periodical, but in the past two or three decades the articles have in many instances taken an advocacy position vis-à-vis the environment and conservation, for example. "The Incredible Potato" may not have the ring of *Clear and Present Danger,* but it goes on the shelves belonging to tens of millions of Americans who carefully preserve the magazine for posterity, to be handed down to following generations like precious heirlooms.

That the popular stereotype of Peru is of an Indian, or of an Indian artifact, or of an Indian tomb recently discovered, makes Peru in the American mind largely an exotic land filled with exotic indigenous peoples and items, where the rafting is pretty good and the mountain vistas and river streams are spectacular. Within this scenario, fast twin-engine Cessnas and Pipers roar in and out of the Upper Huallaga

Valley at night, picking up coca paste for the laboratories of Colombia and the ultimate consumers in the streets and homes of the United States, while the operators pay off army officers and terrorists to keep the wheels of the machine greased.

But that, of course, is too simple. The valleys and plateaus of Peru, highlands and lowlands, deserts and coastal oases, are populated only very thinly with drug runners and terrorists, tied in one fashion or another to the American economy.

Tongues of Fire

Picking up where we left off on another cultural contact from an earlier chapter, what about the effect of more than one million Pentecostal Protestant Christians in Peru, most of them members of evangelical churches which originated in the United States?[73] There were a number of "waves" of Protestantism that arrived at Peru's shores in the last century. Scholars have identified as many as seven, but the most important can be divided into two: the traditional Protestant sects that sent representatives in the nineteenth and twentieth centuries, and the arrival of Pentecostal Protestantism beginning in the 1940s and 1950s. It is this latter form of Protestantism that has dramatically altered the religious context of modern Peru, and, indeed, of modern Latin America, especially in such countries as Guatemala, Brazil, and Chile where sizable Pentecostal communities exist. Some scholars suggest that the religious landscape is being radically transformed by the Pentecostal movement, gradually ending the long domination of the Roman Catholic Church. And as the religious context is altered, so are other elements of Peruvian and Latin American life, from traditional social and family relationships to the distribution of economic and political power.[74] "The four pillars of Protestantism," wrote W. Stanley Roycroft, an English missionary with long experience in Peru, "namely, the priesthood of all believers, justification by faith, the right of private intervention and the authority of the Word of God, are also of fundamental importance in the development of a democratic society."[75]

Whether the cause-and-effect sequence of Pentecostal Protestantism and political democracy is quite so clearly drawn is a subject of some debate among students of the phenomenon, but there is little doubt that Pentecostal Protestantism, largely introduced from the United States, has altered the political landscape. The question is how, especially since the Pentecostals have publicly shunned participation in the political world around them and have been very conservative in their politics. They looked first to the inward conversion of man's soul, the born-again experience, as the transcending act of their faith. If one allowed the spirit of God to enter one's life, then the outward, secular changes associated with Christian living—giving up alcohol and tobacco for instance—would follow.

Since many of these Pentecostal communities were begun by American missionaries, what was their influence on modern Peruvian-U.S. relations? First, however, some general definitions, realizing that in the subculture of Christian sects and denominations there are many shades of distinctions beyond those that follow.

The immense increase in the number of Pentecostals, especially from the 1950s through the 1980s, prompted the beginnings of scholarly examination that continue today, which attempts to assess the impact on Latin America. Evangelical is a term used almost interchangeably with Pentecostal, and, indeed, most Latin American Pentecostals call themselves *"evangélicos."* Charismatics is another term and is sometimes applied equally loosely.

Some of the denominations that came to Latin America bearing the Pentecostal/evangelical standard were the Assemblies of God, the Churches of God, Seventh Day Adventists, and a host of smaller denominations. Jehovah's Witnesses and Mormons also spread into Peru, and although both are considered cults by mainline Christians, they were associated with the movement.

Some of the Pentecostals are loosely categorized as "Word" churches, where the emphasis is on the words of the Bible not only as messengers of God's will, but as having power in and of themselves. Many of them take their cue from the opening verses of the Book of John:

> In the beginning was the Word,
> and the Word was with God,
> and the Word was God.

There is also something called, colorfully and wonderfully redolent of the modern world, the "electronic church," by which is meant the electronic transmission of the gospel via television, radio, videotapes, and other modern media. The fallen evangelist Jimmy Swaggart was perhaps the best known of the televangelists who reached into Latin America, although Swaggart was preceded, sometimes by decades, by Christian radio broadcasts that pioneered the Protestant evangelization of this largely Catholic reserve.

The term Pentecostal derives from the day of Pentecost, which is the fiftieth day after the Sabbath of Passover week. Also called the Feast of Weeks or the Feast of Harvest in Jewish ritual, it took on a special meaning for Christians when the Holy Spirit descended on the Apostles at Pentecost after Jesus's crucifixion. Filled with the Holy Spirit, the Apostles spoke in tongues, or languages, they had not previously known. As recorded in the Second Book of Acts, "They saw what seemed to be tongues of fire that separated and came to rest on each of them. All of them were filled with the Holy Spirit and began to speak in other tongues as the Spirit enabled them." Other instances of speaking in tongues occur in the New Testament. There is some controversy over certain aspects of this gift, but that theological hair-splitting need not detain us here. So, Pentecostals are defined as Christian Protestants who speak in tongues when moved by the Holy Spirit.

They also practice faith healing, or the healing of the body by the laying on of hands, by prayer, by faith. Many examples from Jesus's ministry testify to his powers of healing and performing miracles, but, perhaps less well known, are also the examples of healing mentioned in other books of the New Testament.

Pentecostals are also distinguished by other characteristics. They are marked more by an oral rather than written tradition, an egalitarian organization stressing the individual rather than the formal hierarchical and patronal structures of Catholicism and traditional Protestantism, and a spiritual appeal that has found its most powerful and numerous adherents among the poorer, illiterate classes of Latin America. Pentecostals, evangelicals, Charismatics—whatever term one uses—now represent between 3 and 5 percent of Peru's population, but in countries such as Guatemala, Chile, and Brazil, the increases have been dramatic, rising to more than 20 to 30 percent in the 1980s and 1990s.

Why this increase? Perhaps a sentence from a nonbelieving (by his own definition) but immensely astute student of Protestantism in Latin America helps explain. "By appealing to the deepest needs of a people," wrote David Stoll, "evangelical churches help them redefine themselves, reorganize their lives, and move in dramatic new directions."[76]

"When one attends the worship of a large Pentecostal congregation," Stoll observed, "it is hard to avoid a sense of the immense social power in those praying masses of believers. 'There was a spontaneous audible prayer by the whole congregation which made one feel as though a volcano had erupted,' William Read reported of a six-thousand-person service. 'It continued for a while and then suddenly ended as if by pre-arranged signal. With this, the Monday service of Missionary Manoel de Melo was over.'"[77]

There is a new power at work here in the relations between the United States and Peru—and Latin America in general. Believers easily define it as the power of the Holy Spirit, while skeptics attribute it to a host of secular influences, such as poverty, spiritual and mystical needs, magic, and even to various conspiracies by such disparate agencies as the CIA or the Reverend Sun Myung Moon's Unification Church. But, whatever one ascribes it to, it is present. How has this power been made manifest in the modern relations between the United States and Peru?

While the Summer Institutes of Languages/Wycliffe Bible Translators (SIL/WBT) described in chapter 6 spread their version of civilization and Christianity among Peru's Amazonian Indians, the Pentecostals—as noted, but also including Methodists, Baptists, Jehovah's Witnesses, Mormons, and others—made inroads in the more thickly populated areas of coastal and sierra Peru. They found fertile grounds, as the excellent Jesuit historian Jeffrey Klaiber noted, "among the marginalized classes in town and country . . . where they filled a void in the lives of many poor people who have either lost contact with the Catholic Church or have not found a response to their deepest human needs in the parish nearest them."[78]

There is also a democratizing tendency within the Pentecostal movement. Whether attributable to Protestantism's general nature, to the special egalitarian trends of Pentecostalism, or to the U.S. origins of these religious movements does not seem to matter as long as this phenomenon is noted.

"Many more participate in the Pentecostal than in the Catholic church," wrote Klaiber, "and they rapidly take on positions of responsibility which endow them with a feeling of importance in their lives." Or as the sociologist David Martin wrote, "the crucial characteristic of evangelical Christianity in the vast urban agglomerations of Latin America is self-government."[79]

Pentecostals have been considered basically apolitical in some of the literature. They tend to abstain from direct participation in the political processes of the nation, instead emphasizing that the conversion process is more important to evangelical Christianity than more visible, external stands on social or political reforms. In other words, as earlier missionary Protestants argued, the internal conversion to Christ, manifested outwardly in the churches by living a new life free of alcohol, improving family relationships, and a spiritual life imbued with egalitarian sentiments, inherently carries beyond the confines of the house of worship. In Peru in 1990, seventeen evangelicals were elected to congress, along with President Fujimori's second vice president. This is definitely not a sign of an apolitical view of life, but, rather, is directly taking one's convictions into the marketplace of political ideas and actions.

And the relationship of all this to the United States? "In a sense," David Martin observed, "the USA is the protecting power of Protestantism everywhere. . . . Clearly . . . the influence of the United States is immense."[80]

Pentecostals have given Fujimori strong support in his administration, which itself drew closer to the United States in its economic restructuring of the nation between 1990 and 1999. One perhaps can make more of the relationship than it really merits. Max Weber, the founder of modern sociology, emphasized that the "Protestant work ethic" drove such nations as the United States to the material heights it reached, and Weber's relationship between Protestantism and prosperity was accepted as near gospel for many years. However, when non-Protestant nations such as Japan rose to prominence, the argument was considerably diluted, although certainly not discarded. After all, there was a definite relationship between the Puritan's religious and secular values, which did encourage capital accumulation and material prosperity as godly and good, within certain restraints.

In Peru, Pentecostalism, as in other parts of Latin America, has essentially been viewed as an apolitical, anti-Communist, conservative phenomenon when it was studied as a movement beyond the confines of its religious context. It also has evolved apart from its original U.S. sponsors, taking on a life of its own. But there is little denying that the conservative direction of U.S. political life since the election of Ronald Reagan in 1980, accompanied by the rise of the politically powerful Christian right, the crash of communism in the late 1980s, and the coming to power of Newt Gingrich and the Republicans in Congress in 1994, has found sympathetic listeners in Peru, especially among the Pentecostals so prominent in Fujimori's administrations.

As we near the end of this book, it is perhaps fitting to stress those "softer" cultural, intellectual, and even spiritual influences that flowed between Peru and the United States, the ones that could make political, military, and economic decisions easier within a common vision of what was best for one's people.

Schools, Coca-Cola, and Cyberspace

There are other actors who have stepped onto this stage of Peruvian-U.S. relations over the years. Americans in Peru established their own schools—as did the British, French, Italians, Swiss, and Germans—and some of these schools became important conduits of U.S. values and education. The most important of the "American" schools in Peru, the Franklin Delano Roosevelt School, came into being shortly after World War II, precisely when there was a rapidly increasing American presence in Peru.

Panagra Airlines, with its operating headquarters in Lima, was looking to the postwar expansion as were the other airlines of the world. It ordered four-engine Constellations for its long inter-American routes, which required two pilots and a flight engineer. William D. Kent, a flight engineer at the Pan American base at Treasure Island in San Francisco Bay, was selected to train twelve new flight engineers for the Panagra routes. In preparation for his transfer to Lima, Kent flew down to look at housing and schooling.

"I found the schooling inadequate," Kent remembered, "particularly for those who expected to gain admission into colleges and universities in the United States."[81] Kent persuaded the principal of a Burlingame, California, grammar school, Elsiann Irvin, to come to Lima, live in the Kent home with his wife and five children, and teach his children at home in the manner of the Burlingame curriculum.

"When I returned to Lima," Kent wrote, "and told other Panagra personnel that a U.S. school principal was coming to Lima to teach our children I was deluged with requests to let other children join the classes." That was the genesis of the Franklin D. Roosevelt School.

With too many children to accommodate in Kent's home located in the pleasant Miraflores neighborhood of Lima, another house was located nearby, two other teachers were contracted, and the Franklin Delano Roosevelt School (a name suggested by a Peruvian in the Ministry of Education, which had to approve the school's establishment) was launched in 1946.

The Roosevelt school evolved into one of the premier K-12 schools in Lima over the years. Not only Americans, but hundreds of Peruvians over the years learned in a U.S.-style environment that invariably predisposed them to favor the system and the country from which it sprang. In 1996 more than 90 percent of the graduates went on to two- and four-year colleges and universities, 50 percent of those in the United States. Enrollment had grown from Kent's five children to almost fourteen hundred students.[82]

The Instituto Peruano Norteamericano dates from the late 1930s and emerged in the post–World War II period as not simply a place to learn the English language but as a vehicle of U.S. culture. Funded and administered in part for a long time by various U.S. government agencies—most notably the U.S. Information Agency (USIA)—the institute not only sponsored language courses, but U.S. movies, art exhibits, and other cultural events that opened windows into the United States.

And if one did not attend the Roosevelt School or take a language course at the institute, one could always participate in U.S. culture by going to McDonald's or perhaps the local Kentucky Fried Chicken outlet to order a Big Mac or crispy southern fried chicken and wash it down with a Coca-Cola. It may have been that the generals directing the country's foreign policy in the early 1970s were supranationalists, but the very nature of modern Peruvian society, wedded in so many ways to the United States, sometimes subverted their attempts to wean Peru from dependency upon the United States.

This writer can well remember being in Peru in the early 1970s, when the government was mandating the Inca Quechua language for all schoolchildren and even espousing a locally made soft drink, Inca Cola, as a "Peruvian" drink. "What good is Quechua going to do when my daughter applies for a job at IBM-Peru?" asked one outraged parent.

The failure of the generals to respond to that question—to hundreds and thousands of others related to work, to savings, to basic freedoms—eventually contributed to the undoing of the Peruvian Revolution, although certain key elements, such as the massive land reform that dispossessed the old landholding elites, were never reversed.

And how did the image of the United States fare at the very height of the revolution? On May 30, 1970, an earthquake in the Callejón de Huaylas triggered a massive landslide that buried the city of Yungay. "Twenty-five thousand dead," the cable from the U.S. embassy in Lima to the Canal Zone in Panama said. "I thought the text was garbled," said the U.S. army officer on duty at the receiving end of the cable.[83]

It was not. The earthquake broke up a lake high on the slopes of Mt. Huascarán. The water came rushing down and loosened a terrifying avalanche of mud and rocks that buried the city in a few minutes and instantly entombed virtually all its inhabitants who had gathered there for a regional carnival.

The disaster assistance team in the Panama Canal Zone immediately was activated. Eventually a U.S. aircraft carrier was sent to Chimbote to provide hospital support, U.S. helicopters flew in critical relief supplies, and even the beleaguered I.P.C. threw its considerable resources into the relief effort. It would seem that the revolution—pronationalist, pro–Third World, and determined to free Peru from the perceived hegemony of the United States—was not radically altering the old relationship based ultimately on the generally positive attitudes that still prevailed between the two countries.

Many linkages between Peru and the United States were occasionally frayed by the nature of the times. Tourism suffered during the height of the war against Sendero Luminoso from the mid-1980s through the early 1990s.[84] Oil exploration, on the other hand, increased in the eastern jungle areas of Peru, while new investments were made in traditional areas of copper and gold mining for example.[85] In education the Fulbright Program continued to provide a flow of students and scholars in both directions, although the economic depression and the war against terrorism in the 1980s tended to dampen the exchange for a while. One of the premier agricultural research centers in the world, the Potato Institute at La Molina, sponsored by the United States and Peru, continued to promote new research on the potato, thus improving one of the great food crops of the world, which was first domesticated in ancient Peru. This, even while the former rector of La Molina and now president of Peru, Fujimori, sparred with Washington over the nature of the war on drugs.

The depressed economy and uncertain political conditions of the late 1980s tended to promote new areas in the relationship between Peru and the United States, even while dampening traditional ones such as tourism. By the mid- to late 1980s Peruvians were emigrating in ever-increasing numbers to the United States and Europe, escaping the frustrations of an economy in a tailspin, looking for education and opportunity abroad. This writer remembers one of his graduate assistants in 1988 at the University of Lima who had begun law school at the national university, San Marcos, several years earlier. Thoroughly frustrated by the constant interruptions of her education, she would gladly have gone abroad to complete her work. Thousands of her peers did, not simply looking for education, but for opportunities to work in the relatively tranquil political environment of the United States. By the mid-1990s, hundreds of these Peruvians abroad—most of them in the United States—were linked together in cyberspace. Through the Internet, many Peruvians were in near instant communication through e-mail lists, not only with each other, but with their colleagues in Peru and across the world as networks, nodes, and other forms of electronic information and communication innovations were put into place.

Even the long hand of Sendero reached out into cyberspace. In the spring of 1995, a *Senderista* participating under the pseudonym of Adolfo Olichea kept the Peruvian list in an uproar with his/her prickly comments, sometimes fashioned in a crude and offensive manner. In this instance a largely American invention, the Internet, became a vehicle for communications between Peruvians (assuming Olichea was a Peruvian, an assumption questioned by some on the net) who ordinarily would not have been in contact in Peru. Olichea's communications were issued from an e-mail address in Great Britain, emphasizing the internationalization of domestic affairs.

Whether the marvelous world of e-mail and the instant live broadcasts of CNN have made the world more or less understanding is a question for other social scientists, armchair analysts, commentators, and pollsters to answer. In the case of the United States and Peru, the almost negligible relations between the two at the dawn of the nineteenth century have been replaced by almost instant relations two centuries later. These, however, are meaningless without a context. It is hoped this volume leads the reader backward a bit in time to understand better the present and future relations between these two Western Hemisphere countries that have shared the experience of evolving together in modern times.

Conclusion

There is no true historical conclusion to this story, for it continues. Unlike an historical event, let's say a great battle or war, or a defined period in time with a beginning and end, or a biography of an individual who has long since gone to his reward, the relations between the United States and Peru have a past, present, and future. This book is rendered, for example, quickly obsolete with respect to contemporary events, for by the time you read it, at least one year, perhaps two or more, will have passed since the manuscript was composed.

Having said that, we can still review the passage of two centuries and come to some conclusions. We began this book with the observation that the United States looked at Peru from two angles—one was idealistic and the other pragmatic. From these two views flowed much of the behavior and actions that characterized the history between these two nations. Peru, too, possessed a "bifocal" view, if you will, of the United States. On the one hand, the United States was viewed in idealized terms as land of democracy and equality, not to mention of peace and material prosperity; while on the other hand the United States was always suspect in terms of its ultimate intentions, described in imperial, aggressive terms.

The history of the Summer Institutes of Languages/Wycliffe Bible Translators and of I.P.C. in Peru offers, for example, remarkably vivid examples of how two representative institutions from the United States were viewed differently. The SILs were welcome, while I.P.C. eventually was ostracized. Each represented a different face of the United States in Peru.

The "presence" of the United States in Peru has constituted a significant proportion of Peru's national life, while the opposite has not been true until very recently with the rise of the cocaine trade, or narcotraffic. In the nineteenth century, the United States emerged as Peru's closest ally among the great powers, especially during and after the War of the

Pacific. The United States attempted to maintain Peru's territorial integrity in the face of the victorious Chileans who were strongly supported, in the eyes of many Americans, by the United States' principal commercial and political competitors in Latin America, the British. The rapid growth of U.S. investments in Peru after the turn of the century, especially in the mining sectors, added to the integration of Peru's export economy into the U.S. orbit. And a shared understanding of political and social issues, built around laissez-faire capitalism, tended to harmonize the views of the business and political leadership in both countries.

The apex of U.S. influence was reached during the 1920s when President Augusto Leguía almost slavishly sought U.S. advisers, U.S. finances, and U.S. models in helping determine the nature of his administration. It was a time when business values and individual liberty were extolled in the United States. This mood was mirrored in Leguía's Peru, leading to a confluence of vision and actions between the two nations. This era tended to confirm another major framework proposed for understanding Peruvian-U.S. relations: the confluence, or divergence, in attitudes toward liberty and equality. When they dovetailed, as in the 1920s, relations were harmonious.

The rise of APRA in the 1920s and 1930s proved to be a double-edged sword in the relations between the two countries. On the one hand, APRA was viewed by the old ruling elements of Peru as a socialist threat to the very survival of Peruvian society as they understood it. On the other hand, APRA found many sympathetic echoes in the United States of the 1930s and 1940s as the United States too struggled to come to terms with the depression and capitalism's apparent failure.

The Cold War brought Peru and the United States closer because major sectors in both societies despised communism, although they viewed the threat of communism from different angles. Americans saw Soviet-style communism as a threat to world order internationally and as un-American domestically, while *Apristas* in Peru viewed the Communists as dangerous rivals for political power. For whatever reasons, the threat of communism tended to firm Peruvian-U.S. relations for almost two decades after the end of the Second World War.

While Washington and Lima marched together with respect to communism, U.S. private investments in Peru also increased dramatically in the postwar era. The already large U.S. participation in the mining sector vigorously expanded, as did other American enterprises, from Sears Roebuck to Goodyear Tires. By the 1960s however, the widening gulf between the haves and have-nots in Peru—as elsewhere in Latin America—produced a decade-long crisis. Part of the U.S. response was the Alliance for Progress created by President Kennedy in 1961 to bridge the gap between the poor and the rich in a democratic context, a plan and policy forged in large part to meet the threat of the Cuban Revolution of 1959.

In Peru the International Petroleum Company came to symbolize much of what intensely nationalistic individuals sought to eliminate— a strong foreign presence that undermined true Peruvian sovereignty and continued dependence on the United States. Negotiations between Peru, the United States, and I.P.C. almost succeeded by 1968 in coming to a satisfactory conclusion, but those negotiations collapsed in what amounted to a failure of goodwill, and, perhaps most important, an increasingly divisive vision of Peru's future. The generals who overthrew President Belaúnde in October 1968 almost immediately nationalized I.P.C. and went on to dramatically reject U.S. leadership in the context of the Cold War.

Peru's revolutionary leaders, especially President Velasco Alvarado, wished to break the cycle of dependency, another paradigm suggested early in this book for analyzing the relationship. To this end these leaders initiated a new political, social, and economic agenda with dramatic nationalizations of U.S. properties and a turn to the Soviet Union and other nontraditional suppliers and buyers of Peruvian needs and products, respectively. Equality was the password of the Peruvian Institutional Revolution of 1968, while the United States under the administration of Richard Nixon was more concerned with containing the effects of the Vietnam War and communism. As the search for social and economic justice pushed the pendulum of liberty versus equality far into the equality end of the arc in Peru, relations deteriorated. To many in Washington, it seemed Peru was fast-stepping to the beat of Marxism, and the result was probably the most divisive time in the long history of the relationship.

Yet old and new forces drew the two countries together in the contemporary period—or from the 1980s through the turn of the century.
The rise of the cocaine trade intermingled the largest producer—Peru—
with the largest consumer—the United States—in fashions neither desired, but that neither could resist. The two countries' views of the threat
of narcotraffic often dramatically conflicted, even as they tried to cooperate in eliminating, or, at the least, curtailing the production and
trafficking of cocaine. The United States viewed the narcotraffic as an
immensely corrupting business that had to be—literally—uprooted
and destroyed at its source, principally among the small farmers of
Peru's Upper Huallaga Valley. Peru's national existence, on the other
hand, was being sorely tested by the Shining Path revolutionary movement that reached its apex in the late 1980s. The cultivation of coca—
a plant long known in Peru and whose leaves were chewed by millions
of Indians in the same way Americans chewed tobacco—did not seem
like such a serious threat. Besides Peruvians quite rightly pointed out
that Americans were being a bit hypocritical about the entire business.
Shrink the demand among the millions of American consumers and the
supply would automatically diminish. It was an American problem as
much as, if not more so, than a Peruvian problem. The old adage of having a tiger by the tail comes to mind. In this instance both Peru and the
United States had a grip on the narcotraffic tiger. Neither could afford
to let go; neither could afford to move too far from the other.

The election of Fujimori in 1990, and again in 1995, served to turn
Peru around from the near desperate straits of the 1980s, hamstrung by
debt, inflation, and terrorism. Fujimori began to break down the State's
participation in the economy, following the lead of so many countries
after the collapse of communism and the general discrediting of Marxism around the world. Fujimori's neoliberal economic measures once
again seemed to bring Peru and the United States into sync as the
pendulum swung toward liberty in both countries, emphasizing free
trade, marketplace-driven policies, and the general privatization of the
economy.

Underscoring and emphasizing the growing nexus between the two
nations at the turn of the century are cultural, intellectual, religious, and

educational ties that are inherently less quantifiable and self-evident than economic, military, and political events and trends for example. American schools in Peru, Pentecostal missions, American-style mass-retailing, fast foods, and the growing ease of communications via the Internet and World Wide Web have made the flow of information and values much faster and easier than in the past. Thousands of Peruvians study and live in the United States, facilitating the multiple exchanges that make up the complex relationship.

Today Peru and the United States are drawn together by such disparate historical elements as drugs, computers, and the collapse of communism around the world. Yet, while the cocaine culture, the Internet, and shared conservative political views of the 1990s mark a possible confluence of destinies, one can argue that nationalism, both the American and the Peruvian variety, still very much courses powerfully just below the surface of relations.

Each country and the people therein have had much to admire and deplore in their relations over the past two centuries. Each has had to come to grips with a quicksilver definition of their nationality—because the United States is so immense and diverse, and because Peru has historically been "two" Perus, one of the coast and one of the sierra. One is tempted to editorialize and perhaps sentimentalize at the end of such a book as this. Relations have been strained occasionally but wonderful in the main over the years. They are getting better. A rosy world lies ahead. Perhaps.

More important is that those interested in knowing each country better might find something useful—and truthful—in these pages, which tell how human beings have interacted over the space of two hundred years through the most rapidly changing circumstances in history. If there has been baseness and nobility in the relationship, then it simply reflects the human condition. Nonetheless the high points and the successes over the years seemed to have had the upper hand on the low points and the failures. One finds throughout the history of these two peoples a manifestation of goodwill and a spirit to do right with respect to each other. That is as it should be, and with that note we close.

Notes

Introduction

1. In keeping with the spirit of modern research, this footnote is to a document I downloaded off the World Wide Web. "The Americas in 1997: Making Co-operation Work: A Report of the Sol M. Linowitz Forum, Inter-American Dialogue," an on-going research project of the North-South Center at the University of Miami, which can be accessed by going through the home-page of the University of Miami—www.miami.edu.

2. In this area of analysis, political scientists and other observers vary greatly in their interpretations. One school, for example, claims the old U.S. he-gemony is in serious decline, if not broken, by the realities of late twentieth-century power structures in the world. See Abraham F. Lowenthal's *Partners in Conflict: The United States and Latin America* (Baltimore: The Johns Hop-kins Press, 1987), 25, for example, where the subtitle of Lowenthal's chap. 2 is "Hegemony in Decline." He refers to asymmetry in the following fashion: "Asymmetry between the United States and Latin America has persisted, and it has been reinforced since the onset of Latin America's current eco-nomic and financial crisis, but it was substantially reduced during the 1960s and 1970s." In the same volume, a report by a distinguished group of ob-servers, on the other hand, easily describes the relationship as "this huge asymmetry of power and resources between the United States and the other countries of the hemisphere. . . ."

Chapter 1: Getting to Know You

1. Among those works I have found most helpful are Mariano Baptista Gu-mucio, *Latinoamericanos y norteamericanos: cinco siglos de dos culturas* (La Paz: Editorial Artistica, 1987); Fredrick B. Pike, *The United States and the Andean Republics: Peru, Bolivia, and Ecuador* (Cambridge, Mass.: Harvard University Press, 1977); Carlos Rangel, *The Latin Americans: Their Love-Hate Relationship*

315

with the United States (New York: Harcourt, Brace, Jovanovich, 1977); and Leopoldo Zea, *The Latin-American Mind* (Norman, Okla.: University of Oklahoma Press, 1963).

2. Pike, *The United States and the Andean Republics*, 12–13, drawing upon the writings of the anthropologist George Foster.

3. Pike, *The United States and the Andean Republics*, 16; Mariano Baptista, *Latinoamericanos y norteamericanos*, 114.

4. William Tudor to Henry Clay, May 12, 1826, Lima, William R. Manning, ed. *Diplomatic Correspondence of the United States Concerning the Independence of the Latin-American Nations* (New York: Oxford Univ. Press, 1925–26), 3:1797.

5. Lawrence S. Kaplan, *Entangling Alliances with None: American Foreign Policy in the Age of Jefferson* (Kent State, Ohio: Kent State University Press, 1987), 166, quoting from James H. Hopkins, ed., *The Papers of Henry Clay* (Lexington, Ky., 1959–), 2:520.

6. Especially helpful in this area is John J. Johnson's *Latin America in Caricature* (Austin: University of Texas Press, 1980).

7. Much of this discussion is borrowed from John Johnson's *Latin America in Caricature,* a clear and sensitive exposition of the subject, especially between pp. 9–21.

8. Ibid., 9–21.

9. Tudor to Secretary of State Henry Clay, May 23, 1827, in William R. Manning, ed., *Diplomatic Correspondence of the United States, Inter-American Affairs, 1831–1860,* 8 vols. (Washington, D.C.: Carnegie Endowment for International Peace, 1938), 3:1830.

10. Ibid., 183. Randolph also expressed the southern point of view that saw the "abolitionist and Negrophil tendencies manifested by some of the new governments" as abhorrent, reflecting, of course, the essence of American racism.

11. Arthur P. Whitaker, *The United States and the Independence of Latin America, 1800–1830* (1941; rpt., New York: Russell & Russell, 1962), 178ff. I would refer the reader to those pages for Whitaker's assessment of Brackenridge's influence and importance as an observer of the Latin American scene; basically, Whitaker places Brackenridge within the context of being one of several observers, not all in agreement. The general point, however, being that Brackenridge's views tended to be shared "by those who controlled the government, and that he was one of the first to make a systematic, comprehensive application of these ideas to the Latin American problems in the light

of the best information then available." I have followed Whitaker closely over the next several pages of text, in some instances quoting his assessments verbatim.

12. Félix Denegri Luna, "Los primeros contactos entre el Perú y los Estados Unidos," *Revista Histórica* (Instituto Histórico del Perú) 31: 71–97. This work is valuable for its exploration of early contact between North America and the west coast of South America. Denegri used standard English and Spanish-language sources, such as Samuel Eliot Morison, *The Maritime History of Massachusetts, 1782–1860* (Boston: Houghton Mifflin Co., 1941) and Eugenio Pereira Salas, *Los primeros contactos entre Chile y los Estados Unidos, 1778–1809* (Santiago: Editorial Andres Bello, 1971). See also Whitaker, *The United States and the Independence of Latin America,* especially chap. 1, "Opening the Door to Latin America."

13. Whitaker, ibid., 13–14.

14. Louise Clinton Nolan, "The Diplomatic and Commercial Relations of the United States and Peru, 1826–1875" (Ph.D. diss., Duke University, 1935), 65–68.

15. Ibid., 66.

16. Donald E. Worcester, *Sea Power and Chilean Independence* (Gainesville: University of Florida Press, 1962), 61.

17. Jorge Basadre, *Historia de la República del Perú, 1822–1933,* 11 vols. (7th ed.; Lima: Editorial Universitaria, 1983), 1:1.

18. Whitaker, *The United States and the Independence of Latin America,* 383; Nolan, "Diplomatic and Commercial Relations," 76–77; William Spence Robertson, "The Recognition of the Hispanic-American Nations by the United States," *Hispanic American Historical Review* 1 (August 1918): 239–69. Formal recognition came on May 2, 1826, when the United States appointed James Cooley of Ohio as chargé d'affaires to Peru.

19. J. B. Prevost, the first U.S. agent to the Andean nations, wrote Secretary of State John Quincy Adams in 1821 that "our countrymen generally have not been of a class to claim respect, the few who are so have been and are cherished, the majority are adventurers, who have either been engaged in privateering or in devising some other mode of livelihood alike disgraceful." Quoted in Whitaker, *The United States and the Independence of Latin America,* 150.

20. Ibid., 583.

21. Asbury Dickins and John W. Forney, eds., "Documents, Legislative and Executive, of the Congress of the United States," *American State Papers, Naval*

Affairs, 4 vols. (Washington, D.C.: Gales and Seaton, 1860), 2:512.

22. Monroe's Message in Thomas G. Paterson, ed., *Major Problems in American Foreign Policy: Documents and Essays Vol. 1: to 1914* (Lexington, Mass.: D. C. Heath & Co., 1978), 167–68.

23. For more on the Panama Congress see Whitaker, *The United States and the Independence of Latin America*, 564–602; John Edwin Fagg, *Pan Americanism* (Malabar, Fla.: Robert E. Krieger, 1982), 12–17; Basadre, *Historia*, 1:69–74.

24. Simón Bolívar, *Selected Writings of Bolívar*, 2 vols., Vicente Lecuna, comp. Harold A. Bierck, Jr., ed. (New York, 1951), 2:732.

25. Ibid., 1:30.

26. Clements R. Markham, *A History of Peru* (1892; rpt., New York: Greenwood Press, 1968), 278–80.

27. William Tudor to J. Q. Adams, Lima, December 22, 1824, in Manning, *Diplomatic Correspondence*, 3:1775.

28. Lester D. Langley, *America and the Americas: the United States in the Western Hemisphere* (Athens: University of Georgia Press, 1989), 55.

29. Tudor to Clay, August 24, 1826, Lima, in Manning, *Diplomatic Correspondence*, 3:1808.

30. Pickett to Secretary of State John C. Calhoun, March 3, 1845, Lima, in Manning, *Diplomatic Correspondence*, 10:537.

31. Nolan, "Diplomatic and Commercial Relations," 109.

32. Commo. Jacob Jones to Secretary of the Navy (hereinafter cited as SecNav), Commanding Officer, Pacific Squadron (hereinafter cited as CO PacRon), January 15, 1828, in Letters Received by the Secretary of the Navy from Captains ("Captains' Letters"), in the Naval Records Collection of the Office of Naval Records and Library, National Archives, Washington, D.C. (hereinafter cited as NA:ND).

33. Paul Gootenberg, *Between Silver and Guano: Commercial Policy and the State in Postindependence Peru* (Princeton: Princeton University Press, 1991), presents a more complicated framework for the period, identifying protectionists and nationalists in competition with free trade liberals, all battling for control of Peru's commercial and foreign policies.

34. Acting Secretary of State Richard K. Crallé to John A. Bryan, Washington, D.C., October 30, 1844, in Manning, *Diplomatic Correspondence*, 10:232–33.

35. Buchanan to Jewett, Washington, D.C., March 19, 1847, in Manning, *Diplomatic Correspondence*, 10:237; see also Basadre, *Historia*, 3:132–33.

36. Nolan, "Diplomatic and Commercial Relations," 140, quoting from *American Farmer* 7 (December 24, 1824): 316–17.

37. Nolan, "Diplomatic and Commercial Relations," 140–41.
38. Basadre, *Historia,* 4:58–59; Mark J. van Aken, *King of the Night: Juan José Flores and Ecuador, 1824–1864* (Berkeley: University of California Press, 1989), 230–33.
39. On this point the Jackson administration had already demonstrated that it would not apply the Monroe Doctrine in the Falkland Islands (Malvinas) controversy of the early 1830s, while President Polk had narrowed the application of the Monroe Doctrine to areas north of Colombia.
40. For an interpretation of the Congress in the broader Pan-American perspective, see Arthur P. Whitaker, *The Western Hemisphere Idea: Its Rise and Decline* (Ithaca, N.Y.: Cornell University Press, 1954), 50–60.
41. Basadre, *Historia,* 4:129–30.
42. David P. Werlich, *Admiral of the Amazon: John Randolph Tucker, His Confederate Colleagues, and Peru* (Charlottesville: University Press of Virginia, 1990), 141.
43. Nolan cites 32d Congress, 2d sess., House Executive Document, no. 43 (serial 678); 32d Congress, 2d sess., Senate Executive Document, no. 36 (serial 663–664), while Werlich cites Donald M. Dozier, "Pathfinder of the Amazon," *Virginia Quarterly Review* 23 (autumn 1947): 554–67.
44. Nolan, "Diplomatic and Commercial Relations," 201, citing Eugene Schuyler, *American Diplomacy and the Futherance of Commerce* (1886; rpt., New York: C. Scribner's Sons, 1895), 332.
45. Nolan, "Diplomatic and Commercial Relations," 202; 33d Congress, 1st sess., House Miscellaneous Document, no. 22 (serial 741).
46. Nolan, "Diplomatic and Commercial Relations," 202.
47. Most of the following on Tucker and the Amazon from Werlich, *Admiral of the Amazon,* 135ff.
48. Werlich, *Admiral of the Amazon,* 227–28. Orton's book was *The Andes and the Amazon; or, Across the Continent of South America* (New York: Harper and Brothers, 1870).
49. Werlich, *Admiral of the Amazon,* 255–56.
50. Marvin C. Ross, ed., *George Catlin: Episodes from Life Among the Indians and Last Rambles* (Norman: University of Oklahoma Press, 1959). Catlin traveled through South America in 1852–55 and sketched a good deal along the Peruvian Amazon.
51. Katherine Emma Manthorne, *Tropical Renaissance: American Artists Exploring Latin America, 1839–1879* (Washington, D.C.: Smithsonian Institution Press, 1989), 55. This book is a magnificently illustrated volume on the theme expressed in the title with a sensitive and most informative text. All of the

following section on American artists and scientists in Andean America between 1839–1879 is drawn from this source.

52. Basadre, *Historia*, 4:71–72.
53. Ibid., 4:72.
54. Basadre, *Historia*, 4:377.
55. Ibid., 4:388–89.
56. Ibid., 4:333–34.
57. Ibid., 4:333–34.
58. Nolan, "Diplomatic and Commercial Relations," 293.
59. Werlich, *Admiral of the Amazon*, 86ff.
60. Nolan, "Diplomatic and Commercial Relations," 318–19.
61. Nolan, "Diplomatic and Commercial Relations," 307–8; see also George Baker, ed., *The Works of William H. Seward*, 5:444–45.
62. Nolan, "Diplomatic and Commercial Relations," 309–10.
63. Werlich, *Admiral of the Amazon*, 90ff, for all the information on Tucker.
64. Ibid., 90ff.
65. Forrest MacDonald, *The American Presidency: An Intellectual History* (Lawrence, Kans.: University Press of Kansas, 1994), 147ff, and personal conversation.
66. John Lynch, *The Spanish-American Revolutions, 1808–1826* (New York: W. W. Norton, 1973), 170.

Chapter 2: The War of the Pacific

1. For the best study of Bolivian-U.S. relations focusing on the lost Bolivian Pacific coast, see Jorge Gumucio Granier, *Estados Unidos y el mar boliviano* (New York: privately published, 1985). The English translation is *United States and the Bolivian Seacoast* (La Paz, Bolivia: Ministerio de Relaciones Exteriores y Culto, 1988).
2. For a good summary of the failure of U.S. diplomacy in this war, see A. Nayland Page, "United States Diplomacy in the Tacna-Arica Dispute, 1884–1929" (Ph.D. diss., University of Oklahoma, 1958), 24ff.
3. Much of this section from L. A. Clayton, *Grace, W. R. Grace & Co: the Formative Years, 1850–1930* (Ottawa, Ill.: Jameson Books, 1985), 108ff.
4. Granier, *United States and the Bolivian Seacoast*, 39, citing U.S. Astronomical Expedition to the Southern Hemisphere during 1849-'50-'52. Lt. J. M. Gillis,

Superintendent. Executive Document No. 121, 33d Congress, 1st sess., House of Representatives, Washington, D.C., 1855.

5. Nolan, "Diplomatic and Commercial Relations," 217ff.

6. Jacinto Lopez, *Manuel Pardo* (Lima: Imprenta Gil, 1947), quoted in Heraclio Bonilla, *Guano y burguesía en el Perú* (Lima: Instituto de Estudios Peruanos, 1974), 58, quoting from the Lopez biography of Pardo.

7. Basadre, *Historia*, 5:136.

8. Ibid., 5:122.

9. Watt Stewart, *Henry Meiggs: Yankee Pizarro* (Durham, N.C.: Duke University Press, 1946).

10. Basadre, *Historia*, 5:136.

11. Ibid., *Historia*, 5:135.

12. For a full biography of William Russell Grace, see Marquis James, with introduction by L. A. Clayton, *Merchant Adventurer: The Story of W. R. Grace* (Wilmington, Del.: Scholarly Resources Press, 1993).

13. For more on Flynt, see his autobiography, *Charles R. Flynt, Memories of an Active Life: Men, Ships and Sealing Wax* (New York: G. P. Putnam's Sons, 1923). Stephen Topik of the University of California at Irving has done a series of fascinating articles on Flynt and his multitudinous activities.

14. Page, "United States Diplomacy in the Tacna-Arica Dispute," 29.

15. Ronald Bruce St. John, *The Foreign Policy of Peru* (Boulder, Colo.: Lynne Rienner, 1992), 112. This is a good narrative history of the subject, brief and selective, but founded on a wide array of sources—both U.S. and Peruvian.

16. Grace, *Merchant Adventurer*, 115. For more on Charles Flynt as arms merchant, see Steven Topik's short article "Man o' War" in *World Trade* (May 1991): 110ff.

17. Flynt, *Memories of an Active Life*, 87.

18. Clayton, *Grace*, 126.

19. Ibid., 126.

20. Walter R. Herrick Jr., *The American Naval Revolution* (Baton Rouge: Louisiana State University Press, 1966), 19–20.

21. V. G. Kiernan, "Foreign Interest in the War of the Pacific," *Hispanic American Historical Review* 35 (February 1955): 14–36.

22. St. John, *Foreign Policy of Peru*, 119ff.

23. J. P. Christiancy to J. G. Blaine, May 4, 1881, United States Department of State, *Papers Relating to Foreign Relations of the United States* (Washington, D.C.: U.S. Government Printing Office, 1881).

24. Charles S. Campbell, *The Transformation of American Foreign Relations, 1865 – 1900* (New York: Harper & Row, 1976), 94ff.

25. Ibid., p. 95, quoting fn. 29, Spenser St. John to Foreign Secretary Lord Granville, September 28, October 4, 1881, Foreign Office 61/334.

26. Campbell, *Transformation of American Foreign Relations,* 95, quoting in fn. 28, Hurlbut to Blaine, October 4, 5, 26, December 22, 1881, Senate Executive Documents, 47th Congress, 1st sess., no. 79, pp. 526–28, 530–31, 537–39, 591–93; David M. Pletcher, *The Awkward Years: American Foreign Relations Under Garfield and Arthur* (Columbia: University of Missouri Press, 1972), 49; Herbert Millington, *American Diplomacy and the War of the Pacific* (New York, 1948), 93.

27. Campbell, *Transformation of American Foreign Relations,* 95, quoting fn. 32, Blaine to Hurlbut, November 22, 1881, Senate Executive Documents, 47th Congress, 1st sess., no. 79, pp. 565–66.

28. Morton Keller, *Affairs of State: Public Life in Late Nineteenth Century America* (Cambridge, Mass.: Harvard University Press, Belknap Press, 1977), 267.

29. M. P. Grace to Petrie, July 12, 1881, Grace Papers, Columbia University, New York.

30. Campbell, *Transformation of American Foreign Relations,* 98.

31. Ibid., 94, citing fn. 27, House Reports, 47th Congress, 1st sess., no. 1790, passim. For indictments of Blaine, see Congressional Record, 47th Congress, 1st sess., 5639–47 (July 5, 1882), and Perry Belmont, *Recollections of an American Democrat* (New York: Columbia University Press, 1941), chaps. 7 and 8.

32. Campbell, *Transformation of American Foreign Relations,* 97.

33. Ibid., citing fn. 38, Frelinghuysen to Trescot, January 3, 1882, in Papers Relating to the Foreign Relations of the United States 1882 (Washington, 1883), 56; Frelinghuysen to American consul at Panama (for Trescot), January 4, 1882, ibid., p. 57; Frelinghuysen to Trescot, January 9, 1882, January 9, 1882, ibid., pp. 57–58.

34. Campbell, *Transformation of American Foreign Relations,* 98.

35. Clayton, *Grace,* 137–38.

36. Ibid., 138.

37. Campbell, *Transformation of American Foreign Relations,* 98, citing fn. 40, W. E. Graham to Granville, March 30, 1882, Foreign Office 61/399.

38. St. John, *Foreign Policy of Peru,* 121.

39. Cited in Granier, *United States and the Bolivian Seacoast,* 84.

Chapter 3: The Ascendant American Eagle

1. Pike, *The United States and the Andean Republics,* 195.
2. Ibid., 193.
3. Ibid., 40.
4. Ibid., 159; see also Pike's newest work, *The United States and Latin America: Myths and Stereotypes of Civilization and Nature* (Austin: University of Texas Press, 1992), for a wide-ranging exploration of the ideological and cultural images and stereotypes that so often influenced the relations between Latin America and the United States.
5. Pike, *The United States and the Andean Republics,* 161.
6. Charles H. McArver Jr., "Mining and Diplomacy: United States Interests at Cerro de Pasco, Peru, 1876–1930" (Ph.D. diss., University of North Carolina, 1977), 105; McArver cites the following: Jesús Chavarría, "The Intellectuals and the Crisis of Modern Peruvian Nationalism: 1870–1919," *Hispanic American Historical Review* 50 (May 1970): 268; Augusto Salazar Bondy, *Historia de las ideas en el Perú contemporáneo; el proceso del pensamiento filosófico,* 2 vols. (2d ed.; Lima: Francisco Moncloa, 1967), 1:70–71, 142.
7. M. P. Grace to chairman of Bondholders Committee, May 18, 1885, Grace Papers.
8. Edward Eyre to M. P. Grace, July 10, 1886, Grace Papers.
9. Basadre, *Historia,* 6:2755.
10. Clayton, *Grace,* 155–56.
11. Basadre, *Historia,* 6:2754–57.
12. W. R. Grace to Secretary of State Bayard, December 19, 1887, Grace Papers.
13. M. P. Grace to Aurelio Denegri, February 20, 1888, Grace Papers.
14. Ibid.
15. W. Ivins to Edward Eyre, July 9, 1888, Grace Papers.
16. Rory Miller, "The Making of the Grace Contract: British Bondholders and the Peruvian Government, 1885–1890," *Journal of Latin American Studies* 8 (May 1976): 93; Basadre, *Historia,* 6:2760–61.
17. Basadre, *Historia,* 6:2770.
18. St. John, *Foreign Policy of Peru,* 119 passim. Most of the information on the Chimbote naval station is from St. John's book and Dale William Peterson's dissertation (see next note).
19. Dale William Peterson, "The Diplomatic and Commercial Relations Between the United States and Peru from 1883 to 1918" (Ph.D. diss., Univer-

sity of Minnesota, 1969), 135ff. Peterson deals with the Chimbote station at length.

20. Ibid., 140ff.
21. Ibid., 143ff. In part, quoting verbatim.
22. McArver, "Mining and Diplomacy," 105ff.
23. Ibid., p. 189.
24. Pike, *The United States and Latin America*, 163.
25. Peterson, "Diplomatic and Commercial Relations," 83.
26. Ibid., 85. The Inca Mining Company ceased operations in 1912.
27. Basadre, *Historia*, 7:465–68; also John Melby, "Rubber River: An Account of the Rise and Collapse of the Amazon Boom," *Hispanic American Historical Review* 22 (August 1942): 452–69; Peterson, "Diplomatic and Commercial Relations," 86–88; Rosemary Thorp and Geoffrey Bertram, *Peru, 1890–1977: Growth and Policy in an Open Economy* (New York: Columbia University Press, 1968), 69ff.
28. Basadre, *Historia*, 7:466–68.
29. Interspersing biographical materials from Basadre and Alberto Tauro, *Enciclopedia Ilustrada del Peru* (2d ed.; Lima, Peru: Editorial Inca, 1988), 2:809–10.
30. Peterson, "Diplomatic and Commercial Relations," 87–88.
31. Adalberto J. Pinelo, *The Multinational Corporation in Peru as a Force in Latin American Politics: A Case Study of the International Petroleum Company in Peru* (New York: Praeger, 1973), 6. Pinelo's study is the most comprehensive on I.P.C. in Peru. See also Thorp and Bertram, *Peru*, 98ff.
32. L. A. Clayton, *Caulkers and Carpenters in a New World: The Shipyards of Colonial Guayaquil* (Athens, Ohio: Center for International Studies, Ohio University Press, 1975), 22, and Richard N. Goodwin, "Letter from Peru," *The New Yorker*, May 17, 1969: 44ff.
33. This writer lived on Calle Herbert Tweddle, Barranco, Lima, Peru, in 1988 while teaching at the University of Lima on a Fulbright grant. Now he knows who Herbert Tweddle was.
34. Thorp and Bertram, *Peru*, 99.
35. See Bennett H. Wall's *Growth in a Changing Environment: A History of Standard Oil Company (New Jersey), Exxon Corporation, 1850–1975* (New York: Harper & Row, 1988), for some details from the corporate perspective and on Walter Teagle.
36. Peterson, "Diplomatic and Commercial Relations," 91; Peterson cites five or six sources in his fn. 28 for this information.
37. Pinelo, *The Multinational Corporation*, 17–20.

38. Goodwin, "Letter from Peru," 54.
39. Ibid., 48.
40. Ibid., 52.
41. Ibid., 54.
42. See, for example, Hiram Bingham's numerous articles in the *National Geographic Magazine:* "Explorations in Peru" (April 1912): 417–22; "In the Wonderland of Peru" (April 1913), 387–573; "The Story of Machu Pichu: The Peruvian Expeditions of the National Geographic Society and Yale University" (February 1915): 172–217; and others as well as numerous books on the subject.
43. J. Valerie Fifer, *United States Perceptions of Latin America, 1850–1930: A "New West" South of the Capricorn* (Manchester, Eng.: Manchester University Press, 1991), 161ff.
44. Basadre, *Historia,* 11:227–228; Fifer, *United States Perceptions,* 158–60.
45. Basadre, *Historia,* 11:275–76.
46. Pike, *The United States and Latin America.*
47. See Fagg, *Pan Americanism,* for a good introduction to the general subject. See also Whitaker, *The Western Hemisphere Idea.*
48. Basadre, *Historia,* 11:110.
49. James C. Carey, *Peru and the United States, 1900–1962* (Notre Dame, Ind.: Notre Dame University Press, 1964), 23, fn. 11; see also Tauro, *Enciclopedia,* 3:115–120.
50. Pike, *The United States and the Andean Republics,* 144–45; Tauro, *Enciclopedia,* 6:2250–2351.
51. Carey, *Peru and the United States,* 24–25.
52. Robert Bacon and James Brown Scott, eds., *Latin America and the United States: Addresses by Elihu Root* (Cambridge: Harvard University Press, 1917), xiv.
53. Pike, *The United States and the Andean Republics,* 19ff.
54. St. John, *Foreign Policy of Peru,* 157–58.
55. Thorp and Bertram, *Peru,* 143.

Chapter 4: The Leguía Years

1. Fredrick B. Pike, *The Politics of the Miraculous in Peru: Haya de la Torre and the Spiritualist Tradition* (Lincoln, Nebr.: University of Nebraska Press, 1986), 35.

2. For those interested in some of the major sources consulted for the writing of this chapter, see the following: for Cerro de Pasco, see McArver, "Mining and Diplomacy"; for Grace, see Clayton, *Grace;* for I.P.C., see Goodwin, "Letter from Peru"; plus, Carey, *Peru and the United States,* Pike, *The United States and the Andean Republics,* and a nice M.A. thesis by Mary A. Jurjevich, "American Interests in Peru During the Leguía Administration, 1919–1930" (University of Alabama, 1950).

3. Goodwin, "Letter from Peru," 46; Pike, *The United States and the Andean Republics,* 199.

4. Pinelo, *The Multinational Corporation,* 34.

5. Ibid., 36–37.

6. Ibid., 36–37.

7. Alfonso W. Quiroz, *Domestic and Foreign Finance in Modern Peru, 1850–1930: Financing Visions of Development* (Pittsburgh: University of Pittsburgh Press, 1993), 206.

8. Pinelo, *The Multinational Corporation,* 37; Quiroz, *Domestic and Foreign Finance,* 210.

9. Pinelo, *The Multinational Corporation,* 37–38.

10. Ibid., 38.

11. Ibid., 39.

12. Ibid., 39–40.

13. Harry E. Vanden, *National Marxism in Latin America: José Carlos Mariátegui's Thought and Politics* (Boulder, Colo.: Lynne Rienner, 1986), 24.

14. McArver, "Mining and Diplomacy," 188.

15. Ibid., 189ff.

16. Most of this information on Cerro is from the excellent McArver dissertation.

17. McArver, "Mining and Diplomacy," 209.

18. Ibid., 219.

19. Ibid., 237, citing Harry L. Foster, *The Adventures of a Tropical Tramp* (New York: Dodd, Mead and Company, 1927), 59.

20. McArver, "Mining and Diplomacy," 213, 214.

21. Thomas F. O'Brien, *The Revolutionary Mission: American Enterprise in Latin America, 1900–1945* (New York: Cambridge University Press, 1996), 123.

22. This incident, as most of the detail on Cerro, from McArver, "Mining and Diplomacy," 269ff.

23. Ibid., 266–67.

24. Ibid., 276, with invented dialog but based on the actual conversation as reported by McArver.

25. Ibid., 279.

26. Interview, John C. Duncan, August 1979, New York City.

27. L. A. Clayton, *Grace,* 303. Most of the following information extracted from this source.

28. William Kooiman, *The Grace Ships, 1869–1969: An Illustrated History of the W. R. Grace & Co. Shipping Enterprises* (Point Reyes, Calif.: Komar Publishing Co., 1990).

29. Most of the foregoing on the Santa Maria's maiden voyage from "The 'Santa Maria's' Maiden Voyage," *Grace Log* 11, no. 4 (July-August, 1928): 69–71. *The Grace Log* was W. R. Grace & Co.'s public relations magazine, which was published on an almost regular basis for almost half a century.

30. We have drawn from a wide range of sources for this discussion on loans. The most important are James C. Carey, *Peru and the United States,* 66–80; Quiroz, *Domestic and Foreign Finance,* 199–205; Pike, *The United States and the Andean Republics,* 193–201; and Jurjevich, "American Interests in Peru." The Jurjevich thesis is a little gem that explores, among a number of topics, the investigations held in the U.S. Senate in 1932 and 1933 over loans to Latin America. Finally, we have dealt separately with the fascinating Kemmerer missions to the Andean nations covered well in Paul W. Drake, *The Money Doctor in the Andes: The Kemmerer Missions, 1923–1933* (Durham, N.C.: Duke University Press, 1989).

31. Pinelo, *The Multinational Corporation,* 34–35.

32. Quiroz, *Domestic and Foreign Finance,* 203.

33. Carey, *Peru and the United States,* 75.

34. Various sources were used in writing about early aviation in Peru. Among them, Basadre, *Historia,* 10:401ff; Wesley Phillips Newton, *The Perilous Sky: U.S. Aviation Diplomacy and Latin America, 1919–1931* (Coral Gables, Fla.: University of Miami Press, 1978), 157ff; Daniel M. Masterson, *Militarism and Politics in Latin America: Peru from Sánchez Cerro to Sendero Luminoso* (Westport, Conn.: Greenwood Press, 1991), 31; Carey, *Peru and the United States,* 84ff; Jorge Ortiz Sotelo, "El capitán de navío Davy y la Mision Naval norteamericana en el Perú (1920–1930)," *Revista del Instituto de Estudios Histórico-Marítimos del Perú* 8–9 (1987–90): 117–26.

35. By far the best and most complete study of this area is Newton, *The Perilous Sky.*

36. Ortiz Sotelo, "El capitán de navío Davy," 228.
37. Naim A. Benavente, "140 Years of Naval Relations Between Peru and the United States," research paper by then-cadet Benavente, U.S. Naval Academy, Annapolis, Maryland, February 1962, 10, 19. Personal possession of author.
38. Jorge Ortiz Sotelo, "Sucesos a bordo del BAP Almirante Grau con motivo de la caida de Leguía," *Revista de Marina, año 78* 374 (May-June 1985): 175.
39. Interview with Harold R. Harris, November 5, 1979, Falmouth, Mass.; "Sixty Years of Aviation History: One Man's Remembrance," speech by Harris at Tenth Annual Northeast Historians Meeting, Windsor Locks, Connecticut, October 12, 1974; Manuel Pareja Bueno, "Faucett: Aguila en Cielo de los Condores," *Transportes peruanos* 50 (July 1988): 19–21. Thanks to Sra. Sonia Figuerola for calling my attention to this article.
40. Basadre, *Historia,* 9:407, for the Moore flights.
41. Pareja Bueno, "Faucett," 20.
42. See Newton, *The Perilous Sky,* for full details of this fascinating period in the extension of U.S. aviation to Latin America.
43. Harris interview.
44. Carey, *Peru and the United States,* 88.
45. We have used a number of sources to reconstruct the Tacna-Arica dispute. Among them Arturo García Salazar, *Historia diplomática del Perú* (Lima: Imprenta A. J. Rivas Berrio, 1930), vol. 1.; Basadre, *Historia,* vol. 9; Page, "United States Diplomacy in the Tacna-Arica Dispute"; and St. John, *Foreign Policy of Peru.*
46. Page, "United States Diplomacy in the Tacna-Arica Dispute," 133ff.
47. Pershing quotes from Page, "United States Diplomacy in the Tacna-Arica Dispute," 133ff.
48. St. John, *Foreign Policy of Peru,* 164.

Chapter 5: The Good Neighbor

1. Barry Eichengreen, "House Calls of the Money Doctor: The Kemmerer Missions to Latin America, 1917–1931," in Paul W. Drake, *Money Doctors, Foreign Debts, and Economic Reforms in Latin America from the 1890s to the Present* (Wilmington, Del.: Scholarly Resources Press, 1994), 110. Eichengreen is quoting from Carlos Díaz Alejandro, "Stories of the 1930s for the 1980s,"

in Pedro Aspe Armella, Rudiger Dornbusch, and Maurice Obstfeld, eds., *Financial Policies and the World Capital Market: The Problem of Latin American Countries* (Chicago: University of Chicago Press), 5.

2. Drake, *The Money Doctor,* 229, quoting from *El Comercio* (Lima), January 13, February 18, March 18, 1931; E. W. Kemmerer, Diary, March 17, 1931, 76. We have depended on Drake's superb study for most of this section on Kemmerer in Peru.

3. Ibid., 229–30.

4. Ibid., 226.

5. Ibid., 229.

6. Ibid., 228.

7. Ibid., 247.

8. St. John, *Foreign Policy of Peru,* 166.

9. Carey, *Peru and the United States,* 98, for U.S. aviators serving as civilian instructors in Colombia; interview with Harold Harris, August 1979, Woods Hole, Massachusetts, in which General Harris, then the general manager of Panagra in Peru, told how Leguía impressed some of Panagra's aircraft to ferry men and supplies across the Andes into the Leticia region.

10. St. John, *Foreign Policy of Peru,* 176.

11. Ibid., 182; Internet article, downloaded from Peru list server, *El Comercio,* February 21, 1995.

12. I am deeply indebted to the brilliant biography of Haya de la Torre by Pike, *Politics of the Miraculous,* to which most of the following observations are due.

13. Pike, *Politics of the Miraculous,* 124ff.

14. Thomas M. Davies Jr., *Indian Integration in Peru: A Half Century of Experience, 1900–1948* (Lincoln, Nebr.: University of Nebraska Press, 1970), 157.

15. Pike, *Politics of the Miraculous,* 39–40.

16. Rosa del Carmen Bruno-Jofré, *Methodist Education in Peru: Social Gospel, Politics, and American Ideological and Economic Penetration, 1888–1930* (Waterloo, Ontario: Published for the Canadian Corporation for Studies in Religion by Wilfrid Laurier University Press, 1988), 97.

17. Masterson, *Militarism and Politics,* 46.

18. Pike, *Politics of the Miraculous,* 188.

19. Ibid., 188.

20. Ibid., 188.

21. Ibid., 189.

22. Ibid., 191.
23. Ibid., 191–92.
24. Ibid., 198.
25. Thorp and Bertram, *Peru*, 147ff.
26. Pike, *Politics of the Miraculous*, 210.
27. Ibid., 210.
28. Ibid., 201–2.
29. For fascism in Peru in this period see Orazio Cicarelli, "Fascism in Peru during the Benavides Regime, 1933–39; The Italian Perspective," *Hispanic American Historical Review* 70 (1990): 403–32, and Cicarelli, "Fascist Propaganda and the Italian Community in Peru during the Benavides Regime, 1933–1939," *Journal of Latin American Studies* 20 (1988): 361–88.
30. Quiroz, *Domestic and Foreign Finance*, 209–11.
31. Ibid., 209–11.
32. Pike, *The United States and the Andean Republics*, 274, paints Beltrán more as an opportunist than idealist.

    A staunch defender of Peru's wealthiest capitalist sectors who had previously shown little social conscience, Beltrán had by now [early 1950s] acquired the foresight to understand that the established order was threatened unless a vast amount of additional spending was channeled into social projects. Above all, he wished to spare the native oligarchies the burden of contributing their own funds to social spending. Therefore he directed his 'eloquent plea' [an appeal to Milton Eisenhower, so described, in his influential book on Latin America, *The Wine Is Bitter: The United States and Latin America* (Garden City, 1963)] to the United States, pointing constantly to the rising communist menace so as to bolster his arguments—and often fabricating communist threats through the irresponsible journalism of his influential Lima daily, *La Prensa*.
33. Carey, *Peru and the United States*, 107ff.
34. Pike, *Politics of the Miraculous*, 204.
35. Ibid., 204.
36. Ibid., 204–5.
37. Joseph E. Persico, *The Imperial Rockefeller: A Biography of Nelson A. Rockefeller* (New York: Simon and Schuster, c. 1982), 34.
38. Ibid., 33.
39. Claude C. Erb, "Prelude to Point Four: The Institute of Inter-American Affairs," *Diplomatic History* 9 (summer 1985): 249–69.

40. Ibid. Most of the above and what follows on the origins of Point Four is from the excellent Erb article.
41. Carey, *Peru and the United States,* 121–23.
42. Erb, "Prelude to Point Four," 254.
43. Ibid., 252–53.
44. Ibid., 266–67.
45. Ibid., 266–67.
46. Persico, *The Imperial Rockefeller,* 35.
47. Erb, "Prelude to Point Four,", 267.
48. Persico, *The Imperial Rockefeller,* 35–36.
49. Ibid., 35–36.
50. Ibid., 35–36.

Chapter 6: The Early Cold War Period

1. Catherine Marshall, *A Man Called Peter: The Story of Peter Marshall* (New York: Avon Books, 1951), 277. Peter Marshall's widow, Catherine, published some of Marshall's sermons in their entirety, including this one, at the end of the biography of her husband.
2. The above and following are from *Declaración del Ministerio de Relaciones Exteriores y Culto, Doctor Enrique García Sayan, sobre el plan Marshall y sus relaciones con la America Latin* (Lima: Ministerio de Relaciones Exteriores y Culto del Peru, 1948).
3. Luis Alberto Sánchez, *Haya de la Torre y el Apra. Crónica de un hombre y su partido* (Santiago de Chile: Editorial del Pacífico, 1955), 418. Sánchez quoting from an interview that Haya gave to the magazine *Cromos* in 1946 while traveling through Latin America.
4. John Foster Dulles, January 1953, cited in Robert Dallek, *The American Style of Foreign Policy: Cultural Politics and Foreign Affairs* (New York: Alfred A. Knopf, 1983), 187.
5. Roscoe Drummond and Gaston Coblenz, *Duel at the Brink: John Foster Dulles' Command of American Power* (Garden City, N.Y.: Doubleday & Co., 1960), 13–17.
6. Ibid., 13–17.
7. Sánchez, *Haya de la Torre y el Apra,* 433–34.
8. Ibid., 433–34.
9. Pike, *Politics of the Miraculous,* 69.

10. Pike, *Politics of the Miraculous,* 242.

11. J. W. Fulbright, *The Arrogance of Power* (New York: Random House, 1966), thanks to Colette Anderson Gill, for notes taken January 1988, while a teaching assistant in the Program in Latin American Studies.

12. Benavente, "140 years," 10–11.

13. Frank R. Pancake, "Military Assistance As an Element of U.S. Foreign Policy in Latin America, 1950–1968" (Ph.D. diss., University of Virginia, 1969), 193.

14. Masterson, *Militarism and Politics,* 120–21.

15. Pancake, "Military Assistance," 196.

16. Masterson, *Militarism and Politics,* 140; Pancake, "Military Assistance," 184.

17. Masterson, *Militarism and Politics,* 216–17.

18. Pancake, "Military Assistance," 199ff; Masterson, *Militarism and Politics,* 221.

19. Pancake, "Military Assistance," 200.

20. Masterson, *Militarism and Politics,* 221–22.

21. St. John, *Foreign Policy of Peru,* 200.

22. Thomas Wolff, *In Pursuit of Tuna: The Expansion of a Fishing Industry and Its International Ramifications—The End of an Era* (Tempe, Ariz.: Center for Latin American Studies, Special Studies No. 19, 1980), 53–54.

23. Rex A. Hudson, *Peru: A Country Study* (Washington, D.C.: Federal Research Division, Library of Congress, 1993), 149–50.

24. For the following discussion of the "tuna wars" between Peru and the United States, I have drawn, principally, on Wolff's *In Pursuit of Tuna,* and an article by David C. Loring, "The Fisheries Dispute" in Daniel A. Sharp, ed., *U.S. Foreign Policy and Peru* (Austin: Institute of Latin American Studies, University of Texas, 1972).

25. St. John, *Foreign Policy of Peru,* 200. For example, the Pelly Amendment, a provision attached to the 1968 Foreign Military Sales Act, required suspension of military aid to any country that illegally seized U.S. fishing boats.

26. Bruno-Jofré, *Methodist Education in Peru,* 98.

27. Pike, *Politics of the Miraculous,* 47–48.

28. MacKay later distinguished himself as the president of the Princeton Theological Seminary. Presumably, his memoirs, archives, and books all reflect upon this part of his early career in Peru.

29. Paul E. Kuhl, "Protestant Missionary Activity and Freedom of Religion in Ecuador, Peru, and Bolivia" (Ph.D. diss., Southern Illinois University, 1982),

52ff, an excellent source of information, almost exhaustive in its treatment of the subject.

30. Bruno-Jofré, *Methodist Education in Peru,* 67, quoting from John MacKay, "Renacimiento," *Renacimiento* 10 (July 1921): 101.

31. Jeffrey Klaiber, S.J., *La iglesia en el Perú* (Lima: Pontifica Universidad Católica del Perú, 1988), 310.

32. Jeffrey Klaiber, S.J., *Religion and Revolution in Peru, 1824–1976* (Notre Dame, Ind.: University of Notre Dame Press, 1977), 23–25.

33. Ibid., 23–25. Father Klaiber quoting from John A. MacKay's own *The Other Spanish Christ* (London: Student Christian Movement Press, 1932). Mac-Kay's other books include *That Other America* (New York: Friendship Press, 1935) and *Christianity on the Frontier* (New York: Macmillan, 1950).

34. Pike, *Politics of the Miraculous,* 47–48.

35. Ibid., 47–48.

36. Ibid., 47–48.

37. Ibid., 199.

38. Ibid., 128.

39. Bruno-Jofré, *Methodist Education in Peru,* 96, quoting from Luis Alberto Sánchez.

40. Klaiber, *Religion and Revolution,* 134. The rest of the account of Haya and Lisson follows Klaiber.

41. Ibid., 134. Father Klaiber quoting from the newspaper *La Semana* (Arequipa), May 20, 1923, pp. 6–8.

42. Ibid., 137.

43. This other biographical detail from David Stoll, *Fishers of Men or Founders of Empire?: The Wycliffe Bible Translators in Latin America* (London: Zed Press, 1982), 22ff, 28ff.

44. Ibid., 4.

45. Ibid., 99.

46. Ibid., 102.

47. Ibid, 103.

48. Margarita Guerra, *Historia general del Perú: la república contemporanea (1919–1950)* (Lima: Editorial Milla Batres, 1984), 12:30.

49. Pike, *The United States and the Andean Republics,* 275–80.

50. Stoll, *Fishers of Men,* 104.

51. Ibid., 107.

52. Ibid., 110.

334 *Notes to Chapter 6*

53. Ibid., 112, quoting from *National Geographic Magazine* (March 1956): 350.
54. Stoll, *Fishers of Men,* 116.
55. Gustavo Gorriti, "Shining Path's Stalin and Trotsky," in David Scott Palmer, ed., *The Shining Path of Peru* (New York: St. Martin's Press, 1992), 154ff. Gorriti writes that "Morote would be torn between his desire to maintain the academic standards of the university and to help with the 'politically progressive' measures of opening it up to masses of new students and allowing proselytizing work. Thanks to Guzmán, he never had much of a choice, and ultimately he would be overcome by events to a nightmarish extent." Two of his children would become members of the Shining Path and Morote saw his vision of a progressive University of Huamanga monstrously distorted by Guzmán and his followers.
56. Stoll, *Fishers of Men,* 120, wrote that

    [t]o Efrain Morote Best, the bilingual teacher was a frugal, temperate, abstinent man possessed by an apostolic Christian mission. At the annual exodus from the Yarinacocha, he reported, the teachers returned to their people "carrying pigs, chickens, turkeys, ducks, seeds and seedlings of fruit trees, outboard motors, shotguns, victrolas, flashlights, bicycles, clothes, medicines and, together with all this, a good pile of books, notebooks, pencils and primers. . . . From that time on, the bilingual teacher is an adviser to the group. He is looked upon as the symbol of advancing civilization."

    Stoll quoting from Efrain Morote Best, "Tres temas de la selva," *Tradición* (Cuzco): 19–20.
57. Burns may have left the university (and Peru as the text indicates) in 1970, but a communication from David Scott Palmer to University of Georgia Press, July 14, 1997, indicates that Burns probably stayed in Ayacucho in the new Ministry of Education bilingual teachers' education facility in the San Juan Bautista neighborhood directing the 34 bilingual primary schools in that area until at least 1972.
58. Stoll, *Fishers of Men,* 205ff.
59. Ibid., 210–11.
60. Ibid., 161, 202.
61. Much of the detail on U.S. investments and trends is from Thorp and Bertram, *Peru,* 210ff. Also, Charles T. Goodsell, *American Corporations and Peruvian Politics* (Cambridge, Mass.: Harvard University Press, 1974), 154ff.
62. Other shareholders were the Phelps Dodge Corporation (16 percent) and

the Newmont Mining Corporation (10 percent), Goodsell, *American Corporations*, 49.

63. Ibid., 169–70.
64. Carey, *Peru and the United States*, 166.
65. Goodsell, *American Corporations*, 3, 4.
66. So ubiquitous was Casa Grace that some critics nicknamed it *"el pulpo,"* or the octopus.
67. Goodsell, *American Corporations*, 201–2.
68. Ibid., 55ff.
69. Ibid., 56.
70. Ibid., 197–98.

Chapter 7: The Peruvian Institutional Revolution of 1968

1. Goodsell, *American Corporations*, 42.
2. Ibid., 68.
3. Ibid., 76.
4. Ibid., 96–97. "Cash payments are definitely received by Peruvian government officials," Goodsell noted, "and American corporations definitely make them."
5. Interview with John C. Duncan, August 1979, New York City.
6. Goodsell, *American Corporations*, 169ff.
7. Pike, *The United States and the Andean Republics*, 329.
8. They were big enough to scare this writer who remembers them as brutes who he was not sure would distinguish between him—a little gringo son of a U.S. manager—or the *obreros* who occasionally went on strike and were sometimes the targets of the dogs.
9. Goodsell, *American Corporations*, 58–59. This writer can remember driving past the *obrero* housing at Paramonga when he visited the plantation with his father, a Grace manager in the 1940s and 1950s. I can close my eyes and remember dust, lots of dust, one-story, open-doored, brown "houses" that all seemed tied together, flat roofed, open to the sun, and more dust. My older brother, William Harold Clayton, also remembered that a mixture of molasses and some other ingredients was periodically sprayed over the unpaved roads to keep the dust down, and the sweet smell of treacle permeated that part of the plantation.

10. Goodsell, *American Corporations*, 58–59.
11. Ibid., 58–59.
12. Ibid., 60–61.
13. Ibid., 60–61.
14. Jeffrey Meyers, *Hemingway: A Biography* (New York: Harper & Row, 1985), 492–93.
15. Ibid., 492–93.
16. Goodsell, *American Corporations*, 182–83.
17. Klaiber, *La iglesia en el Perú*, 360.
18. Pike, *The United States and the Andean Republics*, 329–31, argues this well.
19. Goodsell, *American Corporations*, 187–89.
20. Ibid., 189.
21. The Imperial Oil Company was Standard Oil of New Jersey's Canadian subsidiary which managed I.P.C. until after World War II when I.P.C.'s operations were put under Esso Inter America of Coral Gables, Florida, thus, in fact, "Americanizing" the top management of I.P.C.
22. A theme well developed and argued by Goodsell, *American Corporations*, in his chap. 8, "Aspects of National Integration."
23. Stoll, *Fishers of Men*, 107ff.
24. Goodsell, *American Corporations*, 204–5.
25. Carey, *Peru and the United States*, chap. 11, 186–207. Most of the Nixon affair described above is drawn from this excellent report by Carey. The Nixon quote from Richard M. Nixon, *Six Crises* (New York: Doubleday, 1962), 202.
26. Carey, *Peru and the United States*, 201.
27. Harold Molineu, *U.S. Policy Toward Latin America: From Regionalism to Globalism* (Boulder, Colo.: Westview Press, 1986), 100.
28. Robert Freeman Smith, ed., *The United States and the Latin American Sphere of Influence, Vol. 2: Era of Good Neighbors, Cold Warriors, and Hairshirts, 1930–1982* (Malabar, Fla.: Krieger Publishing Co., 1981–83), 60.
29. See Pike, *The United States and the Andean Republics*, 308, and his entire chap. 11 as well on the ideological origins of the Alliance for Progress.
30. Pike, *The United States and the Andean Republics*, 304ff.
31. Ibid., 305.
32. This section on Vicos is drawn from a number of sources, including Carey, *Peru and the United States*, 154–56; Pike, *The United States and the Andean Republics*, 323; Sharp, *U.S. Foreign Policy and Peru*, 176–77.
33. Carey, *Peru and the United States*, 156.

34. Sharp, *U.S. Foreign Policy and Peru*, 208–9.

35. Pike, *The United States and the Andean Republics*, 323, quoting from Henry F. Dobyns, *The Social Matrix of Peruvian Indigenous Communities* (Ithaca, N.Y.: Dept. of Anthropology, Cornell University, 1964), 96.

36. Sharp, *U.S. Foreign Policy and Peru*, 182.

37. Robert G. Myers, "Peruvian Educational Development," in Sharp, *U.S. Foreign Policy and Peru*, 350.

38. Goodwin, "Letter from Peru," 48.

39. Masterson, *Militarism and Politics*, 184ff.

40. Goodwin, "Letter from Peru," 48ff.

41. Pinelo, *The Multinational Corporation*, 120.

42. I have deliberately avoided details of each one of these agreements and accords reached over the years as I.P.C. and Peru negotiated. They are dealt with at length in sources such as Pinelo's *The Multinational Corporation*, Goodwin's "Letter from Peru," and others. Basically at issue was the ownership of La Brea and Pariñas and, if these were given up by I.P.C., how Peru would compensate I.P.C. through relief of tax claims, giving I.P.C. operating privileges, etc.

43. Goodwin, "Letter from Peru," 48ff.

44. Pinelo, *The Multinational Corporation*, 121.

45. Goodwin, "Letter from Peru," 48ff.

46. Pinelo, *The Multinational Corporation*, 121–22.

47. Goodwin, "Letter from Peru," 48ff.

48. Pinelo, *The Multinational Corporation*, 125.

49. Ibid., 126, 125.

50. Goodwin, "Letter from Peru," 48ff.

51. Account of this meeting recreated from Goodwin, "Letter from Peru," 48ff.

52. Masterson, *Militarism and Politics*, 226–227.

53. Scene recreated using Pinelo and Goodwin.

54. Scene recreated from Goodwin, "Letter from Peru."

55. The two principal sources, Pinelo and Goodwin, disagree on whether Espinosa went home thinking the final agreement was fixed or knowing it was not. Goodwin: "finally, at about 2 A.M. on August 13th, thinking that final agreement had been reached on the price to be paid by I.P.C. for the crude oil from La Brea, Espinosa went home to prepare for the scheduled dawn flight to Talara," 48ff. Pinelo: "By mid-night, the negotiations broke down again. . . . the Ambassador . . . persuaded I.P.C.'s general manager, Fernando

Espinosa, to return to the Presidential Palace and accept the government's terms," 140.

56. Pinelo, *The Multinational Corporation*, 147.

57. Masterson, *Militarism and Politics*, 232.

58. Juan Velasco Alvarado, *Velasco: La Voz de la Revolución: Discursos del Presidente de la República General de División Juan Velasco Alvarado, 1968–1970* (Lima: Oficina Nacional de Difusión del SINAMOS, 1972), 3–4.

59. Sharp, *U.S. Foreign Policy and Peru*, table of contents.

Chapter 8: Contemporary Times

1. Lowenthal, *Partners in Conflict*, 25.

2. Pike, *The United States and Latin America*, 337ff.

3. St. John, *Foreign Policy of Peru*, 200.

4. Helan Jaworski C., "Peru: The Military Government's Foreign Policy in Its Two Phases (1968–1980)" in Heraldo Muñoz and Joseph S. Tulchin, eds., *Latin American Nations in World Politics* (Boulder, Colo.: Westview Press, 1984), 208.

5. Personal communication, R. Kaufman to L. Clayton, July 7, 1995, Litchfield, Connecticut.

6. Term applied by Abraham Lowenthal in *The Peruvian Experiment: Continuity and Change under Military Rule* (Princeton: Princeton University Press, 1975), although certainly not an exclusive phrase.

7. Shane Hunt, "Direct Foreign Investment in Peru: New Rules for an Old Game," in Abraham Lowenthal, ed., *The Peruvian Experiment*, 312.

8. Molineu, *U.S. Policy Toward Latin America*, 101.

9. Goodsell, *American Corporations*, 133.

10. Lowenthal, *The Peruvian Experiment*, 12.

11. Velasco Alvarado, *Voz de la revolución*, 41.

12. Goodsell, *American Corporations*, 134ff.

13. This account largely from Goodsell, *American Corporations*, 134ff.

14. Actually, Cerro was not nationalized officially until 1973. The fishing industry, half owned by foreigners, was also nationalized that year. See E. V. K. Fitzgerald, *The State and Economic Development: Peru Since 1968* (Cambridge: Cambridge University Press, 1976), Department of Applied Economics, Occasional Paper 49), 68ff.

15. Felipe Osterling, "Comentario," in Eduardo Ferrero Costa, ed., *Relaciones*

del Peru con los Estados Unidos (Lima: Centro Peruano de Estudios Internacionales, 1987), 365.

16. Ibid., 366.
17. James D. Rudolph, *Peru: The Evolution of a Crisis* (Westport, Conn.: Praeger, 1992), 58.
18. Osterling, "Comentario," 365.
19. Masterson, *Militarism and Politics,* 258–59.
20. Masterson, *Militarism and Politics,* 261, summarized them: "The world recession, coinciding with OPEC's oil embargo, however, generated an economic crisis in Peru, which exposed the structural weaknesses of the military government's economic program. Heavy dependence upon the import of foodstuffs (including even potatoes) and industrial goods, a refusal to reform the tax structure, an inconsistent manufacturing policy, and limitations on export expansion weakened an economy already made vulnerable by a sharp decline in the world price of copper and sugar and poor yields in the once-booming fishing industry."
21. Rudolph, *Peru,* 104.
22. St. John, *Foreign Policy of Peru,* 214.
23. Richard L. Burger, "An Overview of Peruvian Archaeology (1976–1986)," *Annual Review of Anthropology* 18 (1989): 37–69.
24. St. John, *Foreign Policy of Peru,* 214.
25. Felipe E. MacGregor, Jonathan Cavanagh, and Rosemary Underhay, trans., *Coca and Cocaine: An Andean Perspective* (Westport, Conn.: Greenwood Press, 1993), quote from a review of the book by Paul Daughty in *Hispanic American Historical Review* 75 (May 1995): 307–8.
26. Palmer, *Shining Path,* 1.
27. See, for example, Raymond Bonner, "A Reporter at Large: Peru's War," *The New Yorker* (January 4, 1988): 31–58; Peter T. White, "An Ancient Herb Turns Deadly: Coca," *National Geographic Magazine* 175 (January, 1989); Gustavo Gorriti, "The War of the Philosopher-King," *The New Republic* (June 18, 1990): 15–22; Mario Vargas Llosa, "Inquest in the Andes," *New York Times Magazine* (July 31, 1983): 18–23ff; and a PBS documentary on the assassination of seven Peruvian journalists in 1983.
28. See for example, "The Shining Path after Guzmán: The Threat and the International Response," hearing before the Subcommittee on Western Hemisphere Affairs, House of Representatives, 102d Congress, 2d sess., September 23, 1992.
29. From Partido Comunista del Perú-Sendero Luminoso, "Desarrollar la

guerra popular sirviendo a la revolución mundial," mimeo, 1986, cited by Carlos Iván Degregori, "The Origins and Logic of Shining Path: Two Views, Return to the Past," in Palmer, *Shining Path,* 38.

30. Gustavo Gorriti, "Shining Path's Stalin and Trotsky," in Palmer, *Shining Path,* 151.

31. Gorriti, in "Shining Path's Stalin and Trotsky," writes "the incident that precipitated Kawata's downfall seemed to have very little to do with his politics, and is one more example of how major historical events are often explained by a footnote." Then he describes how Kawata was discovered by Guzmán in bed with two women, one of them allegedly Guzmán's mistress. So Presidente Gonzalo drummed Kawata out of the party, although Kawata remained a part of Sendero until at least the early 1990s, although marginalized and ostracized by the maximum leader.

32. Ibid., 167.

33. Ibid., 164.

34. Ibid., 165.

35. Gaddis Smith, *Morality, Reason, and Power: American Diplomacy in the Carter Years* (New York: Hill & Wang, 1986), 53ff.

36. Rensselaer W. Lee, *The White Labyrinth: Cocaine and Political Power* (New Brunswick, N.J.: Transaction Publishers, 1989), quoted by Rensselaer W. Lee III in a file received via the Internet, May 2, 1995. No page cited but specifically pointed to a USIA public opinion poll.

37. Alma Guillermoprieto, "Letter from Lima: Down the Shining Path," *The New Yorker* (February 8, 1993): 65.

38. Ibid., 66.

39. Ibid., 66.

40. Sor Juana Inez de la Cruz, seventeenth-century Mexican nun and poetess, one of the premier poets of colonial Latin America.

41. Much of this section is drawn from a wonderful little article by Pola Reydburd, "Who Are the Bad Guys? Literary Images of Narcotraffickers," in Bruce M. Bagley and William O. Walker III, eds., *Drug Trafficking in the Americas* (Miami, Fla.: University of Miami North-South Center, 1994), 535ff.

42. Ibid., 535ff.

43. Figures from various sources including José E. Gonzales, "Guerrillas and Coca in the Upper Huallaga Valley," in Palmer, *Shining Path,* 106, and Edmundo Morales, "The Andean Cocaine Dilemma," in Bagley and Walker, *Drug Trafficking in the Americas,* 162–63.

44. Scott B. MacDonald, *Dancing on a Volcano: The Latin American Drug Trade*

(Westport, Conn.: Praeger, 1988), 14–15. For most of the history of cocaine that follows this footnote, we have relied on MacDonald's excellent chap. 1, "Historical Perspective."

45. Again, following MacDonald, *Dancing on a Volcano,* 18ff.

46. As MacDonald notes, it is a simple process: "the leaf is placed in a tub, mixed with diluted sulfuric acid, trodden into a paste; alcohol is added, the syrup is siphoned off, left to solidify, and the cocaine is then washed in either ether or acetone," 19.

47. David Scott Palmer, "Peru, Drugs, and Shining Path," in Bagley and Walker, *Drug Trafficking in the Americas,* 181, cites the following: "A 1988 survey concluded that coca prices ranged anywhere from 4 to 34 times higher than leading alternative crops—cacao and corn respectively," 181.

48. Lee, *White Labyrinth,* 34.

49. Ibid., 41.

50. Ibid., 46, and Palmer, "Peru, Drugs, and Shining Path," 183. This writer can remember hearing—he thought incorrectly—that his colleagues at the University of Lima in 1988 made about three to four hundred dollars per month while he was there teaching on a Fulbright. My Fulbright stipend was, if I remember correctly, somewhere in the neighborhood of two thousand dollars per month, modest by U.S. salary standards. That my colleagues were making 20–25 percent of my modest stipend I found incredible.

51. Lee, *White Labyrinth,* 193.

52. Palmer, "Peru, Drugs, and Shining Path," 182.

53. Ethan A. Nadelmann, *Cops Across the Borders: The Internationalization of U.S. Criminal Law Enforcement* (Penn State: Pennsylvania State University Press, 1993), from chap. 5, 251–312, "The DEA in Latin America: Dealing with Institutionalized Corruption," excerpted by Sergio Rivera (srayala@suvm.acs.syr.edu) and copied from an online document provided by Rivera, spring 1995.

54. Ibid.

55. *Tuscaloosa News,* June 7, 1995.

56. José E. Gonzales, "Guerrillas and Coca in the Upper Huallaga Valley," in Bagley and Walker, *Drug Trafficking in the Americas,* 106ff.

57. Bruce M. Bagley, "After San Antonio," in Bagley and Walker, *Drug Trafficking in the Americas,* 63.

58. Gonzales, "Guerrillas and Coca," 113ff.

59. Account put together from Gonzales, "Guerrillas and Coca," 112ff, and

Palmer, "Peru, Drugs, and Shining Path," 183, in Bagley and Walker, *Drug Trafficking,* and Rudolph, *Peru,* 124.

60. Rudolph, *Peru,* 114ff.

61. "We pay $50,000 per helicopter flight," one trafficker told me, "$30,000 for the commanding officer and $20,000 for the crew," reported Francisco Reyes in "Peru's Deadly Drug Habit," *The Washington Post* (February 28, 1993), p. C4.

62. The preceding discussion is based on my article "The Nisei and the Novelist: Alberto Fujimori, Mario Vargas Llosa, and the Peruvian Presidential Election of 1990," *The World & I* (May 1991): 561–83.

63. Hudson, *Peru,* appendix, table 15, "Principal Trading Partners, 1980 and 1990," drawn from Richard Webb and Graciela Fernández Baca, eds., *Perú en números, 1990* (Lima, 1990), 4.

64. St. John, *Foreign Policy of Peru,* 213.

65. St. John, *Foreign Policy of Peru,* 208.

66. Rudolph, *Peru,* 112.

67. The quotes in the preceding section are taken from Clayton, "The Nisei and the Novelist."

68. Much of this discussion from a fine paper by Maria Eugenia Mujica, "The Antidrug Policy in Peru During the Fujimori Administration: Rhetoric Alternative Development V. Actual Increased Militarization," presented at the Interamerican Relations Conference, University of North Florida, Jacksonville, Fl., September 22–24, 1994.

69. Paper graciously loaned to me by Maj. David A. Palmer, USA, entitled "South American Insurgencies: From Communists to Criminals?" written for Dr. Donald M. Snow, Political Science, University of Alabama, while Palmer was studying for his M.A. in Latin American Studies at University of Alabama. Palmer cites Dan W. Hammack in *Security Management* 37 (January 1993): 26.

70. Daniel M. Masterson, "Little Time Left to Negotiate: The United States and the Peru-Ecuador Border Dispute in Historical Perspective," paper delivered at the Second Inter-American Relations Conference, University of North Florida, Jacksonville, Fl., October 10–12, 1996, pp. 24ff.

71. Gabriel Marcela, *War and Peace in the Amazon: Strategic Implications for the United States and Latin America of the 1995 Ecuador-Peru War* (n.p.: Strategic Studies Institute, 1995), 22ff.

72. Ibid., 25.

73. Roger S. Greenway, "Protestant Mission Activity in Latin America," in

Daniel R. Miller, ed., *Coming of Age: Protestantism in Contemporary Latin America* (Lanham, Md.: University Press of America, 1994), 197–201.

74. Among the growing literature on Protestantism in Latin America that reflect on and analyze these movements are David Stoll, *Is Latin America Turning Protestant? The Politics of Evangelical Growth* (Berkeley: University of California Press, 1990), David Martin, *Tongues of Fire: The Explosion of Protestantism in Latin America* (Oxford, Eng.: Blackwell Publishers, 1990), Virginia Garrard-Burnett and David Stoll, eds., *Rethinking Protestantism in Latin America* (Philadelphia: Temple University Press, 1993), Miller, *Coming of Age,* and Stoll's earlier work, *Fishers of Men.*

75. W. S. Rycroft, *Religion and Faith in Latin America* (Philadelphia: Westminster Press, 1958), 152, cited and quoted in J. Samuel Escobar, "The Promise and Precariousness of Latin American Protestantism," in Miller, *Coming of Age,* 14.

76. Stoll, *Is Latin America Turning Protestant?,* 13.

77. Ibid., 321.

78. Klaiber, *La iglesia en el Perú,* 479.

79. Martin, *Tongues of Fire,* 285.

80. Martin, *Tongues of Fire,* 267, 280. Martin's argument is complex, erudite, and, in some instances, he carries his arguments further than the facts might warrant, but his book is the sociological treatise most respected by students of the expansion of Protestantism and its significance in Latin America.

81. This, and all other information on the founding of the Franklin Delano Roosevelt School is from William D. Kent, "The American School of Lima, Colegio Franklin Delano Roosevelt, School History," published on the Web at the following location: http://www.fdralumni.com/fdr06.html.

82. This information from the Franklin Delano Roosevelt School website at http://www.amersol.edu.pe/.

83. Personal communication, R. Kaufman to L. Clayton, July 7, 1995, Litchfield, Connecticut.

84. Hudson, *Peru,* "Tourism" section, 165. Not only terrorism and insurgency, but common crime and the 1990–91 cholera epidemic all contributed to a dramatic decline. Between 1988 and 1992, for example, there was a decline of 76 percent in the number of tourists visiting Peru's premier tourist location, Machu Picchu.

85. Ibid., 328–29, tables 14 and 16. Oil production actually peaked in 1980, but exploration has continued. Copper, lead, and zinc exports all increased.

Bibliographical Essay

This essay is devoted primarily to a discussion of books in English on the relations of the United States with Peru. A few of the seminal works in Spanish have been included for Spanish-language readers. Many fine articles have also appeared over the years dedicated to various aspects of the subject. Reference to these can be found in the endnotes.

There are some bibliographies on United States–Latin American relations that are essential for any student beginning or continuing research in the area. The most comprehensive bibliography of U.S.–Latin American relations is David Trask, Michael C. Meyer, and Roger Trask, *A Bibliography of United States–Latin American Relations Since 1810* (Lincoln, Nebr.: University of Nebraska Press, 1968), with a *Supplement* (Lincoln, Nebr.: University of Nebraska Press, 1979). More recent citations to the literature are included in the multi-volume *Handbook of Latin American Studies* (Cambridge, Mass., Gainesville, Fla., and Austin, Texas, 1936–). The *Handbook* represents an exhaustive bibliography in all fields of Latin American studies. The *Guide to American Foreign Relations Since 1700* (Santa Barbara, Calif.: ABC-Clio, 1983), edited by Richard Dean Burns, has sections devoted to Latin America.

In the broad field of U.S.-Latin American relations, I have found particularly useful an insightful set of observations on the differences in the ways Americans and Latin Americans behave in Mariano Baptista Gumucio, *Latinoamericanos y norteamericanos: cinco siglos de dos culturas* (La Paz: Editorial Artistica, 1987). In this same genre are the books by Carlos Rangel, *The Latin Americans: Their Love-Hate Relationship with the United States* (New York: Harcourt, Brace, Jovanovich, 1977), and John J. Johnson, *Latin America in Caricature* (Austin: University of Texas Press, 1980), especially good for popular stereotyping between North Americans and Latin Americans.

Studies of United States–Latin American relations that all contain materials on Peru include Lester D. Langley, *America and the Americas: the United States in the Western Hemisphere* (Athens: University of Georgia Press, 1989), Harold Molineu, *U.S. Policy Toward Latin America: From Regionalism to Globalism* (Boulder, Colo.: Westview Press, 1986), Robert Freeman Smith, *The United States and the Latin American Sphere of Influence* (Malabar, Fla.: Krieger Publishing Co., 1983),

345

Abraham F. Lowenthal, *Partners in Conflict: the United States and Latin America* (Baltimore: The Johns Hopkins Press, 1987), Heraldo Muñoz and Joseph S. Tulchin, eds., *Latin American Nations in World Politics* (Boulder, Colo.: Westview Press, 1984).

For the early period, indispensable are Arthur P. Whitaker, *The United States and the Independence of Latin America, 1800–1830* (1941; rpt., New York: Russell & Russell, 1962), and Whitaker's authoritative study of *The Western Hemisphere Idea: Its Rise and Decline* (Ithaca, N.Y.: Cornell University Press, 1954).

A number of books focus directly on the subject of the U. S. and Peru, the best of these being Fredrick B. Pike's *The United States and the Andean Republics: Peru, Bolivia, and Ecuador* (Cambridge, Mass.: Harvard University Press, 1977), a magisterial interpretation based on a profound understanding of the differing natures of Peruvian and North American society and culture. Pike's study was preceded by the excellent piece by James C. Carey, *Peru and the United States, 1900–1962* (Notre Dame, Ind.: Notre Dame University Press, 1964) and followed by Ronald Bruce St. John's *The Foreign Policy of Peru* (Boulder, Colo.: Lynne Rienner, 1992). Another genre is the edited collection of articles. Among these is a helpful group of essays focusing on contemporary matters edited by Eduardo Ferrero Costa, *Relaciones del Perú con los Estados Unidos* (Lima: Centro Peruano de Estudios Internacionales, 1987). An earlier compilation by Daniel A. Sharp, ed., *U.S. Foreign Policy and Peru* (Austin: Institute of Latin American Studies, University of Texas Press, 1972) brought together many different specialists in a conference whose papers later made up the core of this book. Ironically much of the impetus for this book was occasioned by the rather anti–United States nature of the Peruvian Institutional Revolution of 1968.

That revolution sparked a miniboom of literature exploring the aftermath of the event. Among the most useful are Abraham F. Lowenthal, *The Peruvian Experiment: Continuity and Change under Military Rule* (Princeton: Princeton University Press, 1975), E. V. K. Fitzgerald, *The State and Economic Development: Peru Since 1968* (Cambridge: Cambridge University Press, 1976), and James D. Rudolph, *Peru: the Evolution of a Crisis* (Westport, Conn.: Praeger, 1992).

General histories of Peru, all of which contain considerable materials on the relationship with the United States, include the standard work by Jorge Basadre, *Historia de la república del Perú, 1822–1933*, 11 vols. (7th ed.; Lima: Editorial Universitaria, 1983). A classic narrative by Clements R. Markham, *A History of Peru* (1892; rpt. New York: Greenwood Press, 1968) is dated but is a wonderful read with many insights. Always helpful, especially for very contemporary details, are the area studies published by the U.S. Government. The latest is Rex A.

Hudson, *Peru: A Country Study* (Washington, D.C.: Federal Research Division, Library of Congress, 1993).

Books dealing with politics and economics that one can mine successfully for various components of both the foreign policy of Peru and relations between Peru and the United States include Paul Gootenberg, *Between Silver and Guano: Commercial Policy and the State in Postindependence Peru* (Princeton: Princeton University Press, 1991), which identifies protectionists and nationalists in competition with free trade liberals, all battling for control of Peru's commercial and foreign policies. Rosemary Thorp and Geoffrey Bertram, *Peru, 1890–1977: Growth and Policy in an Open Economy* (New York: Columbia University Press, 1968) provide a well-documented, insightful, sometimes iconoclastic, view of the Peruvian economy and especially its relationship to foreign investors, entrepreneurs, and influences. Paul W. Drake, *The Money Doctor in the Andes: the Kemmerer Missions, 1923–1933* (Durham, N.C.: Duke University Press, 1989), thoroughly presents the influence of Edwin Kemmerer, a financial adviser much sought after by Latin Americans—including Peruvians—in the 1920s and 1930s. Drake followed this book with one he edited, *Money Doctors, Foreign Debts, and Economic Reforms in Latin America from the 1890s to the Present* (Wilmington, Del.: Scholarly Resources Press, 1994), which contains a number of useful essays. Alberto W. Quiroz, *Domestic and Foreign Finance in Modern Peru, 1850–1950: Financing Visions of Development* (Pittsburgh: University of Pittsburgh Press, 1993) demonstrates the relationship between foreign investors and bankers in Peru and provides an excellent road map to Peru's financial history.

Foreign corporations in Peru are the focus of numerous studies. Lawrence A. Clayton, *Grace, W. R. Grace & Co.: the Formative Years, 1850–1930* (Ottawa, Ill.: Jameson Books, 1985) traces the history of the first multinational in Peru and its role in Peruvian-U.S. relations. Adalberto J. Pinelo, *The Multinational Corporation in Peru as a Force in Latin American Politics: A Case Study of the International Petroleum Company in Peru* (New York: Praeger Publishers, 1973) portrays the long and tumultuous relationship between I.P.C. and Peru in a fashion that sympathizes with the corporation. Thomas F. O'Brien, *The Revolutionary Mission: American Enterprise in Latin America, 1900–1945* (New York: Cambridge University Press, 1996) examines a number of U.S. corporations and their role in inculcating a corporate culture in Latin America. Among his case studies are several set in Peru. Wesley Phillips Newton, *The Perilous Sky: U.S. Aviation Diplomacy and Latin America, 1919–1931* (Coral Gables, Fla.: University of Miami Press, 1978) focuses especially on the rise of Pan American Airways and its founder Juan Trippe and contains much useful information on the early development of U.S.

aviation in Peru. Charles T. Goodsell, *American Corporations and Peruvian Politics* (Cambridge, Mass.: Harvard University Press, 1974) is an excellent study by a political scientist regarding the way in which American corporations expressed their economic and political objectives within Peru.

Excellent biographies include David P. Werlich, *Admiral of the Amazon: John Randolph Tucker, His Confederate Colleagues and Peru* (Charlottesville: University Press of Virginia, 1990), which presents the odd interweaving of American and Peruvian destinies in the post–Civil War period. Two-time Pulitzer Prize–winning biographer Marquis James, *Merchant Adventurer: The Story of W. R. Grace* (Wilmington, Del.: Scholarly Resources Press, 1993) describes the career of the founder of W. R. Grace & Co., a man who also became prominent in American politics and was the first foreign-born mayor of New York in 1881. Watt Stewart, *Henry Meiggs: Yankee Pizarro* (Durham, N.C.: Duke University Press, 1946) is the standard study of that fascinating and flamboyant railroad builder and entrepreneur who helped forge Peru's modern destiny. Fredrick B. Pike, *The Politics of the Miraculous in Peru: Haya de la Torre and the Spiritualist Tradition* (Lincoln, Nebr.: University of Nebraska Press, 1986), examines a lesser known side of the great leader of the APRA party by focusing on the intellectual and religious elements that contributed to his evolution as a charismatic political leader. Harry E. Vanden, *National Marxism in Latin America: José Carlos Mariátegui's Thought and Politics* (Boulder, Colo.: Lynne Rienner, 1986), provides a sympathetic overview of one of Peru—and Latin America's—seminal Marxist thinkers whose legacy certainly had an impact on the modern relations between Peru and the U. S.

Among the excellent studies focusing on cultural, artistic, religious, and intellectual influences are Katherine Emma Manthorne, *Tropical Renaissance: American Artists Exploring Latin America, 1839–1879* (Washington, D.C.: Smithsonian Institution Press, 1989), which provides insights into the artistic and cultural influences at work between the countries in the mid-nineteenth century, J. Valerie Fifer, *United States Perceptions of Latin America, 1850–1939: A "New West" South of the Capricorn* (Manchester, Eng.: Manchester University Press, 1991), and Fredrick B. Pike, *The United States and Latin America: Myths and Stereotypes of Civilization and Nature* (Austin: University of Texas Press, 1992), a wide-ranging exploration of the ideological and cultural images and stereotypes that so often influenced the relations between Latin America and the United States.

More narrowly focused on religion are the works by Jeffrey Klaiber, S.J., *Religion and Revolution in Peru, 1824–1976* (Notre Dame, Ind.: Notre Dame University Press, 1977) and Klaiber's more comprehensive *La iglesia en el Perú* (Lima:

Pontifica Universidad Católica del Perú, 1988), each of which contains sections dedicated to the influence of foreign entities in the evolution of the Roman Catholic Church in Peru.

Among the growing literature on Protestantism in Latin America, some with specific focus on Peru are Rosa del Carmen Bruno-Jofré, *Methodist Education in Peru: Social Gospel, Politics, and American Ideological and Economic Penetration, 1888–1930* (Waterloo, Ontario: Published for the Canadian Corporation for Studies in Religion by Wilfrid Laurier University Press, 1988), David Stoll, *Fishers of Men or Founders of Empire: the Wycliffe Bible Translators in Latin America* (London: Zed Press, 1982), Stoll's *Is Latin America Turning Protestant? The Politics of Evangelical Growth* (Berkeley: University of California Press, 1990), David Martin, *Tongues of Fire: the Explosion of Protestantism in Latin America* (Oxford, Eng.: Blackwell Publishers, 1990), Virginia Garrard-Burnett and David Stoll, eds., *Rethinking Protestantism in Latin America* (Philadelphia: Temple University Press, 1993), and Daniel R. Miller, ed., *Coming of Age: Protestantism in Contemporary Latin America* (Lanham, Md.: University Press of America, 1994).

Daniel M. Masterson, *Militarism and Politics in Latin America: Peru from Sánchez Cerro to Sendero Luminoso* (Westport, Conn.: Greenwood Press, 1991) not only examines and explains the domestic side of the military in politics in Peru, but also how the Peruvian and U.S. militaries interacted and, in some key areas, affected the course of major events in modern Peruvian history.

The "tuna wars" from the 1950s to the 1970s are covered in Thomas Wolff, *In Pursuit of Tuna: the Expansion of a Fishing Industry and Its International Ramifications—the End of an Era* (Tempe, Ariz.: Center for Latin American Studies, Special Studies No. 19, 1980).

Another point of contact between the two nations in the modern period has been the narcotraffic. Useful for this subject are Felipe E. MacGregor, *Coca and Cocaine: An Andean Perspective* (Westport, Conn.: Greenwood Press, 1993), Jonathan Cavanagh and Rosemary Underhay, trans., Rensselaer W. Lee, *The White Labyrinth: Cocaine and Political Power* (New Brunswick, N.J.: Transaction Publishers, 1989), Bruce M. Bagley and William O. Walker III, eds., *Drug Trafficking in the Americas* (Miami, Fla.: University of Miami North-South Center, 1994), Scott B. MacDonald, *Dancing on a Volcano: the Latin American Drug Trade* (Westport, Conn.:, Praeger, 1988), and Ethan A. Nadelmann, *Cops Across the Borders: the Internationalization of U. S. Criminal Law Enforcement* (Penn State: Pennsylvania State University Press, 1993).

David Scott Palmer, *The Shining Path of Peru* (New York: St. Martin's Press, 1992), contributed to and edited a series of insightful articles on the most violent modern terrorist movement in Latin America that kept Peru tense and off balance for almost a decade and a half in the 1980s and early 1990s.

One of the most important resources is the growing access to information through the World Wide Web. The *Handbook of Latin American Studies,* for example, is available online through the Library of Congress by going to the following Web address: http://lcweb2.loc.gov/hlas/. Virtually anyone with a browser, such as Netscape or Microsoft Explorer, can review the entire collection online. Access to the handbook online is only touching the proverbial tip of the iceberg. There exist vast amounts of discreet and detailed information on the relations between Peru and the United States. One of the best guides into this online information is through the Latin American Network Information Center maintained by the Institute of Latin American Studies at the University of Texas: http://lanic/utexas.edu/.

Index

absolutism, 17

Achilles, Theodore C., 224

Adams, Alvin, 295

adventurers, 32

African-Peruvians, 18

agreement theory, 10

agriculture, 307

Air Force, Peruvian: equipment of, 177–78; firing on Hercules, 295–96

airports, 205–6

air services, 58, 106, 122, 134, 136, 205–6, 222, 260, 304–5; Jungle Aviation and Radio Service (JAARS), 222. *See also* aviation

Alianza Popular Revolución Americana. *See* APRA

Allende, Salvador, 286

Alliance for Progress, 6–7, 101, 227–29, 233–34, 311

Almirante Cochrane, 52, 64, 65

Alzamora, Isaac, 85

Amazonian region, 37–39; geography of, 149

Amazon River, 37–40, 88

ambiguity: in values of Peru, 98; theory of, 10, 12–13

amendments, 257

America, 24

American Bible Society, 186

American Bridge Company, 113

American Civil War, 49, 50

American Corporations and Peruvian Politics (Goodsell), 209, 250

American dream, 170

American Economic Association, 144

American Geographical Society, 96

American International Association (AIA), 167–68

Americanization, 6

Americans: academic works of, on Peru, 248–50; attitudes of, toward Peru, 6, 9, 12–13, 20; early Peruvian visits of, 2; in Peruvian governmental positions, 100, 105; nature of, 153, 228

Amerindians, 2, 18, 19; and American opinions, 156; and Haya, 151; and Summer Institutes of Languages, 195; isolation of, 231–32; and labor relations, 116–17, 118; civilization of, 90; in Vicos, 230, 231; racism toward, 75–76; rebellions of, 152; relationship with Fitzgerald, 89; stereotypes of, 299; sue Cerro de Pasco, 115

Ancón, Treaty of. *See* Treaty of Ancón

Andes: artistic works depicting, 41, 42; colonization of jungle area, 223; early flights in, 131–33

Andes and the Amazon (Orton), 40

The Andes of Southern Peru, 96

Angamos, Battle of, 63

anti-American demonstrations, 6

APRA, 5, 111, 310; and Haya, 150–51, 154; and Kemmerer mission, 145; and land reform, 230; loses election of 1931, 155; position on communism, 172, 173

Apristas, 119, 120, 146, 151; and assassination of Graña Garland, 174–75; assassination of Sánchez Cerro by, 155; and Confederation of Peruvian Workers, 174; and Nixon's visit, 226